D0305528

TOBIAS SMOLLETT

TOBIAS SMOLLETT

Jeremy Lewis

JONATHAN CAPE
LONDON

First published by Jonathan Cape 2003

1 3 5 7 9 10 8 6 4 2

© Jeremy Lewis 2003

Jeremy Lewis has asserted his right under the Copyright, Designs and
Patents Act 1988 to be identified as the author of this work

First published in the United Kingdom in 2003 by Jonathan Cape,
Random House, 20 Vauxhall Bridge Road, London SW1V 2SA

Random House Australia (Pty) Limited
20 Alfred Street, Milsons Point, Sydney
New South Wales 2061, Australia

Random House New Zealand Limited
18 Poland Road, Glenfield
Auckland 10, New Zealand

Random House South Africa (Pty) Limited
Endulini, 5a Parktown Road, Parktown 2193, South Africa

The Random House Group Limited Reg. No. 954009
www.randomhouse.co.uk

A CIP catalogue record for this book
is available from the British Library

Papers used by Random House are natural,
recyclable products made from wood grown in sustainable forests.
The manufacturing processes conform to the environmental
regulations of the country of origin

ISBN 0–224–06151–8

Typeset by Palimpsest Book Production Limited,
Polmont, Stirlingshire
Printed and bound in Great Britain by
Biddles Ltd, Guildford and King's Lynn

To the memory of
Alan Ross and Dennis Enright:
my mentors and my friends

Contents

Illustrations

Tobias Smollett by an unknown artist (*By Courtesy of the National Portrait Gallery, London*)

The Court of Glasgow University, 1761

Amputation instruments used by a naval surgeon (*The Wellcome Library, London*)

'Amputation' by Thomas Rowlandson (*The Wellcome Library, London*)

British Men-of-War, c.1720-30 (*British Men-of-War and a Sloop, c.1720-30 (oil on canvas) by Peter Monamy (1681-1749) Yale Center for British Art, Paul Mellon Collection, USA/Bridgeman Art Library*)

Cartagena under siege (*A Prospect of the Town and Harbour of Cartagena, 1741 (engraving) Private Collection/Bridgeman Art Library*)

Admiral Charles Knowles by Faber

'Starving Poet and Publisher' by Thomas Rowlandson

'The Distrest Poet' by William Hogarth

James Quin by Thomas Gainsborough (*By Courtesy of the National Portrait Gallery of Ireland*)

David Garrick by Thomas Gainsborough (*By Courtesy of the National Portrait Gallery, London*)

Henry Fielding by an unknown artist (© *Hulton Archive*)

William Hunter by Joshua Reynolds (*Hunterian Art Gallery, Glasgow*)

William Hogarth, self portrait (© *Tate, London*)

Mary Wilkes and John Wilkes by Johan Zoffany (*By Courtesy of the National Portrait Gallery, London*)

John Wilkes by William Hogarth (© *Hulton Archive*)

'The Bruiser' by William Hogarth (*Witt Library, Courtauld Institute of Art, London*)

'Englishman at Paris, 1767' by Bunbury

'Petit Maitre and his Valet' by Charles Grignion

Every effort has been made to contact all copyright holders. The publishers will be glad to make good in future editions any errors or omissions brought to their attention.

Apologia, and Acknowledgements

Although I embarked on this book with the purest of motives – I have long admired *Roderick Random*, *Humphry Clinker* and *Travels through France and Italy* – I am not, and never will be, a scholar of the eighteenth century; nor can I pretend that this is a work of original research. I have not spent long hours poring over yellowing manuscript pages, or comparing one version of a text with another, or tracking down long-lost letters in the attics of remote and draughty country houses. Nor have I read more than a tiny percentage of the tidal wave of words that flowed from Smollett's pen: to have done so might well have proved a lifetime's work, and I would almost certainly have died from boredom before reaching the end. I have been more than happy to rely on those scholars, mostly American, who have kept Smollett's reputation alive – and, above all, on Lewis Knapp, the great authority on the life and work. A calm and reassuring presence, and a well-respected academic, Knapp seems to have devoted his entire career to the study of his hero. Much of his published work consisted of articles in learned journals: almost all were given over to Smollett, and the few that escaped the net concerned related matters such as Smollett's wife, Anne, or his collaborator on the *Critical Review*, John Armstrong. Knapp's *Tobias Smollett: Doctor of Men and Manners* was published in 1949 by Princeton University Press, and it remains the standard, and the most recent, biography; he went on to edit Smollett's *Letters* for Oxford University Press, bringing to the proceedings the same air of dependability and omniscience that infuses all his work.

Knapp's minutely detailed biography has been my mentor and my crutch, and although scholars have amplified aspects of the story, his account of Smollett's life remains as true and accurate as ever it was. As a book for the lay reader, however, it has its drawbacks. It is curiously likeable, and very fluent, but was written by a scholar for other scholars: learned footnotes are devoted to wondering whether such-and-such a school friend of Smollett's did or did not end his days as Provost of Glasgow, but, on the assumption that such things are already known to the initiated, little is done to provide the context in which the life was lived. We are told that, as a young man, Smollett went to sea as a ship's surgeon, and took part in the siege of Cartagena; but no effort is made to describe what doctors were taught in the early eighteenth century, or the workings of the Royal Navy, or what the War of Jenkins's Ear was all about. Smollett longed, in vain, to succeed as a playwright, but we are told next to nothing about the theatre; he spent his life in the literary world, but the mechanics of publishing are barely examined; he was more bruised than most by the Scottophobia that blighted English society, but the whole shameful business receives little attention, and his battle with John Wilkes, once a close friend and kindred spirit, is dismissed in less than a page. Drawing on the writings of historians and Knapp's fellow-Smollettians, I have tried to relate the modest details of Smollett's life to the social, intellectual and political history of his times; and because, in the last resort, the only thing that matters about a writer is his writing, I have quoted as much as possible from Smollett's own works. Since he has been neglected and under-valued for far too long, this can only be to the good.

Biographies of writers tend to be short of drama and adventures, if only because their subjects spend most of their lives at a desk, staring at an empty sheet of paper, the scratch of the pen or the clack of the keyboard enlivened only by hangovers or illicit love affairs. Despite his time at sea, and a short spell in prison, Smollett was no exception to the rule, nor – as far as we know – were his domestic arrangements disturbed by drunkenness or infidelity;

because his life was both brief and uneventful, I have occasionally deserted my chronological framework in order to take a particular strand through to its conclusion.

I have not provided reference notes: the sources of most quotations are, I hope, self-evident, and to refer the reader on to other secondary sources seems a pointless exercise. I have, however, provided a full bibliography; on this side of the Atlantic, at least, Smollett remains *terra incognita*, and my list may, with luck, be of use to genuine scholars in the future.

Nothing here will be unfamiliar to the Smollett scholars I have consulted. I am extremely grateful to Paul-Gabriel Boucé of the Sorbonne, the doyen of Smollett scholarship, a naval man whose dedication to a writer so ill-disposed to the French is a model of magnanimity, and a reproach to those academics on this side of the English Channel who have shown so little interest in one of the great masters of the English novel; to Ian Campbell Ross of Trinity College, Dublin, who not only provided me with his own writings on the subject, but urged me to read John Sekora's *Luxury: The Concept in Western Thought, Eden to Smollett*, intellectual history at its best, and one of the few works devoted to Smollett that I would happily have read in civilian life; to William Gibson, whose PhD thesis, 'All Together Exquisite: Tobias Smollett and Fine Art', was invaluable as a source of information about Smollett's interest in the visual arts, and is far too well written and stimulating not to have found a publisher; and to Henry Fulton and Fiona Macdonald, both of whom provided details of Smollett's training as a surgeon in Glasgow which made unfamiliar terrain spring suddenly into focus. None of these, I hasten to say, is remotely responsible for what follows. My wife, Petra, remembering how, over thirty years ago, I read her *Roderick Random* while she did the ironing, suggested him as a subject, and urged me to write about him for the general reader; I am also extremely grateful, for help and advice, to Piers Brendon, D.J. Enright, A.D. Harvey, Richard Ingrams, Crispin Jackson, Michael Mason, Jane Moore, Tony Mott, William Palmer, Tom Rosenthal, Jane Ross, Deborah Singmaster, Adam Sisman, Charles Sprawson, Paul Wigham and Charles Wilkinson. I'm more grateful than I can say to Dan Franklin of Jonathan Cape and Will Sulkin of Pimlico for commissioning the book without a backward glance (or so it seemed), and to Tony Whittome, James Nightingale and Beth Humphries for the care they have taken in editing my typescript. Once again I am in debt to Douglas Matthews, an indexer sans pareil.

Prologue

As a teenager, I sought refuge in the eighteenth century. A timid, clumsy, ill-coordinated youth with rotten eyesight, flailing limbs and a loathing for organised games, I liked to lurk in a far corner of the school library on windswept autumn afternoons, reading about Boswell and Wilkes and Goldsmith and the raffish William Hickey, and so losing myself in Covent Garden or the Mitre or Ranelagh Gardens that the horrid clunk of boot on ball, the peremptory blast of the referee's whistle and the oafish cries of the supporters on the touchline faded into a faint and unimportant background hum. Heavily dosed on secondary sources – T.H. White's scandalous stories of rakes and debauchees, Austin Dobson's gossipy *Eighteenth-century Vignettes*, the works of Sir Albert Richardson, an authority on the period and the architect responsible for Post Office Georgian – I loved the eighteenth century because it seemed both elegant and boisterous, simple and sophisticated. Rude and Arcadian all at once, it combined a liking for lavatory jokes with decorum and formality, brimming chamber-pots with periwigs and tasselled canes, brutality and coarseness with a gift for graceful living that has never been equalled since. I told myself that, compared with what I was used to in the late 1950s, life in Georgian England would have been brief, brutish, painful and malodorous, but none of that seemed to matter when set against the beauty of the houses and cities, clothes and furnishings. I envied the men their everyday dress – not the fops in lace and gold braid, but the dashing young heroes, like Smollett's Roderick Random, setting out to seek their fortunes in sky-blue swallowtail jackets, canary waistcoats, buff-coloured knee breeches, white stockings and buckled shoes, their hair held back in a black velvet band: so very different from my grey worsted trousers that concertinaed over scuffed black lace-up shoes, or my white school shirt which, however often I tucked it in, flapped loose like a badly furled sail in the wind. The most shy and gauche of schoolboys, I dreamed of one day resembling Dr Johnson's dapper friend Topham Beauclerk – Boswell's *Life* was beyond me, so I judged him by his name alone – and struggled through some pages of the Everyman edition of Lord Chesterfield's pompous *Letters to His Son* in the futile hope that some of the old gentleman's urbanity and *savoir-faire* would come my way. Desperate to avoid the rapidly looming world of cars and commuter trains and the dreaded telephone, my mind awash with George Morland's saccharine rustic idylls and Rowlandson's bosomy delights and the melancholic Cowper's 'A Winter Walk at Noon', I pined for a pre-industrial England in which an empty, unblemished, russet-hued countryside was inhabited by beaming, rubicund yokels in smocks, worldly clerics in rusty black, raucous, bottle-nosed hunting squires, sea-dogs with wooden legs, lisping macaronis and a profusion of saucy wenches.

All these, plus assorted highwaymen, medics, fraudsters, duplicitous grandees, rapacious landlords and ladies of ill repute, could be found in abundance in Tobias Smollett's *Roderick Random*, the novel which, above all others, chimed with my notion of the eighteenth century. Unlike their nineteenth-century descendants, and Dickens in particular, the novelists of the period had proved a disappointing crew. I read *Roxana* and *Moll Flanders* like a middle-class slummer sampling low life at a safe remove, but although I admired Defoe's robust, Orwellian prose, I found his successors tougher nuts to crack. I liked the *idea* of *Tom Jones* and *Joseph Andrews*, but was unnerved by Fielding's authorial interjections and abstract ruminations; I found, and still find, the Sterne of *Tristram Shandy* entirely unreadable, part of an impenetrable tradition that culminated in *Ulysses* and *Finnegans Wake*; Richardson, like Trollope, is probably a novelist best read in middle age; but *Roderick Random* was a very different matter. At the age of seventeen, I thought it one of the most fast-moving, boisterous and consistently entertaining novels I had ever read; that was over forty years ago, and it has lost none of its allure. Smollett, it seemed, was a Scot, and his opening paragraph had the direct, button-holing approach I associated with *Kidnapped* and *The Thirty-nine Steps*, both works by his fellow-countrymen:

> I was born in the northern part of this united kingdom, in the house of my grandfather; a gentleman of considerable fortune and influence, who had, on many occasions, signalised himself in behalf of his country; and was remarkable for his abilities in the law, which he exercised with great success, in the station of a judge, particularly against beggars, for whom he had a singular aversion.

Never too good at following a plot, I was grateful for the novel's loose, episodic structure, reminiscent of *Don Quixote* and LeSage's *Gil Blas*, both of which Smollett had translated; I liked, too, the way in which he sustained such a cracking pace, as he took his young hero to sea as a surgeon on a creaking man-of-war, and on to the crowded, raucous streets of Hogarthian London. I relished the physicality of his writing, his eye for detail, and the ruthless, often brutal ways in which he itemised bodily attributes and failings. A good example, encountered in a coach as Roderick makes his way south to London, was the pot valiant Captain Weasel. A precursor of the bombastic and cowardly Captain Dowler in *The Pickwick Papers* – Dickens was a great admirer, and his early, picaresque novels resound to echoes of Smollett – Weasel cowers behind the ladies when a highwayman heaves to; nor does his appearance match his bold, stentorian voice:

> But how was I surprised, when I beheld the formidable captain in the shape of a little thin creature, about the age of forty, with a long withered visage, very much resembling that of a baboon, through the upper part of which two little grey eyes peeped: he wore his own hair in a queue that reached to his

rump . . . Having laid aside his great coat, I could not help admiring the extraordinary make of this man of war: he was about five feet and three inches high, sixteen inches of which went to his face and long scraggy neck; his thighs were about six inches in length, his legs resembling spindles or drumsticks, two feet and a half, and his body, which put me in mind of extension without substance, engrossed the remainder; so that, on the whole, he resembled a spider or grasshopper erect.

The mildest of youths myself, I delighted in Smollett's bluntness and brutality – qualities he shared with my other hero, R.S. Surtees, along with a good line in bounders and blackguards, and an eye for the details of clothing, touching and revelatory as they always are. Keener than most on lavatory jokes, I was thrilled to find a brimming chamber-pot being emptied over an unsuspecting sleeper early on in the proceedings, when Roderick and his manservant Strap are caught up in one of those scenes, reminiscent of an old-fashioned French farce, in which the guests in an inn find themselves straying into the wrong beds. J.H. Plumb once observed of the Georgians that 'an exceedingly frank acknowledgement, one might almost say a relish, of man's animal functions was as much a part of the age as the elegant furniture or delicate china', and no sooner have Roderick and his Sancho Panza arrived in London than another pot is emptied over Strap's head from a first-floor window, and he has to wring the urine from his wig; as I eventually discovered, Smollett's novels are relentlessly scatological, crammed with laxatives and emetics, often administered on the sly, and pulsating to the gasps of the afflicted, some of them suffering the full horrors of what he refers to, more than once, as 'double evacuation'.

Medical men, like Smollett, tend to have no illusions about human nature and bodily attributes, and I found this aspect of his writing, and his personality, familiar and congenial. My father was a urologist, and when I was very young, back in the early 1950s, the mantelpiece was decorated with bladder stones, the size and shape of a marble, like Maltesers with the chocolate sucked off, or tiny balls of pumice: later I learned that lithotomy, the removal of such stones, was one of the very few 'internal' operations to be successfully performed by eighteenth-century surgeons, and that a fashionable practitioner like Sir William Cheselden could charge as much as £500 for (or so he boasted) five minutes' work at the most. I longed, in those days, to be a sailor: short sight and physical ineptitude soon put paid to that, but the Hornblower stories more than made up for the loss; and, a decade or so later, I thrilled to the naval scenes in *Roderick Random*, to the ship's timbers groaning in a gale, the tyrannical Captain Oakum, the rations infested with maggots, and the terrible siege of Cartagena, far off on the Spanish Main. Smollett's account of life at sea had all the brightness and exhilaration of a voyage under sail, as well as providing a model and an inspiration for Captain Marryat, Robert Louis Stevenson, Melville and C.S. Forester himself.

After leaving school, I sought refuge from the perils of office life by reading under my desk or on park benches during the lunch hour. Dickens was my preferred means of escape, but in between heavy doses of *Martin Chuzzlewit* and *Nicholas Nickleby* I found time for *Humphry Clinker* – Smollett's last novel, published only weeks before his death in 1771 – and his curmudgeonly, xenophobic *Travels through France and Italy*. Written in epistolary form, and luridly evocative of the smells and din of Georgian England, *Humphry Clinker* seemed to lack the jaunty, tireless energy of *Roderick Random*; nowadays I happily subscribe to the conventional view that it is Smollett's masterpiece, but his diatribes against the corrupting effects of luxury and the vulgarity of the mercantile *nouveaux riches* left me writhing in my chair. As for the *Travels*, I hugely enjoyed the bug-ridden beds, filthy meals and insolent innkeepers, and his invectives against the French and the use of garlic in cooking, but, as I still do, happily skipped the pages devoted to Roman antiquities or the economy of Nice. I never got round to *Peregrine Pickle*, all 800 pages of it, let alone *Ferdinand Count Fathom* or *Sir Launcelot Greaves*: this was probably just as well, since despite a few redeeming moments, they have not survived the passing of time, and – like *The Complete History of England*, the Swiftian satire *Adventures of an Atom*, the *Compendium of Authentic and Entertaining Voyages*, *The Present State of All Nations*, the *Essay on Water*, the translations of Voltaire, Cervantes and LeSage, and the innumerable polemics, poems, book reviews, editorials and hackwork churned out to keep Smollett afloat in Grub Street – are best left to the scholar and the specialist.

In due course I made my way to university, where I read history. Most of my friends read English and, like the majority of those who teach and study the subject, they seldom strayed from the 'canon'. To my irritation, none of them read a word of Smollett, and they treated my enthusiasm with bafflement or derision: neither *Roderick Random* nor *Humphry Clinker* was a set book, so neither needed to be read, any more than *Mr Sponge's Sporting Tour* or *Mr Facey Romford's Hounds*. Nor, I suspect, were their lecturers any better informed. Given their anxieties about English being a 'soft' or easy subject, Eng. Lit. academics tend to concentrate on authors who are 'difficult', like Sterne, or sporadically sententious, like Fielding (whom Smollett dubbed 'that sagacious moraliser', envying him his literary success and his grand connections but finding him, in print, something of a windbag). Smollett's standing was not enhanced by the fact that so many of his characters are 'humours' or grotesques, incapable of the introversion, the subtleties and the ambivalences prized by the academic mind. They knew Smollett's name as one of the founders of the English novel, passed on such information to their students, and left it at that. On this side of the Atlantic at least, his admirers have not been academics but fellow-writers, Arnold Bennett, George Orwell and V.S. Pritchett among them.

Since leaving university in the mid-1960s, I have spent my life in the literary world, working, at various times, for five publishers, two literary agencies and two magazines, as well as writing my own books and innumerable book reviews. I knew little about Smollett's life until I decided to write this biography, but soon discovered that he was – like Cyril Connolly, my previous subject – something of a kindred spirit, in that he inhabited a world with which I was all too familiar. He spent most of his life in Grub Street, at a time when the professional author was learning to depend on the market rather than the whims of a patron, and the book trade was assuming forms still recognisable today. For much of his life he was financially embattled, and, like any denizen of Grub Street, he would turn his hand to anything. With Dr Johnson, he was the quintessential eighteenth-century man of letters, writing novels, poems, histories, polemics and reviews, editing collections of travel writing and the standard work on obstetrics, founding and editing three magazines, and ruining his health in the process; his novels abound with self-important, scheming, indigent hacks, and familiar complaints about the parsimony of publishers, the lowering effect of hackwork, the impossibility of refusing a commission, and the need to meet deadlines. A hack who was also a master of English prose, he is, like Johnson, Thackeray, Gissing and Connolly, one of the great chroniclers of writing as a way of life that is both addictive and oppressive.

He was also, of course, a masterly travel writer, and the first in a line of loose-limbed, anecdotal, comical and socially observant novelists that stretches through Surtees and the early Dickens to the clerking novels of H.G Wells and the Sinclair Lewis of *Babbitt*, *Dodsworth* and *Elmer Gantry*. Re-reading his three great books, I found them as vigorous and colourful and opinionated and fast-moving as ever, literature's equivalent to the great Thomas Rowlandson, the artist he most resembles, and his posthumous illustrator; and as I learned more about his life, I became increasingly fond of Smollett the man, as well as the writer. Brought face-to-face with a portrait of Smollett, A.L. Rowse once noted that its subject looked 'the converse of what one would have expected: not jovial, coarse or brutal, but sensitive, almost finicking, with small upcurved mouth and oval face like a lady of the period'. A lugubrious-looking character with a long face, sad eyes, a drooping nose and a wide, humorous mouth, he was peppery, thin-skinned, hypochondriacal, proud, vindictive and, in his views on the social order, as reactionary as an empurpled colonel of the old school; but he was also generous to a fault, kind, encouraging, convivial, brave and far too hard-working for his own good.

All biographies have, or should have, an element of autobiography as well, whether explicit or oblique, or a mixture of the two; hence these prefatory musings. Having delivered the explicit part, I shall now bow out, and leave the rest to Smollett.

1

Arcadia on the Clyde

Like many others before and since, Tobias Smollett occasionally indulged in mild speculation about his family origins, with special reference to the Normans; and since family trees and genealogies are invariably the most tedious part of any biography, it is a relief to find him pondering the matter for us from his home in Chelsea in the spring of 1756. 'I begin to think we were originally Malet or Molet and came from Normandy with the Conqueror,' he told his cousin 'Commissary' James Smollett, the Sheriff-Depute of Dumbartonshire and future owner of Cameron House, an elegant property on the shore of Loch Lomond. Not long after the Battle of Hastings, he continued, a certain William Malet had made his mark as 'governor of York and a very gallant officer', but although the Smolletts were 'freeholders in Dumbarton four hundred years ago', somehow acquiring a preliminary 'S' in the process, and the novelist had tracked down a publican in the 'skirts of Chelsea' by name of James Mollet, the trail had run cold. 'I should be very glad to know if you have any anecdotes of our little family,' he told the Commissary.

Whether the Commissary was able to oblige his cousin with a fund of anecdotes is something we shall never know, but by the seventeenth century the Smolletts were distinguishing themselves as lawyers and soldiers. A Whig by political persuasion and a Presbyterian by religion, the novelist's grandfather, Sir James Smollett,

I

also referred to as 'Commissary', played a role in the Glorious Revolution, was knighted by William III ten years later, and took part in public life in Edinburgh and Glasgow as well as in the county town of Dumbarton. Like many young Scotsmen of the day, especially those anxious to study medicine or the law, his three sons were sent to university at Leyden in Holland. Archibald, the youngest and the father of Tobias, was taken poorly in Holland and probably remained sickly for the rest of his short life. Undecided in terms of a career, he was, like Roderick Random's father, rash enough to get married without the approval of his strong-minded father. His bride, Barbara Cunningham, was described as a 'woman of distinguished understanding, taste and elegance, but no fortune', while Smollett's cousin and future biographer John Moore – whose son became the Sir John Moore of Corunna fame – remembered her as 'very entertaining in conversation, being endowed with an uncommon share of humour'. Widowed while young, she lived on until 1770, and Smollett, who shared her conversational gifts and her humour, would make a point of visiting her on his rare trips back to Scotland.

Despite Archibald's poor health and Sir James's initial disapproval, the happy couple produced three children: James, who became a captain in the Army, and was lost at sea off America ('I know what a man of Jack's sensibility must feel upon such an occasion,' Smollett once wrote, on learning that the playwright John Home had lost a brother, 'for I once sustained the same calamity, in the death of a brother whom I loved and honoured'); Jane, 'ill-natured looking, with a high nose – but not of a bad temper', a demon card-player who later married Alexander Telfer of Scotstoun and went on to outlive both of her brothers, her husband and 'Commissary' Smollett; and Tobias George, who was born in his parents' house at Dalquhur, a plain, three-storeyed building overlooking the Leven Valley, no distance from Sir James's mansion at Bonhill, and was baptised in the parish church of Cardross on 19 March 1721.

Dumbarton, with its rock and its castle, and much of the Leven Valley, linking Loch Lomond with the Clyde, were long ago subsumed into the outskirts of Glasgow, but back in the 1720s Glasgow was a trim little city of 13,000 people, some distance from the verdant, rolling countryside of Smollett's childhood. Towards the end of his life, ill, exhausted and prematurely aged, Smollett looked back on the Leven Valley and the banks of the Clyde as a paradise lost, a green and uncorrupted idyll far removed from the noisy, dirty, pestiferous, luxury-loving London in which he had spent his adult life, and the ideal manifestation of that innocent, time-less rural bliss to which all his fictional heroes invariably return. 'Everything here is romantic beyond imagination,' reported his *alter ego* Matthew Bramble in *Humphry Clinker*, completed in Italy and published five years after Smollett's final visit to Scotland in 1766, during which he revisited the scenes of his childhood. Part travel book, part social commentary, and epistolary novel throughout, *Humphry Clinker* takes Bramble and his family party on a circular tour of Britain: Scotland proves the high point of their journey, its beauty and civility comparing favourably with the squalor and corruption south of the Border, and the country where Smollett grew up 'is justly styled the Arcadia of Scotland; and I don't doubt but it may vie with Arcadia in every thing but climate'. Not for the first time, Smollett brings himself and his family into the novel. Bramble and his party are staying at Cameron, the Commissary's house on Loch Lomond, 'so embosomed in an oak wood, that we did not see it till we were within fifty yards of the door'. 'I have seen the Lago di Garda, Albano, de Vico, Bolsena, and Geneva, and, upon my honour, I prefer Lough Lomond to them all,' Bramble tells his old friend Dr Lewis back in Wales. The banks of the loch 'partake of the sublime', displaying 'a sweet variety of woodland, corn field, and pasture, with several agreeable villas emerging as it were out of the lake, till, at some distance, the prospect terminates in huge mountains covered in heath, which being in the bloom, affords a very rich covering of purple'. Deer abound, and the air and water seem miraculously pure after the horrors of London, where 'human excrement is the least offensive part' of the water on offer, which is otherwise 'composed of all the drugs, minerals, and poisons, used in mechanics and manufacture, enriched with the putrefying carcasses of beasts and men; and mixed with the scourings of all the wash-tubs, kennels, and common sewers, within the bills of mortality'. Although, ideally, the house should be a little further from the lake, which almost washes against the windows, 'we make free with our landlord's mutton, which is excellent, his poultry yard, his garden, his dairy and his cellar, which are all well stored'. It all makes a refreshing change from London, where the bread is made from 'chalk, alum, and bone-ashes', the greens are boiled with half-pennies to improve their flavour, and the fish on sale are too putrescent and malodorous to be borne. So carried away is Squire Bramble by the delights of it all that he encloses with his letter a copy of the 'Ode to Leven Water', a composition 'by Dr Smollett, who was born on the banks of it, within two miles of the place where I am now writing. It is at least picturesque and accurately descriptive, if it has no other merit':

> On Leven's banks, while free to rove,
> And tune the rural pipe to love;
> I envied not the happiest swain
> That ever trod th' Arcadian plain.
> Pure stream! In whose transparent wave
> My youthful limbs I wont to lave;
> No torrents stain thy limpid source;
> No rocks impede thy dimpling course . . .

And so on for another twenty lines, demonstrating Smollett's nostalgia and affection for his native patch, and his competence as an occasional if entirely conventional poet.

The Clyde itself, Bramble noted, was 'a delightful stream, adorned on both sides with villas, towns and villages. Here is no want of groves, and meadows, and corn-fields interspersed . . .' It sounds indeed like a vanished Arcadia, but by the time of his visit Scotland had undergone more than sixty years of momentous change following the Act of Union with England, and more would occur in the years ahead as the Industrial Revolution, already in its infancy, blighted and enriched Glasgow and the Clyde Valley. Sir James had been one of the commissioners appointed to negotiate the terms of the Union, as a result of which the Scottish Parliament had voted itself out of existence, trading political independence for – it was hoped – the economic benefits that would flow from unlimited access to the markets of England and its colonies overseas. England's reasons for favouring the Union were political and strategic, in that an independent Scotland – albeit one that had shared a monarch since 1603, and a Stuart at that – could prove a liability during the inevitable wars with France, and a united island of Britain would be less exposed, in military terms, to wily Frenchmen keen to exploit the Auld Alliance. The benefits to Scotland were altogether more prosaic, and the loss of independence in 1707 was initially resented by many – the majority, perhaps – as a national humiliation. Scottish representation at Westminster seemed insultingly modest, with 45 Scottish MPs joining the 513 elected from England and Wales, and a mere 16 Scottish peers travelling down to the House of Lords, where 190 English equivalents were already installed. It was hardly surprising that whereas English politicians, in those rare moments when they gave thought to the matter, claimed, with a certain condescension, that Scotland had been 'merged' with England on terms of rare generosity, many Scots grumbled that they had been 'sold' by Sir James and his fellow-commissioners, and hinted at bribery and worse.

Although sceptics like the battered, cantankerous old soldier Lismahago in *Humphry Clinker* continued to complain that Scotland had gained nothing from the Union, the famine of the 1690s, the last to occur on British soil, and the failure of the Darien Scheme, widely blamed on the English, had underlined the vulnerability and the backwardness of the Scottish economy. The immediate effects of the Union seemed to vindicate those who had prophesied doom and disaster. Some industries, hitherto protected, suffered badly from English competition; unused to English forms of taxation, the Scots resented customs and excise duties on such staples as beer, linen, soap and salt, and riots broke out in 1725 when Sir Robert Walpole's ministry decided to apply the Malt Tax north of the Border. But the Scottish legal system, so very different from the English, and the central role of the Presbyterian Kirk had been unaffected, though the Kirk was to shed some of its grimmer and more repressive features, including its hostility to the theatre. Edinburgh remained an important centre of law and administration, a city of advocates and civil servants, and Scotland's semi-independent status was reinforced when, in the 1720s, a new Secretary for Scotland was appointed in the shape of the forceful Earl of Islay – whose ancestral castle, Inverary, was on Loch Lomond, and would be visited in due course by Matthew Bramble and party. Islay, who became the Duke of Argyll in 1743, dominated Scottish politics until his death in 1761, and may have done more than anyone to reconcile his fellow-Scots to the benefits of the Union: so much so that although Bonnie Prince Charlie's rising in 1745 posed more of a threat to the unity of the kingdom than that led by his father, James Stuart, in 1715, Jacobitism and the drinking of toasts to the King over the Water became, on both sides of the Border, more a matter of sentiment and nostalgia than practical politics. Islay ran the country like a private fiefdom, advancing Scotland's interests at Westminster, and – via the powers of patronage that loomed so large in eighteenth-century life – building up an elaborate network of dependants in the law, the Church, the universities and the administration. Apart from a momentary lapse in 1745, he provided political stability and order: London was happy to let him get on with it, and left to its own devices, Scotland flourished from benign neglect.

Many enterprising young Scotsmen, like Smollett in due course, set out to make their fortunes in England, where despite – or because of – their success as doctors, lawyers, soldiers and administrators in the rapidly expanding British Empire, they often encountered prejudice and hostility of the kind later reserved for immigrants from Ireland, the West Indies and the Indian subcontinent. Others preferred to stay at home, and nowhere did they prosper more than in Glasgow and the Clyde Valley. Although some Scottish traders and smugglers had done business with the English tobacco colonies of Virginia, Maryland and North Carolina before the Act of Union, they were now free to do so on a legitimate basis, and were entitled to the protection of the Royal Navy as well. Glasgow's famed 'tobacco lords' soon outwitted and outsold their English competitors: sharper off the mark, and nimble at selling their tobacco on to customers as far afield as Russia, Glasgow's merchants accounted for 15 per cent of the British tobacco trade by the 1720s, and thirty years later their business was worth that of all the English ports combined, London included. It was important to carry goods on the outward voyage as well, and other industries flourished as the tobacco lords diversified into banking, linen manufacture, glass-blowing, the importing of sugar and citrus fruits and, in 1759, an ironworks at Carron.

Such changes were not restricted to Glasgow. The Highlands remained as primitive and as poverty-stricken as ever, as baffling to Scots like Smollett as to English visitors like Dr Johnson, but throughout the eighteenth century Scottish society was in a state of rapid flux. Up-to-date agricultural methods were introduced from England and Holland, with lawyers and literary men like Lord Kames bending their minds to the rotation of crops and suchlike matters; Scottish architects like Robert Adam and William Chambers found an eager clientele among peers and landed gentry happy to knock down gaunt and draughty baronial keeps in favour of pedimented and pillared mansions designed along fashionably classical lines. In Edinburgh, a famously filthy city, ancient and unwholesome practices, including sewage in the stairwells and the emptying of chamber-pots out of tenement windows on to the heads of unsuspecting passers-by, alerted only by a strangled cry of 'gardey-loo', coexisted with the conscious cultivation of the arts and gracious living. In due course the city's reputation as the 'Athens of the North' would manifest itself in the squares and crescents of the New Town, where the professional middle classes could establish their homes in an urban setting matched only by Bath; those who were proud to be both Scots and British, and wanted to make their way in the new united kingdom, fought hard to eliminate embarrassing and parochial-seeming 'Scotticisms' in speech and on the written page. Smollett was to embody this combination of a prickly pride in being Scottish with an appreciation of the broader horizons and opportunities offered by the new status of a 'Briton'. As the centre of the publishing and literary world, London would offer him all he needed as a writer and editor, and when travelling in Latin countries he swelled with pride at the thought of English roast beef and Protestant liberties, and grew misty-eyed when the white cliffs of Albion hove into view; yet during his years in London he was to consort almost exclusively with fellow-exiles, loathed the recurrent waves of Scottophobia which ran through English society, and, as he grew older, exalted the virtues of his native land at the expense of his adopted country. Such feelings of ambivalence were aroused by his home town of

Dumbarton. Its famous rock had been a stronghold of the Scottish patriot William Wallace, renowned for his defiance of the English in the thirteenth century. According to John Moore, the youthful Smollett, inflamed by a popular version of Blind Harry's 'Wallace' written in the 1720s during a resurgence of cultural nationalism, wrote a poem of his own in praise of the great man; yet in *Humphry Clinker*, and his letter to Commissary Smollett, he delights in the more 'British' notion that the people from his part of Scotland were by origin Welsh-speaking Britons from a long-lost Cumbrian kingdom, far longer established than the Scots, 'who came from Ireland but yesterday', and argued that the name Dumbarton was a corruption of 'Dunbritton'.

Whatever the truth of the matter, young Tobias was sent at the age of six or seven to Dumbarton Grammar School. Then as now, Scottish education was held to be superior to the English variety. The School Act, passed by the Edinburgh Parliament in 1696, had decreed that every parish should be provided with a school and attendant master; competition between the burghs or town councils responsible for the running of schools kept up standards, and the fact that the ubiquitous Sir James was one of the commissioners responsible for Scottish schools and universities may have weighed heavily at Dumbarton. Most of the lessons were in Latin; Smollett would have become proficient in it and, at the very least, acquainted with Greek. On top of this he probably studied English, music and calligraphy. His spare time may have been spent playing ninepins and handball, and writing satirical verses, none of which has survived; no doubt he was a bright and nimble-witted boy, like Roderick Random 'allowed by everybody to be the best scholar in the school'. *Roderick Random* is vividly evocative of particular aspects of his career, but it is generally of intermittent value to the biographer; much to his annoyance and embarrassment, Smollett – like innumerable novelists since – was to fall foul of the assumption that novels are covert autobiography, especially those which have a first-person narrator, follow his episodic career from birth to wedding-bells, and have enough real or apparent similarities to justify the charge. The treacherous Squire Gawky was said to have been based on James Buchanan, a future Provost of Glasgow, but since they had fallen out, that was neither here nor there; rather more worrying was the matter of his old headmaster. The schoolmaster in the novel is an all too familiar type, in that he bullies his pupils while grovelling to the mighty – in this case, Roderick's tyrannical old grandfather. Though neglected at home, Roderick is a bright and fairly tiresome child. The schoolmaster has agreed to teach him free of charge in order to keep in with his patron, and takes it out on his pupil. Not only is Roderick 'inhumanly scourged for crimes I did not commit', but, on the pretext that he had written impertinent letters to his grandfather, the schoolmaster 'caused a board to be made with five holes in it, through which he thrust the fingers and thumb of my right hand, and fastened it with a whip cord to my wrist, in such a manner as effectually debarred me from use of my pen'.

Salvation is to hand in the form of Roderick's uncle Tom Bowling, the first of a series of good-hearted if voluble sea-dogs to feature in Smollett's novels. Vengeance is invariably a brutal, even sadistic business, and Tom Bowling is the man for the job. 'Egad, I'll play him a salt-water trick; I'll bring him to the gangway, and anoint him with a cat o' nine tails; he shall have a round dozen doubled, my lad, he shall, and be left lashed to his meditations,' cries the outraged tar, his customary benevolence quite forgotten. He and his nephew burst into the classroom in the middle of a lesson, lash the pedant to his desk, pull down his trousers to the accompaniment of a 'loud huzza' from the assembled pupils, and set to work with the cat-o'-nine-tails. 'This smart application to the pedant's withered posteriors gave him such exquisite pain, that he reared like a mad bull, danced, cursed and blasphemed, like a frantic bedlamite.' His humiliation is greeted with a loud cheer, and afterwards Tom Bowling entertains Roderick and his schoolfriends in a nearby public house.

'I am not a little mortified to find the characters strangely misapplied to particular men whom I never had the least intention to ridicule,' Smollett told his friend Alexander 'Jupiter' Carlyle after the publication of the novel in 1748: 'some persons, to whom I have been extremely obliged, being weak enough to take umbrage at many passages of the work, on the supposition that I myself am the hero of the book, and they, of consequence, concerned in the history'. Among those to have taken particular offence was John Love, headmaster of Dumbarton Grammar in Smollett's day, and an eminent 'controversialist and grammarian'. Smollett's initial reaction was one of irritation and defiance. He would, he told Carlyle, treat Love's indignation 'with the contempt it deserves – the more so, as I am informed that he has by way of revenge propagated many lies to my disadvantage'. Such bluster may well have masked spasms of guilt. The most thin-skinned of men, Smollett always combined pride and irritability with kindness and generosity, and years later he wrote to John Wilkes in the hope that he could advance the naval career of Robert Love, 'son of the man from whose instruction I imbibed the first principles of my education'.

For years to come, Smollett would protest that his first novel should not be read as autobiography. 'Christian reader, I beseech thee, in the bowels of the Lord, remember this example while thou art employed in the persual of the following sheets; and seek not to appropriate to thyself that which equally belongs to five hundred people,' he wrote in an 'Apologue' to the 1760 edition:

> If thou shouldst meet with a character that reflects thee in some ungracious particular, keep thy own counsel; consider that one feature makes not a face, and that though thou art, perhaps, distinguished by a bottle nose, twenty of thy neighbours may be in the same predicament.

And to an American admirer he insisted that

> The only similitude between the circumstances of my own fortune and those I have attributed to Roderick Random consists in my being born of a reputable family in Scotland, in my being bred a surgeon, and having served as a surgeon's mate on board a man of war during the expedition to Carthagene. The low situations in which I have exhibited Roderick I never experienced in my person.

This was a shade disingenuous – quite apart from the naval scenes, the novel also included a detailed account of Smollett's mortifications as a would-be playwright – and there may just have been a grain of truth in the story. Much of Smollett's early life is filtered through rumour and second-hand gossip, but according to the Edinburgh lawyer John Ramsay of Ochtertyre, a former pupil of Love's claimed that 'there had been a violent mutiny among the boys in which an uncle of his had a share'. As for young Smollett, according to Ramsay, 'Even while at school and college, his pride and cynical humour which turned everything into ridicule made him be considered as no safe companion or easy friend.'

All of which proves that a way with words is a double-edged gift, and that writing novels can prove a hazardous business. In the meantime, Tobias – like Roderick Random – had put his schooldays behind him, and was preparing to go on to university.

Although, in the nineteenth century, Glasgow came to be thought of as a handsome but alarming city of vertiginous, blackened tenement blocks and squalid, malodorous courts and alleyways, it was associated in Smollett's youth with wide streets, clean air and flagstoned pavements. Writing in 1727 about a visit he had made some twenty years before, Daniel Defoe described it as a 'large, stately and well-built city, standing in a plain in a manner four-square, and the five principal streets are the fairest for breadth, and the finest I have ever seen in one city together. The houses are all of stone, and generally uniform in height as well as in front . . . In a word, 'tis one of the cleanliest, most beautiful and best built cities in Great Britain.' Some fifty years later Dr Johnson, not noted for kind words about the Scots or their country, was – or so Boswell assures us – overwhelmed by 'this beautiful city' and 'expressed his admiration of the beautiful buildings'. Since Defoe's visit, Glasgow had begun to enjoy the benefits of the Act of Union, and new mansions belonging to tobacco lords, cotton brokers, distillers and sugar importers were springing up to the west of the city, inching their way down the Clyde in the direction of Matthew Bramble's Arcadia. Alexander Carlyle, who spent two years at Glasgow University after studying at Edinburgh, found it a 'very industrious, wealthy and commercial city', but less sophisticated than the capital. 'The manner of living, at this time, was but coarse and vulgar,' he declared. Despite the wealth of the merchant class, few families had manservants; there were no post-chaises or hackney carriages, and only a handful of sedan chairs. Though keen on coffee-houses, the merchants tended to shun dinner parties and the theatre in favour of an early supper and bed at nine: but they had great respect for learning and intellectual life, sending their sons on to university and meeting in clubs which combined jollity with debate and rumination. 'Few of them could be called learned,' in Carlyle's view, but they admired those who were, and were eager to find ways in which new and persuasive ideas could be put into practical effect. Many attended a society founded by Andrew Cochrane, the city's Provost, to 'inquire into the nature and principles of trade in all its branches': Adam Smith, who went up to Glasgow University in 1737, and may have been a contemporary of Smollett's, made use of the society's findings when researching *The Wealth of Nations*.

This combination of intellectual energy and practicality, of a delight in the play of ideas with an insistence on their application to the world at large, was characteristic of Scottish universities in the early eighteenth century, and of what came to be known as the Scottish Enlightenment. At a time when Oxford and Cambridge were sinking into Gibbonian torpor, the Scottish universities were heading in the opposite direction. Despite the hostility of the unreformed Kirk to liberal notions or new ideas, they had proved open to the ideas of Locke and Newton in the 1690s; in 1708 the tenor and quality of academic life was radically improved when William Carstares, the Principal of Edinburgh University, replaced the antiquated system of 'regenting', whereby students were allocated to a particular professor who taught them everything from Greek to mathematics, with the Dutch system, whereby subjects were taught by specialists. This approach was adopted in Glasgow by the influential Francis Hutcheson, an Ulster Scot who, at the instigation of the Earl of Islay, was appointed Professor of Moral Philosophy in 1729, remained in the job till 1746, and must have numbered Smollett among his pupils. Carlyle remembered him as an eloquent speaker who dispensed with notes and strode up and down while addressing a class; he broke with the tradition of lecturing in Latin, and encouraged the technique of 'catechising', whereby professors encouraged their pupils to discuss matters raised in class on a more informal basis, with him and among themselves.

Hutcheson shared, and was influenced by, Lord Shaftesbury's optimistic view of human nature. Man was naturally a social animal,
possessed of an innate moral sense, and good conduct was both
natural and pleasurable. Great store was laid on the power of disinterested benevolence; both men emphasised the power of reason,
rejected arbitrary authority and benighted intolerance, and were
convinced that knowledge and reason should be used to improve
the conditions of life. Unlike Fielding, who was in sympathy with
Shaftesbury's views, Smollett had a darker, more Hobbesian cast of
mind, convinced – as he put it in the Preface to *Roderick Random* –
of the 'sordid and vicious disposition of the world', yet prone to
surges of 'generous indignation' all the same; but Hutcheson's ideas
had a great influence on close friends like Carlyle, John Home and
the historian William Robertson, all of them liberal-minded
Presbyterian clergymen, founders of the Moderate Party in the Kirk,
and representative figures in the Scottish Enlightenment.

The practicality espoused by Hutcheson and his successor William
Leechman, the Professor of Theology, was reflected in the avail-
ability of vocational courses like law and, in due course, medicine.
That in itself must have recommended the university to the merchant
classes: it also had the gravitas that went with being a medieval
foundation, its quadrangles were more attractive than anything on
offer in Edinburgh, and the fact that, at £5 per annum, its fees were
a tithe of those at Oxford and Cambridge made it possible for the
sons of artisans, farmers and shopkeepers to attend, along with
Dissenters banned from the English universities and students from
Ireland and the north of England. Some of the 400-odd students
were as young as fourteen, Smollett among them. Since there is no
record of his having matriculated or taken a degree, one can only
guess at the course of his studies. Roderick Random tells us that 'in
the space of three years, I understood Greek very well, was pretty
far advanced in the mathematics, and no stranger to moral and
natural philosophy; logic I made account of; but above all things I
valued myself on my taste in *belles letters*, and a talent for poetry,
which had already produced some pieces that met with a favourable
reception.' According to John Moore, Smollett continued to 'direct

the edge of boyish satire against such green and scanty shoots of affectation and ridicule as the soil produced', but none of this has come down to us: a piece of dreary doggerel could just have been his, but the fact that it is signed 'Toby' Smollett – a diminutive he always loathed – suggests that it was not. According to the *Emmet*, a magazine published some fifty years after his death, Smollett was already displaying his characteristic combination of satirical sharpness and private generosity: 'Good Lord, what a lodging has honesty taken up with!' he is said to have exclaimed after a beggar pointed out that he had handed him a guinea instead of a shilling, or even a penny, and promptly gave him another. When not directing satirical barbs, he probably studied Latin, Greek, logic, mathematics, metaphysics and 'pneumaticks', science 'as improved by Sir Isaac Newton', and 'Lessons of the Law of Nature and Nations'. Whatever the ingredients, his studies gave him an extraordinarily wide-ranging general knowledge, on the strength of which he would, in due course, write a multi-volume history of England and topographical surveys of places as far apart as Siberia and South America, prepare for press the standard work on obstetrics, translate from the French and the Spanish, and review innumerable books on science, medicine, history, politics and literature.

Smollett's father had been long dead, and Sir James had died in 1731: as the youngest son of a youngest son, Smollett had to think in terms of career, and to bend his mind to the matter while still in his early teens, Like others in his position, he had to choose between the Army, the Navy, the professions – the Church, law and medicine – or trade: impoverished gentry on both sides of the Border were not above dabbling in commerce, and some had even been apprenticed to silversmiths, drapers, flax-dressers and ships' carpenters. More snobbish than some, Smollett was proud of being descended from a long line of gentry, and, like Roderick Random, he would always set great store on being a 'gentleman'. He would never have contemplated trade, for – as he once told John Moore – commerce was 'a subject quite foreign to my taste and understanding' and although, as a writer, he was to prove adept at exploiting the market, and liked to boast of his independence of both patrons and the state, he was to devote a good deal of his literary energy to fulminating against the vulgarity and ostentation of the mercantile *nouveaux riches*, whose appetite for luxury was corrupting and undermining the health of society and the body politic. The Army might have been a possibility, but his brother James had already embarked on that path, and it may be that Smollett – whose health was never robust – was thought too frail for such a life, or indeed for the Navy; law, too, ran in the family, but that seems not to have been an option – which may have been just as well, since his dealings with lawyers were to prove unhappy, leaving him with a deep loathing for their kind. He was almost certainly too sceptical to have summoned up the necessary modicum of faith for the Church: in due course he became a supporter of the Church of England as part of the glue holding a stable social order together, abominating Methodism and other over-enthusiastic sects on the grounds that they appealed to that mindless monster, the mob, and were socially disruptive.

Medicine was the only alternative, and it may be that he decided to try it out after consorting with surgical apprentices and finding them good company. Although Glasgow University's medical school was to become famous throughout Europe after the appointment of the great William Cullen to the Chair of Medicine in 1744, it was still, in Smollett's day, lagging behind the rest of Scotland, and Edinburgh in particular. The charters of all the Scottish universities except Glasgow offered medicine on the curriculum; a chair in medicine had been established, but nothing was done about it until Cullen's arrival, though outsiders like John Gordon, to whom Smollett was apprenticed, did occasional teaching, and Smollett may have attended lectures by John Paisley, the Professor of Anatomy. The Faculty of Physicians and Surgeons, which was not part of the university, opposed the development of a medical school on the grounds that it alone should supervise the training of surgeons and the licensing of physicians. The university was slow in shaking off the influence of strict Presbyterians, who took a dim view of the new medical notions emanating from Leyden and Edinburgh; and there was as yet no large teaching hospital comparable to the Edinburgh Royal Infirmary, founded in 1729. Smollett would have to learn his trade in another way, at a time when, north of the

Border at least, the theory and practice of medicine were rapidly changing.

Scotland has long been famous for its doctors and its medical schools, and during the eighteenth century, when this enviable tradition took root, Scottish medicine was far more advanced than its English equivalent in terms of knowledge, practice and organisation. The English medical world had, at its apex, the Royal College of Physicians, fellowship of which was restricted to graduates of Oxford and Cambridge. Neither place made much effort to keep up with medical advances or encourage undergraduates to study medicine: prospective Fellows were examined in Greek, due attention was paid to Hippocrates and Galen, the medieval master of humours, and much emphasis was laid on the unbridgeable social and professional gulf set between physicians, the aristocrats of the medical world, and the humbler surgeons and apothecaries. Scottish medicine was, by contrast, flexible and pre-eminently practical. Many Scottish medics had studied under the mighty Hermann Boerhaave in Leyden, and the enthusiasm with which they embraced his ideas made Edinburgh, and later Glasgow, among the most advanced centres of medical learning and instruction in Europe. Much value was placed on anatomy, on seeing and studying the body as a working whole, and on breaking down the absurd and artificial distinctions between the three branches of medicine. In 1726 Alexander Monro, who had studied under Boerhaave, became the first Professor of Anatomy and Surgery at Edinburgh University, teaching both trainee physicians and indentured or apprentice surgeons. His teaching was hospital-based, and made effective use of the anatomy lesson, in which students gathered round a corpse laid out on a table and dissected for their edification. Practical instruction was combined with the notion of medicine as an intellectual discipline, and with the teaching of surgery, chemistry, medical theory, biology and other relevant subjects. Equally influential was William Cullen, who believed that diseases should be seen in a coherent framework, the key to which lay in the nervous system. Known as 'Old Spasm' on account of his belief that disease was caused by a 'spasm' or disordered reaction of the nerves, he included among his pupils Smollett's future friend William Hunter, who went on to achieve fame and fortune in London for his social skills as an *accoucheur* or male midwife to the aristocracy, his private anatomy lessons and demonstrations, attended by the likes of Burke and Gibbon, and his bizarre collection of anatomical specimens, fossils, coins and assorted curios.

Nowadays surgeons see themselves as the aristocrats of the medical world, but matters were very different then. Never as fixed in Scotland as in England, the distinctions between the three branches of medicine became increasingly blurred as the century wore on, and although London physicians still thought themselves a cut above the rest, much of the work we now associate with a general practitioner was undertaken in Scotland and the English provinces by surgeon-apothecaries. But the ancient snobberies persisted, and were much resented by the better-trained Scottish practitioners who flowed south in search of work, making their marks in the armed forces and in the colonies as well as in London practice. Among their number were the urbane and dapper William Hunter, his brilliant but untutored brother John, William Smellie the great obstetrician, and John Pringle, who went on to become Physician-General to the Army, a pioneer in the fields of epidemiology and cross-infection, and the originator, at the Battle of Dettingen, of the concept of the military hospital as occupying neutral ground: all later formed part of Smollett's circle of expatriate Scots in London.

Whereas surgeons remained plain 'Mr', physicians were entitled to the prefix of 'Dr'. Physicians did not demean themselves by touching or handling their patients. John Rutherford of Edinburgh, an influential practitioner, recognising that modesty forbade the inspection of more private parts, stressed the importance of a patient's facial appearance and of noting the colour of the gums, and most physicians relied on the traditional 'five senses' – feeling the pulse, sniffing for gangrene, tasting the urine, listening for irregular breathing, and observing the colour of skin and eye. Surgeons, on the other hand, were regarded as medical artisans, unpleasantly involved in the sordid actualities of their patients' bodies. Since the nineteenth century, when the status of surgeons soared, the Royal Society of Surgeons has been a very grand body, a cut above the physicians' equivalent, but until 1745, when they went their separate ways, surgeons and barbers were lumped together, sharing membership of their United Company; the once familiar red-and-white barber's pole symbolises both disciplines, the red standing for surgery and the white for barber's skills. Surgery was seen as a manual job, akin to hairdressing; learning how to excise tumours, wens, gangrenous limbs and syphilitic chancres formed part of a practical rather than a liberal education. A surgeon's day-to-day work included lancing boils, dressing abrasions, pulling teeth, treating skin ulcers and – the universal panacea – phlebotomy or blood-letting. More daring spirits might attempt the removal of a bladder stone and cataracts, but operating inside a patient's body was usually out of bounds. Internal ailments were treated with medicines concocted by the still humbler apothecaries; the risks of trauma, blood loss and sepsis were great; and major surgery was anyhow impossible in an age when anaesthetics and antiseptics had yet to be discovered.

Like many other tradesmen, trainee surgeons were expected to serve an apprenticeship of between five and seven years. They were indentured to a master, usually at the age of fourteen, and would be expected to do chores about the surgery, attend lectures, visit hospitals, watch demonstrations of amputations and the like, and eschew pubs, gambling dens, loose women, theatres and other causes of sin. Smollett was apprenticed, in May 1736, to what was then the best-known surgical partnership in Glasgow, that of Stirling and Gordon. William Stirling retired in 1740 to devote himself to his linen business, but John Gordon seems to have been a more memorable figure. He had studied under Boerhaave, and his pupils included William Smellie, to whom he suggested the use of the obstetrical hook, and Smollett's cousin John Moore, who later worked in London under Smellie and William Hunter before returning to Glasgow, where he went into partnership with his old mentor. Gordon was closely involved with Glasgow's Town's Hospital, which specialised in treating the city's poor, and may well have taken Smollett with him on his visits. Moore celebrated him as 'a man esteemed by all who knew him for good sense, integrity and benevolence'. Later in life he became a physician, and Smollett – worried, perhaps, that Gordon might have assumed that the repellent Launcelot Crab, to whom Roderick is briefly apprenticed, was in some way modelled on him – made a point of looking up his old master on his last trip to

Scotland, acclaiming him in *Humphry Clinker* as a 'patriot of a truly noble spirit' who, had he lived in Ancient Rome, 'would have been honoured with a statue at the public expense'. Sir James had had dealings with Gordon, which doubtless smoothed the way, and James Smollett of Bonhill may well have paid his nephew's premium. Judging by an earlier indenture agreement drawn up by the firm, Smollett would have agreed to 'faithfully honestly and obediently serve and obey his said Masters in the foresaid arts and calling (of chyrugerie and pharmacie)', refuse to give away trade secrets or discuss patients' ailments with third parties, and steer clear of alehouses and the like; in return for a premium of £40 or so, the two surgeon-apothecaries – as 'surgeons in company' to the Town's Hospital, they were also contracted to supply drugs and medicines – provided tuition, board and lodgings. The surgeons' shop was on the ground floor of a seventeenth-century building; quite how Smollett, still a mere child, combined his surgical apprenticeship with his university studies, and to what extent they overlapped, remains a mystery.

Although John Gordon's apprenticeships were supposed to last five years, it was customary to spend the last two of these gaining practical experience, very often as a surgeon's assistant in the armed forces. John Moore broke off after three years to join the British Fusiliers during the War of the Austrian Succession. Smollett himself did not serve out his apprenticeship, nor did his masters try to hold him to his contract. 'There is no question of Tobias staying, for as he is sometimes troubled with a cough, I was satisfied that he got a week or two in the country. I hope he will do well,' Gordon wrote to James Bonhill. Such sentiments suggest that the benevolent Gordon was far removed from the hard-drinking Launcelot Crab, who was

> about five feet high, and ten round the belly; his face was capacious as a full moon, and much of the complexion of a mulberry; his nose, resembling a powder-horn, was swelled to an enormous size, and studded all over with carbuncles; and his little grey eyes reflected the rays in such an oblique manner, that, while he looked a person full in the face, one would have imagined he was admiring the buckle of his shoe.

Roderick is introduced to Crab in a pub, where the eminent surgeon, with two of his fellow-practitioners, is draining 'a liquor called *pop-in*, composed of mixing a quartern of brandy with a quart of small beer'. 'Studied surgery! What? In books, I suppose,' Crab greets his new apprentice.

> 'I shall have you disputing with me one of these days on points of my profession. You can already account for muscular motion (I warrant) and explain the mystery of the brain and nerves – ha? You are too learned for me, damn me. But let's hear no more of this stuff. Can you bleed and give a clyster, spread a plaster, and prepare a potion?'

A 'clyster' was an enema, and Smollett would exploit to the full the comic potential of enemas, laxatives and emetics; the reference to 'potions' suggests that Crab may have trained as an apothecary as well as a surgeon. To the annoyance of its Fellows, the College of Physicians' monopoly in England on prescribing pills and medicines had been ended in 1704, when apothecaries were also allowed to prescribe; in Edinburgh, the Incorporation of Surgeons and Apothecaries offered increasing competition to the College of Physicians, which, like its sclerotic London equivalent, was exclusive and limited in membership.

Despite his poor health, Smollett seems to have been a sprightly, sardonic figure, writing his satirical verses and, on one occasion, making his point with a snowball. According to a story printed in the *Emmet*, he was throwing snowballs with other boys of his age, all of them surgical apprentices. One of the boys was reprimanded by his master for leaving the shop unattended, but claimed that he had been hit on the head with a snowball while making out a prescription, and had set out in pursuit of the offender. The master thought this an unlikely tale, adding, 'I wonder how long I should stand here before it would enter any mortal's head to throw a snowball at me' – only to be hit full in the face by a snowball thrown by the disrespectful Smollett. Rather less frivolous is his account in *Travels through France and Italy* of a botched suicide attempt which succeeded thanks to a well-meant but ill-informed rescue attempt:

A young man of uncommon parts and erudition, very well esteemed at the university of G——w, was found early one morning in a subterranean vault among the ruins of an old archiepiscopal palace, with his throat cut from ear to ear. Being conveyed into a public house in the neighbourhood, he made signs for pen, ink and paper, and in all probability would have explained the cause of this terrible catastrophe, when an old woman, seeing the windpipe which was cut, sticking out of the wound, and mistaking it for the gullet, by way of giving him a cordial to support his spirits, poured into it, through a small funnel, a glass of burnt brandy, which strangled him in the tenth part of a minute.

But medicine would never engage his full attention, and, like so many of his fellow-Scots, he was determined to move to London. James Smollett of Bonhill died towards the end of 1738: it could be that Smollett, who combined pride of origin with an acute shortage of funds, was disappointed at not inheriting something in his uncle's will, and felt he had to make his own way in the world. Or perhaps, like Roderick Random, he was told that the forthcoming war would provide opportunities to complete his apprenticeship with practical experience. 'What's to hinder you from profiting by the war which will certainly be declared in a short time against Spain?' Crab asks Roderick. 'You may easily get on board of a king's ship in quality of a surgeon's mate; where you will certainly see a good deal of practice, and stand a chance of getting prize money.' Above all, though, he had been bitten by the literary bug: he had written a play called *The Regicide*, and he was determined to bully and pester London's theatrical managers into staging it. Roderick set out for London with 'one suit of clothes, half a dozen of ruffled shirts, as many plain, two pair of worsted, and a like number of thread stockings, a case of pocket instruments, a small edition of Horace, Wiseman's "Surgery", and ten guineas in cash'; after running up a bill for £11 18s 10d. with a Glasgow cloth merchant – two years later, it had yet to be settled – Smollett left for London in the summer of 1739, his play in his pocket.

2

A Scotch Sea-Surgeon

Quite how Smollett made his way to London is something we shall never know, but it must have been a long and uncomfortable business. It took up to a fortnight to travel between Edinburgh and London, and it was quicker to go by sea than by road. Turnpikes – the eighteenth-century motorways – had been introduced in the 1720s, but only began to snake their way across country at appreciable length in the 1750s and 1760s, partly as a result of the Forty-Five, and there was as yet no turnpike road north of Grantham. Turnpikes tended to be unpopular with the locals, who resented the charges levied by their operators for the cost of maintaining the roads, and sporadically vented their disapproval by rioting. The roads were often splattered with dung and deeply rutted by the weight of heavy wagons trundling slowly along: according to some travellers' tales, the Great North Road was so bad in places that men and horses had drowned in the pot-holes. Road-users inching their way south changed down to a funeral pace, or sometimes ground to a halt altogether, if they were unlucky enough to come up behind some of the 40,000 Highland cattle making their annual trip to Norfolk, or the 150,000 gobbling turkeys *en route* from Suffolk to market in London.

It may be that Smollett travelled in a stage-coach, a springless box on wheels covered in black leather held in place with studded nails, the six passengers inside peering dimly out through oval, red-framed windows, or in a huge stage wagon carrying up to twenty passengers and moving at a walking pace. Like Roderick Random, he may have hitched lifts with passing farmers and – depending on how much luggage he had with him – walked when no transport was available. Highwaymen, cheating landlords, sharing an unlit bedroom with other travellers and clambering into the wrong bed in the middle of the night were familiar hazards encountered by Roderick on his long journey south: particularly memorable are the pot-valiant Captain Weasel and the sanctimonious host who expatiates about the wickedness of his fellow-men all evening, quoting liberally from the classics, and presents an extortionate bill the following morning. Smollett may have enjoyed similar encounters, but bearing in mind his caveats about the hazards of reading fiction as autobiography, especially where 'low situations' are concerned, it may be safer to assume that life was duller than fiction.

The London in which he eventually found himself was tiny by modern standards, but with a population approaching 700,000 it was already the biggest city in Europe. One Englishman in ten lived in the capital. Although the aristocracy and the richer merchants were building on green fields to the north and west of London, where the air was fresher and less pestiferous – Cavendish and Hanover Squares were laid out in the 1720s, Grosvenor and Berkeley in the following decade – the City, Covent Garden, Soho, Southwark and the streets off the Strand remained, in the words of a contemporary, 'a hotchpotch of half-moon and serpentine narrow streets, close, dismal, long lanes, stinking alleys, dark gloomy courts and suffocating yards'. Then, as now, London was a grubby, scruffy city: the most celebrated and enthusiastic Londoner of all, Dr Johnson, regretted that

The filth, Sir, in some parts of the town, and the inequality and ruggedness of others, cannot but in the eyes of foreigners disgrace our nation, and incline them to imagine us a people, not only without government, but without delicacy, a herd of Barbarians, or a colony of Hottentots. The most disgusting part of the character given by travellers, of the most savage nations, is their neglect of cleanliness, of which, perhaps, no part of the world affords more proofs, than the streets of the British capital:

a city famous for wealth, commerce and plenty, and for every
other kind of civility and politeness, but which abounds with
such heaps of filth, as a savage would look on with amazement.

Quite apart from the dirt and the stench, it was a famously noisy
place, though despite the best endeavours of those who make tele-
vision costume dramas, it is hard to believe that the clank and rasp
of iron-shod wheels over cobbles, and the apparently incessant cries
of costermongers, flower girls and town criers in any way approached
today's din of police sirens, pneumatic drills, burglar alarms, snarling
motorbikes and aeroplanes roaring overhead. It was also a fairly brutal
and violent place. Part of the problem is encapsulated in Hogarth's
famous etching of *Gin Lane*. A prohibition on the importing of
French brandies during the Anglo-French wars of the late seventeenth and early eighteenth centuries, combined with low corn
prices and a relaxation of the rules whereby distillers had to serve
a seven-year apprenticeship, led to a frenzy of distilling and gin
consumption: anyone was free to brew the stuff, and there were no
restraints on how or where it was sold. Sporadic efforts were made
to control its sale, usually through excise duties, but it was not
until the 1750s that the tidal wave of alcohol began to recede.
Excessive boozing led to fights and assaults on innocent passers-
by, but little help could be expected from a friendly policeman:
maintaining law and order was in the hands of local wards, vestries
and parishes, each of which guarded its jurisdiction so jealously
that constables in pursuit of a villain were reluctant or unable to
stray into neighbouring territory. It was not until the novelist Henry
Fielding was appointed chief or stipendiary magistrate in Bow Street
in 1749 that some kind of metropolitan police authority came into
being.

Although Lincoln's Inn Fields, hitherto a vast rubbish dump, had
been enclosed in 1735, and various Lighting Acts were passed in
the same decade, Smollett arrived in London too early for many of
the improvements that, during his lifetime, were to make London a
safer, cleaner and more agreeable place to live. Most of the streets
were not only narrow but darkened, even at midday, by huge hanging
signs creaking in the wind. Short-sighted or inattentive pedestrians

could easily topple into uncovered coal chutes and cellars, as well as being deluged by rain-water untrammelled by gutters and pipes. Some houses were so shoddily built that collapsing masonry presented another hazard as, in Dr Johnson's words, 'falling houses thunder on your head'.

Much was to be improved by a series of Paving Acts: Purbeck stone flagstones replaced cobble pavements, the open 'kennel' that ran down the middle of the road gave way to less squalid gutters on either side, and the creaking signs were taken down in favour of house numbers, a radical innovation. Rain-water on the roof began to make its way down to street level via pipes and gutters, and the relevant authorities were made responsible for cleaning or 'scavenging' the streets. In 1747 the fetid Fleet Ditch, with its cargo of raw sewage, dead dogs, rotting vegetables and rubbish, was covered over to make way, in due course, for the Farringdon Road. An embankment was built along the Thames between the Fleet and London Bridge, and some decrepit old buildings were knocked down in the process; the last of the old City gates were removed, and movement between the north and south banks was made easier by the building of Westminster Bridge in 1750, and Blackfriars in 1769. Smollett's vision of London is, for the most part, hellish and unflattering, anticipating those of Dickens, Mayhew and Gustave Doré, but in his *Travels through France and Italy* he was to note that none of the bridges he had seen in either country was a patch on Westminster 'either in beauty, magnificence, or solidity', and that 'when the bridge at Black-Friars is finished, it will be such a monument of architecture as all the world cannot parallel'. Reminders of an older London, still in evidence when Smollett arrived there, were the heads of executed criminals impaled on spikes above Temple Bar: Horace Walpole remarked on how 'people made trade of letting spy-glasses at a half-penny a look', but those of Jacobites condemned to death after the Forty-Five marked the end of a long tradition.

Anyone writing about the London of Hogarth and Fielding feels duty bound to mention the long, ritualised processions that accompanied condemned criminals from Newgate to Tyburn tree, on the site of the present Marble Arch; debtors' and other prisons, each like a small, self-contained city; the pleasure-gardens of Ranelagh

and Vauxhall; Covent Garden and the Strand, aswarm with prostitutes, con-men and pickpockets; the proliferation of coffee-houses,
often catering for particular professions, political groupings or nation-
alities, for writers or Scotsmen or theatricals, where men met to
gossip, read the papers and pick up business; the little boats scur-
rying about the river like so many water beetles, ferrying passengers
from one bank of the Thames to the other, the great dome of St
Paul's looming up behind like a vast, benevolent egg. Tyburn
excepted, Smollett was to write about them all with an energy, a
satirical edge and an eye for detail reminiscent of Hogarth, a painter
he hugely admired, and of those unflinching Dutch interiors in which
bottle-nosed men, inflamed by drink, pick fights, pee in corners and
thrust their hands in the bosoms of cherubic, smiling wenches.

London was also at the centre of changing patterns of behaviour
which Smollett would profit from as a freelance writer and editor
while at the same time abominating their effects on society at large.
The eighteenth century saw the emergence of what came to be
known as the consumer society – a world in which, among the
middle and even some of the artisan classes, there was enough
disposable income to spend on books, furnishings, gardens, silver-
ware, pottery, fashionable clothes, travel and the occasional flutter
at the races. Everything, authorship included, had its price and its
market value: the provinces followed where London led, newspapers
and advertising spread the word, and each class sought to emulate
its betters. Although the landed aristocracy was as rich and powerful
as ever, and would remain so until the agricultural depression of
the 1870s, or even the First World War, a rival centre of wealth
and power was emerging, based on commerce and the City. In
London itself, ancient crafts and light industries such as silk-weaving
and clock-making gave way to clerical, administrative and financial
occupations. Stockbrokers, bankers, brokers and commission agents
flourished and grew fat; men hurried to the City to work in insurance
offices and banks. Rich City merchants and traders – many of whom
chose to go on living in the cramped streets between St Paul's and
the Tower rather than move to airier quarters out west – came to
see themselves as embodying the true interests of the nation,
building up Britain's overseas trade and embryo Empire, forming a

kind of permanent opposition to the landed interests while emulating their taste and style, buying themselves country estates and marrying their daughters into the aristocracy. Each class sought to imitate those above, while drawing up the ladder firmly behind them: Fielding noted how 'the Nobleman will emulate the grandeur of a Prince and the Gentleman will aspire to the proper status of a Nobleman; the Tradesman steps from behind his counter into the vacant place of the Gentleman', and the *British Magazine* observed that 'the present rage of imitating the manners of high life hath spread itself so far among the gentlefolks of lower life, that in a few years we shall probably have no common folk at all'. Even so benign a figure as Jonas Hanway, a well-known philanthropist and the inventor of the umbrella, was outraged by the subversive notion of labourers drinking tea and taking sugar. For Smollett, and other social conservatives, the appetite for luxury and the increasing power of the mercantile *nouveaux riches* were the root of all evil, and London the devil's lair.

Smollett had arrived in London with a sheaf of introductions to influential and well-connected fellow-Scots, including the publisher Andrew Millar and the poet James Thomson, author of *The Seasons* and 'Rule, Britannia', which was set to music by Thomas Arne in 1740 as part of his masque of *Alfred*. It may well be that, like Roderick Random, Smollett was cheated by con-men and, as a 'Sawney', mocked for his impenetrable accent and exposed to wearisome jokes about kilts and oatmeal; it is less likely that he was reduced to taking a room for two shillings a week above a chandler's shop in St Martin's Lane, just round the corner from the crime-infested 'rookeries' of Seven Dials, the alleys and courts of which pullulated with Irish labourers, prostitutes, sailors and derelicts.

Keen as he was to find a theatrical manager willing to take on *The Regicide*, Smollett had to bide his time before embarking on his career as a playwright. War with Spain broke out in October 1739, and he decided to enlist as a surgeon's mate on board a man-of-war. Scotland, James Thomson observed, was 'fruitful of surgeons; they come here like vultures every day . . . The Change is quite full of them. They peruse the ship-bills and meet the sea-captains.' Those applying to be taken on as ships' surgeons were shunted between the

Navy Office, the branch of the Admiralty responsible for personnel, food and uniforms, and the Surgeons' Hall, where the lucky candidates – luckier still, in Roderick Random's experience, if they had the wherewithal to tip or bribe their examiners – were supplied with the necessary paper qualifications. Roderick encountered a 'swarm of Scotch surgeons', and his examiners told him that 'We have scarce any other countrymen to examine here; you Scotchmen have overspread us of late as the locusts did Egypt.' After jumping through the requisite hoops, Smollett's efforts to enlist paid off, and he joined HMS *Chichester* – an 80-gun 'third-rate' ship of the line – as a surgeon's second mate in October 1740.

Fondly remembered for its unusual name by generations of schoolchildren, the War of Jenkins's Ear was fought at the behest of City merchants who resented any restraints on their right to trade and do business anywhere in the world, and especially in the West Indies. The aggressor – or victim, depending on the point of view – was the once-mighty but ailing Spanish Empire, with its fabulously rich colonies in the Caribbean and South and Central America. Fuelled by dreams of El Dorado, English merchants and pirates had coveted Spanish gold and Spanish galleons since the great days of Drake and Hawkins. The lure remained as strong as ever, and never more so than when the enormous *azogues* or treasure ships, laden with Mexican silver and Peruvian gold and taking three or four years to make the round trip from Spain and back, lumbered slowly across the Atlantic from Porto Bello on the Panamanian coast, where they had taken on their cargoes, to their home ports of Ferrol and Cadiz. Spain, for all its riches, was a predominantly agricultural country and had to rely on others to provide its colonies with manufactured goods; nor did it have a toehold in Africa, which would have enabled it to send out slaves of its own to make up a shortage of unpaid labour. Under the terms of the Treaty of Utrecht, which concluded the War of the Spanish Succession in 1713, Britain – in the form of the newly established South Sea Company – was granted the much-coveted 'Asiento' for the following forty years. Previously held by Portugal and, more recently, by France, the Asiento gave the South Sea Company the monopoly in supplying slaves to Spain's American colonies. The Royal African Company, operating from its forts on the West African coast, sold slaves to the South Sea Company, which was also allowed to send out a ship of 500 tons, laden to the gunwales with British manufactured goods, to the annual fairs at Vera Cruz on the Mexican coast, and Cartagena in Colombia.

Such legitimate traffic tantalised but hardly satisfied, and the Spanish were uneasily aware that English traders, licit and illicit, hovered round their possessions like so many feeding sharks. Already bruised by the loss of Gibraltar and Minorca to the British under the Treaty of Utrecht, they flared up at the slightest provocation. They resented the English colony of Georgia, which abutted on to their own colony of Florida and had been founded by the eccentric philanthropist General Oglethorpe to enable debtors from the Fleet prison to make a fresh start in life, minus slaves and strong drink; they objected when English sailors were spotted collecting salt in the Tortugas and felling mahogany – the fashionable wood for furniture – in Honduras; they complained that, in contravention of the rules, the annual ship attending the fairs was accompanied by illegal 'provision tenders' selling extra goods for sale. As it turned out, the trade permitted under the terms of the Asiento was never enough to justify the wildly over-optimistic speculation that led to the collapse of the South Sea Bubble in 1720, and only seven fairs were held between 1719 and the outbreak of war twenty years later. The reason was all too obvious, both to the Spanish authorities and – though they might not have openly admitted it – to the City merchants: much of the trade with the Spanish colonies was essentially contraband and in the hands of English smugglers, who saw themselves as the heirs to the Elizabethan buccaneers.

The Spaniards employed *guarda costas* or coastguards to intercept and board suspected smugglers, and – if necessary – confiscate both ships and cargoes. Their activities aroused a frenzy of righteous indignation among the English merchant classes. Horror stories were told of stout-hearted English tars rotting in putrid Spanish jails, and of how the innocent crew of the *Robert* had been tortured with screws and vices by diabolical *guarda costas*; the South Sea Company claimed that the *guarda costas* were no better than pirates. The cry of 'no search' went up, and the pacific First Minister, Robert Walpole, who had no desire to go to war with Spain, came under incessant pressure to take revenge on the 'Spanish poltroon'. The leading opposition paper, the *Craftsman*, castigated Walpole for his failure to protect British merchantmen, and the 'Patriot' leader William Pulteney prophesied that if things went on as they were the *guarda costas* would shortly be blockading the Thames. But nothing proved quite as inflammatory as Robert Jenkins and his celebrated ear. In 1731, or so he claimed, his ship, the *Rebecca*, was boarded by a notoriously cruel *guarda costa* called Fandino; Jenkins, as master, was lashed to the mast, and his ear was then cut off by the brutish Spaniards. Seven years later, when agitation over Spanish 'depredations' was reaching a climax, Jenkins appeared to dramatic effect in the House of Commons, waving above his head what he claimed was his lopped-off ear, wrapped in cotton-wool. Alderman Beckford – an immensely rich City merchant who made his fortune from the West Indian sugar trade, and fathered the languid and aesthetic William, the builder of Fonthill and author of *Vathek* – later suggested that had anyone taken the trouble to lift the flaps of the sea-dog's wig, he would have found both ears firmly in place; but that was neither here nor there. What Horace Walpole described as the 'clamour of the merchants' was in full spate. William Pitt, who would devote his career to the mercantile interests and the pursuit of a 'blue water policy', exercised, for the first time, his fabled oratorical powers in the House of Commons on behalf of the supposedly embattled merchants and ship-owners. Sir Robert Walpole, his back against the wall, ordered the British Minister in Madrid to start immediate negotiations in order to avert war. Under the terms of the Convention of Prado, the Spanish government agreed to compensate British merchants to the tune of £200,000, provided the South Sea Company itself paid some £68,000 owing in arrears. By the time a further sum had been deducted to cover the sinking of a Spanish fleet at Pasarro, the amount to be paid by the Spaniards had been whittled down to a mere £27,000. The South Sea Company refused to pay up; the Asiento was suspended; Admiral Vernon was dispatched to the West Indies in July, and war was declared three months later. 'It is your war, and I wish you well of it,' Walpole told the Duke of Newcastle, his eccentric and belligerent Secretary of State for the Southern Department.

Although the reforms of the mid-century were to turn the Royal Navy into an effective and efficient fighting force, ready for Nelsonian inspiration, it was, when Smollett joined up, a fairly shambolic organisation. English men-of-war were often elderly, dating back to the previous century in some cases; they were also less seaworthy and weaker in firepower than their French or Spanish equivalents, and their tendency to roll excessively in high seas often made it impossible for the lowest tier of guns to be used. Wooden ships were expensive to maintain, and few were kept in a state of high alert: out of a total of 124 ships of the line, only 30 were ready for action in 1739. There was also an acute shortage of manpower. Conditions in the merchant navy were much milder, the pay was better, and many of those who might have enlisted were already on the high seas, dodging the *guarda costas*. Since squadrons were always on duty in the Channel, the Mediterranean and the West Indies, some 10,000 sailors were normally employed in peacetime; in wartime the demand went up to around 60,000, and the shortfall had to be met. Bounties were paid to those who enlisted voluntarily, and even the humblest members of the crew were entitled to, and tantalised by, a proportion, however tiny, of the prize money resulting from the capture of a well-stocked enemy ship; but much use was also made of the notorious press-gangs. For all his efforts to enlist as a surgeon's mate, Roderick Random was himself press-ganged into service; merchant sailors, returning from a two- or three-year voyage, had barely set foot in an English port before being bustled on board a Navy ship and forcibly enrolled. Innocent civilians, many of them, in Admiral Hawke's words, 'poor sickly little fellows that are of no service', were seized while strolling along a street or emerging from the pub; it was rumoured that among those forcibly enlisted for Anson's expedition of 1740 to harry the Spanish treasure fleets off the coasts of Chile and Peru – which turned into a four-year circumnavigation of the globe – was a party of pensioners from the Greenwich naval hospital, with an average age of over seventy.

There was little co-ordination between those responsible for the various facets of naval life. The Secretary of State ordered the movement of fleets around the world; the Admiralty Board was responsible for the Navy being in a state of readiness, or not; the Navy

Office, where Roderick (and Smollett, presumably) presented his credentials, was in charge of personnel, uniforms and food. There was also a separate Pay Office, and a Sick and Wounded Board. Those at the top were, like the Greenwich pensioners, of an advanced age: Wager, the First Sea Lord, was seventy-three in 1739; Norris, the First Lord of the Admiralty, was seventy-nine; even the bustling, warlike Vernon, who was made Vice-Admiral that year, was fifty-five. The ships themselves were 'rated' according to the number of guns they carried: a third-rate, like the *Chichester*, carried between 64 and 80 guns and a crew of around 600 men. Fifth-rates had one deck, fourths had two, and three and above had three; all were four-masted and square-rigged.

Quite how harsh and brutal life was aboard ship is a matter of debate. Vernon, a disciplinarian who also believed in taking care of his men, once described the Navy as being 'manned by violence and maintained by cruelty'; Dr Johnson, who had no direct experience of the matter but probably reflected the views of his age, decreed that 'No man will be a sailor who has contrivance enough to get himself into a jail; for being in a ship is being in a jail, with the chance of being drowned', and claimed that 'A man in jail has more room, better food, and commonly better company.' Smollett himself once wrote that whereas the merchant seaman had plenty to eat, was free to come and go, had no worries about being court-martialled, and was reasonably well paid, his military equivalent was 'restricted to an allowance of provision, and that not always of the best species; he is subject to control and personal outrage, under a succession of officers, from the captain to the boatswain's driver; he is exposed to flagellation, stripes, shackles, court-martials, death and maiming from the enemy'. Writing as an historian, he referred to the sailors' tedious diet of 'putrid beef, rusty pork, and bread swimming with maggots' – salt meat, biscuits, dried fish, beer, onions, dried peas and huge cubes of 'portable soup' formed the staple, with no meat available on the 'banyan' days of Monday, Wednesday and Friday – but his most famous, influential and damning account of life at sea was in the pages of *Roderick Random*.

Like his creator, Roderick signs up as a surgeon's second mate. He soon falls foul of the ship's surgeon, Mackshane, a cowardly Irish crypto-Catholic, and Crampley, the bullying first mate; Captain Oakum is a half-crazed nautical dictator. Upright and defiant to the end, Roderick finds himself in a sadistic, half-demented hell-hole, redeemed only by honest Jack Rattlin and Morgan, the good-hearted if verbose Welsh surgeon's first mate. Sick sailors are ordered to parade on deck, with fatal results, the cat-o'-nine-tails is applied with gruesome relish, and Roderick himself is manacled to the deck, unprotected from the tropical sun, and left there during the course of an engagement with some French warships: at one point in the battle, 'the head of the officer of the marines, who stood near me, being shot off, bounced from the deck athwart my face, leaving me well nigh blinded with brains'.

Such goings-on – echoes of which reverberate through Melville's *Billy Budd* and innumerable films about life on board the *Bounty* – fail to impress the eminent naval historian N.A.M. Rodger. Smollett, he warns us, is 'a poor, or rather an over-rich substitute for documentary evidence'. The notion that the early eighteenth-century warship was akin to a 'floating concentration camp' should, in his view, be scotched, and Smollett must shoulder much of the blame for its entering the popular imagination. Rodger concedes that the lash was employed for such anti-social practices as buggery and theft, and that sailors tended to degenerate into a drunken rabble when on shore or in the event of a shipwreck, but he has an 'organic' view of life on board ship, with captain, officers and men bound together by ties of dependence and obligation. Discipline, he suggests, was 'lax to the point of anarchy': the captain was, in effect, a kind of patron or father figure, whose crew would often follow him from one ship to another. Brutality carried to excess, in the manner of Captain Oakum, would cause the ship's fragile ecosystem to crumble. Despite the occasional martinet, Rodger's account rings true; but he seems to forget that Smollett was writing a novel, and that lurid villains and intolerable conditions make for a more compelling read than a temperate version of events.

Like the purser, the master and the navigator, the ship's surgeon was a warrant officer, appointed by the Navy Board; all were one tier down from the commissioned officers – the captain and the lieutenants – appointed by the Admiralty. Since few physicians or apothecaries joined the Navy, the surgeon and his mates were expected to combine all three medical disciplines – which, together with a shortage of work back home, explains the preponderance of Scottish surgeons at sea. Before being appointed, they had to be examined and approved at the Surgeons' Hall by the famously corrupt and inefficient Company of Barber Surgeons; like the purser, who supplied the ships' provisions, and was often accused of short-changing his customers, the surgeon was expected to provide his own instruments and drugs. He earned £5 a month, and as one of the ship's 'idlers' he was exempt from having to stand watch or turn out when all hands were piped on deck, very often in the middle of the night. Many were alarmingly ill-qualified: Thomas Blakeway, a surgeon's mate on board the *Cambridge*, had been a 'very eminent operator in London for nails and corns' (i.e. a fashionable chiropodist). Surgeons were expected to visit the sick twice a day, present the captain with a daily sick list, and, if possible, provide their patients with freshly caught fish.

The surgeon berthed on the orlop deck, just on or above the waterline, and messed either with the lieutenants in the wardroom, or with the warrant officers in the gun-room; the surgeon's mates shared the dark and malodorous cockpit with the midshipmen. Roderick, newly arrived on the *Thunder*, is 'filled with astonishment and horror' when, after descending 'by divers ladders to a space as dark as a dungeon, which I understood was immersed several feet under water', he finds himself in the cockpit, where 'my nose was saluted with an intolerable stench of putrified cheese and rancid butter' emanating from the purser's store cupboards. His colleague Thomson – who later throws himself overboard, unable to bear life on board ship a moment longer – shows him to his mess, 'a square of about six feet, surrounded with the medicine chest, that of the first mate, his own, and a board, by way of a table, fastened to the after powder-room; it was also enclosed with canvas, nailed round to the beams of the ship, to screen us from the cold, as well as from the view of the midshipmen and quarter-masters, who lodged within the tiers on each side of us'.

A dinner of boiled peas, onions, butter and pepper, known to sea-dogs as salmagundi, has a restorative effect, but worse is to come when Thomson suggests that they visit the sick and make up their prescriptions. 'I was much less surprised that people should die on board, than that any sick person should recover,' Roderick declares, for

> Here I saw about fifty miserable distempered wretches, suspended in rows, so huddled upon one another, that not more than fourteen inches space was allocated for each with his bed and bedding; and deprived of the light of day, as well as of fresh air; breathing nothing but a noissome atmosphere of the morbid steams exhaling from their own excrements and diseased bodies, devoured with vermin hatched in the filth that surrounded them, and destitute of every convenience necessary for people in that helpless condition.

Nor was that the end of the horrors in store. After watching how Thomson administers 'clysters' or enemas – he removes his wig, strips down to his waistcoat, creeps along the floor below the hammocks, enema in hand, forces two hammocks apart with his head and shoulders, administers the clyster, and resubmerges like a submarine – Roderick tries his hand. Unfortunately the ship rolls at a critical moment: he tips over, or treads in, a pot brimming over with more than mere urine, and the stench wafts round the already reeking sick-bay. Such hazards were not simply the by-product of Smollett's lavatorial imagination. Some twenty years after Smollett joined the Navy, a Captain Blake urged that

> the hospital room be provided with one or more strong-armed chairs, which may then be lashed to the deck, each having in its bottom a close stool-pan made of metal, which may be more easily emptied and washed clean than the wooden buckets directed by the present regulation of the navy to be used, which always retain a smell, though washed ever so clean, and are very inconvenient for a sick man to sit upon, frequently overset with him, by the sudden rolling of the ship, and produce very offensive and unwholesome consequences; and on such occasions fill the ship with a stench, which not only annoys the

whole company but retards the cure of the sick, and even contributes to infect those who are well.

The medical authorities of the time set great store on the notion that illnesses were caused, and spread, by an unhealthy environment. The 'ague' and 'marsh fever' were thought to be most common among those living by estuaries or in wetlands; 'spotted' and 'putrid' fevers, including typhus, afflicted slum-dwellers and those cooped up in barracks, in workhouses and on board ship. 'Miasmatic' diseases were allegedly caused by poisonous exhalations from rotting meat and vegetation and stagnant water, and much was made of the pestilential effects of bad air, dirty clothes and filthy living conditions. The eminent and influential William Cullen was among those medical men who believed that whereas some diseases, like smallpox, were contagious, others were associated with particular places and ways of life, and he paid close attention to external influences such as climate, food, drainage and humidity, and to the role of dirt, bad air and poor ventilation in spreading diseases in hospitals and prisons. Despite the stench of putrefying cheese and the overturned chamber-pot aboard HMS *Thunder*, such ideas had been warmly welcomed in the Navy. English warships were far cleaner than their French equivalents. The decks were washed down regularly with vinegar, sand and water, and to reduce the risk of infection, especially from those recently delivered by the press-gangs, surgeons recommended the fumigation of clothes. The great naval doctor James Lind suggested that, in the event of an outbreak of disease, the area below decks should be fumigated with brimstone burned in pots, foul bedding destroyed, and infected clothes baked in the oven. Gunpowder was sporadically ignited to clear the air; sailors were urged to keep their clothes as clean as possible, but since fresh water was scarce and had to be kept for drinking, and soap was ineffectual in salt water, they had to resort to 'chamberlayne' or urine as a detergent.

For all these precautions, life below decks was an unsavoury affair – and three-deckers like the *Chichester* and the *Thunder* were less well-aired and hygienic than single-decked frigates. After weeks at sea, the bilge water in the ship's well stank; rats gnawed the provisions, and spread their fleas; clothes became mildewed in the damp, and butter and cheese turned rancid. Ventilation was a perennial problem, especially in winter or bad weather, when the ports and hatches were closed. The air in the bowels of the ship was sometimes suffocatingly bad, and those unlucky enough to descend to the depths would lower a candle in a lantern to test whether or not it stayed alight. Much ingenuity was devoted to the circulation of air. Admiral Wager, in the year that war broke out, recommended a system of pipes and fires; Stephen Hales, the inventor of a windmill-operated scheme for use in Newgate Prison, came up with 'ships' lungs', driven by bellows in a box. Mr Sutton, the progenitor of a rival air pump, conceded that Hales's ventilators 'will keep a prison sweet, but my pipes will sweeten even a boghouse'.

Keeping healthy under such conditions would have been hard enough, the ship's diet could only make matters worse. Too little fresh water and too much booze caused that unpleasant if faintly comical-sounding complaint called the 'gravel', and a lack of fresh fruit and vegetables did nothing for the health of the crew. Oil, raisins, rice and other imperishables might be added to the purser's stores on exotic stations, and cows and chickens were sometimes kept on board for the officers' use, but the combination of fraudulent contractors, cheese-paring pursers and the need to stock items that would last for weeks or even months at sea meant that the food was invariably tedious, often rotten and never health-inducing. According to the waggish William Thompson, the ships' biscuits swarmed with black-headed maggots, while the rounds of nautical cheese were so hard that they could be carved into buttons or incorporated whole into the ship's mast. Lieutenant Robert Watkins, who served on the *Chichester* at the same time as Smollett, condemned a huge quantity of cheese as inedible; Anson, who set out on his famous circumnavigation of the globe a year later, found two-thirds of the dried beef supplied to his pursers by the Victualling Board to be 'stinking'.

The most famous naval ailment of all, of course, was scurvy. Few died of it, except on long voyages – Anson lost a third of his men that way, many of them on the interminable voyage across the Pacific from South America to the Philippines, and another 300-odd from dysentery and fever – but its debilitating effects limited the amount of time squadrons could spend at sea, or on blockade. Its symptoms included spots on the body, putrid gums, lassitude, ulcers, wounds that failed to heal and an unwholesome bodily stench. For many years it was assumed, quite wrongly, to be a venereal disease, and the standard anti-scorbutic consisted of elixir of vitriol – sulphuric acid diluted and flavoured with alcohol, sugar and spices. The first to advocate the use of citrus fruits was James Lind, an Edinburgh-trained medic who joined HMS *Salisbury* in 1739 as a surgeon's mate, and went on to become the Physician-General to the Haslar Naval Hospital in Portsmouth. Incensed by the poor accommodation and food and water on board men-of-war, Lind noted that 'The number of seamen in time of war, who died by shipwreck, famine, fire and sword, are but inconsiderable, in respect of such as are destroyed by the ship diseases, and by the usual maladies of intemperate climates.' Smollett reached much the same conclusion after his experiences on the doomed expedition to Cartagena. Nowadays the Scots are famed for their aversion to fresh fruit and veg, but although Smollett went to sea some fifteen years too soon to take advantage of Lind's *Treatise on the Scurvy*, he seems to have shared his countryman's faith in their salutary properties: towards the end of the siege of Cartagena, when his shipmates were dying like flies from yellow fever, Roderick sourly observes that 'a great many valuable lives might have been saved, if the useless transports had been employed in fetching fresh stock, turtle, fruit and other refreshments from Jamaica, and other adjacent islands . . .'

Fever – described in Aubrey's *The Sea Surgeon, or the Guinea Man's Vade Mecum* of 1729 as 'a preternatural heat all over the body excited by a vicious kind of air altering the fluids and depriving them of their natural motion' – was treated by various means, including emetics and laxatives made from rhubarb, bark or cream of tartar; a 'gentle puke' was deemed effective, as was the inevitable blood-letting, said to alleviate overheating of the system. Other ailments tended by Smollett and his fellow-surgeons included tetanus, the 'wind of a ball' (the numbing of part of the body caused by a cannonball passing too close for comfort), 'flash burns' resulting from accidental explosions, and an alarmingly high incidence of insanity, with the afflicted banging their heads on the timbers and occasionally hurling themselves overboard. Still more hair-raising were the demands made on the surgeon and his mates in the height of battle. They were expected to keep swabs, tourniquets, lint, needles, knives and splints ready for an emergency, and men wounded in action were treated either in the cockpit, at the aft end of the orlop deck, or on a platform in the hold below the waterline: when, in the heat of battle, Captain Oakum refuses Mackshane's request to have a platform raised in the after-hold where he can treat the wounded, the lily-livered surgeon, whose sole interest is self-preservation, invokes Article IX of the 1734 *Instructions to Surgeons*, and carries the day. As Roderick discovers when the vindictive Mackshane tries, quite unnecessarily, to whip off honest Jack Rattlin's leg, amputation was the universal panacea for shattered limbs. The two most widely used manuals, Aubrey's *The Sea Surgeon* and John Atkins's *The Navy Surgeon*, both emphasised the importance of speed, since 'the heat and surprise in action make it the properest time for amputation, men meeting their misfortune with greater strength and resolution than when they have spent a night under thought and reflection'. Describing the hazards of operating in the Indian Ocean in the 1750s, Edward Ives noted that they were constantly interrupted by the cries of the wounded while amputating, and that 'the very shaking of the lower gun deck, owing to the recoil of the large cannon which are placed just over his head, is of itself sufficient to incommode a surgeon'.

The War of Jenkins's Ear got off to a sluggish start, and was bedevilled thereafter by dithering, delays and ineptitude. The fact that it had been debated so long and so loud in the press and in Parliament had long ago alerted the Spaniards; Walpole's lack of enthusiasm and divisions within the ministry made matters worse. Walpole, who was far more interested in maintaining the peace through a network of Continental alliances, worried that naval entanglements in far-away places left Britain exposed to Jacobites and the like. 'May not one poor ship be left at home?' he pleaded. He worried, too, about aggravating the French, who were neutral in theory but pro-Spanish in fact: both countries now had a Bourbon on the throne, and much of the trade between Spain and its American colonies was carried in French ships. Keen to prevent Spanish reinforcements and news of British intentions from crossing the Atlantic, Norris, the Admiral of the Fleet, favoured blockading Spanish ports to prevent the *flota* or treasure fleet from setting sail. Haddock, the admiral in charge of the Mediterranean, had only ten ships with which to patrol the entire Spanish coast: Cadiz was watched, but Ferrol was unguarded, and the Spaniards made their getaway, taking with them 2,000 men as reinforcements for the garrison at Cartagena.

Although Smollett came to despise him, and to blame him for the disaster at Cartagena, Vice-Admiral Vernon was a good deal more energetic and effective than his fellow-admirals – apart, that is, from Anson. Short and dark, with a 'piercing eye, a searching look and a majestic bearing', ridiculed by Horace Walpole as a 'silly, noisy admiral', Edward Vernon had been born in 1684. As a schoolboy at Westminster, he could 'discuss any subject in Latin'; while still at Oxford, he was taught by Newton how to calculate latitude by the North Star. He joined the Navy at the age of seventeen, took part in the siege of Gibraltar in 1704, and then spent time on the West Indies station, operating against pirates and Spanish privateers: his experiences there convinced him that the Spaniards had little stomach for a fight, and that the Royal Navy was more than a match for the 'bully Don'. He was also made uneasily aware that a fleet operating so far from home was at the end of a long and tenuous line of supply, and that keeping ships in trim and indenting for men and supplies was a hazardous and unreliable business: supply convoys sailed every two months during the War of Jenkins's Ear, and Vernon complained to the Victualling Board that his men would starve if they had to rely on the American colonies for alternative provisions. He served for twelve years as a voluble and energetic MP, loudly supporting the mercantile interests and the 'blue water policy', and denouncing Walpole for his neglect of British interests. When war broke out in the autumn of 1739 he immediately button-holed Wager, the First Sea Lord, and persuaded him that he was the man to lead an expedition to the Caribbean to sort out the Spaniards.

As an MP, Vernon had once boasted that if he were given six ships he could capture Porto Bello, the Panamanian port which was a base for the *guarda costas* and an entrepôt for the treasure fleets. In November 1739 he took Porto Bello, becoming a national hero when the news eventually filtered back to England: he was made a Freeman of the City, his features were replicated on jugs and medals, and both he and the port he had captured lent their names to innumerable pubs and streets. He went on to capture the port of Chagres – but Cartagena, which he bombarded, proved a tougher nut to crack: it was difficult to mount an assault on the main part of the town, which lay within a U-shaped bay, and rolling, shallow seas made anchorage a tricky business. Vernon withdrew to Jamaica, from where he urged Newcastle to send out reinforcements. With time on his hands, he set about implementing his ideas about how life should be conducted at sea, and how to deal with the perennial problem of nautical drunkenness. Because the smoke from gunfire made it impossible to peer through the murk of battle, let alone decipher the messages flagged from the Admiral's ship, Vernon made a virtue of necessity by delegating authority to his captains. A disciplinarian who believed in keeping his men busy and made effective use of confinement, the occasional flogging and the power of prayer to keep his men in order, he was determined to tackle that 'formidable dragon, drunkenness'. 'We are now in a great hurry for sailing, and I in a sad pickle, with my whole ship's company drunk,' Admiral Keppel had once confessed to Anson. Vernon wanted none of that. The sailors drank beer in northern climes, and wine in the Mediterranean, but in the West Indies they were supplied, to lethal effect, with local rum, issued at midday in half-pint measures. Vernon issued his celebrated memorandum forbidding raw spirits to be served to ships' companies, who had to make do instead with 'grog', named after the Admiral's grogram cloak. Each half-pint of rum was diluted with a quart of water and served out at eleven in the morning and five in the evening. The effect on discipline and general well-being was said to be instantaneous; 'grog' passed into the language, and Vernon was immortalised.

Back in England, there was keen debate about whether the grateful inhabitants of Porto Bello and Chagres were planning to throw off the Spanish yoke, embrace Protestantism and, like good Englishmen, elect a mayor and corporation; but, once again, everything moved at a snail's pace. Sir Chaloner Ogle, who had served as Commander-in-Chief Jamaica, and recently been elevated to Rear-Admiral of the

Blue, was said to be assembling a fleet off the Isle of Wight, but was subject to endless delays. 'You ask me, why does not Sir Chaloner Ogle sail,' Newcastle remarked to his ministerial colleague, Lord Hardwicke. 'I cannot answer because he is not ready. If you ask another question, why is he not ready? To that I cannot answer.' In October 1740 Sir Chaloner finally assembled his fleet of twenty-five ships – reduced by one when the *Augusta* lost its rudder on leaving harbour – and set out for the Caribbean with some 8,500 soldiers and marines on board.

Smollett, duly equipped with his warrant as surgeon's second mate, had joined the *Chichester* on the Medway back in March. Built in Chatham in 1694, she was, although a third-rate, one of the largest ships in the Navy, and rolled heavily in high seas. She was manned by a mixture of veterans and press-ganged novices. Crews' uniforms were not introduced in the Navy until 1748, so the men were clad in a motley of blue jackets, check or spotted shirts, loose necker-chiefs, waistcoats and calf-length white trousering; most were clean-shaven, wore their hair in a pigtail, and were barefooted. Once out of the Channel, the fleet encountered a horrific storm in the Bay of Biscay. The *Superb* lost its three masts, and the *Chichester*'s mainsail split. 'Of all the fleet, seven sail only were to be seen, and of these two had lost their masts, while the others scudded under reefed main-sails,' Smollett wrote in his 'Account of the Expedition against Cartagena'. A water barrel broke free of its lashings and maimed sixteen men; one of the yardarm braces gave way with such force that four men were hurled overboard, two of them lost for ever, and another man's knee was horribly mangled. 'I was wakened by a most horrible din, occasioned by the play of the gun carriages upon the deck above, the cracking of cabins, the howling of the wind through the shrouds, the confused noise of the ship's crew, the pipes of the boatswain and his mates, the trumpets of the lieutenants, and the clanking of the chain pumps,' he recalled in *Roderick Random*, adding that 'The sea was swelled into billows mountain high, on the top of which our ship sometimes hung as if it was about to be precipitated to the abyss below! Sometimes we sunk between two waves that rose on each side higher than our topmast head, and threatened, by dashing together, to overwhelm us in a moment!' All seemed chaos on board:

A number of officers and sailors ran backwards and forwards with distraction in their looks, halloing to one another, and undetermined what they should attend to first. Some clung to the yards, endeavouring to unbend the sails that were split into a thousand pieces flapping in the wind; others tried to furl those which were yet whole, while the masts, at every pitch, bent and quivered like twigs . . .

It is during this storm that Jack Rattlin is hurled from the yardarm on to the heaving deck and breaks his leg so violently that splintered shin bones poke through the surrounding skin, leading Mackshane to attempt an amputation – only to be thwarted by Roderick and Morgan, who saw off the protruding piece of bone, dress the wound, apply the 'eighteen-tailed bandage, and put the leg in a box, *secundum artem*'.

The *Chichester*'s Lieutenant Watkins refers to the gale in his journal, as well as to the health of his men. Almost every day he recorded a death on board ship. When the ship reached Dominica in December, 110 sick men – a sixth of the crew – had to be sent ashore. Tents were pitched for them on the shore, and those with scurvy were, as if in anticipation of Lind's proposals, treated to limes, lemons and oranges, as well as fresh air and water. Although the ship's bill of health was no worse than average, Smollett and his colleagues were kept busy throughout the voyage. 'At a certain hour of the morning, the boy of the mess went round all the decks, ringing a small hand-bell, and, in rhymes composed for the occasion, invited all those who had sores to repair before the mast, where one of the doctor's mates attended, with applications to dress them,' he recorded. Watkins noted, on 19 November, that they 'began to serve wine to the sick men', and the following day they 'sold some of our dead men's clothes at the mast': Smollett eventually had £2 15s. deducted from his pay for the cost of a set of dead sailor's clothes. The men enjoyed watching the dolphins as the fleet entered tropical waters, but Smollett remembered that a man threw himself overboard 'in resentment for having undergone the shameful discipline of the ship for vermin'; Atkins recorded that 'Samuel Murray was whipped for mutiny because the steward would not give him raw meat, and for beating the cooper', and that 'eighteen hundred and ninety-five pounds of cheese' had been condemned as inedible

After spending a week in Dominica, taking in water and allowing the sick to recuperate, Sir Chaloner's fleet reached Port Royal in Jamaica in January 1741, and joined up with that of Admiral Vernon. It had taken a year for the reinforcements to arrive, bringing with them such essentials as replacements for rotted rigging. Vernon's fleet now included not just men-of-war, but frigates, fireships, bomb-ketches and tenders: 'Never was an armament more completely equipped; and never had the nation more reason to hope for extra-ordinary success,' Smollett was to write in his *Complete History of England*. The soldiers and marines, many of them Scots, who had come out from England, were supplemented by an 'American regi-ment of four battalions, and a body of Negroes enlisted at Jamaica', and now totalled some 12,000 men. Unfortunately, their commanding officer, Lord Cathcart, whom Smollett thought a 'nobleman of approved honour', was taken ill and died the day after the fleet arrived in Dominica, and was replaced by Brigadier Wentworth, 'an officer without experience, authority or resolution'. But despite the delays and – more worryingly – the approach of the rainy season and its lethal fevers, Vernon seemed in no hurry to set out for Cartagena. Time was wasted watching and giving chase to a French fleet under the Marquis d'Antin; but the *Chichester* was not involved, nor were the French yet at war with Britain.

The fleet anchored to the windward of Cartagena on 4 March. Situated at the far end of a bay, Cartagena was strongly fortified with castles, batteries, booms, cables and men-of-war, and the garrison had recently been reinforced by a squadron of ships commanded by Don Blas de Leso, whom Smollett described as 'an officer of expe-rience and resolution'. Vernon, in Smollett's disapproving words, 'lay inactive' till the ninth, when – acting in conjunction with Wentworth's soldiers – he began to lay siege to the forts that lined the Boca Chica or 'little mouth' at the entrance to the harbour. To begin with all went well, and they succeeded in capturing the Spanish admiral's flagship, the *Galicia*. But from then on the assault on Cartagena disintegrated into what Smollett describes as 'a scene of misery and disgrace'.

Part of the problem, as Smollett saw it, was that the soldiers were inexperienced and of poor quality. The officers tended to be 'young gentlemen of family, chiefly North Britons, who had learned the rudiments of the military art in Holland and other foreign services', but most of their soldiers had been 'taken from the plough-tail a few months before'. This could be seen as a naval man giving voice to the widespread eighteenth-century preference for the Navy over the Army, which was associated with unwelcome Continental alliances and the use of Hanoverian and Hessian mercenaries, were it not that Smollett condemns Vernon and Wentworth with equal severity. He thought them dilatory, incapable of taking advantage of Spanish weaknesses, and so riven by resentment and suspicion of each other as to be quite incapable of cross-service co-operation. The two men, he wrote, 'had contracted a hearty contempt for each other, and took all opportunities of expressing their mutual dislike: far from acting vigorously in concert, for the advantage of the community, they maintained a mutual reserve, and separate cabals; and each proved more eager for the disgrace of his rival, than zealous for the honour of the nation'. In his 'Account of the Expedition against Cartagena' he was harsher still about the military prima donnas. Vernon was 'a man of weak understanding, strong prejudices, boundless arrogance, and over-boiling passions', while Wentworth, 'though he had some parts, was wholly defective in point of experience, confidence and resolution'. Both officers held separate councils of war, pausing occasionally to send 'irritating messages to each other', and while 'each of them piqued himself on doing barely as much as would screen himself from the censure of a court martial, neither seemed displeased at the neglect of his colleague; but, on the contrary, both were in appearance glad of the miscarriage of the expedition, in hope of seeing one another stigmatized with infamy and disgrace'. Vernon, Smollett thought, was particularly culpable in that he failed or refused to bring his warships into the harbour to provide supporting fire when, after the usual dithering, Wentworth finally mounted an abortive land attack on the citadel of San Lazar, in the town of Cartagena itself. The assault proved a futile business: the scaling ladders were too short to reach up the walls, the soldiers were weakened by the heat and incipient fever, and although Vernon eventually agreed to send in the *Galicia* as a floating battery, it carried a mere sixteen guns and was far less effective than Vernon's own warships and bomb-ketches might have proved. (The *Galicia* was under the temporary command of a Captain Hoare, seconded from the fireship *Success*. After his retirement from the Navy, he built himself a house near Warrington designed to look like a ship: bells sounded the time of day, the lawn in front, terminating in a ha-ha, was referred to as the 'quarter deck', and visitors were supposed to doff their hats, shipshape and Bristol fashion. Smollett used him as a model for his most famous and voluble sea-dog, Commander Trunnion in *Peregrine Pickle*, whose house, known as the 'garrison', is run on similarly naval lines.)

Matters were made immeasurably worse by the climate and disease. The rainy season had arrived with a vengeance. It was intolerably hot, and the men sweated like pigs under a 'vertical' sun. Water was in short supply, and the vessels used to contain it – including old pork tubs and beef barrels – were so filthy, and the 'water was so corrupted, and stunk so abominably', that 'a man was fain to stop his nose with one hand, while with the other he conveyed the can to his head'. Nor was the Admiral's grog the answer: it was, in Smollett's opinion, 'a most unpalatable drench, which no man could swallow without reluctance'. Two hundred men were killed in the assault on Fort Lazar, and twice as many wounded, but whereas those captured by the Spaniards were 'treated with great humanity', the British sick and wounded 'languished in want of every necessary comfort and accommodation'. Smollett's first-hand accounts in *Roderick Random* and 'An Account of the Expedition against Cartagena' are strikingly similar. He tells us of how the wounded were 'destitute of surgeons, nurses, cooks, and proper provision; they were pent up between decks in small vessels, where they had not room to sit upright; they wallowed in filth; myriads of maggots were hatched in the putrefaction of their sores, which had no other dressing than that of being washed by themselves in their own allowance of brandy'. Those unwise enough to peer over the side of the ship 'beheld the naked bodies of their fellow soldiers and comrades floating up and down the harbour, affording prey to the carrion crows and sharks, which tore them to pieces without interruption, and contributed by their stench to the mortality that prevailed'.

It rained almost continuously, and the lightning was so incessant that 'one might have read a small print all night by the illumination'. 'Such a change of the atmosphere is always attended by an epidemical distemper,' Smollett declared, and the Caribbean was famed, and dreaded, for the fevers which struck down Europeans in particular. Most lethal of all was yellow fever – also known as Black Vomit, Yellow Jack and Breakbone Fever – which had been brought from West Africa in slave ships during the previous century and was especially prevalent in Colombia and Ecuador. It struck with disconcerting rapidity. The face and eyes turned yellow, the bile in the vomit was mixed with blood, red patches appeared on the body, and the victim haemorrhaged from the ears, mouth and anus. Cures were, at best, hit and miss: John Hume, a surgeon in Jamaica at the time of the expedition, recommended bleeding, clysters of oil and wrapping patients in thick blankets to increase perspiration.

Some fifteen years earlier, in 1726, Admiral Hosier had lost five-sixths of his men, and his own life, in just such an epidemic while laying siege to Porto Bello, and the capture of the town by Vernon in 1739 had been both celebrated and lamented in Richard Glover's well-known poem 'Admiral Hosier's Ghost':

> As, near Portobello lying,
> On the gently swelling flood,
> At midnight, with streamers flying,
> Our triumphant navy rode;
> There, while Vernon sat all-glorious
> From the Spaniard's late defeat,
> And his crews, with shouts victorious,
> Drank success to England's fleet;
>
> On a sudden, shrilly sounding,
> Hideous shrieks and yells were heard;
> Then, each heart with fears confounding,
> A sad troop of ghosts appeared;
> All in dreary hammocks shrouded,

Which for winding sheets they wore;
And with looks by sorrow clouded,
Frowning on that foreign shore . . .

Now, down the coast in Cartagena, history was repeating itself
for those 'Sent in this foul clime to languish/ . . . Wasted with disease
and anguish/ Not in glorious battle slain.' The deduction of 10s. 8d.
from his wages suggests that Smollett himself may have been taken
ill: either way, he resented the shortage of doctors and surgeons to
cope with the contagion – unfairly, perhaps, since Vernon had been
worried by the shortage of surgeons' mates and had asked the
Admiralty Board to send some more. The soldiers in particular, he
tells us, suffered from 'the bilious fever, attended with such putrefaction of the juices, that the colour of the skin, which is at first
yellow, adopts a sooty hue in the progress of the disease, and the
patient generally dies about the third day, with violent atrabilious
discharges upwards and downwards'. His remedy, like Lind's for
scurvy, consisted of 'plenty of sweet water, fresh provision, and a
liberal use of vegetable acids, such as limes, lemons, oranges, ananas,
and other fruits natural to the West Indies'.

Thwarted in their attempt to capture the port, and brought low
by disease, Vernon and Wentworth met on board the Admiral's flagship and, agreeing for once, decided to withdraw. After blowing up
the forts they had captured, they set sail for Jamaica from where,
after attempting an equally futile landing on the Cuban coast, they
set sail for England.

It is hard to know how much action, if any, Smollett saw at first
hand, and to what extent he relied on other people's accounts.
According to Watkins, the *Chichester* was not involved in the fighting
and lost no men in action; she seems not to have taken part in the
early stages of the campaign, when Vernon destroyed several Spanish
men-of-war and captured the forts of St Louis and St Philip, but she
may have played an auxiliary role, landing troops, supplies and
artillery. But although Smollett's name appears on the *Chichester*'s
musters or roll-calls all the way from the Medway to Jamaica, with
a brief leave of absence while the fleet was gathering below the
Downs, it is absent during the Cartagena campaign, and it may be

that he transferred to the *Prince Frederick*, and saw action against the Boca Chica forts. Nor does he appear to have been on board the *Chichester* during the return voyage to Jamaica, so he may have been tending the sick on another ship.

One of those who emerged with credit from the whole sorry story was Charles Knowles, the captain of the *Weymouth* and, in later years, an admiral and the proud bearer of a knighthood. He would also prove famously litigious, as Smollett learned to his cost. Some twenty-five years older than Smollett, Knowles was rumoured to be the illegitimate son of the fourth Earl of Banbury. A bright, ambitious young man – he spoke fluent French, and was something of a prodigy at mathematics and mechanics – he had joined the Navy in 1718 as a ship's servant. As captain of the *Diamond*, he took part in Vernon's capture of Porto Bello: the bomb-ketches and fireships were under his command, an eyewitness noting how 'the shells fell into the town pretty successfully, particularly into the principal church, the Jesuits' college, and beat down several houses'. He bombarded the port once more at the siege of Chagres, and Vernon appointed him its governor. Unlike his dilatory seniors, he seems to have been ubiquitous during the attack on Cartagena, blasting St Joseph's Fort with his mortars, picking the *Weymouth*'s way past the booms and sunken warships that cluttered the harbour mouth, and demolishing the Castillo Grande. In both his *History of England* and his 'Account of the Expedition against Cartagena', Smollett gives this unattractive, petulant character due credit, albeit without much enthusiasm. He would have been unamused by the suggestion, made after his death, that he had served as a 'loblolly boy' – an unflattering epithet for a surgeon's mate – on board Knowles's ship during an unsuccessful attempt to take the Spanish fort of La Gueira, near Caracas, in 1743, and that Knowles had 'behaved toward him with paternal kindness'. In later years he would ridicule Knowles's efforts to take La Gueira, noting how the Commodore, as he had then become, had trailed back to the Leeward Islands 'without having added much to his reputation, either as to conduct or resolution'. Such things rankle, and worse was to come. A more endearing, if over-talkative, legacy of Smollett's time at sea is the steady stream of garrulous and kind-hearted sea-dogs who populate the novels; like

Captain Crowe in *Sir Launcelot Greaves*, all, once on land, prove to be innocents abroad, 'as little acquainted with the world as a suckling child'.

Since nothing is known about Smollett's movements between September 1741, when the *Chichester* finally returned to England, and May 1744, when he set up as a surgeon in London, it could just be that he did serve under Knowles, and that his animus against him was the result. The fact that he was unable to collect the £38 5s. 11d. owing in back wages in Plymouth in February 1742, but arranged for the money to be paid over to a lawyer friend instead, suggests that he may have gone back to the West Indies as a surgeon's mate, in a warship or a merchant ship. What we do know is that he spent some time in Jamaica, and that while he was living in Kingston he met and fell in love with his future wife, Anne Lassells. She, too, had been born in 1721; her family, wealthy planters and slave-owners, had been established on the island since the previous century. Her father died when she was two, leaving assets worth a mere £782, £140 of which took the form of four slaves; in his will he left his 'dear daughter Anne' £100 and two slave girls. Anne's mother had then married a merchant called William Leaver, who died in 1736 leaving £19,948 and twenty-four slaves. Anne had great expectations, since she and her two brothers would inherit the hefty sums left by their stepfather on their mother's death. Her brother Charles died in 1752, and left his 'well beloved sister' £250, with further sums due at a later stage; and throughout their married life the Smolletts were to benefit from the income from property in Jamaica, and the sporadic sale of slaves and land. According to Robert Chambers's mid-Victorian biography of Smollett, 'His wife, as we know from authority, was a Creole, with a dark complexion, though upon the whole rather pretty – a fine lady, but a silly woman.' The 'though' may be the most revealing part of Chambers's account. Anne was to remain a shadowy figure; no pictures of her survive, and the references to her in Smollett's letters are perfunctory in the extreme. Whether they were married in Jamaica or in England, when she joined him in London, remains a mystery.

3

The Perils of a Playwright

Back in London and, for a time, on his own, Smollett is next sighted in 1744, living in a house in Downing Street, a cul-de-sac between Whitehall and St James's Park built by Sir George Downing towards the end of the previous century and described in 1720 as 'a pretty open space especially at the upper end where are four or five very large and well built houses fit for persons of honour and quality; each house having a pleasant prospect into St James's Park'. One of the large and well-built houses, No. 10, had been acquired by the Crown in 1732 and offered by George II as a personal gift to Sir Robert Walpole, since when it has been the official residence of what later became known as the Prime Minister. At a less elevated level, reprobates like James Boswell and William Hickey, his equally over-sexed fellow-diarist, were soon to enjoy the delights offered by milkmaids and others doubling up as prostitutes behind the bushes in the Park. The rent of £26 a year reflected the fashionable address, and it may be that Anne contributed to the cost.

Until his death the previous summer, the house had been lived in by John Douglas, a successful Scottish surgeon specialising in lithotomy. Douglas's brother, James, was even more eminent, and it may have been through him that Smollett was introduced to the self-sustaining world of Scottish medics practising in London. Trained in Edinburgh and Holland, James Douglas was then in his seventies, and could look back on a successful career as an obstetrician or male midwife. An associate of the Chamberlens, who had invented obstetrical forceps in the sixteenth century but kept them a family trade secret until the early eighteenth, he had been appointed Physician to Queen Caroline in 1727. The previous year he was one of two eminent midwives asked to pronounce in the celebrated case of Mary Tofts of Godalming, who claimed to have given birth to a litter of rabbits: a male midwife in Guildford declared that he had seen the rabbits leaping about in her uterus – 'this particular fact was unanimously agreed upon by most of the people of Guildford' – but eventually Mary Tofts, to general disappointment, confessed that she had been put up to it by a friend, who had supplied the baby rabbits and somehow pushed them inside her. Smollett may have been introduced to the Douglas brothers by Robert Foulis, a fellow-student at Glasgow University and a protégé of Francis Hutcheson who, after working for a time as a bookseller, made a name for himself as an elegant and influential printer, designing new typefaces and specialising in Greek and Latin texts renowned for their accuracy. Through James Douglas Smollett probably met the old man's most distinguished pupil, William Hunter, who was to become one of his closest friends as well as a fashionable and extremely well-paid society obstetrician and anatomy lecturer.

Most of Smollett's closest friends were Scots, but not all of them were medics. John Home was an ambitious young clergyman-cum-playwright who, like Smollett and Dr Johnson, arrived in London with a play in his pocket, and an introduction to Smollett from Alexander Carlyle. He could find no takers for *Agis*. Smollett had no better luck with *The Regicide*, and his efforts to place it with theatre managers was to absorb both time and emotional energy, and drive him almost mad with anger and resentment. He may have tried placing it before he left for the West Indies, and he persisted with his increasingly desperate efforts until 1747, when he finally abandoned hope: as he wrote in the Preface to the published version of the play, 'Had some of those who were pleased to call themselves my friends been at any pains to deserve the character, and told me ingenuously what I had to expect in the character of an author, I should, in all probability, have spared myself the incredible labour and chagrin I have since undergone.' Smollett was, even by authorial standards, unusually thin-skinned, sniffing out insults where none existed and hot in revenge, and his experiences with *The Regicide* stoked his incipient literary paranoia. Although John Cleland, the author of *Fanny Hill*, declared of the published version that 'the diction is everywhere animated, nervous and pathetic', and that it was 'one of the best theatrical pieces that have appeared these many years', the few who have struggled to the end have tended to agree with the raffish poet-clergyman Charles Churchill, who declared that

> Whoever read the Regicide, but swore
> The author wrote as man ne'er wrote before?
> Others for plots and underplots may call,
> Here's the right answer – have no plot at all

Given the hostility of the Kirk to the theatre – the staging in Edinburgh of Home's *Douglas* was to lead to a ferocious battle between the old and the new guard, with the Moderates finally carrying the day – it is surprising that Smollett, who may never have been near a theatre in his life, should have written a play as a teenager in Scotland; but, miraculous as that may be, *The Regicide* is a sub-Shakespearian stinker that reads like one of Max Beerbohm's parodies or the celebrated spoof in *Beyond the Fringe*. A blank verse drama, it deals with the assassination of James I of Scotland, and may have been inspired by Smollett's reading, as a schoolboy, of Buchanan's history of Scotland. A random extract should suffice.

Athol:	Curse on the smooth dissembler! Welcome, Grime!
	My soul is wrought to the sublimest rage
	Of horrible revenge! If aught remained
	Of cautious scruple, to the scatt'ring winds
	I give the phantom. May this carcase rot,
	A loathsome banquet to the fowls of heav'n,
	If e'er my breast admit one thought to bound
	The progress of my hate!
Grime:	What means my prince?

Athol:	Th' unhappy youth is slain!
Grime:	Ha! Hell be prais'd! (*Aside*)
	He was a peevish stripling, prone to change,
	Vain is condolence. Let our swords be swift
	To sate his hov'ring shade . . .

And so on, and on.

Smollett's most vivid account of his travails with *The Regicide* can be found towards the end of *Roderick Random*, when Roderick, enjoying a spell in the Marshalsea, the famous debtors' prison, meets a fellow-inmate called Melopoyn, a hapless poet and would-be playwright. Roderick agrees to read Melopoyn's unstaged tragedy, and is 'not a little amazed at the conduct of the managers who had rejected it'. In his opinion – and Smollett's, no doubt – 'the incidents [were] interesting, the characters beautifully contrasted, strongly marked, and well supported; the diction poetical, spirited, and correct; the unities of the drama maintained with the most scrupulous exactness; the opening gradual and engaging, the *peripeteia* surprising, and the catastrophe affecting'. Smollett's wounded pride was still evident when he published *Peregrine Pickle*, four years after he had abandoned all hope of seeing his play performed. The first edition includes derisive portraits of two of those involved, David Garrick and James Quin, as well as shafts of worldly wisdom denied to the youthful and idealistic Smollett and his *alter ego*, Melopoyn. Peregrine attends a meeting of literary hacks, grandly termed the College of Authors, and they are harangued by a 'noisy North Briton, who complained (in a strange dialect) that he had, in the beginning of the season, presented a comedy to the manager of a certain theatre, who, after it had lain six weeks in his hands, returned it to the author, affirming there was neither sense nor English in the performance'. The President of the College, a Johnsonian figure, has some soothing words of advice. Managers don't read plays, he tells the indignant Scotsman: 'There are only two methods, by which you have any chance of introducing your play upon the theatre: one is compulsive, by the interposition of the great, whom a patentee dare not disoblige; the other, insinuation, by ingratiating yourself with the manager.' If a playwright doesn't take the trouble to butter up the manager, 'Why the devil should he put himself to the expense and trouble attending the representation of a new play, and part with three benefit nights, to please the vanity and fill the pockets of a stranger?' The 'patentees' were the managers of Covent Garden and Drury Lane, the two London theatres licensed by royal patent to stage spoken drama; on 'benefit nights', the manager paid over all that evening's proceeds, minus agreed costs, to the otherwise un-remunerated author. Benefits were normally paid on the third, six and ninth nights: if opponents of a play succeeded in 'damning' it, and it was taken off after the second night, the playwright would receive nothing for his labours.

Although Garrick would do much to raise the social standing of theatricals, actors were widely regarded as riff-raff: under the terms of the 1714 Vagrancy Act, they were liable to the same penalties as rogues and beggars, and both the main theatres were in a part of London famed for low life and prostitution. Attending the theatre was a raucous and sometimes riotous affair, and at both theatres there were spikes along the front of the stage to keep drunk or over-stimulated spectators at bay. Every now and then riots broke out over the price of seats, or to protest against a particular play or production. French plays were especially vulnerable to the fury of xenophobic theatre-lovers, and when, in 1755, Garrick brought over a team of French dancers, well-heeled spectators joined the groundlings in tearing up benches, destroying the scenery and inflicting £4,000-worth of damage. The actor James Quin – who was once charged with murder after stabbing a fellow-actor in the eye with his cane during a quarrel over a wig – did battle with a drunken Earl who forced his way on to the stage during a performance of *Macbeth* and tried to attack the manager, who was cowering in the wings: Quin rushed to the manager's aid with sword drawn, while the Earl's equally drunken friends slashed the sets with such vigour that the theatre had to close for two days. John Rich, the manager involved, had introduced the pantomime to England, and until Garrick made his influence felt, a night at the theatre was closer to circus or music hall than to the sedate, one-item experience of today. Most performances lasted at least three hours, and the main play, often a sentimental offering by George Lillo or Colley Cibber, would be preceded by an overture and followed by an 'afterpiece'. Much to Garrick's irritation, serious work was interlaced with acrobatics or juggling. According to Edmund Burke, Garrick 'raised the character of his profession to the rank of a liberal art': he not only pioneered a more natural manner of acting, but, as the hugely influential actor-manager of Covent Garden from 1746, he reinstated Shakespeare at the centre of theatrical life.

John Rich may have been uneducated and almost illiterate, but he mounted one of the century's great successes in John Gay's *The Beggar's Opera* at the Lincoln's Inn Theatre in 1728. It ran for a record sixty-two nights: hoping to emulate its success, theatres unlicensed by the Lord Chamberlain proliferated, among them the Goodman's Fields Theatre, the Little Theatre and the opera house in the Haymarket, while playwrights enjoyed an insatiable demand for their wares. The Lord Chamberlain's efforts at prosecution usually fizzled out, but in 1737 Walpole rushed through restrictive legislation after learning of a play called *The Golden Rump*, which referred to George II's flatulence and piles. Under the 1737 Act, all plays needed government approval, and theatres without a specific licence or a royal patent were declared illegal. Plays had to be submitted to the Lord Chamberlain's office fourteen days before their planned opening, and he was still free to change his mind. Among the theatres to close down were those in Lincoln's Inn Fields and Goodman's Fields, and the Little Theatre, which Henry Fielding had been managing for the past year. Fielding had been a prolific playwright in the 1730s, but fear of prosecution and the closing of unlicensed theatres made life harder for aspiring playwrights: he diverted his literary energies into the less risky business of writing novels. Smollett would follow his example.

Smollett's efforts to put *The Regicide* on stage form a tale of broken promises, hopes that are dashed, revived, and dashed again, endless postponements, and revisions and rewritings vainly undertaken. According to his Preface to the published edition, a 'nobleman of great weight' showed interest in reading it, but then sat on the manuscript for four months, at the end of which 'it was retrieved by pure accident (I believe) from the most dishonourable apartment of his lordship's house' – a fate even worse than that reserved for poor

Melopoyn's play, which was carried off to the kitchen, where 'a negligent wretch of a cook-maid, mistaking it for waste-paper, has expended it all but a few leaves in singeing fowls upon the spit'. Smollett first showed his play to an ineffectual patron in 1739, and revised it before setting out for the West Indies. On his return, he sent it to Fleetwood, the patentee of Drury Lane. In *Roderick Random*, Fleetwood appears as Supple, an engaging and seemingly good-natured character who apologises profusely for allowing the manuscript to fall into the hands of his kitchen maid, warmly urges Melopoyn to rewrite it from memory, and, after promising that it will be put into production, pleads the lateness of the season as an excuse for delay. In reality, Charles Fleetwood was a well-mannered, gout-ridden debauchee who had frittered away the £6,000 he had inherited at the age of twenty-one and, as the patentee of Drury Lane from 1733 to 1745, brought his theatre to the verge of bankruptcy. After his play had been retrieved from the nobleman's lavatory, a bruised Smollett withdrew it from circulation for a couple of years. In 1745 a well-intentioned patron, Lord George Graham, submitted it to James Lacy, the new manager of Drury Lane. Lacy – Brayer, in the novel – received it in June: an effusive, apologetic, complimentary character, judging by his fictional equivalent, he promised Smollett that he would stage *The Regicide* that winter. The promised time approached, but Lacy opted instead for the actor Charles Macklin's first play, *King Henry VII, or the Popish Imposter*. It ran for three days only, but *The Regicide*'s chance had been lost.

Lord Rattle, Melopoyn's patron, then recommends him to Bellower, Smollett's unsubtle pseudonym for the bombastic James Quin. Bellower is, he tells him, not only an eminent actor, but the effective 'prime minister' to Vandal (i.e. John Rich), the patentee of 'the other house' (i.e. Covent Garden). Vain, fat, peppery and warm-hearted, painted by Hogarth and described by Matthew Bramble as 'a real voluptuary in the articles of eating and drinking', Quin featured unflatteringly in Smollett's first two novels, and fondly in his last. The Donald Wolfit or Laurence Olivier of his age, much given to roaring declamation, emphatic gestures and much pounding of the stage, he was the kind of forceful, flamboyant actor around whom anecdotes accrue: Richard Cumberland remembered him as dominating the stage 'in a green velvet coat embroidered down the seams, an enormous full-bottomed periwig, rolled stockings and high-heeled square shoes', and how he delivered his set pieces 'in a deep, full tone, accompanied by a sawing kind of action'. A Dubliner, he had been educated at Trinity College, Dublin, where, according to his biographer, he 'laughed at those who read books'. He made his first appearance at Drury Lane in 1714; he was on stage at the opening night of Covent Garden in 1732, and worked there with Rich from 1742 when he retired to Bath, where he encountered Squire Bramble and party. The more refined Garrick, his great rival, was to make Quin's technique seem cumbrous and melodramatic. According to Smollett, Quin suggested the 'despair of a great man' by 'beating his own forehead and bellowing like a bull'; he was keen on the pregnant pause, so much so that, as Thomas Davies recalled in his *Memoir of Garrick*,

> When Lothario gave Horatio the challenge, Quin, instead of accepting it instantaneously, made a long pause and dragged out the words 'I'll meet thee there!' in such a manner as to make it appear absolutely ludicrous. He paused so long before he spoke that somebody, it was said, called out from the gallery, 'Why don't you tell the gentleman whether you will meet him or not?'

His favourite part was Falstaff, and when, in *Humphry Clinker*, Squire Bramble's nephew, Jery Melford, dines with him at the Three Tuns in Bath, Quin is 'carried home with six good bottles of claret under his belt'.

When, after the usual delays, Melopoyn is finally favoured with an audience with the great actor, only to be told that Bellower has not yet got round to reading his play, he asks if he can have his script back:

> 'Ay,' said he, in a theatrical tone, 'with all my heart.' Then pulling out a drawer of the bureau at which he sat, he took out a bundle, and threw it upon a table that was near him, pronouncing the word 'There' with great disdain. I took it up,

and perceiving, with some surprise, that it was a comedy, told him it did not belong to me; upon which he offered me another, which I also disclaimed. A third was produced, and rejected for the same reason. At length he pulled out a whole handful, and spread them before me, saying 'There are seven – take which you please – or take them all.'

Smollett did not repeat this story in his Preface, but according to the *Life of Quin*, published in 1766, a poet who had submitted a tragedy to Quin waited on the great man and

in a faltering voice desired to have his piece returned. 'There,' said Quin, 'it lies in the window.' Upon which poor Bayes repaired to the window and took up a play which proved to be a comedy, and his muse had brought forth a direful tragedy; whereupon he told Quin of the mistake; who very pleasantly said, 'Faith, then, sir, I have certainly lost your play.' '*Lost my play!*' cries the poet, almost thunderstruck. 'Yes, by ———, but I have,' replied Quin, 'but look ye, here is a drawer full of both comedies and tragedies – take any two in the room of it.'

Still smarting from his treatment, Smollett took revenge in *Peregrine Pickle*, published in the year Quin retired from Covent Garden. 'His utterance is a continual sing-song, like the chanting of vespers, and his action resembles that of heaving ballast into the hold of a ship,' Peregrine is told: he 'performs such strange shakings of the head, and other antic gesticulations, that when I first saw him act, I imagined the poor man laboured under that paralytical disorder which is known by the name of St Vitus's dance'. Smollett returns to the subject later in the novel, ridiculing the way in which Quin 'throws all his limbs into a tremulous motion' and 'assumes a wild stare' while playing Othello. In later years he mellowed towards the old ham. 'Quin excelled in dignity and declamation, as well as exhibiting some characters of humour equally exquisite and peculiar,' he declared in his *Complete History of England*, and he wrote warmly of him in *Humphry Clinker*. But even then he found it hard to resist taking a dig at Quin's acting technique. '"I was once vastly entertained with your playing of the Ghost of Gimlet at Drury Lane, when you rose up through the stage, with a white face and red eyes, and spoke of *quails upon the fretful porcofine* – Do, pray, spout a little of the Ghost of Gimlet,"' Tabitha Bramble, an embryonic Mrs Malaprop, begs of 'Mr Gwynn'. '"Madame (said Quin, with a look of ineffable disdain) the Ghost of Gimlet is laid, never to rise again."'

But help was now at hand, it seemed, in the impressive and influential form of the Earl of Chesterfield – a 'Maecenas in the nation', as Melopoyn described his fictional incarnation, Earl Sheerwit. Best remembered for his exhortatory *Letters to his Son*, and for the contempt with which Dr Johnson spurned his belated support for his *Dictionary* ('Is not a Patron, my Lord, one who looks with unconcern on a man struggling for life in the water, and, when he has reached ground, encumbers him with help?'), Chesterfield was both a statesman and a patron of the arts: Smollett probably met him in 1746, when the great man came back to London after a stint as Lord-Lieutenant in Ireland. Although Smollett was to write scathingly in his novels about aristocratic patrons who promise support to his heroes but turn out to be ineffectual, self-serving or corrupt, he let Chesterfield off lightly in his Preface, merely noting that the 'eminent wit' suggested a few improvements before recommending his play to Rich and Garrick at Covent Garden. In *Peregrine Pickle*, however, he took mild revenge on his would-be patron. One of those attending the College of Authors, an 'author of some character', tells of how a 'certain nobleman of great pretensions to taste' had 'eagerly courted his acquaintance', begged him to 'breakfast with him at least three times a week' and expressed himself 'highly entertained' by the manuscript he had left with him; but before long the author notices that his lordship is no longer at home when he calls. He overhears one of the footmen asking, 'Will your lordship please to be at home, when he calls?' and is 'not a little irritated at the silly peer's disingenuity'.

'I have a play now with me, sent by my Lord Chesterfield and wrote by one Smollett,' Garrick wrote to a friend in September 1746. 'It is a Scotch story, but it won't do, and yet recommended by his Lordship and patronized by Ladies of Quality: what can I say or do?

Must I belie my judgement or run the risk of being thought impertinent and disobliging by ye grand folks?' Poor Garrick was in an
embarrassing and all too familiar quandary: it was no easy matter for
a young and ambitious provincial, eager to make his way in the
world, to turn down a recommendation from the likes of Chesterfield.
And, as a friend recalled, 'He would, in the ardour of a moment,
promise what his cooler reflections told him he ought not to perform;
nay, he would sometimes be betrayed into promising what indeed
he neither could, nor ought, to fulfil. This failing accompanied him,
more or less, through life, and brought with it much vexation.'

This must have been cold comfort to Smollett, who took his
revenge for Garrick's inevitable rejection of *The Regicide* by savaging
him in *Roderick Random* with due ferocity. Marmozet (i.e. Garrick)
is working in tandem with Vandal (i.e. Rich of Covent Garden).
Marmozet, a 'celebrated player', has recently 'appeared on the stage
with astonishing éclat, and bore such sway in the house where he
acted, that the managers durst not refuse anything he recommended'.
He speaks warmly of Melopoyn's play, and seems to admire it so
much that he may well appear in it himself; the overjoyed author
hugs himself 'in the expectation of seeing it not only acted, but acted
to the greatest advantage'. The weeks go by, and nothing happens.
Marmozet then tells him that he should try to place it elsewhere,
since he is not sure that he will be appearing on stage that winter,
and his influence with Mr Vandal isn't as strong as it had been: in
real life, Garrick was about to leave Covent Garden for Drury Lane,
the theatre with which he would be associated for the rest of his
life. Melopoyn learns, indirectly, that for all his fulsome praise,
Marmozet had told Sheerwit that the play was 'altogether unfit for
the stage'. If Melopoyn's play was anything like as bad as *The Regicide*,
Marmozet was stating the obvious, but the playwright's rollercoaster
ride from despair to exultation and back is far from over. Marmozet
passes Melopoyn on to Vandal, who assures him that he has such
respect for Lord Sheerwit's opinion that he will 'put it into rehearsal
without loss of time'; but after reading the play, Vandal declares it
to be 'improper for the stage'. Vandal's change of mind can be
forgiven since 'the poor man's head, which was not naturally very
clear, had been disordered with suspicion, and he laboured under

the tyranny of a wife, and the terrors of hell-fire at the same time', but Marmozet's treachery is of a different order. He is charged with being hypocritical, lying, insinuating and avaricious, a 'little parasite' whose 'grovelling manner' would inevitably 'create contempt and abhorrence of him in his patrons, and effectually deprive him of the countenance and protection he now enjoys in such an eminent degree'.

Harsh words indeed – and worse were to follow in *Peregrine Pickle*, where Garrick and his old enemy Quin are lumped together as the epitome of thespian ineptitude. Nowhere but in England, Peregrine is assured by a French theatre-goer, would such actors be able to make a living. Attention is drawn to Garrick's renditions of Richard III and Hamlet:

> At a juncture, when his whole soul ought to be alarmed with terror and amazement, and all his attention engrossed by the dreadful object in view, I mean that of his friend whom he had murdered; he expresses no passion but that of indignation against a drinking-glass, which he violently dashes in pieces on the floor, as if he had perceived a spider in his wine . . . He represents the grief of an hero, by the tears and manner of a whining schoolboy, and perverts the genteel deportment of a gentleman, into the idle buffoonery of a miserable tobacconist; his whole art is no other than a succession of frantic vociferation, such as I have heard in the cells of Bedlam, a slowness, hesitation and expression of speech, as if he were troubled with asthma.

The 'tobacconist' is particularly fine, but after conceding that Garrick was 'blessed with a distinct voice, and a great share of vivacity', the Frenchman apologises for 'treating this darling of the English with so little ceremony'. Smollett could have distanced himself from these views by pointing out that they were expressed by a mere Frenchman, albeit one with knowledge of Bedlam, London's notorious lunatic asylum; but later in the novel he returns to the attack, comparing Garrick's rendition of a libertine in Nicholas Rowe's *The Fair Penitent* to 'a lively representation of a tinker oppressed with gin, who staggers against a post, tumbles into the kennel, makes diverse convulsive efforts to rise, and finding himself unable to get up, with many intervening hiccups, addresses himself to the surrounding mob'.

'I am vain of your approbation with regard to my tragedy,' Smollett wrote to Alexander Carlyle, adding that his efforts to have it staged had been thwarted by 'that little rascal Garrick', who had persuaded Rich to reject it after displays of misleading enthusiasm and encouragement. He had, he went on, made further alterations 'as agreed upon by the manager of Drury Lane', and had been assured that it would be staged before Christmas. A 'Lady of Quality' – possibly the raffish Lady Vane, whose rackety memoirs of her marital infidelities loom large in *Peregrine Pickle* – had persuaded James Lacy to reconsider; but that had come to nothing, possibly because Garrick had recently joined Lacy as co-patentee at Drury Lane. The time had come to abandon all hope of seeing *The Regicide* performed: as a final twist of the knife, Smollett was shown a letter in which it was claimed that, two years earlier, Lacy had thought well of the play, but had already promised the only available opening to his friend James Thomson, whose *Tancred and Sigismunda* was staged at Drury Lane in March 1745.

That was almost, but not quite, the end of Smollett's theatrical ambitions. *The Regicide* was published by subscription in 1749, and was read, if at all, for its plaintive Preface, in which Smollett describes his sufferings at the hands of theatrical managers. Samuel Richardson sent his friend Margaret Collier a copy, but she remained unimpressed: 'By what I have read of it, I think Mr Garrick is very much obliged to the author for showing the world how much he was in the right for refusing it.' According to Horace Walpole – who took a dim view of Smollett as a 'sea surgeon, turned author' – Lord Lyttelton, a patron of authors unkindly mocked in *Peregrine Pickle*, advised Smollett to abandon comedy. It was rumoured that he dutifully produced a comedy with the improbable title of *Charles XII, or the Adventures of Roderick Random and his man Strap*, but if it ever existed it has, mercifully, vanished into oblivion – as have another comedy, *The Absent Man*, and a play he may have written in the 1740s with James Hunter, the younger brother of John and William. All was not lost, however. Eight years after he finally abandoned hope for *The Regicide*, a comedy, all his own work, was staged at Drury Lane, by courtesy of David Garrick.

'I have planned a comedy which will be finished by next winter,' Smollett told Carlyle in the summer of 1748 apropos, presumably, *Charles XII*. 'Garrick, who was inexpressibly galled at the character of Marmozet, has made some advances towards an accommodation with me, but hitherto I have avoided a reconciliation, being determined to turn the tables upon him, and make him court my good graces in his turn.' Quite how Garrick felt about the further drubbing he received, three years later, in *Peregrine Pickle*, is unknown, but Smollett – whether in mellow mood, or in a spirit of theatrical self-interest – removed the offending passages when the novel was reprinted in 1758; and two years earlier he had been sufficiently reconciled to the increasingly famous actor-manager to deplore the poverty of the plays in which he appeared while admitting that 'he has the art, like the Lydian king, of turning all he touches into gold'. 'Mr Garrick in a very civil letter gave me to understand that it will be proper to defer the representation of my piece until after the holidays,' Smollett told his friend Dr Macaulay in December 1756. The 'piece' was a short, farcical play called *The Reprisal: or the Tars of Old England*. First produced the following January as an after-piece to Aaron Hill's *Merope*, it coincided with the court-martial and sentencing to death of the luckless Admiral Byng for his failure to prevent Port Mahon in Minorca from falling into the hands of the French during the early stages of the Seven Years War, and its contrasting of rugged, plain-speaking English sea-dogs with their affected and ineffectual French counterparts was seen as a modest boost to sagging morale. National stereotypes abound: the Irishman Oclabber gives vent to cries of 'ochrone' and 'grammachree', the Scot Maclaymore obliges with 'Hoot-fie' and bonny lasses, and Champignon, the French *petit maître* sea captain, speaks a variant of Franglais ('Permettez donc, madame, dat I 'ave the honour to languisse before your feet – 'ave pitie of me – take my sword – plongez dans my bosom'). An English buttock of beef is carried in on the shoulders of 'four meagre Frenchmen', and the quintessentially Gallic combination of frivolity and squalor is summed up by the description of a French man-of-war as 'all gingerbread work, flourish and compliment aloft, and all rags and rottenness below'. Dr Johnson's friend Arthur Murphy remembered that the actor playing Block was 'made by the author to lie down, and whimper and cry, in a manner that gave no adequate idea of a British tar'.

Bad as it was, *The Reprisal* was performed eleven times at Drury Lane, and frequently revived thereafter, three times in Smollett's own lifetime; and although Garrick himself did not deign to play a part, his occasional appearance in the accompanying play drew the crowds. The reviews were understandably harsh, the *Theatrical Review* suggesting that its acceptance 'might be brought as incontestable proof, by Mr Garrick's friends, that, whatever people might say, he is not over-nice in acceptance of works for the stage'. Despite the mockery, Smollett seemed delighted – and not least by his belated fondness for Garrick. 'You will give me leave to express my warmest acknowledgements for the frank and generous manner in which you received my performance, and the friendly care you have exerted in preparing it for the stage,' he wrote. He was particularly grateful to Garrick for allowing him a benefit night on the sixth performance, and for appearing in the accompanying play that evening; as a result, 'I shall ever retain the most grateful sense of your friendship.' Arthur Murphy suggested that Smollett 'reaped the profits of a very large benefit', and after the usual deductions he probably cleared £140. To make sure that Garrick fully appreciated his gratitude, and the friendliness of his feelings towards his old enemy, he emphasised elsewhere that 'if any person accuses me of having spoken disrespectfully of Mr Garrick, of having hinted that he solicited for my farce, or had interested views in bringing it upon the stage, he does me wrong, upon the word of a gentleman'. As for any 'former animosities', they were – on Smollett's side at least – 'forgotten and self-condemned'. Garrick seems to have been happy to let bygones be bygones. He visited Smollett when he was locked up in the King's Bench Prison in 1761 for libelling Admiral Knowles; and in his *Complete History of England*, Smollett declared that Garrick 'greatly surpassed all his predecessors of this and perhaps every nation, in his genius for acting; in the sweetness and variety of his tones, the irresistible magic of his eye, the fire and vivacity of his action, the elegance of attitude, and the whole pathos of expression'.

The only part of *The Reprisal* to survive is the rousing chorus of tars with which it concludes:

> While British oak beneath us rolls,
> And English courage fires our souls,
> To crown our toils, the fates decree
> The wealth and empire of the sea.

Smollett's first published work had been a poem, 'A New Song', which appeared in 1744 with a musical setting by James Oswald, the 'Scottish Orpheus', an Edinburgh-born fiddler and composer who settled in London in 1741, became a friend of Charles Burney, the musicologist, and was appointed Court Composer to the King in 1761: Smollett may have attended meetings of his Society of the Temple of Apollo, the members of which were mostly Scots. The song appeared, in slightly altered form, in *Roderick Random*. Roderick, reduced to working as a servant in her aunt's house, struggles to express his thwarted passion for the seemingly inaccessible Narcissa:

> When Sappho struck the quiv'ring wire,
>   The throbbing breast was all on fire:
> And, when she raised the vocal lay,
>   The captive soul was charm'd away.
>
> But had the nymph possess'd with these,
>   Thy softer, chaster power to please:
> Thy beauteous air of sprightly youth
>   Thy native smiles of artless truth . . .

And so on, via the kind of rapturous declaration typical of Smollettian heroes in love,

> For while I gaze, my bosom glows,
>   My blood in tides impetuous flows;
> Hope, fear, and joy alternate roll,
>   And floods of transport whelm my soul!

to the tragic finale:

> Condemn'd to nurse eternal care,
> And ever drop the silent tear,
> Unheard I mourn, unknown I sigh,
> Unfriended live, unpity'd die!

Roderick's verses, incidentally, upstage those produced by Narcissa's kind but demented aunt, who ponders long and hard in her study before delivering such lines as 'Nor dare th' immortal gods my rage oppose'. A prototypical bluestocking, with sandy disordered locks, a scattering of snuff down the front of her dress and a 'chin peaked like a shoemaker's paring knife', she suffers periodical bouts of lunacy, imagining herself to be a hare and bounding about the room on all fours, or, convinced that the house is about to catch fire, suffering fearful problems of urine retention in her anxiety to have enough liquid to hand with which to quench the flames.

Early in 1749, Smollett was tantalised by the possibility of having more of his words set to music. 'I have a sort of tragedy on the story of Alceste, which will (without fail) be acted at Covent Garden next season, and appear with such magnificence of scenery as was never exhibited in Britain before,' he told his friend Alexander Carlyle that February. John Rich had approached him with the suggestion that he should write the libretto for an opera or oratorio, the music for which was to be provided by Handel. The sets would be the work of the Italian Servandoni, who had recently designed the firework display that had accompanied Handel's 'Water Music', written to celebrate the Peace of Aix-la-Chapelle in October 1748. Once again, Smollett's theatrical ambitions were doomed to disappointment. Some suggested that Handel's music was too grand for the play, no trace of which has ever been found, and Rich and Smollett soon fell out. 'Two days ago, I sent my masque to Rich, that it may be put into rehearsal immediately; but he is such a compound of indolence, worthlessness and folly, that I cannot depend on anything he undertakes,' Smollett complained to Carlyle that October, adding that 'Tho' he has no objection to the piece, which has again and again been approved of by the very judges he himself appointed; tho' he has no other prospect of being saved from destruction than that of exhibiting it immediately; and tho' he is almost certain of uncommon success on its appearance, he is such an infatuated miscreant that he has told some of his friends in common that the performance was crammed down his throat.' 'That Scotchman is ein tam fool; I vould have made his vork immortal,' was Handel's apocryphal comment when he learned that *Alceste* was no more; for his part, he recycled some of the music in his cantata *Alexander's Feast*, while Servandoni's elaborate sets eventually resurfaced in an opera house in Poland in 1755. And with that sad story, we can finally draw the curtain on Smollett's theatrical ambitions.

Smollett's best-remembered verses were inspired by the aftermath of one of the most romanticised episodes in British history. The story of Bonnie Prince Charlie and the Forty-Five has been told again and again: of how Prince Charles Edward Stuart, the Young Pretender, was landed from a French ship with a handful of supporters on the tiny Hebridean island of Eriskay in the summer of 1745; of how he marched south with his army of Jacobite Highlanders, gathering support as he went; of how he routed the numerically superior forces of the English general 'Wee Johnnie' Cope at Prestonpans, so decisively that – as Alexander Carlyle vividly recorded in his memoirs – the battle was over in quarter of an hour; of how he crossed the Border into England, marching as far south as Derby, while panic prevailed in London and the Hanoverian settlement seemed to totter; of how he turned back, saw his army thrashed by 'Butcher' Cumberland at the Battle of Culloden in April 1746, slipped away into permanent exile, and spent his last, long years in Rome, a bloated, drunken figure far removed from the glamorous prince of popular legend.

What is less often remembered is that the Scots themselves were deeply divided about the whole affair. Lowlanders were stoutly pro-Hanoverian, as were the merchants of Glasgow and the new professional classes; and although myth has it that the Highlanders were Jacobites to a man, as many as half the clans owed their allegiance to the House of Hanover, and the Duke of Cumberland's army at Culloden included Lord Loudoun's regiment of Highland volunteers as well as three Scottish battalions. We have no record of how Smollett felt about the Young Pretender's advance on London, but although, in later years, hostile hacks and Scottophobes like Wilkes liked to imply that he was a crypto-Jacobite as well as an unrepentant Tory, he had been brought up in a Whig family and, however much he resented English jibes about the Scots, was a Unionist and a proud North Briton. Many of his closest friends in Scotland – Carlyle, John Home, William Robertson – had taken part in the vain attempt to defend Edinburgh against the Young Pretender's advance, and had he remained in Scotland he might well have been among them. But he was deeply shaken by the news of Culloden: as a patriotic Scot and a kindly man who combined, as a writer, an apparent delight in coarseness and brutality – or, at least, a refusal to avert the gaze – with an outraged loathing for cruelty inflicted in practice, he was filled with fury when he learned of what had happened in the aftermath of the battle. Outnumbered and outgunned, Charles's Highland army had been shot to bits at close range by Cumberland's artillery; many of those who survived were bayoneted as they tried to escape, and the wounded were left untended on the battlefield for up to a day after the fighting had ended. Alexander Carlyle was in either the British or Forrest's Coffee House – he couldn't remember which, but both were near Charing Cross – when 'news of the Battle of Culloden arrived, and London all over was in a perfect uproar of joy'. Carlyle wanted to join a friend for dinner in New Bond Street, so

> I asked Smollett if he was ready to go, as he lived in Mayfair; he said he was, and would conduct me. The mob were so riotous, and the squibs so numerous and incessant that we were glad to go into a narrow entry to put our wigs in our pockets, and to take our swords from our belts and walk with them in our hands, as everybody then wore swords; and, after cautioning me against speaking a word, lest the mob should discover my country and become insolent, 'For John Bull,' says he, 'is as haughty and valiant tonight as he was abject and cowardly on the Black Wednesday when the Highlanders were at Derby.' After we got to the head of the Haymarket through incessant fires, the

Doctor led me by narrow lanes, where we met nobody but a few boys at a pitiful bonfire, who very civilly asked us for sixpence, which I gave them.

They were wise to hide their nationality, for dislike of the Scots, already virulent, had been inflamed by events, and it was widely believed that – in the words of a pamphleteer writing as 'Old England' – 'a Scot is a natural hereditary Jacobite, and incurable by acts of lenity, generosity and friendly dealing'. Scottophobia was to reach an inglorious climax in the 1760s, when Wilkes and the *North Briton* mounted their campaign against the ministry of Lord Bute; in the meantime, the Forty-Five had done little to endear Smollett and his fellow-Scots to their English compatriots. Writing, a few years later, to Alexander Carlyle, John Home mentioned that he had seen nobody in London 'but Smollett, whom I like very well'. Home was 'a good deal disappointed at the mien of the English, which I think but poor. I observed it to Smollett after having walked at the High Mall, who agreed with me.' The Scots in London clung together more than ever – to the evident pleasure of Home, who, a year later, reported on 'your friend Smollett, who has a thousand, nay, the best qualities, and whom I love much more than he thinks I do'.

Smollett may have had his reservations about the amiable young clergyman-playwright, but there was no doubting his indignation at Cumberland's treatment of the rebel Highlanders. Crofts were burned with their inhabitants inside, cattle were confiscated, ploughs and agricultural equipment deliberately destroyed; of nearly 3,500 men taken prisoner, 120 were executed, and hundreds more transported to the West Indies. In his *Complete History of England* Smollett noted that whereas, after Prestonpans, Bonnie Prince Charlie had 'borne his good fortune with moderation' and made sure that enemy wounded were humanely treated, after Culloden 'the glory of the victory was sullied by the barbarity of the soldiers'. Rebel clansmen were 'either shot upon the mountains, like wild beasts, or put to death in cold blood, without form of trial; the women, after having seen their husbands and fathers murdered, were subjected to brutal violation, and then turned out naked with their children, to starve on the barren heaths'. Cumberland's revenge was 'the triumph of low, illiberal minds, untinctured by humanity' – so much so that 'the humane reader cannot reflect upon such a scene without grief and horror'.

Among the low, illiberal minds to welcome the activities of the royal duke were the dons of St Andrews University, who elected 'Butcher' Cumberland their Chancellor in a spasm of craven gratitude. Altogether more praiseworthy were rebel peers like Lord Balmerino, who, according to Smollett, 'eyed the instruments of death with the most careless familiarity, and seemed to triumph in his sufferings', or Lord Lovat, then in his eighties, who was executed after being impeached in Westminster Hall and charged with high treason; he 'surveyed the crowd with attention, examined the axe, jested with the executioner, and laid his head upon the block with the utmost indifference'. Nor, in later years, could Smollett help pitying Jacobites in exile, like those encountered by Peregrine Pickle in Boulogne: 'They were his own countrymen, exiled from their native homes, in consequence of their adherence to an unfortunate and ruined cause . . . They were gone to the seaside, according to their daily practice, in order to indulge their longing eyes with the prospect of the white cliffs of Albion, which they must never more approach.' Among these unhappy figures was David Hunter of Burnside, 'who seemed to be about thirty, wept bitterly over his misfortune, which had involved a beloved wife and three children in misery and distress; and in the impatience of his grief, cursed his own fate with frantic imprecations'. Hunter of Burnside wrote to Smollett about his predicament. Smollett showed the letter to Lady Vane, in the hope that she would put in a word with her cousin, the Duke of Newcastle; but since, shortly after Culloden, the Duke had confessed that 'As to Scotland, I am as little partial to it as any man alive', it seems unlikely that their intervention had any effect.

All this lay in the future: more immediately, Smollett gave vent to his sadness and his anger through verse. Writing to Carlyle, Smollett mentioned that he had recently published 'a ballad set to music under the name of the Tears of Scotland, a performance very well received at London, as I hope it will be in your country which gave rise to it'. In his autobiography, Carlyle tells of how Smollett showed him the manuscript of his poem, adding that Smollett 'though a Tory, was not a Jacobite, but he had the feelings of a Scotch gentleman on the reported cruelties that were said to be exercised after the Battle of Culloden'. Years later, Smollett's friend and colleague Oliver Goldsmith wrote that 'The Tears of Scotland' 'does rather more honour to the author's feelings than his taste'; but it has a fine ring to it, and is, with the 'Ode to Leven Water', one of the few Smollett poems to resurface in anthologies.

> Mourn, hapless Caledonia, mourn
> Thy banished peace, thy laurels torn!
> Thy sons, for valour long renown'd,
> Lie slaughter'd on their native ground;
> Thy hospitable roofs no more
> Invite the stranger to the door;
> In smoky ruins sunk they lie,
> The monuments of cruelty.

runs the first of its seven stanzas. According to John Moore, the concluding stanza was added later, 'after remonstrances to stop it'; Robert Graham of Gartmore claimed that Smollett was sitting with some friends in a pub, and that after reading them the first six stanzas and being told that 'the termination of the poem, being too strongly expressed, might give offence to persons whose political opinions were different', he picked up his pen and 'with an air of great indignation, subjoined the concluding stanza'. Its political import is very different from that of its predecessors, in which the desolation that has befallen Caledonia is seen as the result of a fratricidal falling-out, whereby 'The sons against their father stood/ The parent shed his children's blood' and 'What foreign arms could never quell/ By civil rage and rancour fell'. Scotland is now seen as the victim, arousing patriotic fury:

> While the warm blood bedews my veins,
> And unimpair'd remembrance reigns,
> Resentment of my country's fate
> Within my filial breast shall beat;
> And, spite of her insulting foe,

No sympathizing verse shall flow:
'Mourn, hapless Caledonia, mourn
Thy banish'd peace, thy laurels torn.'

According to John Moore, Smollett's friends worried about his open avowal of the poem's authorship but 'he was little influenced by prudential considerations, and never intimidated from avowing his sentiments by the fear of making powerful enemies'. By a curious irony, one of the poem's many admirers was the Earl of Chesterfield, and it could be that he interested himself in Smollett's theatrical endeavours as a result. Chesterfield was particularly vindictive towards the Jacobites, urging Cumberland to massacre rebel clansmen and suggesting a naval blockade to prevent food from reaching starving Highlanders. 'The Tears' was set to music by James Oswald, whose other compositions included a setting of Collins's 'Ode Written in 1746', also inspired by Culloden.

The events of 1745 are referred to in two other poems written at this time. Like Samuel Johnson, whose denunciatory poem *London* had appeared in 1738, Smollett was a keen admirer of Pope's Juvenalian satirical verses, and in 'Advice' and 'Reproof' he sought, like his mentor, to savage the 'insuperable corruption and depravity of manners' of the metropolitan world. Neither poem bears re-reading, and both are replete with topical references to, and digs at, long-forgotten politicians, quacks, financiers and theatrical folk. Each consists of a dialogue between the idealistic poet, horrified by the venality and corruption he sees all about him, and his more worldly friend.

Look round and see
What vices flourish still, unprun'd by me:
Corruption, roll'd in a triumphant car,
Displays his burnish'd front and glitt'ring star . . .

laments the poet. 'Two things I dread, my conscience and the law,' he tells his friend, who warns him that

Too coy to flatter, and too proud to serve,
Thine be the joyless dignity to starve . . .

Rich, Newcastle, Pitt and Colley Cibber are all harshly treated; the heroes include Handel, Pope, James Thomson and the philanthropic Scottish lawyer Daniel MacKercher, whose benevolent endeavours on behalf of the hard-done-by 'Annesley claimant' were to occupy a self-contained section of *Peregrine Pickle*. 'Wee Johnnie' Cope is ridiculed on two accounts: as an inept and cowardly soldier, whose exoneration by a board of inquiry provided further evidence of the all-pervading corruption denounced in the poems, and as a homosexual:

> Eternal infamy his name surround,
> Who planted first that vice on British ground!
> A vice that 'spite of sense and nature reigns,
> And poisons genial love, and manhood stains!

the poet declares of homosexual love; and both here and in *Roderick Random* Smollett takes a dim view of the matter. As the *Thunder* prepares to return to England after the Cartagena fiasco, Captain Oakum is replaced by Captain Whiffle, a tall, thin young man whose hair flowing down to his shoulders in ringlets and is partly tied at the back with a pink ribbon; he wears a pink silk coat, a white satin waistcoat embroidered in gold, crimson velvet breeches, white gloves held in place with a ring on each little finger, a plethora of diamonds and lace, and has an amber-headed cane dangling from his wrist. The members of his retinue 'seemed to be of their patron's disposition', Roderick tells us, disapprovingly, 'and the air was so impregnated with perfumes, that one may venture to affirm the clime of Arabia Felix was not half so sweet-scented'. Brought face-to-face with coarse, malodorous, check-shirted sea-dogs, the captain swoons away, and has to be brought round with dabs of scent and smelling salts; much to the relief of both parties, Roderick's efforts to bleed him are interrupted by the arrival of the new surgeon, Simper, 'a young man gaily dressed, of a very delicate complexion, with a kind of languid smile on his face, which seemed to have been rendered habitual by a long course of affectation'. They fly into each other's arms, and the captain's activities during the rest of their short stay on board 'gave Scandal an opportunity to be very busy with his character, and accuse him of maintaining a correspondence with the surgeon not fit to be named'.

Smollett's account of the homosexual peer Lord Strutwell is even more damning. Adrift in London, Roderick is trying to make his way in a corrupt, self-serving society in which advancement depends on getting to know the right people, and finding a patron to put in a word with the powers-that-be. Lord Straddle and Lord Swillpot, both adept practitioners, offer to intercede on Roderick's behalf with Earl Strutwell, who 'was hand-in-glove with a certain person who ruled the roost'. Strutwell promises to take Roderick's career in hand, but then ruins it all by clutching him too tightly to his chest, urging him to read Petronius Arbiter, and subjecting him to a short lecture on the delights of homosexual love – which, he assures his outraged protégé, is all the rage in London and 'in all probability will become in a short time a more fashionable vice than simple fornication'. Roderick denounces homosexuality as an 'appetite unnatural, absurd, and of pernicious consequence'; Strutwell turns out to be a con-man and a thief: 'it was a common thing for him to amuse strangers whom his jackals ran down, with such assurances and caresses as he had bestowed upon me, until he had stripped them of their cash, and every thing valuable about them – very often of their chastity – and then leave them a prey to want and infamy.'

It has been suggested that, for all his apparent outrage, Smollett wrote more explicitly about homosexual behaviour than any other writer between the classical world and the twentieth century; but his homophobia – which he seems to have shared with his admirer, George Orwell – is of less import than his sense of English society, and metropolitan society in particular, as a sink of venality, mendacity and vulgar ostentation, in which a writer was hard pressed not to become a Grub Street hack of the kind that Pope had denounced and ridiculed in *The Dunciad*, paid by the line to churn out party propaganda and reduced by penury to a life of incessant toil. Both themes were to loom large, in his writing and his life.

The facts of Smollett's life are few and hard to come by at the best of times, and seldom more so than in these early London years. Some time in 1746 he moved from Downing Street to Chapel Street in

Mayfair, where the rent was a modest £8 per annum; Anne may have joined him from Jamaica in 1747, and their only child, Elizabeth, was born the following year. The success of *Roderick Random*, published in 1748, enabled them to move into more expensive lodgings in Beaufort Street, between the Strand and the river, conveniently close to the theatres and pubs of Covent Garden and the booksellers of Fleet Street and St Paul's. He had yet to make his mark as a novelist, let alone embark on the hazardous life of a full-time man of letters, but was still trying to make his way as a doctor-cum-playwright. Carlyle remembered him from this time as 'a man of very agreeable conversation and of much genuine humour; and, though not a profound scholar, [he] professed a philosophical mind, and was capable of making the soundest observations of human life, and of discerning the excellence or seeing the ridicule of every character he met with'. At a meeting with fellow-Scots at the Golden Ball in Cockspur Street, the 'frugal fare' and 'little punch' – 'the finances of none of the company were in very good order' – were 'enlivened by Smollett's agreeable stories, which he told with peculiar grace'.

With only half his mind on the job, Smollett was not a particularly effective or enthusiastic doctor. He is said to have been too brusque and impatient to appeal to the lucrative society market: according to a memoir published after his death, he 'could not render himself agreeable to the women', and John Moore noted that he 'could neither stoop to impose on credulity, nor humour caprice'. In order to practise as a physician as well as a surgeon, he obtained an MD from Aberdeen University in 1750, paying £28 for the privilege. Despite the superiority of the medical training in Scotland, Scottish physicians – much to their indignation – were unable to become Fellows of the Royal College in London, and had to make do with 'licenciates' instead. MDs from the Scottish universities were ridiculed by the grander London practitioners: writing to Dr Cullen in Glasgow, William Hunter complained of 'how contemptuously the College of Physicians here have treated all Scotch degrees indiscriminately', while noting that 'the professors of one Scotch university at least shamefully prostitute their degrees still to any one who can pay them a small sum of money, and procure, perhaps purchase, a recommendation from some necessitous doctor'. MDs from Aberdeen and St Andrews were especially easy to come by, and could be acquired, like Smollett's, by post, but they improved their owners' professional standing and made it possible to charge higher fees. William Smellie, the great obstetrician, acquired his Scottish MD by post at the age of forty-five, and William Jenner of vaccination fame was among those who paid for the privilege.

Born in Lanarkshire in 1697, and a former pupil of John Gordon, Smellie had come to London at the age of forty-two, and established himself as the most influential of the new breed of male midwives. Midwifery had been, until the early years of the century, an exclusively female preserve, the domain, perhaps, of bibulous and unhygienic Sarah Gamps, licensed to practise by the local bishop. An awkward, ungainly character, lacking the smooth manners and social graces of William Hunter or James Douglas, the kind and benevolent Smellie was more than happy to treat poor women free, provided his pupils could look on; but this did not prevent his being savaged by Elizabeth Nihell, the leading female midwife of the day, who denounced his enthusiastic advocacy of obstetrical forceps and claimed that the male midwives included in their ranks tailors, barbers and pork butchers, including one who 'after passing half his life in stuffing sausages, is now turned an intrepid physician and man-midwife'. Smollett edited and prepared for press Smellie's authoritative, three-volume *Treatise in the Theory and Practice of Midwifery*, and later reviewed it as well. When, after observing an abnormal delivery, he thought he had made an important discovery about the separation of the pubic joint, he hurried round to share the good news with his mentor, only to be told that this was nothing new to those in the know.

Thanks to the success of *Roderick Random*, Smollett was able to retire from medical practice in 1752 or 1753, but although his only formal contribution to medical literature was his *Essay on the External Use of Water* – he always had strong views on the therapeutic qualities of sea bathing and immersion in cold water – he put his knowledge of the medical world to satirical use in his novels; nowhere more so than in his third novel, *The Adventures of Ferdinand Count Fathom*, published in 1753. A demonic incarnation of evil, whose career is given over to ruthless seduction and betrayal, Fathom decides to try his luck as a physician. Spa towns have always provided rich pickings for medical men, real or bogus, so he makes his way to Tunbridge Wells, where – according to the pamphleteer and social commentator Ned Ward – 'physicians swarm like pick-pockets at a fair'. Realising that 'the success of a physician, in a great measure, depends upon the external equipage in which he first declares himself an adept of the healing art', Fathom does his homework by consulting a few textbooks, and then descends on his patients – or victims – clad 'in the uniform of Aesculapius, namely a plain suit full trimmed, with a voluminous tie periwig'. His expertise in writing out a prescription impresses an apothecary, who tells him that 'in England, nothing could be more honourable, or indeed profitable, than the character of a physician, provided he could once wriggle himself into practice'. Poaching patients is fair game, but Fathom soon falls foul of a rival doctor of the old school, who denounces him as 'one of those who graduate themselves, and commence doctors, the Lord knows how: an interloper, who, without license and authority, comes hither to take the bread out of the mouths of gentlemen, who have been trained to the business in a regular manner, and bestowed great pains and expence to qualify themselves for the profession,' and refuses to work with 'any physician who has not taken his degree at either of the English universities'.

Fathom then moves to London, where, as part of the equipment essential for the fashionable practitioner, he buys and repaints a 'chariot' and hires a footman in laced livery. 'Every shabby retainer to physic', it seems, needs a chariot: they are used 'by way of a travelling signpost, to draw in customers', and a physician who goes about on foot is thought of as no better than an 'obscure pedlar'. He visits the medical coffee-houses, where fellow-practitioners meet to gossip and drum up business, and learns how 'confederacies' of physicians, surgeons, apothecaries, nurses and midwives work together, passing patients down the line from one to another and, as a last resort, maintaining a 'correspondence with one particular undertaker'. Already a master of low cunning, he is quick to learn the tricks that are used to drum up trade – being summoned ostentatiously from church to attend to an urgent case, or knocked up loudly in the middle of the night – and soon realises how important it is to be talked about: 'When a physician becomes the town talk, he generally concludes his business more than half done, even though his fame should wholly turn upon his malpractice . . .'

Such cynicism was not entirely misplaced. The eighteenth century saw the rise of the 'celebrity doctor', and if some provincial physicians could earn as much as £1,000 a year, their fashionable London equivalents often made a great deal more. 'There are two ways, my boy, for a physician to treat his patients: either to bully or cajole them. I have taken the first course, and done very well, as you see. You may take the latter, and perhaps do just as well,' John Radcliffe told a pupil towards the end of the previous century. Cajoling patients involved developing a bedside manner, exploiting charm and flattery to the full, and making use of what Fathom described as 'that decorum and urbanity which ought to distinguish the deportment of every physician'. The physician's character, Smollett elsewhere declared, 'not only supposes natural sagacity, and acquired erudition, but it also implies every delicacy of sentiment, every tenderness of nature, and every virtue of humanity'. It also called for a fairly tough hide. If the eighteenth century saw the first manifestation of the consumer society, medicine was – like novels, theatre-going, fashionable clothes, racing and interior decoration – one of the ways in which disposable income could be put to use. There was a large and ever-expanding market for books on medical matters written for the layman, the more adventurous or hypochondriacal of whom were more than happy to diagnose their own ailments and take responsibility for their own health; those in a position to call on a physician expected to shop around, take a second or even third opinion, and – then as now – combine orthodox and fringe medicine, according to taste. Doctors had to be prepared to listen and, where the grander patients were concerned, defer to their social superiors. Placebos were widely used; 'stale' blood was 'evacuated' by phlebotomy or bleeding, and toxins or 'peccant humours' were expelled by means of sweating, vomiting and purging with laxatives or enemas made from rhubarb or senna.

Good health resulted from an orderly working of the constitution, and maintaining 'balance' and 'equilibrium'; sickness was the result of an imbalance or disequilibrium. It was essential to keep a balance of bodily fluids or humours, of hot and cold, wet and dry: a system that was too hot and dry resulted in a fever, while one that was too wet and cold led to a cold; with too little blood the patient languished, but too much – caused, perhaps, by an excess of red meat or port – put him or her in danger of a stroke or apoplexy. Like many of his contemporaries, Smollett was a keen believer in the importance of exercise: in the war against malignant 'contra-naturals', emphasis was laid on the virtues of regular bowel movements, uninterrupted sleep, a healthy environment, fresh air, a sensible diet and moderation in all things, including amorous inclinations and alcoholic intake. One extremely influential advocate of 'dietetick management' was George Cheyne, a fashionable London physician trained in Edinburgh. As a young medic-about-town eager to make his way in society, Cheyne had so over-indulged that 'I swelled to such an enormous size that upon my last weighing I exceeded 32 stones.' Once back to a more manageable size, Cheyne set about preaching good health. He urged his patients to avoid liquids that were too viscous or too saline, to eat white meats like chicken, rabbit and mutton rather than the much-vaunted English beef, and to take plenty of exercise on the grounds that it promoted circulation of the blood, perspiration and fluidity of the bodily juices, 'their viscidity broken and dissolved'. Such notions, and the language in which they were expressed, recur again and again in Smollett's writings and correspondence: as a hypochondriac who always suffered from poor health, he was more than happy, even after he retired from practice, to pass on medical advice to his friends, while at the same time keeping a keen eye on his own ailments. He shared, too, Cheyne's belief in the enervating and corrupting effects of luxury, which promoted excess and diseases like gout, and prevented the upper classes in particular from taking as much exercise as they needed.

One way in which physicians could bump up their earnings was by charging for medicines. According to Cheyne, some doctors were 'continually cramming their patients with nauseous and loathsome potions', obtained usually from apothecaries but sometimes from large druggists like Thomas Corbyn, who stocked over 2,500 items.

Herbs still formed the basis of the 'materia medica', and herbal remedies were widely used as laxatives and purgatives. The 'Fifth London Pharmacopia' of 1746 still included such arcane items as woodlice, bezoar, coral and viper, while dropping such old favourites as spiders' webs, moss from human skulls and unicorn horns; among the newer drugs listed were aconite, sarsaparilla, castor oil and liquid opium. Opium, which could be bought over the counter, was used for diarrhoea and fevers, and as an analgesic. Under the influence of the Paracelsians, increasing use was made of mineral- and metal-based drugs like calomel and antimony, and mercury in the treatment of syphilis; cocktails of drugs were sometimes prescribed as purgatives, and if they proved too violent the side effects were countered with a dose of belladonna, so poisoning the system still further. Many apothecaries, like Lavement in *Roderick Random*, were nimble at concocting prescriptions:

> I have sometimes been amazed to see him, without the least hesitation, make up a physician's prescription, though he had not in his shop one medicine mentioned in it. Oyster shells he could invent into crabs' eyes; common oil, into oil of sweet almonds; syrup of sugar, into balsamic syrup; Thames water, into aqua cinammoni; turpentine, into capivi; and a hundred more costly preparations were produced in an instant, from the cheapest and coarsest drugs of the materia medica . . .

And in *An Account of My Own Constitution and Illness, with some Rules for the Preservation of Health; for the Use of my Children*, the effete Lord Hervey – the 'Sporus' of Pope's *Epistle to Dr Arbuthnot*, the inspiration for Smollett's 'Advice' and 'Reproof' – wrote of doctors that

> They all jog on in one beaten track; a vomit to clear your stomach, a glister to give you a stool, laudanum to quiet the pain, and then a purge to cleanse your bowels, and what they call 'carry it off'. This was their method in every attack; and, during the intervals, if bitters to restore my appetite, spa-waters to raise spirits, and ass's milk with powder of crabs' eyes and

oyster shells to sweeten my blood, would not prevent the return of my distemper, they none of them knew what else to try . . .

Physicians claimed the right to visit apothecaries' shops and remove drugs which were not up to standard; their motives were not entirely disinterested, since they wanted to increase their own involvement in the lucrative drugs business, and a fierce 'battle of the dispensaries' was fought in the 1730s.

It must have been hard, at times, to distinguish the wilder shores of orthodox medicine from folk remedies and outright quackery. The 'London Dispensatory', issued by the College of Physicians, recommended the use of viper's fat and crabs' eyes; folklore cures included stroking a stye with the tail of a black cat, holding a pigeon to the side of the head to cure inflammation of the brain, and staunching wounds with toasted cheese. Newspapers and brand-name remedies were often sold and promoted together: John Newbery, one of the most distinguished booksellers of the age, and a publisher specialising in children's books, made a second fortune from selling the highly dubious but hugely popular 'St James's Powder', said by some to have hastened Oliver Goldsmith's untimely end. (For all Dr Lind's good work on behalf of citrus fruits, it was also recommended to the Navy as an antidote to scurvy – as were the equally fraudulent and ineffectual pills produced by the notorious quack Dr Joshua 'Spot' Ward, MP.) Years later, Newbery and Smollett were to come together through publication of the British Magazine, and two of Smollett's most virulent and vindictive Grub Street enemies – Drs John Hill and John Shebbeare – were either quacks or involved in the shadier end of the medical spectrum.

Although Smollett's practical involvement in the medical world would soon be over, his work as a writer is inseparable from the experiences, and the view of life, he absorbed as a surgeon and a physician; nor was the use he made of his knowledge restricted to satirical accounts of practitioners or lurid descriptions of how they put theory into practice. He is among the most physically aware of all novelists, acutely sensitive, in print as in person, to the din and stench and bustle of everyday life, on board ship, in the assembly rooms of Bath, or on the raucous streets of Covent Garden; and although, compared with the great nineteenth-century novelists, he showed little interest in, or ability to deal with, the internal and subjective lives of his characters, in the subtleties of change and ambiguity, he had a keen eye for the external manifestations of personality, for the small, revealing details of clothes and physiognomy. In his obsession with externals, he was merely carrying over into his writing the techniques and methods of medical men who, unable to examine or cure the inner man, set great store by surface symptoms and the outward expressions of ill health. The fact that his comical and villainous characters are essentially 'humours' reflects his training in a tradition that, in literature as well as medicine, had a long and honourable ancestry, but was nearing the end of its day. It was not the only way in which Smollett, a deeply conservative man, would be fighting a rearguard action.

4

The Glories of Grub Street

'I have finished a romance in two small volumes, called the Adventures of Roderick Random,' Smollett wrote to Alexander Carlyle towards the end of 1747. 'It is intended as a satire on mankind, and by the reception it has met with in private from the best judges here I have reason to believe it will succeed very well.' Quite who the 'best judges' were remains obscure, but Smollett's optimistic forecast was amply justified – so much so that he was to become an early example of the novelist whose first work enjoys greater commercial and popular success than those which come after. Being best remembered for your first book is an invidious business; *Roderick Random* may have inspired a comic opera and given his name to a racehorse nimble enough to earn 1,000 guineas for Lord Eglinton and the Earl of March, but on the other hand Smollett's later novels, published anonymously, were all attributed on the title page to 'the author of *Roderick Random*', as if basking in remembered glory.

Though Roderick is no match for Matthew Bramble in *Humphry Clinker* as a rounded, sympathetic and plausible central character – by the end of his adventures we know little about him except that he is Scottish, red-haired, proud, thin-skinned and vindictive, and, defiantly, a gentleman throughout – his adventures embody Smollett at his most fast-moving and rumbustious, with none of the longueurs

84

that blight *Peregrine Pickle*, *Count Fathom* and *Sir Launcelot Greaves*. Quite apart from his forays into naval, medical and literary life, Roderick – like any good picaresque hero – samples an extraordinary range of eighteenth-century life, high and low, before settling down to rustic and squirearchical bliss with his beloved if duly anodyne Narcissa. He consorts with prostitutes, con-men, peers of the realm, highwaymen, eccentric maiden aunts and pot-valiant soldiers; he survives a shipwreck, is left for dead, writes poems for Narcissa, misbehaves in Covent Garden, fights a duel, gambles in Bath, finds himself on the French side at the Battle of Dettingen, serves time in prison, sails on a slave-trader to Africa and South America, meets up with his long-lost father in the kind of coincidence that Dickens, his great admirer, could only marvel at, and – since such novels have to end with a satisfactory financial settlement as well as the sound of wedding bells – comes into a sizeable inheritance at last. The characters he meets along the way are, unless of the dutifully good variety, one-dimensional humours or grotesques, and all the more enjoyable for it; as in an Elizabethan farce, most have names to match, from Mr Cringer the obsequious politician to Potion the medical man and Lavement the apothecary (*lavement* was a contemporary French euphemism for Smollett's old favourite, the enema). Roderick is accompanied for much of the time by a loyal and long-suffering manservant, Strap, who practises as a barber when not rescuing his master from his latest scrape: as such, he occupies an honourable fictional niche between Sancho Panza and Sam Weller – though his simple-mindedness, and his tendency to leap and caper with joy on hearing good news, are more reminiscent of poor Tom Pinch in Martin Chuzzlewit than of Mr Pickwick's wily henchman. As a result of all this non-stop activity, the reader, or so Smollett tells us in his Preface,

> gratifies his curiosity in pursuing the adventures of a person in whose favour he is prepossessed; he espouses his cause, he sympathises with him in distress; his indignation is heated against the authors of his calamity; the humane passions are inflamed; the contrast between dejected virtue and insulting vice appears with greater aggravation; and every impression having a double force

on the imagination, the memory retains the circumstance, and the heart improves by the example . . .

He goes on to pay homage not just to Cervantes, his most obvious model, but to the contemporary French picaresque novelist LeSage, whose most famous novel, *The Adventures of Gil Blas*, he translated while working on *Roderick Random*. LeSage, Smollett tells us, 'has described the knavery and foibles of life, with infinite humour and sagacity', but Smollett has chosen to differ from him in that

> The disgraces of Gil Blas are, for the most part, such as to excite mirth rather than compassion: he himself laughs at them; and his transitions from distress to happiness, or at least ease, are so sudden, that neither the reader has time to pity him, nor himself be acquainted with affliction. This conduct, in my opinion, not only deviates from probability, but prevents that generous indignation which ought to animate the reader against the sordid and vicious disposition of the world.

Roderick does indeed find himself adrift in a brutal, coarse-grained and, except where true love is concerned, unsentimental world, and Smollett himself was never the man to dodge 'generous indignation'. But back to his Preface. 'I have attempted,' he continues,

> to represent modest merit struggling with every difficulty to which a friendless orphan is exposed, from his own want of experience, as well as from the selfishness, envy, malice, and base indifference of mankind. To secure a favourable prepossession, I have allowed him the advantages of birth and education which, in the series of his misfortunes, will, I hope, engage the ingenuous more warmly in his behalf; and though I foresee that some people will be offended at the mean scenes in which he is involved, I persuade myself that the judicious will not only perceive the necessity of describing those situations in which he must of course be confined, in his low state, but also find entertainment in viewing those parts of life, where the humours and passions are undisguised by affectation, ceremony or education . . .

By 'making the chief personage of this work a North Briton', Smollett could provide Roderick with an education befitting 'the dignity of his birth and character' more cheaply than would have been the case had he started life in England, and 'represent simplicity of manners in a remote part of the kingdom, with more propriety than in any other place near the capital'; quite apart from which, the Scots were already famously 'addicted to travelling'.

With its loose, rambling, episodic structure – Andrew Lang, the well-known Victorian collector of fairy tales, once said of it that 'there is no reason why it should ever stop except at the convenience of printers and binders' – *Roderick Random* is the most famous English example of the picaresque novel. Scholars have debated keenly about what constitutes a picaresque novel, how it differs from the epic (*Tom Jones*, we are told, is a mock epic rather than a would-be picaresque), and whether or not *Roderick Random* – or, indeed, the equally peripatetic *Humphry Clinker* – fully qualifies. The hero, or anti-hero, of the prototypical picaresque novel was developed in sixteenth-century Spain, and *Lazarillo de Tormes* is the quintessence of the form: first published, anonymously, in 1552, it appeared in an English translation in 1576. Like Roderick, Lazarillo is self-reliant and resilient, buffeted by his encounters with an unkind and often malicious world, moving on from one episode or encounter to the next, sampling a wide variety of experiences, most of them disagreeable, yet somehow surviving them all, and remaining remarkably unchanged throughout; but he was also, by definition, an amiable rogue, often from the servant class. LeSage – and some more recent authorities – felt that for a gentleman like Roderick to double up as a *picaro* or rogue would have been a contradiction in terms, so excluding his story from the canon.

Roderick Random did well for itself and its author when it appeared in January 1748. It was published in two volumes at six shillings the pair by J. Osborne of Paternoster Row, a well-respected bookseller who had earlier persuaded the printer Samuel Richardson to try his authorial hand at something more ambitious than indexes and dedication pages, so acting as midwife to *Pamela*. Sales over three impressions between first publication and November the following year amounted to 6,500 copies: not quite as many, maddeningly, as

Fielding's *Joseph Andrews*, published six years earlier, which had sold the same amount within a year – let alone *Tom Jones*, which came out a year later, and sold over 10,000 in under a year – but still a very satisfactory state of affairs.

'*Clarissa* kept us up till two in the morning. Rhoderic [*sic*] will keep us up all night,' declared the Earl of Orrery. 'Have you read that strange new book *Roderick Random?*' Miss Talbot wondered of her fellow-bluestocking Miss Carter. 'It is a very strange and a very low one, though not without some characters in it.' Unlike the high-toned Richardson, both Smollett and Fielding were seen as 'low' novelists who dealt in indelicate matters. The *Gentleman's Magazine* apostrophised *Roderick Random* as 'a warning to one sex, and a remonstrance against t'other'; writing to her daughter, the Countess of Bute, Lady Mary Wortley Montagu suggested that 'There is something humorous in *Roderick Random* which makes me believe the author is H. Fielding,' though Fanny Boscawen, wife to the future admiral, noted in her journal that 'I am told 'tis not Fielding's, but the produce of a Scotch sea surgeon called Smollett . . . I laughed at first, but I grew tired before I was done.' (The Admiral, fondly remembered as 'Old Dreadnought', had been, as a young man, on Hosier's ill-fated venture to the Caribbean. He took part in the capture of Porto Bello, and at Cartagena he distinguished himself by destroying an enemy battery; during both sieges he was charged, by Commodore Knowles, with the destruction of captured enemy forts. He was out of the country when *Roderick Random* was published, attempting, without success, to capture Pondicherry from the French.) Smollett would always be bracketed with, and compared with, Fielding, usually to his discredit; Fielding seems to have been an amiable and easy-going character, but his success as a novelist, playwright, magistrate and recipient of elevated patronage was to inflame his rival's tender sense of grievance

'I am so proud of your panegyric on Roderick that I can no longer resist the inclination I feel to signify how much I am pleased with your approbation. I have had occasion to experience the weakness of vanity in an author which exults even in the applause of a fool. How much then must I triumph in the praise which (I flatter myself) is the result of veracity and taste,' Smollett told Carlyle in June

1748. He went on to say how upset he was that his old schoolmaster had taken umbrage, adding that the novel in its entirety was 'not so much a representation of my life as of that of many other needy Scotch surgeons whom I have known personally or by report'. He apologised for any stylistic faults, the result of his having written the entire book – well over 200,000 words – in 'the compass of eight weeks', during which time he had sometimes failed to pick up his pen for a week or even a month on end; and, combining modesty and boastfulness like 'any true author enamoured of the first person', he informed his friend that he had been approached by two other booksellers about future work.

From now on his life would be ruled by the pleasures, and the travails, of the literary life; and the times could hardly have been more auspicious. The first half of the eighteenth century saw the emergence of the full-time professional writer, unsupported by royal, aristocratic or ecclesiastical patrons and making his way in the world by selling his work to, and accepting commissions from, publishers, newspapers and magazines. Smollett was to prove an exceptionally industrious, prolific, versatile and articulate member of the tribe, and he captured with rare feeling the more humdrum and dispiriting aspects of authorial existence. Few have written better about the exhaustion and demoralisation of Grub Street life, about meeting deadlines and taking on hackwork to pay the bills, and about literary feuds, rife with malice, rivalry and self-importance, and long-forgotten names who loomed so large at the time but mean nothing any more. He was the quintessential man of letters, combining the writing of fiction with work as a publishers' editor, an anthologist, a pamphleteer, an historian, a translator, and a pioneering and influential magazine editor; his life is, in many ways, a cautionary tale, in that years of incessant toil and literary feuding ruined his health and led him to an early grave, and could be read as a useful antidote for those with romantic illusions about the literary life.

Nowadays we tend to assume that social change must have a material or mechanical explanation, and that the emergence of the professional writer is almost certain to have technological causes. The slow improvements in the roads made it possible to distribute books, magazines and even newspapers on a countrywide basis, but printing methods remained much as they had been in the age of Caxton, and would not change in any radical way until the nineteenth century. Although increasing use was made of home-made rather than imported paper, and type-founders and typesetters like William Caslon and John Baskerville freed English printers from their dependence on Continental masters and proved that it was possible to rival and then excel the great European designers and printers, such improvements were neither here nor there. Altogether more important were two items of legislation – one repealed, the other enacted – and that old staple of the history books, the rise of the middle classes, with money enough to spare: the net effect of which was to increase, dramatically, the number, variety and audacity of publications on offer, and accelerate the movement away from an oral culture to one that was dependent on the written word.

Whether Whigs or Tories, eighteenth-century Englishmen – or 'Britons', as they now struggled to term themselves – liked to see themselves as a defiant, freedom-loving people whose liberties had been secured by the Glorious Revolution of 1688 and the subsequent Bill of Rights: both, or so it was claimed, had thwarted Stuart aspirations after absolute rule on the Continental model, and ushered in a strong if delicate balance of power between the conflicting interests of the Monarch, the Lords and the Commons. Among the casualties of Stuart rule was the 1662 Licensing Act, which was allowed to lapse in 1695. Under this Act, no book or pamphlet could legally be printed unless it had first been licensed or passed by the censor. The right to print was reserved to the Crown, and to a limited number of booksellers licensed by the Stationers' Company; only twenty printing houses were allowed to operate in England, and they in turn were restricted to two presses per shop. The Act's repeal triggered an unprecedented proliferation of newspapers, magazines, periodicals, pamphlets and books – all of which had to be written, whether by Grub Street hacks or by Pope, Defoe and Swift. The first daily newspaper, the *Daily Courant*, appeared in 1702; the periodical, consisting of neatly turned essays, was most famously manifested in Richard Steele's *Tatler*, which appeared three times a week for nearly three years, and Addison's *Spectator*, which sold some 400 copies a day between 1711 and 1712. The magazine proper made its appearance in 1731, when Edward Cave produced the first issue of the *Gentleman's Magazine*, a miscellany of essays, poems, news items regurgitated from the London newspapers, details of births, marriages and deaths, and parliamentary reports, written for a time by the young Samuel Johnson. Aimed at the provincial as well as the metropolitan market, it achieved, at its height, a circulation of 15,000, selling through provincial booksellers as well as by subscription. Magazines, periodicals and newspapers all benefited from the proliferation of coffee-houses, where they could be read and discussed. The imposition of stamp duty in 1725 made newspapers too expensive for the labouring classes – always assuming that they could read, a matter of debate among the scholars – but, contrary to government intentions, had the effect of stimulating rather than inhibiting the spread of printed matter, and adding to rather than reducing the number of pages per issue. Newspapers and magazines tended to be short-lived, and their circulations were minute by modern standards; sales of novels and literary reviews, on the other hand, were much the same as they are today. Smollett was to found and edit three magazines, and between 1739 and 1752 Fielding founded and edited the *Champion*, the *True Patriot*, the *Jacobites' Journal* and the *Covent Garden Journal*, none of which lasted more than a year.

Polemical and political journalism, and particularly that which was hostile to whichever ministry happened to be in power at the time, was invariably scurrilous, abusive and *ad hominem*. Sir Robert Walpole was more lambasted than most, incurring the recurrent wrath of Fielding and of the *Craftsman*, which led the opposition in the 1720s. Despite the repeal of the Licensing Act, the government was far from powerless: as well as invoking the laws of libel, obscenity and blasphemy, it could also prosecute on the grounds of seditious libel (so, too, could a private individual, as Smollett learned to his cost). It was, in theory, illegal to question the legitimacy of the House of Hanover, to support the claims of the Stuarts to the throne, or to make personal attacks on the King or members of the royal family: a printer who was hanged at Tyburn for standing up for the Stuarts served as a dreadful warning.

The other influential piece of legislation, positive this time, was the passing of the Copyright Act in 1709. Books that were already in print were entitled to copyright protection for a further twenty-one years; unpublished works were covered for fourteen years from the moment of first publication, at the end of which the copyright could be renewed for a further fourteen years. Authors could assign the copyright in a particular book to a bookseller, as Smollett did with *Roderick Random*, or retain the copyright, as he would do with *Peregrine Pickle*. Pope, a shrewd and influential manipulator of the literary market, who made over £4,000 from his translation of the *Iliad*, was among the first to insist that, at the expiry of the initial fourteen-year period, the copyright should revert from the bookseller to the author, who was then free to do what he liked with the rights for the second term of copyright. Printing had converted books into marketable objects, and the booksellers were, like their modern equivalents, eager to exploit all the rights in the books they published, as well as selling as many copies as possible. The Copyright Act marked the beginning of the end for the notion of perpetual copyright, which, to the fury of those publishers who had earned a steady income from the sale of backlist titles in which they had bought the copyright years before, was finally abolished by a ruling of the House of Lords in 1774. It was of enormous benefit to authors, and crucial to their altered standing in the world, and despite the threat to perpetual copyright, booksellers too had pressed hard for legislation to protect their investments. The Act enabled them to take civil action against pirate publishers, who might well find themselves paying damages should they publish an illegal edition of a copyright book. Publishers in Dublin were exempt from the Act until 1801, while some Scottish lawyers argued that copyright did not exist under Scots law, and that publishers in Glasgow and Edinburgh were free to publish works protected in England. To the intense irritation of their rivals in London, Irish and Scottish publishers would, given half a chance, export their books to England. A Dublin edition of *Roderick Random* was published soon after its appearance in London, and may or may not have found its way into the English market.

Booksellers doubled up as publishers: a typical bookseller would operate from a shop in which he not only sold his own publications – which might include pamphlets and magazines as well as books proper – but those of his rivals, who would be expected to stock his books in their shops. The workings of the retail trade, and the various discounts offered as a book made its way from publisher to purchaser, were spelt out, lucidly and in detail, in a long and helpful letter from Dr Johnson to the Master of University College, Oxford. Publication, and the remuneration of the author, could take various forms. One method – employed in the case of *The Regicide*, that doomed endeavour, but falling out of favour as the century progressed – was publication by subscription: prospective buyers chipped in to the costs of production, paying half in advance and half on publication, and the publisher would go ahead with publication only when an adequate number of subscribers had been enlisted. Some books were published by one bookseller only, others by two or more, sharing the risks, the costs and the profits. Then, as now, publishing was a capital-intensive business – which put pressure on authors to deliver copy on time, and to the right length – and large, long-term and expensive projects, like Dr Johnson's *Dictionary*, or some of the vast works of compilation later undertaken by Smollett, were often funded by a 'conger' or group of publishers, each of whom would own a fraction of the copyright and be entitled to a comparable fraction of the proceeds.

Most authors were paid an outright fee for the copyright. Royalties as we know them had yet to be invented, but increasing use was made of profit-sharing agreements and the payment of a 'refresher' in the event of a new impression or edition. Thomas Cadell and William Strahan paid Gibbon two-thirds of the net profits on the third edition of *The Decline and Fall of the Roman Empire*; Robert Dodsley, one of the most highly regarded publishers of the day, often paid by the sheet, paying Smollett one and a half guineas per sheet for his soul-destroying labours on the *Compendium of Authentic and Entertaining Voyages*. Print runs for most novels were much as they are today, hovering round the 1,500 mark, and they were sold not just to private individuals, but to the circulating and subscription libraries which flourished all over the country, with members paying an annual subscription of 10s. 6d. and a penny a volume per loan. London booksellers and provincial newspapers often worked together, with the booksellers advertising their latest wares in the newspapers and taking advantage of the papers' distribution systems.

Once again, there was a link between the printed word and patent medicines: both books and medicines were centrally produced and distributed, and many provincial bookshops acted as agents for the manufacturers of patent and quack medicines.

The notion of the gentleman-publisher, educated at a major public school and an ancient university, was a product of the 1920s and the 1930s. Like their Edwardian successors, eighteenth-century publishers were, in social if not monetary terms, fairly humble folk; tradesmen who, if they were shrewd and lucky, could do very well for themselves, and even, like Strahan, afford a coach. By ancient tradition, they had congregated in Paternoster Row, in the shadow of St Paul's, spreading west from there along Fleet Street into the Strand and Covent Garden. In 1735, Robert Dodsley, affectionately referred to as 'Doddy' by Dr Johnson, took the bold step of setting up shop in Pall Mall, in the fashionable West End. A former footman, he had started his literary career as a poet and playwright: Pope admired his verses, and encouraged him to publish, by subscription, his *The Muse in Livery; or The Footman's Miscellany*. Dodsley held literary salons in his rooms behind the Tully's Head, employed and encouraged the great type designer John Baskerville (himself a former footman), published Johnson, Burke and Sterne at various stages in their careers, and went on to found a weekly evening paper and the *Annual Register*, with Burke as its editor. Newbery, the publisher of *Jack the Giant-killer*, *Goody Two Shoes*, Goldsmith's *History of England*, the works of his son-in-law, Christopher Smart, and Smollett's *British Magazine*, not only acquired the patent in St James's Powder in 1746, but took the sensible step of marrying, at the age of twenty-four, the widow of the owner of the *Reading Mercury and Oxford Gazette*; Thomas Longman was another aspiring publisher who did well by marrying the master's daughter. But perhaps the best-respected publisher of all, rivalled only by Dodsley, was Andrew Millar, with whom Smollett was to have an often uneasy relationship. A Scot, he opened his shop in the Strand in 1729. Like many of his successors in the trade, he was, according to Dr Johnson, 'so habitually and equably drunk that his most intimate friends never perceived that he was more drunk at one time than another'. Despite this, he was highly regarded by the great man. 'I respect Millar, Sir, he has raised the price of literature,' Johnson once observed, and Millar's readiness to pay ever-larger sums for the novels of Fielding – £183 10s. for *Joseph Andrews*, £700 for *Tom Jones* and £1,000 for *Amelia* – reflected both the increasing power of the author and an expanding market for fiction, not least among female readers.

Millar worked closely with the printer William Strahan, a fellow-Scot who printed *Roderick Random* and, in the years to come, would provide Smollett with help and advice when his financial problems seemed insuperable. Strahan had learned his business in Edinburgh before setting up his own print-shop in Shoe Lane, off Fleet Street. By the 1750s he had the largest print-shop in London, employing over fifty men working flat out on nine presses. With high fixed costs, it was essential to keep the presses running full time: this increased the pressure on hacks to write to order, and since type itself was always in short supply, proofs had to be corrected instantly so that the type could be 'dissed' or redistributed for immediate re-use. Books were often proof-read and printed as they went along: in the case of massive works, like Johnson's *Dictionary* and some of the interminable gazetteers and histories with which Smollett was involved, the author and his team of hack writers would still be at work on the manuscript while earlier pages were being printed and folded in sections, waiting to be bound up once the whole work had been completed, or sold as part-works on their own account. Ambitious and highly successful – he went on to become an MP, as well as owning his own coach – Strahan dabbled in publishing as well. He bought up copyrights, acted as an agent and wholesaler for booksellers, and, as a member of a 'conger', helped finance works like the *Dictionary*. He shared in the publication of *Peregrine Pickle* and *Count Fathom* but, unlike a conventional bookseller, kept his name off the title page. Almost as successful was Samuel Richardson, who started life as a printer before taking up a parallel career as a novelist. His three printing works kept some forty employees busy; his ventures into publishing included backing and financing the mammoth, multi-volume *Universal History*, on which Smollett would be employed as editor and contributor.

'The present age may be styled, with great propriety, *The Age of*

Authors; for, perhaps, there never was a time in which men of all degrees of ability, of every kind of education, of every profession and employment, were posting with ardour so general to the press,' Johnson once declared. Defoe, writing a few years earlier, noted that writing 'is become a very considerable branch of the English commerce. The booksellers are the master manufacturers or employers. The several writers, authors, copiers, sub-writers and all other operators with pen and ink are the workmen employed by the said master manufacturers.' A proliferation of outlets provided unprecedented opportunities for writers, editors, anthologists, critics and reviewers, all of them increasingly dependent on the market rather than the whims of an aristocratic patron. In *The Case of Authors by Profession a Trade*, James Relph recognised that the 'volunteer, or gentleman-writer' had been replaced by the 'writer by profession', who 'serves himself and the public together, has as good a right to the product in money of his abilities, as the landholder to his rent, or the money-jobber to his interest'. As always, there were some who lamented, or half lamented, the passing of the old order, deploring in particular the venomous, ubiquitous Grub Street hacks and the increased power and influence of booksellers: both subjects on which Smollett had strong views, denouncing a trend while actively participating in it. Pope savaged the new order in his poem *The Dunciad*, published in 1728. Print had become an instrument of 'Dulness'; the profusion of hacks, booksellers' readiness to publish anything that would sell, irrespective of quality, and the notion of books as commodities, mechanically produced and sold in bulk, spelt the end of polite letters. Goldsmith, who spent his life in Grub Street, regretted 'that fatal revolution whereby writing is converted to a mechanic trade; and booksellers, instead of the great, become the patrons and paymasters of men of genius'; Fielding, another denizen, lamented a decline of standards in a world in which 'paper merchants, commonly called booksellers' employ 'journeymen of the trade' to keep the mills in motion. A competent hack would try his luck at any kind of writing. In Goldsmith's *The Vicar of Wakefield*, published in 1766, young George Primrose, adrift in London, decides against teaching but is recommended by his cousin to sample authorship:

I see you are a lad of spirit and some learning, what do you think of commencing author, like me? You have read in books, no doubt, of men of genius starving at the trade: at present I'll show you forty very dull fellows about town that live by it in opulence. All honest jogg-trot men, who go on smoothly and dully, and write history and politics, and are praised; men, Sir, who, had they been bred cobblers, would all their lives have only mended shoes, but never made them.

Goldsmith himself was to find the life of a freelance hack more hazardous and less remunerative than his 'jogg-trot men', and the hapless Melopoyn, in *Roderick Random*, is soon sucked into the life of a Grub Street hack. He declines Father O'Varnish's suggestion that he should become a polemical journalist for a weekly paper, but – again at the priest's suggestion – decides to try his hand as a poet: 'I was charmed with this prospect, and having heard what friends Mr Pope acquired by his pastorals, set about a work of that kind, and in less than six weeks, composed as many eclogues, which I forthwith offered to an eminent bookseller, who desired me to leave them for his perusal, and he would give me an answer in two days.' Although the bookseller 'sweetened his refusal by saying there were some good clever lines in them', he has no luck with the poems; he tries his luck with translations from the Latin, but the bookseller recoils in horror when he suggests a rate of 10s. 6d. per sheet, and he is reduced to composing 'halfpenny ballads, and other such occasional essays as are hawked about the streets'. Although he 'studied the Grub Street manner with great diligence, and at length became such a proficient that my works were in great request among the more polite of the chairmen, draymen, hackney coachmen, footmen and servant maids', it proves impossible to keep penury at bay, and he makes ends meet by writing up lurid accounts of rapes and murders, 'my never-failing resource'.

Peregrine Pickle, at a low point in his fortunes, becomes a writer on the grounds that he had, in happier days, 'heard of several authors who, without any pretensions to genius, earned a very genteel subsistence, by undertaking work for booksellers'. One of these, he discovers, does translations at so much per sheet, while another considers compiling a new dictionary; Peregrine himself, like Smollett in the days of 'Advice' and 'Reproof', undertakes an 'imitation of Juvenal', in which he 'lashed some conspicuous characters, with equal truth, spirit, and severity'. At a meeting of the College of Authors he learns about the art of 'puffing' each other's work, and listens sympathetically as members ventilate their grievances about booksellers' deplorable ways; the College solemnly discusses 'the necessity for concerting measures to humble the presumption of booksellers, who had, from time immemorial, taken all opportunities to oppress and enslave their authors; not only by limiting men of genius to the wages of a journeyman tailor . . . but also in taking such advantage of their necessities, as were inconsistent with justice and humanity'.

Melopoyn's bookseller advised him that 'translation was a mere drug, that branch of literature being overstocked with an inundation of authors from North Britain' – including Tobias Smollett. 'I have contracted with two booksellers to translate *Don Quixote* from the Spanish language, which I have studied for some time,' Smollett told Carlyle in the summer of 1748, adding that 'This perhaps you will look upon as a very desperate undertaking, there being no fewer than four translations of the same book already extant, but I am fairly engaged and cannot recede.' Both Smollett's self-proclaimed knowledge of Spanish and his translation of Cervantes's novel have long been viewed with some suspicion. He may have travelled to France and the Low Countries in 1744, so provoking John Shebbeare's jibe that 'the author had been full six weeks to study the language among the native Spaniards at Brussels', the centre of Spanish rule. In 1755, the year in which Smollett's translation was finally published, Ralph Griffiths, later to become a hostile and rival editor, compared in some detail Smollett's translation with that of his most immediate predecessor, Charles Jarvis (sometimes referred to as 'Jervas'). Griffiths declared for Smollett as coming 'nearest the great original', but in more recent times the Spanish-speaking scholar Carmine Linsalata has suggested that Smollett's 'translation' was, in effect, a paraphrase of the Charles Jarvis version, published as recently as 1742. Jarvis had died three years earlier, so was in no position to defend his work; according to Linsalata, Smollett and his team of hacks disregarded the original Spanish, repeated Jarvis's mistakes as well as his footnotes, and even – such was their ignorance of the language – mistranslated the most elementary numbers. Smollett, for his part, declared that his aim had been to 'maintain that ludicrous solemnity and self-importance by which the inimitable Cervantes has distinguished the character of Don Quixote', and to 'retain the spirit and ideas, without servilely adhering to the literal expression of the original; from which, however, he has not so far deviated, as to destroy that formality of idiom, so peculiar to the Spanish'. His translation had been 'conducted with that care and circumspection, which ought to be exerted by every author, who, in attempting to improve upon a task already performed, subjects himself to the most invidious comparison', and he could not 'charge himself with carelessness or precipitation; for it was begun, and the greatest part of it actually finished, four years ago; and he has been for some time employed in revising and correcting it for the press . . .' In the Foreword to a recent reissue of Smollett's translation, Carlos Fuentes hails it as 'the homage of a novelist to a novelist', and enthuses about 'its immediacy and force, its playfulness and freshness': in which case, if Linsalata is right, Jarvis – a novelist *manqué*, perhaps – should be the rightful recipient of praise from a fellow-practitioner. But this could be a case of wishful thinking on the part of Carlos Fuentes. Smollett the novelist comes through with particular immediacy in his Preface to the translation, which he concludes with a portrait of Cervantes:

> His visage was sharp and acquiline, his hair of chestnut colour, his forehead smooth and high, his nose hookish or hawkish, his eye brisk and cheerful, his mouth little, his beard originally of a golden hue, his upper lip furnished with large mustachios, his complexion fair, his stature of the middle size: and he tells us, moreover, that he was thick in the ankles, and not very light of foot.

Despite his use of a team of assistants and amanuenses, such as would later be employed on such mind-numbing chores as *The Universal History*, *The Compendium of Authentic and Entertaining Voyages* and

The Present State of All Nations, seven years were to pass before Smollett's translation was published by a conger of booksellers that included Andrew Millar, T. & T. Longman, J. & J. Rivington and T. Osborne; as a bonus, the book included twenty-eight engravings based on work by Francis Hayman, a friend of Hogarth and one of the founders of the Royal Academy, who later provided illustrations for a reprint of *Roderick Random* and for the first two volumes of the *Complete History of England*. 'I am sorry my friend Smollett loses his time in translations,' Lady Mary Wortley Montagu wrote to her daughter, adding that 'Though I am a mere piddler in the Spanish language, I had rather take pains to understand him in the original, than sleep over a stupid translation.' There is, incidentally, no evidence that Lady Mary ever met her literary 'friend'; that Smollett may have felt vulnerable to charges of being a 'mere piddler' in Spanish is suggested by reference to a member of the College of Authors who has translated the work of a well-known author, only to have the publishers of rival translations suggest that 'he did not understand one word of the language he pretended to translate'.

Smollett steered clear of other translations from the Spanish, but was to prove an assiduous translator from the French in the years ahead, polishing off Voltaire's 'Micromegas' and a tedious-sounding collection of essays published in French under the title *Journal Oeconomique* and described as 'a paultry bookseller's job, in which my name ought not to be mentioned'. His first effort from the French was, appropriately, LeSage's *Gil Blas*, and he worked from the 1747 French edition, published shortly after its author's death. The translation was, according to Smollett, 'a bookseller's job, done in a hurry'; and whereas he dawdled over *Don Quixote*, *Gil Blas* appeared in the same year as *Roderick Random*, with Strahan printing a generous 3,000 copies for Osborne the bookseller. Smollett then moved on to LeSage's *Le Diable boiteux*, published two years later as *The Devil upon Crutches*. How well he read the language was a matter of debate: according to John Moore, who met him in Paris in 1750, 'Dr Smollett had imbibed some of the common English prejudices against the French, of which he never got entirely free. He never attained the power of speaking their language with facility, which prevented him from mixing in their society, and deciding, from his own observation, on their national character.' Such limitations would not prevent him from expatiating on the character of the French in *Peregrine Pickle* and, at far greater length, in his *Travels through France and Italy*.

The earnings from *Roderick Random* and *Gil Blas* enabled the Smolletts to move to Chelsea. The Swedish traveller Peter Kalm visited Chelsea in 1748, two years before their arrival: 'The place resembles a town, has a church, beautiful streets, well-built and handsome houses, all of brick, three or four storeys high,' he noted. It was still, just, a free-standing village, soon to be swallowed up as London proper inched inexorably west, but remote enough to be served by stage-coach. 'I was last night robbed of my watch and money in the stage coach between this and London, and am just going to town to enquire about the robber,' Smollett told Dr Macaulay in December 1754, and a day or two later the crime was reported in the *Public Advertiser* ('On Wednesday eve, between five and six, the passengers in the Chelsea stage were robbed near the water-works going to Chelsea, by two footpads in sailors' habits'). Lawrence Street, where the Smolletts lived, runs down to the river; to the west is Chelsea Old Church, where Smollett's daughter and mother-in-law are buried; to the east are the Physic Garden, established in the previous century, Wren's Chelsea Hospital, and, just beyond that, the site of Ranelagh Gardens, opened in 1742, and rivalled only by Vauxhall, on the south bank of the Thames, as a pleasure garden where men and women of all classes met to eat, drink, flirt, listen to Handel's music and make assignations behind the hedgerows and statuary. The Embankment would not be built for at least another hundred years, and the Thames, still tidal at Chelsea, rose and fell against muddy banks; boats were tied up against the occasional wooden jetty, and on the opposite side of the river, slightly upstream, stood the village of Battersea. Monmouth House was a brick-built, three-storeyed house, shaped like an 'E' minus the central prong, and containing four self-contained houses, one of which was occupied by the Smolletts. It was, according to *Humphry Clinker*, 'a plain, yet decent habitation, which opened backwards into a very pleasant garden, kept in excellent order' and contained, in a far corner, 'a small remote filbert walk' where Smollett used to pace up and down, deep in conversation with one of his literary acquaintances or helpers. Next door to Monmouth House was the Chelsea China Manufactory, famed for its beautiful porcelain. It was said that Dr Johnson visited the works twice a week to try his hand at baking pieces of his own design: it seems unlikely that he made much progress as a potter, but although he and Smollett were never, as Smollett once admitted, 'cater-cousins', or close friends, it may be that Johnson called in at Monmouth House from time to time to stroll beneath the filbert trees.

At some point, Smollett's mother-in-law, Mrs Leaver, came over from Jamaica and took up residence with her daughter and her husband; and this, together with a growing daughter, may have encouraged the move to Chelsea and a larger house. No doubt Smollett found the old lady's permanent presence tiresome and oppressive, but he was maddeningly discreet about his family and domestic life and seldom let his feelings show. Despite his diligence and his literary success, shortage of funds would be a constant worry for years to come; thanks to her properties in Jamaica, Mrs Leaver was fairly well-off, and Smollett combined the urge to benefit from her riches with a reluctance to be dependent on the old lady, or throw her into a tizz. 'You will easily believe that the expense of housekeeping . . . must have thrown me considerably back in a course of four or five years during which I touched not one farthing from Mrs Leaver,' he once told Richard Oswald, a Scottish merchant based in London and responsible for the management of Mrs Leaver's property. Mrs Leaver, he went on, had recently given him £200 out of a £300 remittance recently received from Jamaica, 'a sum which was barely sufficient to quiet the most clamorous of my creditors'; he was now awaiting the next remittance – it was, as ever, months late in arriving – and was loath to ask his mother-in-law for a bridging loan:

> She is naturally obstinate, narrow-minded, and totally ignorant of life, and after having so lately given me two hundred pounds which she looks upon as an infinite sum, she would be alarmed and frightened almost out of her senses at a fresh demand, and conclude that I am either a spendthrift or in debt, for which reason, she might, in the disposal of her effects, take measures

to cut off all my expectations; her fear and suspicions would be communicated to her daughter; a breach between the mother and me would probably ensue, and the peace of my family be utterly destroyed . . .

If only he were 'connected with a sensible woman, who would cordially interest herself in my affairs and behave with that openness and candour which I deserve at her hands', how much easier life would have been – but Mrs Leaver remained 'reserved, distrustful, and as timorously cautious, as if she believed herself environed with thieves and robbers'. Smollett's later letters refer to the old lady's enjoying a sudden and unexpected surge of high spirits, and enduring a ferocious attack of diarrhoea ('our old gentlewoman had such a scouring in my absence that my wife thought she could not have lived till my return'). She died in 1762, unlamented, one assumes, by her son-in-law. Anne Smollett remains an even more shadowy figure, barely mentioned in her husband's letters; and although there is no reason to doubt his devotion to Elizabeth – quite the opposite, in fact – we know nothing about her except that she was said to have written poetry, had whooping cough in the winter of 1759, and went to a school in Chelsea run by a Mrs Aylesworth and Madame Beete, and also attended, at Smollett's recommendation, by John Wilkes's adored daughter, Polly. A touching glimpse of family life is provided in a fragment of a letter – 'Many a time do I stop my task and betake me to a game of romps with Betty, while my wife looks on smiling and longing in her heart to join in the sport; then back to the cursed round of duty' – but since it is excluded from Professor Knapp's exhaustive and authoritative edition of the letters, it may well amount to little more than wishful thinking.

As it was until recent years, Chelsea was favoured by literary and artistic types, including Richard Steele, Lord Bolingbroke, Fielding and Benjamin Franklin, and even if Smollett's home life was unexciting and, at times, embattled, there was convivial company to hand. He may have belonged to a cheerful-sounding outfit called the Chelsea Bowling Green Society, and as a Freemason and a keen member of 'our brotherhood at the Swan', he attended meetings regularly at the White Swan pub. Not far from Lawrence Street, on

Cheyne Walk, stood the famous coffee-house, Don Saltero's, patronised in their day by Swift and Addison and famed for its curiosities presented by, among others, William Hunter and Hans Sloane, whose alternative collection formed the nucleus of what became the British Museum. Among the oddities on display at Don Saltero's were petrified rain, the feet of a Muscovy cat, an elf's arrow (but not his bow), assorted monsters, a pincushion formerly owned by Mary Queen of Scots, two arrows once fired by Robin Hood, and Queen Elizabeth's chamberlain's hat. Those encountered there included John Lewis, a bookbinder, said by some to be the original of Strap in *Roderick Random* (other contenders included two hairdressers and Robert Foulis, the eminent Glasgow printer), assorted sea-dogs, and an eminent botanist called Philip Miller, who worked at the Physic Garden and was later employed by Smollett to review botanical books.

Smollett's most extended account of life – or an aspect of life – at Monmouth House was written years after he had left Chelsea. In *Humphry Clinker*, Matthew Bramble's nephew, Jery Melford, meets up with Dick Ivy, a hard-drinking hack who has recently emerged from a spell in the Fleet; his success with a pamphlet attacking the government has 'enabled him to appear in clean linen', even if his 'breeches are not yet in the most decent order'. Ivy introduces him to some of his fellow-denizens of Grub Street, and the idealistic Jery finds them a dull, dispiriting crew, who 'seemed afraid and jealous of one another, and sat in a state of mutual repulsion, like so many particles of vapour, each surrounded by its own electrified atmosphere'. 'A man may be entertaining and instructive upon paper, and exceedingly dull in common discourse,' the worldly-wise Bramble tells his nephew:

> I have observed, that those who shine most in private company, are but secondary stars in the constellation of genius – a small stock of ideas is more easily managed, and sooner displayed, than a great quantity crowded together. There is very seldom any thing extraordinary in the appearance and address of a good writer; whereas a dull author generally distinguishes himself by some oddity or extravagance.

To give Jery a further taste of London literary life, Dick 'carried me to dine with S——, whom you and I have long known by his writings. He lives in the skirts of the town, and every Sunday his house is opened to all unfortunate brothers of the quill, whom he treats with beef, pudding, and potatoes, port, punch and Calvert's entire butt beer.' Jery joins the assorted hacks at Smollett's dining-room table, 'and I question if the whole kingdom could produce such an assembly of originals'. Apart from their host, all conform to his uncle's cynical suggestion that self-conscious eccentricity coincides with minimal talent. 'What struck me were oddities originally produced by affectation, and afterwards confirmed by habit,' Jery notes. One wears spectacles, though his vision has only ever been impaired by black eyes gained while fighting with an actor; another affects the use of crutches, but proves fleet of foot when chased by a bailiff; another, desperate to be thought odd to the verge of lunacy, affects absent-mindedness and a stutter, 'by means of which he frequently extorted the laugh of the company, without the least expense of genius'; a fourth, much given to winking, insists on wearing yellow gloves throughout the meal. 'The yellow-gloved philosopher', it seems, had initially taken against their host on the grounds that 'he looked and talked, and ate and drank like any other man', and 'talked contemptuously of his understanding' as a result, but had been reconciled to him after learning how a Grub Street poet had promised to publish a panegyric of Smollett if he would allow him to attend his lunches, and a satire if he continued to bar him from Monmouth House: Smollett said he would regard it as an insult to be praised by such a man, and when the poet insisted on publishing the panegyric, he picked up his 'cudgel' and gave him a 'sound drubbing'. Most of the hacks were 'understrappers or journeymen to more creditable authors, for whom they translated, collated and compiled, in the business of book-making; and all of them had, at different times, laboured in the service of our landlord, though they had now set up for themselves in various departments of literature'.

After lunch they move into the garden, where their host takes each of his guests aside for a short audience under the filbert trees. Some then make their way home; but others turn up as the afternoon wears on, including an opulent bookseller, mounted on a gelding and sporting a brand-new pair of expensive-looking boots. The contrast between the very obvious affluence of the bookseller and the penniless hacks proves too much for Tim Cropdale, 'the most facetious member of the whole society' and a man who has 'made shift to live for many years by writing novels at the rate of five pounds a volume': he has had little success recently, since 'that branch of the business is now engrossed by female authors, who publish merely for the propagation of virtue, with so much ease and spirit, and delicacy, and knowledge of the human heart, that the reader is not only enchanted by their genius, but reformed by their morality'. Tim persuades the bookseller to lend him his boots and race him round the garden in his stockinged feet; the bookseller unwisely agrees, and after a couple of circuits Tim nips through the back garden gate and vanishes up the lane with the precious boots. The bookseller swears revenge and threatens to have 'the dog indicted at the Old Bailey' and transported to the colonies, but Smollett lends him a pair of shoes, orders his servant to rub him down like a fractious horse, and consoles him with a glass of rum punch.

After coffee, Jery takes his leave, 'extremely well pleased with the entertainment of the day', but puzzled why their host, 'a man of character in the literary world', should want to waste his time on 'a parcel of authorlings, who, in all probability, would never be able to acquire any degree of reputation by their labours'. As they make their way back to London, Dick tells him that Smollett knows perfectly well that his guests are 'bad men, as well as bad writers'; each of them is, in some way, indebted to their host, and Smollett is far too realistic to imagine that they feel gratitude towards him, or are motivated by anything other than self-interest. One of those present he had bailed out of a sponging-house, the halfway house to a debtors' prison; two others, equally penurious, he had taken into his house to be fed and clothed. 'Those who are in distress he supplies with money when he has it, and with his credit when he is out of cash,' Dick tells Jery:

When they want business, he either finds employment for them in his own service, or recommends them to booksellers to execute some project he has formed for their subsistence. They are always welcome to his table (which, though plain, is plentiful) and to his good offices as far as they will go, and when they see occasion, they make use of his name with the most petulant familiarity; nay, they do not even scruple to arrogate to themselves the merit of some of his performances, and have been known to sell their own lucubrations as the produce of his brain . . .

Jery assumes that Smollett's generosity is reciprocated by a readiness on the part of the hacks to flatter him in private and defend him in public, but nothing could be further from the truth. 'I had often seen this writer virulently abused in papers, poems and pamphlets, and not a pen was drawn in his defence,' Jery recalls – yet he is told that 'those very guests whom you saw at his table today, were the authors of great part of that abuse; and he himself is well aware of their particular favours, for they are all eager to detect and betray one another'. The malice of the hacks is partly inspired by old-fashioned envy, and Smollett's willingness to put up with 'a set of rascals equally ungrateful and insignificant' can, Dick suggests, be attributed to various causes: he can't bear to say 'no', even to the most worthless among them; he secretly rather enjoys holding court to so many 'literary dependants'; he likes hearing them savage and betray each other; he learns all the gossip of Grub Street, for what it is worth; and he may be, quite simply, an 'incorrigible fool'. 'By all accounts,' Jery concludes, 'S—— is not without weakness and caprice; but he is certainly good-humoured and civilised; nor do I find that there is anything overbearing, cruel, or implacable in his disposition.' John Moore remembered his friend as being 'of a disposition so humane and generous, that he was ever ready to serve the unfortunate, and on some occasions to assist them beyond what his circumstances could justify. Though few could penetrate with more acuteness into character, yet none was more apt to overlook misconduct when attended with misfortune.' Hospitable without being ostentatious, he offered all-comers 'a plain but plentiful table'.

It is hardly surprising, in the circumstances, that Smollett was permanently worried about money, and the shortage of funds, and the late arrival of remittances from Mr Bontein, his wife's agent in Jamaica, form a constant, niggling refrain in his letters. 'I have been hedging and lurching these six weeks in expectation of that cursed ship from Jamaica, which has at last arrived without letter or remittance,' he told William Hunter in the early Chelsea years. To have to ask the high-earning Hunter for a loan was 'like fire and brimstone', but it had to be done:

> For heaven's sake, do not look upon me as one of those sneaking rascals who can stoop to subsist upon what they can borrow without shame, remorse, or purpose of repayment. I am an unfortunate dog whose pride providence thinks proper to punish with all the torture of incessant mortification; and I resent my lot accordingly . . .

Nor had matters improved by the winter of 1754. Once again, he told Macaulay, 'that cursed ship' from the West Indies had failed to come through, and 'never was I so much harassed with duns as now.' A month later, and he has had no answer to a begging letter to his brother-in-law, Alexander Telfer; he has promised to pay his tradesmen's bills by Christmas ('my credit absolutely depends upon my punctuality'), but not 'one farthing' has come through from Jamaica. Macaulay lent him £50 against the £1,000 owing from Bontein, and later made him a further loan against an advance promised by Rivington's for *The Complete History of England*. Hunter, too, was to prove a good friend, bailing him out with the odd loan to keep the family afloat. Quite apart from lending money, Hunter must have been a cheering presence. Carlyle remembered him at gatherings at the British Coffee House: he was 'gay and lively to the last degree, and often came in to us at nine o'clock. He had had no dinner, but supped on a couple of eggs, and drank his glass of claret.' After one such convivial evening, he proposed a toast: 'May no English nobleman venture out of the world without a Scottish physician, as I am sure there are none who venture in.'

Smollett's help was not just extended to undeserving literary hacks. Not only did he put in a word with Wilkes on behalf of Robert Love, the son of his aggrieved schoolmaster, but his letters are punctuated with intercessions of a similar kind – including a request to Hunter that he should try to help the son of an apothecary, 'a miserable object, afflicted with scorbutic, leprous or scrophulous ulcers'. His combination of generosity and irascibility turned sour in the spring of 1752, when he found himself hauled before the King's Bench Court and charged with assault and trespass. A former schoolmaster, Peter Gordon was an impecunious and malevolent hack of the kind Smollett invited to Sunday lunch in Chelsea. Smollett had not only rescued him from jail, clothed and fed him, and found him work, but had lent him some £200. Gordon, by now living in a 'paltry alehouse', asked for a further £30, claiming that a refusal on Smollett's part would be of 'the utmost ill consequence' and make it impossible for him to do any work. Smollett's own funds were too reduced for him to come up with ready money, but he unwisely agreed to endorse two promissory notes of £15 each. When Gordon then demanded a further £30, his request accompanied by 'scurrilous and indecent letters and messages', his benefactor's patience finally snapped. According to Gordon's statement to the court, Smollett 'with force and arms, that is to say with swords staves stones knives clubs fists sticks and whips made an assault upon him the said Peter . . . and so ill-treated him his life was greatly despaired of'. Nor was Gordon the only victim of this vicious, multi-weaponed assault: like some frenzied, many-armed Hindu deity, Smollett also assaulted Gordon's friend and landlord, Edward Groom, whom he 'then and there beat wounded and ill-treated . . . so that his life was despaired of'. Though cleared of intended homicide, Smollett was ordered to pay Gordon and Groom £2 10s. each in damages and costs after the jury had been swayed by the lachrymose testimony of Gordon's wife and Groom the publican. According to tradition, his neighbours in Chelsea celebrated his acquittal with a 'general illumination', but Smollett was left bruised by the whole wretched business: he resented having to pay damages to the likes of Gordon and Groom, and the sneering and contemptuous tone of the plaintiffs' counsel aggravated his loathing for the law and its practitioners.

Quite how Gordon and Groom were able to retain Alexander Hume Campbell, MP for Berwickshire, twin brother to the Earl of

Marchmont and a barrister notorious for coarse, abusive language in court, remains a mystery; but after the trial was over, Smollett wrote the lawyer a long and indignant letter, wretchedly revealing of his extreme sensitivity, both as an author and as a gentleman. 'I have waited several days in hope of receiving from you an acknowledgement touching those harsh, unjustifiable (and let me add) unmannerly expressions which you annexed to my name in the Court of King's Bench,' he begins, before demanding 'such satisfaction as a gentleman injured as I am has a right to claim'. Campbell had deliberately set out to 'blacken and asperse' Smollett's character, 'without any regard to veracity or decorum', to 'represent me as a person devoid of all humanity and remorse', as a 'barbarous ruffian' who had behaved in a 'cowardly manner' with intent to murder. Campbell must have known he was innocent, for – and here he strikes a note of authorial pomposity – 'surely I do not overrate my own importance in affirming that I am not so obscure in life as to have escaped the notice of Mr Hume Campbell?' Campbell had undertaken 'the cause of a wretch, whose ingratitude, villainy and rancour are, I believe, without example in his kingdom . . . and endeavoured, with all the virulence of defamation, to destroy the character, and even the life, of an injured person, who, as well as yourself, is a gentleman by birth, education and profession'.

To make matters worse, Campbell had tried to make Smollett the subject of ridicule. Not only did he have the effrontery, while cross-examining a tradesman, to ask him 'if he knew me to be an author', but he did so 'with a view to put me out of countenance, and to raise the laugh of the spectators at my expense'. 'I have assurance enough to stand the mention of my works without blushing, especially when I despise the taste, and scorn the principles, of him who would turn them to my disgrace,' he continues; after which, seemingly oblivious of a barrister's duties, and the tricks of the trade, he reprimands Campbell for browbeating Smollett's witness 'with such artifice, eagerness, and insult, as overwhelmed him with confusion'. It turns out, in Smollett's heightened imagination at least, that Campbell's *ad hominem* approach, the 'bitterness and rancour' with which he had undertaken the prosecution, has a literary basis: as an eminent member of the Bar, he had been outraged by a passage in

Count Fathom, Smollett's third novel, which describes how barristers exert themselves 'with equal industry, eloquence and erudition, in their efforts to perplex the truth, browbeat the evidence, puzzle the judge, and mislead the jury'; and, with the author of these offensive words squirming in the dock before him, he had relished a protracted revenge. Since the novel, though imminent, had not yet been published, it is not clear how Campbell, unless gifted with second sight or a key to the bookseller's warehouse, could have read the offending passage; but the insults endured seem to have brought Smollett to the brink of paranoia. 'For my own part, were I disposed to be merry, I should never desire a more pregnant subject of ridicule than your appearance and behaviour,' Smollett continues, becoming *ad hominem* in his turn: unless he receives 'adequate reparation', he will 'in four days put this letter in the press, and you shall hear in another manner – not from a ruffian and an assassin, but from an injured gentleman'. For all his bluster and bravado, Smollett's letter was never published, and he was almost certainly talked out of sending it by his philanthropic friend Daniel MacKercher, 'the melting Scot': which was just as well, since its combination of pomposity and persecution mania could only have prompted further flurries of ridicule from his enemies and detractors in Grub Street.

Away from the law courts, Smollett was advancing his career as a literary man. *Peregrine Pickle*, his second novel, was published in 1751, the year after the Smolletts moved to Chelsea. A vast, rambling, long-winded piece of work, punctuated, like the early Dickens, with digressions which have little to do with the story – Lady Vane's notorious memoir is over a hundred pages, an eighth of the total – it still has its admirers: Dickens included it among the favourite books of his childhood, and V.S. Pritchett thought the death of the garrulous Commodore Trunnion 'one of the great scenes of English literature, to be compared with that great death scene at the end of Dostoevsky's *The Possessed*'. Each to his taste: but although a novel as long as *Peregrine Pickle* is bound to have its redeeming moments – most of them occur fairly early on, when the over-sexed and unscrupulous Peregrine, just down from Oxford, is on a truncated Grand Tour of France and the Low Countries with his disapproving tutor, Mr Jolter – it is, for the most part, a ponderous, sluggish and seemingly interminable piece of work, with none of the pace or sparkle of its predecessor. Part of the problem lies in Peregrine himself. Like Roderick, he is proud, prickly about his standing as a gentleman, footloose, swift to take offence and avenge an insult, and accompanied by a good-natured and long-suffering Sancho Panza; like Roderick, he inhabits a coarse and brutal world, but whereas Roderick retains our affection and sympathy, Peregrine is too thuggish and too wilful to be borne.

The grandson of a London merchant who has made his pile and moved to the country, Peregrine is, in material terms, much better off than his predecessor. Although he will, as a result of his own profligacy and his exposure to a cynical and predatory world, be reduced to penury and a debtors' prison, he is brought up with money and expectations; nor does he have the disadvantage of being a Scot adrift in England. From an early age, young Perry is addicted to practical jokes of a kind that were the quintessence of hilarity to contemporary readers, but now seem as laboured and unfunny as the comic characters in a Shakespeare play. So unkind are young Perry's pranks that one wonders whether, these days, he might not be labelled a psychopath, or put on a course of soothing drugs. Though a fearful windbag who can't open his mouth without unleashing a torrent of naval imagery, Commodore Trunnion is the soul of goodness, and – given Perry's embattled relations with his immediate family – the nearest thing the wretched boy has to a father figure or kindly uncle: yet from an early age Peregrine likes nothing better than to trample on the Commodore's gouty toe, or hurl his baccy pouch into the fire, or tip the contents of his snuff box into his glass of punch-and-water and watch, delighted, as the old boy writhes with revulsion after the first sip. His best remembered prank, reflecting to the full Smollett's taste for the lavatorial, was to bore holes in Mrs Trunnion's chamber-pot, with the result that

The Commodore, who had just composed himself to rest, was instantly alarmed with a strange sensation in his right shoulder, on which something warm seemed to descend in various streams: he no sooner comprehended the nature of this shower, which in a twinkling bedewed him from head to foot, than he exclaimed 'Blood and oons! I'm afloat!' and starting up, asked with great bitterness if she had pissed through a watering can.

Mrs Trunnion is an unattractive figure, and Perry has not done with her yet. She enjoys a tipple, so he adds a laxative to her brandy. She takes a swig before setting out for church, but

> The service was not half performed, when Mrs Trunnion was suddenly taken ill; her face underwent violent flushings and vicissitudes of complexion; a cold clammy sweat bedewed her forehead, and her bowels were afflicted with such agonies, as compelled her to retire in the face of the congregation. She was brought home in torture, which was a little assuaged when the dose began to operate; but such was the excess of evacuation she sustained, that her spirits were quite exhausted, and she suffered a succession of fainting fits that reduced her to the brink of the grave.

The loathsome youth even adds salt or soot to the family soup, and drives needles into the heads of some guinea fowl; but most horrible of all is his treatment of Mr Keypstick the schoolmaster, 'an old illiterate German quack, who had formerly practiced corn-cutting among the quality, and sold cosmetic washes to the ladies, together with teeth-powders, hair-dying liquors, prolific elixirs, and tinctures to sweeten the breath'. The wretched pedant has a hunch-back and 'distorted limbs', and in order to 'improve his person' he 'wore shoes with heels three inches high, strutted like a peacock in walking, and erected his head with such muscular exertion, as rendered it impossible for him to extend his vision downwards below the preternatural prominence of his breast'. Peregrine scatters dried beans in his path, with the result that Keypstick skids up and lies 'in a very ludicrous attitude for the entertainment of the spectators . . .'

Most modern readers will find the whole episode painful and distasteful, and not remotely entertaining. The sadistic relish with which Smollett the novelist describes such acts of brutality and humiliation sits oddly with his kindness in person, and the loathing and revulsion with which he described the fate of the Highlanders after the Forty-Five, or the way in which Robert Damiens was tortured with red-hot pincers, boiling oil, melted lead and partial dismemberment for his attempted assassination of Louis XV, before dying 'a death shocking to the imagination, and shameful to humanity'.

After Winchester, where he leads a rebellion by the boys, and Oxford, Peregrine – as befits a young man preparing himself for the world – sets off for the Continent with Mr Jolter. The signing of the Treaty of Aix-la-Chapelle in 1748, bringing to a close the War of the Austrian Succession, had liberated an army of ardent English tourists into France. Travelling on the Continent was no longer the preserve of the very rich, but whereas wealthy young aristocrats on the Grand Tour would take in the South of France, Italy and possibly some of the German states as well, their poorer equivalents, like Peregrine, restricted themselves to northern France and the Low Countries. 'The English travel more than any other people of Europe,' wrote the abbé Le Blanc, whose *Letters on the English and French Nations* was translated into English in 1747. 'They look upon their isle as a sort of prison; and the first use they make of their love of liberty, is to get out of it.' Although Smollett visited Paris in the summer of 1750, he had probably completed the first volume of *Peregrine Pickle*, dealing with his hero's adventures on the Continent, before he made the trip, and drew instead on his earlier experiences. After their meeting in Paris, John Moore noted – with Smollett in mind, perhaps – that 'There are instances of Englishmen who, while on their travels, shock foreigners by an ostentatious preference of England to the rest of the world, and ridicule the manners, custom and opinion of every other nation.' Smollett might have preferred 'Briton' to 'Englishman', but in every other respect *Peregrine Pickle*, *Count Fathom* and, most famously of all, *Travels through France and Italy* tally precisely with his cousin's description of the xenophobe abroad.

After a chance encounter in Canterbury with Mr Morgan from *Roderick Random*, Peregrine and Mr Jolter make their way to Dover for the crossing to Calais. 'Calais will always be the port for our Gentry, who had rather go thirty leagues more post by land than cross twenty leagues of water instead of seven,' a newspaper reported in 1769. The relative shortness of the crossing made up for the hazards posed by contrary winds and tides, and a harbour so shallow at the French end that, after tossing interminably on the waves, travellers often ended the journey by being rowed ashore, getting drenched in the process and then wading ashore on the beach. All depended on the weather: although Lady Mary Wortley Montagu once made the crossing in under three hours, Arthur Young spent fourteen hours waiting to land, Lord Fife noted that 'Here have I been three days, tired to death, detained with contrary winds, now getting on board at eleven o'clock at night, but likely to be drove back again', and Charles Thompson set out from Dover for Calais only to be blown down-Channel by so strong a wind that they eventually disembarked at Dieppe. Unaware of the hazards that await him, Mr Jolter, safely aboard ship, launches into a paean for France and the French of the kind that Smollett – always allergic to Francophile Englishmen who adopted French clothes and manners as soon as they reached French soil – loved to ridicule; after 'snuffing up the French air with symptoms of infinite satisfaction' and addressing the French sailors as '*mes enfants*', Jolter is mercilessly jostled and defrauded by a rabble of porters, all of them set on relieving him of his money.

Most English travellers passing through Calais recovered from the voyage at Dessein's. It was the largest hotel in Europe, with 130 beds, shops and a theatre; M. Dessein was happy to exchange guineas for *louis d'or*, and unless the traveller was rich enough to bring his own means of transport, or poor or brave enough to risk the *diligence* or public coach, he could arrange for the hire of a post-chaise, the horses for which would, as in England, be exchanged at regular intervals along the road to Paris. As they trundle towards Paris in their post-chaise, taking in Boulogne and Amiens *en route*, Mr Jolter insists that his pupil note the care with which every inch of the country-side is cultivated, and how symptomatic this is of the 'wealth and affluence of the nation in general'. Peregrine – combining, unusually, his habitual arrogance with genuine indignation on behalf of the underdog – is 'amazed as well as disgusted' by Jolter's wilful blindness, for it seems self-evident that what he ascribed to industry, was the effect of mere wretchedness; the miserable peasants being obliged to plough up every inch of ground to satisfy their oppressive landlords, while they themselves and their cattle looked like so many images of famine; that their extreme poverty was evident from the face of the country, on which there was not one enclosure to be seen, or any other object, except scanty crops of barley and oats, which could never reward the husbandman; that their habitations were no better than paultry huts; that in twenty miles of extent, not one gentleman's house appeared; that nothing was more abject and forlorn than the attire of the country people; and, lastly, that the equipage of their travelling chaise was infinitely inferior to that of a dung-cart in England; and that the postilion, who then drove their carriage, had neither stockings to his legs, nor a shirt to his back.

As always, when writing about foreign parts, Smollett combines the blustering and boastfulness of John Bull with soft-heartedness and genuine outrage. He both reflected and reinforced the notion that, compared to the robust, beef-eating, freedom-loving English, the French were a scrawny, downtrodden, priest-ridden crew who survived, somehow, on a diet of frogs and watery soup, but he also anticipated – and still more so in the *Travels* – the political convulsions that would engulf France at the end of the century. As is so often the case when the British write about the French, the note of defiance is tinged with vague feelings of inadequacy and unease, the sense that, as Laurence Sterne famously put it in the opening sentence of *A Sentimental Journey*, 'They order, said I, this matter better in France.' As the painter Pallet observes in Peregrine Pickle, 'Paris is very rich in the Arts. London is a Goth, and Westminster a Vandal, compared to Paris.'

Far and away the most enjoyable sections of Peregrine's European adventures – indeed, of the whole book – are those in which he pursues various women, including a nun and the smouldering Mrs Hornbeck, a former fishwife gone up in the world whose husband, a dry old stick, Peregrine is determined to cuckold. By now Peregrine has met and fallen in love with the divine and unimpeachable Emilia, with whom he will, after numerous amorous adventures, eventually spend the rest of his life in a state of uxorious and undeserved bliss. In the meantime he feels duty bound to sow as many wild oats as possible, and to treat Emilia with an unpleasant combination of sentimentality and brutality. Emilia, like Narcissa in *Roderick Random*, and all Dickens's heroines, is a saccharine embodiment of goodness; Mrs Hornbeck, on the other hand, radiates sexual allure, and Peregrine's attempts on her honour – and that of the nun, *et al.* – are agreeably reminiscent of an old-fashioned French farce or Goldsmith's *She Stoops to Conquer*, involving much creeping down unlit hotel corridors, mistaken bedrooms and the like. It is coarse, boisterous stuff, and no doubt the young Dickens relished every word: the famous scene in which Mr Pickwick, adrift at night in a hotel in Ipswich, mistakenly lets himself into the bedroom of the outraged lady in the yellow curling-papers is redolent of Peregrine's amorous misdeeds, rendered chaste and whimsical for early Victorian readers. Mrs Hornbeck, a lady of little learning, is given to writing illiterate and misspelt letters ('Pray for the loaf of Geesus keep this from the nolegs of my hussban, ells he will make me leed a hell upon urth'): a vein of humour, replete with indecent puns, which Smollett tapped at greater length in *Humphry Clinker*, in the letters of Tabitha Bramble and her maid, Winifred Jenkins, and which has been hailed by some academics as a precursor of James Joyce.

Altogether less palatable to the modern reader are the wearisome and interminable pages devoted to Peregrine's Parisian encounters with the buffoonish English painter Pallet, and a poet loosely based on the poet-physician Mark Akenside. Akenside may have irritated Smollett with his views on the Scots; his fictional equivalent is obsessed with the ancient world and the strict application of classical rules to every aspect of art and behaviour, culminating in a bizarre and tedious Feast of the Ancients, reminiscent of a facetious *Satyricon*, at which Pallet, the poet and a homosexual couple gorge themselves on Roman delicacies, and live to regret it. It has often been suggested that the verbose, long-winded and bumbling Pallet may have been loosely modelled on the stumpy, blunt-featured figure of Hogarth, who – after the publication in 1749 of his engraved self-portrait featuring his pug Trump and his painter's palette – used a palette as his trademark; but it is unlikely that Smollett, or Hogarth, would have welcomed too close an identification between the real and the fictional painters. Like Fielding, Smollett was a huge admirer of Hogarth, referring frequently to him in his novels as 'inimitable' and 'incomparable', and wishing at times that he had the pen of a Hogarth with which to describe some particularly lurid or convivial scene: he shared Hogarth's taste for – and may well have been influenced by – the more boisterous type of seventeenth-century Dutch interior, and the critic Jerry Beasley has suggested that some of the set pieces in the novels could be seen as the fictional equivalents of Hogarth's narrative paintings, such as *The Rake's Progress* and *Marriage à la Mode*. As editor of the *Critical Review*, Smollett was to prove an ardent and well-informed champion of British art and artists, and in *The Present State of All Nations* he would describe Hogarth as 'an inimitable original with respect to invention, humour, and expression'. He shared and approved Hogarth's tendency to ridicule the French, and was aware that the painter, visiting France after the Peace of Aix-la-Chapelle, had been arrested as a spy while making his sketches for the painting of 'Calais Gate' (itself a pictorial equivalent of the French scenes in *Peregrine Pickle*, or *Travels in France and Italy*, peopled as it is by a corpulent, well-fed friar and a skeletal Frenchman staggering under a gleaming haunch of English beef). However, much as he admired Hogarth's satirical work, he was less impressed by his more conventional historical and mythological paintings, and his Pallet-like attempts to set himself up as an arbiter of taste. There is no firm evidence that the two men ever met, or that Hogarth was aware of, or took offence at, his possible portrayal in *Peregrine Pickle*. Peregrine's practical jokes at Pallet's expense are as unkind and unfunny as ever – one of them involves persuading the stocky little painter to come to a Parisian ball dressed as a woman, filling him up with champagne, and subjecting him to terrible humiliations in his search for a lavatory – while the references to, and jokes about, Akenside's obsession with the classical world have the musty, impenetrable quality of an ancient, long-forgotten scholastic debate.

Back in England, Peregrine, accompanied by his sidekick Pipes – a retired sea-dog, formerly under the command of Commodore

Trunnion – embarks on the peripatetic life of a rake-about-town. He visits Bath, where he outwits some card-sharpers and takes a dim view of the resident medics, noting how 'among the secret agents of scandal, none were so busy as the physicians, a class of animals who live in this place, like so many ravens hovering about a carcase, and even ply for employment, like scullers at Hungerford stairs'. Driven wild by 'an inflammation of desire', he tries to ravish the divine Emilia after dosing her with a soporific, yet she loves him still; he plunges into a life of dissipation after inheriting £30,000 from the Commodore, and, as a devotee of luxury and conspicuous consumption, takes up gambling, buys horses and haunts racecourses; he lends a third of his fortune to a false friend and worthless patron, who persuades him to stand for Parliament and spend a further fortune on bribing and buttering up the electorate, only to be told at the last minute that he must withdraw since the result has been fixed on the side. Utterly disillusioned, Perry 'cursed the whole chain of his court connexion, inveighed against the rascally scheme of politics, to which he was sacrificed'. Reduced to penury, he tries his luck as a hack author: 'this sudden change from his former way of life agreed so ill with his disposition that, for the first time, he was troubled with flatulencies and indigestion', and Smollett too would grumble a good deal about the unhealthy side-effects of the sedentary authorial life. Perry is incarcerated in the Fleet, inherits an even larger fortune when his father dies, and, 'almost fainting with delight', is reconciled to the loyal and long-suffering Emilia. Smollett would have us believe that his intolerable hero has been transmogrified and immeasurably improved by his experiences, and tells us that 'he bore his prosperity with surprising temperance'.

Peregrine Pickle must be at least a third of a million words long: readers who find the slog almost unendurable may be relieved to learn that, halfway through their ordeal, over a hundred pages are given over to what was, in Smollett's lifetime, the novel's most famous, or notorious, ingredient – the true-life amorous adventures of Lady Vane, published in their entirety as 'The Memoirs of a Lady of Quality'. Frances Anne Hawes, the daughter of a director of the South Sea Company, was a few years older than Smollett. Beautiful and louche, she began to attract admirers when, aged thirteen, she first visited Bath. The most ardent and persistent of these was Lord William Hamilton, second son of the Duke of Hamilton, with whom she eventually eloped. Lord William 'conducted me to an house on Blackheath, where we were very civilly received by a laughter-loving dame, who seemed to mistake me for one of her own sisterhood'. Such misunderstandings were soon sorted out and, reconciled to her family, Frances enjoyed two happy years of marriage, moving in high society, being received at court and living on the family estate in Scotland. Devastated by Lord William's early death, she soon found herself under siege from fresh admirers including William Holles, Viscount Vane, who was immensely rich and a cousin of the Duke of Newcastle.

Vane, or so we are told, turned up in a carriage stuffed with hay, and 'when he was lifted out of the chariot, he exhibited a very ludicrous figure to the view: he was a thin, meagre, shivering creature, of a low stature, with little black eyes, a long nose, sallow complexion, and pitted with the small-pox', clad in – among other items of clothing – 'a pair of huge jack-boots'. This unappealing figure then proceeded to press his suit. Lady Vane's friends reminded her of the independence his wealth could buy; he insisted that he did not expect her to love him, and that friendship would suffice. On their wedding night he 'sat moping in a corner, like a criminal on execution day', while his radiant bride 'began to sweat with anguish, at the thought of being subjected to his pleasure', trembled 'as if I had been exposed to the embraces of a rattlesnake', and somehow endured his feeble pawings. Lord Vane's impotence was the subject of widespread gossip, and he was bruised by his wife's reference to it in her 'Memoirs'. According to the *Gentleman's Magazine*, after reading them 'he shut the book, but said not a word, till she asked him what he thought of it. He replied, "I hope they will create no misunderstanding between me and your Ladyship."' For all Lady Vane's indiscretion, and her unconcealed loathing for her spouse, a witty decorum sometimes prevailed. Not long after publication, the story went round that Lord Vane had found his wife asleep, with a copy of *Peregrine Pickle* beside her, and replaced it with *The Practice of Piety*. When she woke up, he congratulated her on her apparent reformation. 'Nay, nay, let our reformation go hand in hand, I beseech you,' she urged him. 'When you, my lord, practice the Whole Duty of Man, then I'll read the Practice of Piety.'

Before long, the marriage was in a parlous state and Lady Vane was attracting the attentions of other men – including Sewallis Shirley, the son of the Earl of Ferrers. Lord Vane tried to remove her from temptation by taking her to Paris, but she fled to the Low Countries to meet her lover who, back in England, settled her in a house in Poland Street in Soho. Lord Vane continued to pester her with his attentions. As was the way with eighteenth-century bounders, Lord Shirley – by whom she now had a daughter – suddenly turned cold after three years of apparently blissful cohabitation, and she took up instead with the Earl of Berkeley: Lady Mary Wortley Montagu – who had herself toyed with the *nom de plume*, 'A Lady of Quality' – reported that 'though she does not pique herself upon fidelity to any one man (which is but a narrow way of thinking), she boasts that she has always been true to her nation, and notwithstanding foreign attacks, has always reserved her charms for the use of her countrymen'. Her harmonious existence in Lord Berkeley's country retreat was rudely interrupted by the arrival of Lord Vane, 'with his night cap in his pocket', but he was sent on his way. Reduced, at one stage, to advertising for the return of his wife, Lord Vane persistently refused to grant her a divorce; she amused guests at her house parties by ridiculing him as a 'dirty little fellow' and entertained a series of lovers, but because she was dependent on him for 'pin money', she returned to him from time to time, and even agreed to share his bed. She raced about the country trying to escape his clutches, locking herself in rooms and even, at one stage, having herself lowered from a window in a basket, but in the end he wore her down. 'After repeated trials, I have given up all hopes of making him happy, or of finding myself easy in my situation: and live with him at present to avoid a greater inconvenience,' she tells Peregrine Pickle, who, in a Smollettian interlacing of fact and fiction, has been introduced to the Lady of Quality by an impoverished widow and has been duly 'smitten with her beauty'. Notorious in her day, Lady Vane spent the last twenty years of her life in bed, reading the ruminations of Lord Chesterfield, and died in 1788.

The 'Memoirs' are faster moving, less verbose and more interesting than most of *Peregrine Pickle*, and attracted far more attention than the novel itself. First off the mark was Dr John Hill, of whom Dr Johnson observed that 'he was an ingenious man, but had no veracity', though 'if he would have been contented to tell the world no more than he knew, he might have been a very considerable man'. Like Smollett's other Grub Street adversary, John Shebbeare, Hill combined the practice of medicine, of a dubious kind, with hackery at its most cynical and vicious. A vicar's son, he styled himself 'Sir John' on the grounds that he was member of a Swedish order of knights; he had been apprenticed to an apothecary, studied botany (shortly before his death from gout, he was appointed Superintendent of Kew Gardens by Lord Bute), incurred the wrath of Henry Fielding and Christopher Smart, written the libretto for *Orpheus; an English Opera*, failed as a playwright, and feuded with Garrick, who wrote of him that 'such a villain never existed'. Not long before *Peregrine Pickle* was published in two volumes, 'Sir John' began to write, under the *nom de plume* of 'The Inspector', a daily gossip column for the *London Advertiser and Literary Gazette* in which, with the ponderous humour all too typical of Grub Street, he ridiculed Smollett as 'Smallhead'. He had learned about the 'Memoirs' in advance of their publication and, posing as a champion of the maligned Lord Vane, determined to profit from the flurry of interest by getting in first with a 'spoiler' or rival version of his own. His *History of a Woman of Quality: or, the Adventures of Lady Frail* appeared early in February 1751, two weeks before *Peregrine Pickle* was published.

Despite Hill's worst endeavours, Lady Vane proved the talking point of Smollett's novel; but although John Cleland praised it at length in the *Monthly Review*, most readers were disappointed.

> Peregrine Pickle I do not admire: it is by the author of Roderick Random, who is a lawyer: but the thing which makes the book sell, is the History of Lady V——, which is introduced (in the last volume, I think) much to her Ladyship's dishonour; but published by her *own* order, from her *own* Memoirs, given to the Author for that purpose; and by the approbation of her *own*

Lord. What was ever equal to this fact, and how can one account
for it?

wrote a confused Lady Luxborough to the poet William Shenstone,
adding, in a later letter, that 'the rest of the book is, I think, ill
wrote, and not interesting'. That waspish gossip Horace Walpole was
soon on the trail of her ladyship. 'Has that miracle of *tenderness and
sensibility* (as she calls it) Lady Vane given you any amusement?' he
wondered of the poet Gray. 'Peregrine, whom she uses as a vehicle,
is very poor indeed with a few exceptions.' To Sir Horace Mann, he
was more censorious: 'My Lady Vane has literally published the
Memoirs of her own life, only suppressing part of her lovers, no part
of the success of the others with her: a degree of profligacy not to
be accounted for; she does not want money, none of her stallions
will raise her credit; and the number, all she has to brag of, concealed!'
Samuel Richardson, who may have shared in the printing of the
novel, referred to the 'Memoirs' as 'that part of a bad book which
contains the very bad story of a wicked woman', and Lady Vane as
one of a 'set of wretches, wishing to perpetuate their infamy'; Mrs
Delaney read *Peregrine Pickle* to her husband by candlelight – an
arduous undertaking – but thought it '*wretched stuff*; only Lady Vane's
history is a curiosity. What a wretch!' The *Royal Magazine* thought
the 'Memoirs' 'most elegantly wrote, and greatly outshine the rest
of the work'; Lady Mary Wortley Montagu agreed that its author's
style was 'clear and concise', but thought the 'strokes of humour' so
much above the talents of Lady Vane that 'I can't help being of
opinion that the whole has been modelled by the author of the book
in which it is inserted.'

Quite who wrote the 'Memoirs', and the extent to which Smollett
wrote, rewrote or edited them, has been keenly debated by
Smollettian scholars; so too has the question of how he got to know
such a notorious figure, and how well he knew her. Lady Vane may
have been the 'humane lady of quality' referred to in the Preface to
The Regicide – and, more obliquely, in Melopoyn's story – as having
tried to help Smollett to find a producer for his doomed play; if, as
seems likely, the Dr S—— referred to, flatteringly, by Lady Vane as
being her doctor was neither Smollett himself nor Dr Shebbeare,

the medic turned Grub Street hack, but Dr William Smellie, then that, too, could have provided a connection, since Smollett was hard at work at the time editing the *Treatise on the Theory and Practice of Midwifery*. A still closer tie was provided by Daniel MacKercher, who may have been one of Lady Vane's ex-lovers. Smollett may have met MacKercher in his Downing Street days: a Scot and a soldier of fortune turned tobacco merchant and philanthropist, MacKercher had devoted much of his energies to championing the cause of James Annesley, a young man whom he believed to have been unjustly done out of his inheritance. Annesley had served as an ordinary seaman during the Cartagena campaign, and Smollett may have been alerted to his cause while on board ship; he described MacKercher in his novel as 'one of the most flagrant instances of neglected virtue which the world can produce' and, once again interrupting the flow of his novel for a factual digression, devotes some forty pages to an account of his friend's career, and the once-celebrated Annesley case.

How close Smollett was to Lady Vane, and how he felt about her, is a intriguing matter. In 1742, when she turned up in the Low Countries, a Colonel Russell wrote home to say that 'the greatest beauty we have here has followed us from England, which is Lady Vane', that she had followed the Brigade of Guards to Ghent and 'walks about each evening with an officer on each side of her'; but eight years later Lady Jane Coke spotted her in Tunbridge Wells, and noted how 'no woman of any rank took any notice of her. In my whole life I never saw anybody altered to the degree she is. I have not seen her since her days of innocence and beauty, and really I should not have known her if I had not been told her name, as there is not the least remains of what she was.' Smollett had to admit that, by the time Peregrine met her, 'the killing edge of her charms was a little blunted by the accidents of time and fortune', but that 'no man of taste and imagination, whose nerves were not quite chilled with the frost of age, could, even at that time, look upon her with impunity'. Indeed, his headstrong hero was so 'smitten by her beauty' that he 'could not suppress his emotions' and decided not to see her again from 'dread of being exposed to her infatuating charm'. Later in the novel, when his fortune is haemorrhaging in the hands of sharks and lawyers, his political hopes have foundered, and he is about to be sent to the Fleet, she visits him in his room and he is smitten again by 'sentiments of a more tender passion'. The Lady of Quality tactfully dissuades him, but not before he has presented her with some verses specially written for the occasion:

> While with fond rapture and amaze,
> On thy transcendent charms I gaze,
> My cautious soul essays in vain
> Her peace and freedom to maintain:
> Yet let that blooming form divine,
> Where grace and harmony combine,
> Those eyes, like genial orbs, that move,
> Dispensing gladness, joy and love,
> In all their pomp assail my view,
> Intent my bosom to subdue;
> My breast, by wary maxims steel'd,
> Not all those charms shall force to yield.
> But, when invok'd to beauty's aid,
> I see the enlighten'd soul display'd;
> That soul so sensibly sedate
> Amid the storms of forward fate!
> Thy genius active, strong and clear,
> Thy wit sublime, tho' not severe,
> The social ardour void of art,
> That glows within thy candid heart;
> My spirits, sense and strength decay,
> My resolution dies away,
> And ev'ry faculty opprest,
> Almighty love invades my breast!

Smollett is far too discreet to let us know to what extent, if any, he shared his hero's feelings about Lady Vane, but having decided to interlace fact with fiction he could hardly dodge the implications. Both the 'melting Scot' and the diabolical Dr Shebbeare have been promoted as possible ghost writers; assuming the raw material to have been Lady Vane's, it seems likely that Smollett himself had, at the very least, some hand in the writing.

Apart from Lady Vane and Commodore Trunnion, *Peregrine Pickle* is best remembered for its unflattering comments about Garrick, Quin, Fielding and Lord Lyttelton – all of which Smollett removed when he revised the novel in 1758, along with assorted indelicacies. His dislike of Fielding was based on jealousy and mild persecution mania, while his readiness to ridicule the hapless Lord Lyttelton reflected the impotence and resentment of an author whose dealings with aristocratic patrons had proved entirely counter-productive. There is no evidence that Smollett and Fielding ever met. William Hunter was a mutual friend, but by the time *Roderick Random* was published Fielding was already a sick man, and six years later he was dead. The notorious references to Fielding in *Peregrine Pickle* are hardly plentiful: apart from the sideways swipe at the 'sagacious moraliser', he has a dig in the pages given over to the College of Authors at 'Mr Spondy' (Fielding) and the patronage he enjoys from 'Gosling Scrag Esq' (Lyttelton). Should Spondy be 'inclined to marry his own cook-wench, his gracious patron may condescend to give the bride away; and finally settle him in his old age, as a trading Westminster justice'. Distraught at the death of his first wife, Fielding had married his housekeeper, Mary Daniel, who was six months pregnant, and this had provoked ignoble and snobbish mirth among his friends; Lord Lyttelton had exerted influence to have him appointed a Bow Street magistrate, but he was to prove the antithesis of the corrupt and venal 'trading' magistrates who had done so much to bring the law in London into disrepute. In return for these favours, Smollett suggested, Spondy had fed his patron with the 'soft pap of dedication'; and he ridicules Lyttelton's 'Monody' on the death of his wife by having a hack poet read, 'with the most rueful emphasis', an 'Ode in Memory of a Grandmother'.

All this smacks of sour grapes, and the fury of a frustrated man who feels himself excluded from a magic circle, real or imaginary. Fielding and Lyttelton had been at Eton together, and Fielding had dedicated *Tom Jones* to his old friend; not only had *Tom Jones* far outsold *Roderick Random*, but for some reason Smollett's first novel had been published in France with Fielding's name on the title page; and although Fielding had advertised *Roderick Random* in his *Jacobites' Journal*, in which he recommended new books, he never gave any sign of having read it, and may have disparaged it as the work of a Scot. Lyttelton was a friend of Akenside and a patron of Garrick; he had advanced the career of Quin, getting him a job teaching elocution to the Prince of Wales's children; he had not only advised Smollett to abandon *The Regicide* in favour of comedy, but had supported James Thomson, whose *Tancred and Sigismunda* had been preferred at Drury Lane to Smollett's ponderous tragedy.

That Smollett had genuine reservations about *Tom Jones* is apparent from a letter to Carlyle from the autumn of 1749. Carlyle had evidently been critical of the novel, and Smollett tells him that he shares his views, which 'are indeed obvious to every reader of discernment'. Fielding must have been aware of Smollett's opinion, and of his own brief appearance as Mr Spondy, for in the second issue of his *Covent Garden Journal*, published in January 1752, he suggested that Smollett was the epitome of Grub Street. Alexander Drawcansir, Fielding's cumbersome *alter ego*, commands the forces of literature against those of hackdom. After setting up his headquarters in Covent Garden, he sends out a contingent under the command of General A. Millar – Andrew Millar, the publisher – to 'take possession of the most eminent printing houses'. The forces of Grub Street quickly cave in, though

a small body, indeed, under the command of one Peeragrin Puckle [*sic*], made a slight show of resistance; but his hopes were soon found to be in vain; and, at the first report of the approach of a younger brother of General Thomas Jones, his whole body immediately disappeared, and totally overthrew some of their own friends, who were marching to their assistance, under the command of one Rodorick [*sic*] Random. This Rodorick, in a former skirmish with the people called critics, had owed some slight success more to the weakness of the critics, than to any merit of his own.

Fielding waged his 'Paper War' not just against Smollett, but against such ubiquitous and venomous embodiments of Grub Street as William Kenrick and 'Sir John' Hill, referred to as 'His Lowness the Prince of Billingsgate'. Although Fielding tired of the long-winded joke after the fourth issue, Smollett was set on revenge, and he took it in kind in a brief but laboured anonymous squib called *Habbakuk Hilding*, published a mere week after the second issue of the *Covent Garden Journal*. Fully entitled 'A Faithful Narrative of the Base and Inhuman Arts that were lately Practised upon the Brain of Habbakuk Hilding, Justice, Dealer and Chapman', allegedly the work of 'Drawcansir Alexander, Fencing-Master and Philomath', and written in a tone of bogus regret, it tells of how Hilding, suffering from 'some temporary paroxysm of delirium' and 'a disordered imagination, originally produced by some unlucky overthrows he had sustained in the warfare of an author', had agreed to head a march against his rivals led by Peregrine Pickle. After draining a large glass of Geneva, Hilding and his blind brother – Fielding's brother, Sir John, the well-known magistrate, was famously blind – lead their rabble down Catherine Street to the Strand, where Millar had his bookshop, 'bellowing defiance at all who should presume to oppose them'. Hilding, mounted on a donkey, is in the forefront, while his blind brother brings up the rear 'under the guidance of one who called himself Jones, and pretended to be a gentleman'. Also present are Jones's right-hand man, Partridge, 'a notorious felon and imposter', and – fresh from the pages of Fielding's recently published novel of that name – Amelia and 'a termagant oyster-wench called Matthews'. When Partridge spots Strap outside Somerset House, and the termagant Matthews catches sight of Miss Williams, the reformed prostitute from *Roderick Random*, both take to their heels, overcome by feelings of guilt. Hilding's troops break up in confusion, and he is left begging for forgiveness. 'Spare me, spare me, good Commodore,' he begs Trunnion. 'I own I have wronged you, as well as your nephew Peregrine, and his cousin Roderick – I have robbed them both, and then raised a false report against them . . .' Suffering one of his bouts of literary paranoia, Smollett had persuaded himself that Fielding had lifted Miss Matthews from Miss Williams, while Partridge had been directly cribbed from Strap: not only were both men barbers, but both had, after a period of separation, recognised and been reunited with their masters while shaving them. The similarities must, in fact, be purely coincidental, since Fielding started writing *Tom Jones* in 1746, and had completed the first eight books, including the shaving scene, well before publication of *Roderick Random*; but Smollett's conviction that he had been plagiarised showed how thin-skinned he had become as a result of his experiences with *The Regicide*, and how vicious was the in-fighting of the literary world. Later, when success had mellowed him a little, he made amends to his fellow-novelist. 'The genius of Cervantes was transfused into the novels of Fielding, who painted the characters, and ridiculed the follies of life with equal strength,' he declared in his *History of England*; and, writing of his old rival in 1762, he pronounced him 'an author who will be read and admired as long as any taste for wit and genuine humour remains in this nation'. In this he proved both prescient and generous, but – as he must have feared – his own novels were never to enjoy the same affection or popularity among critics or general readers.

Writing in the *London Advertiser*, 'Sir John' Hill suggested that the success of *Roderick Random* had 'encouraged this genius to give a greater loose to his ill nature . . . fond as we are of scandal and detraction, unless they are made palatable with wit and humour, they will never go down with us'. To reinforce his disdain for Smollett's second novel, he broke into verse as well:

> Keen, wholesome satire all endure,
> Invective argues want of skill;
> *This*, like the surgeon, cuts to cure,
> *This*, like the doctor, writes to kill.

Writing to his patron, Lord Hardwicke, the Revd Thomas Birch, who seems to have had an unexplained animus against Smollett, had earlier explained that 'the author of *Roderick Random* is printing another set of adventures which are of the low kind,' and that – like the French publishers of *Histoire et aventures de Sir William Pickle*, he seemed unable to get the title right – 'the name of the hero of the new piece is Jeremiah Pickle'. Later he reported, with unchristian glee, on the 'ill success' of the novel, which had 'ruined [Smollett's] reputation among the booksellers in general, against whom he breathes immortal revenge; one of them, Millar, who has particularly offended him by refusing to have any more concern with him'.

Smollett may have offended some members of the trade by his insistence on retaining the copyright, though in this he was no more radical than, for example, Dr Johnson, who made a point of allowing his publishers the right to publish one edition only of his works; but when, seven years later, he brought out the revised and sanitised edition of *Peregrine Pickle* he referred, in the accompanying Advertisement in the press, to the 'art and industry that were used to stifle him [*Pickle*] at birth, by certain booksellers and others, who were at uncommon pains to misrepresent the work, and calumniate the author'. As for the charge that he had 'defamed the character of particular persons to whom he lay under considerable obligations', he could only 'own with contrition that in one or two instances he gave way too much to the suggestions of personal resentment, and represented characters as they appeared to him at that time, through the exaggerating medium of prejudice' while defying 'the whole world to prove that he was guilty of one act of malice, ingratitude or dishonour'. He had, in the revised edition, 'endeavoured to make atonement for these extravagances' by 'retrenching the superfluities of the first [edition], reforming its manners, and correcting its expressions. Divers uninteresting episodes are wholly suppressed; some humorous scenes he has endeavoured to heighten; and he flatters himself, that he has expunged every adventure, phrase and insinuation, that could be constructed by the most delicate reader into a trespass upon the rules of decorum.' Authorial revisions to their published works need to be treated with caution; readers strong enough to embark on *Peregrine Pickle* should eschew the emasculated second edition in favour of the original, perforated chamber-pots, libels, lavatory jokes and all.

5

History and Hot Water

'He is equally qualified to write tragedy, comedy, farces, history, voyages, treatises of midwifery, on physic, and on all kinds of polite letters,' John Shebbeare once wrote of Smollett, whom he had just described as an 'empty author'. 'He undertakes to fit up books by the yard on all subjects,' he continued, many of them written 'for those who cannot write themselves, with great allowance in favour of his countrymen'. A Devon man who had started out as a surgeon-apothecary's apprentice and spent time searching for the philosopher's stone before devoting himself to Grub Street at its most ignoble, Shebbeare enjoyed insulting Scots and women, and was labelled 'the Growler' by Fanny Burney after he had ruined an evening's entertainment for her. Boswell said of him that 'so long as he could find reviews to write at six guineas per sheet and enemies to abuse at three shillings per pamphlet', he was perfectly content, and as such he was hardly in a position to take a high moral tone about his fellow-scribes; but as one of Smollett's inveterate enemies, he was all too well aware of the extraordinary range of subjects and types of writing his adversary was prepared to undertake in order to earn a living.

Like Edward Thomas or Ford Madox Ford in later years, Smollett funded the work by which he is remembered with book reviews, editorial labour, rewrite jobs, compilations and the like, mountainous in volume, exhausting in the execution and long ago lost in the mists of oblivion. He became, for better and for worse, the consummate literary man, able to turn his hand to whatever was asked of him, working all hours of the day, and possessed of little free time. He exploited the new world of publishing, and articulated the resentment felt by ill-paid and overworked writers for their new employers. Reviewing an ill-informed and badly edited history of South America, he savaged those penny-pinching booksellers who, when commissioning histories and gazetteers of the kind that consumed so much of his own time and energy,

cannot distinguish authors of merit, or if they could, have not sense and spirit to reward them according to their genius and capacity. Without considering the infinite pains and perseverance it must cost a writer to form and digest a proper plan of history; compile materials; compare different accounts; collate authorities; compose and polish the style, and complete the execution of the work; he furnishes him with a few books, bargains with him for two or three guineas a sheet; binds him with articles to finish so many volumes in so many months, in a crowded page and evanescent letter, that he may have stuff enough for his money; insists upon having copy within the first week after he begins to peruse his materials; orders the press to be set a-going, and expects to cast off a certain number of sheets weekly, warm from the mint, without correction, revisal, or even deliberation. Nay, the miserable author must perform his daily task, in spite of cramp, colick, vapours, or vertigo; in spite of head-ache, heart-ache, and Minerva's frowns; otherwise he will lose his character and livelihood, like a tailor who disappoints his customer in a birthday suit.

Such grumblings were to become a stock-in-trade of the literary life, as familiar now as in Smollett's day; in the meantime, bills had to be paid, and 'I yesterday met with Provost Drummond and took my leave of him after we had settled the manner of my executing his brother's work,' Smollett told Dr Macaulay in the summer of 1753. George Drummond was an influential Scotsman, six times the Lord

Provost of Edinburgh; his brother Alexander was the British consul in Aleppo; dutifully attending to the interests of his countrymen, as Shebbeare had suggested, Smollett had agreed to edit and, where necessary, rewrite the consul's *Travels through Different Cities of Germany, Italy, Greece and Several Parts of Asia, as far as the Euphrates* for the sum of 100 guineas – the first half of which was more than welcome, since bankruptcy loomed as a result of the Gordon and Groom case, and the persistent tardiness of West Indian remittances. That same year, Smollett signed up with Robert Dodsley, James Rivington and William Strahan to edit A *Compendium of Authentic and Entertaining Voyages*, a compilation which, like the consul's book, reflected the contemporary passion for travel yarns – and, more importantly from Smollett's point of view, the current mania for collating, classifying and synthesising the various forms of knowledge.

This was, after all, the age of Linnaeus, of Johnson's *Dictionary*, of *The Wealth of Nations* and *The Decline and Fall of the Roman Empire*, of Ephraim Chambers's *Cyclopedia* of 1728, itself the inspiration for the far more famous *Encyclopédie* of Diderot and D'Alembert. Smollett, with his medical background, his Glasgow education, his reputation as a writer, and his readiness to make himself an instant expert on matters as diverse as childbirth and the history of Mexico, was to play his part in this movement to make all knowledge accessible to the cultivated general reader. The *Compendium*, which was published in 1736, consisted of twenty-seven articles; only one of these, 'An Account of the Expedition against Cartagena', can definitely be attributed to Smollett, but his editorial influence and control were pervasive. Drawing on 'the best books on these subjects extant', the essays ranged, chronologically, from Columbus to Anson, and interlaced detailed accounts of the adventures of Cortes, Pizarro, Drake and Raleigh, the conquest of Peru and the exploration of the Amazon, with 'a clear view of the customs, manners, religion, government, commerce and natural history of most nations in the known world', from Russia to Ceylon. The aim of the exercise, wrote the editor, was to 'disencumber this useful species of history from a great deal of lumber, that tended only to clog the narration and burden the memory'.

Smollett and his 'understrappers' cheerfully took what they needed from existing histories and travel books; and, like his translation of the *Journal Oeconomique* – published in 1754 under the alluring title *Select Essays on Commerce, Agriculture, Mines, Fisheries and Other Useful Subjects* – Smollett's labours on the *Compendium* provided him with a vast and heterogeneous general knowledge. Bridging all disciplines, it was fitting for an unspecialised age when a literate layman was expected to know about chemistry and the classical world, when Adam Smith and Gibbon attended William Hunter's anatomy lessons in his purpose-built lecture hall in Windmill Street, Thomas Gray devoted the last ten years of his life to the study of natural history, and Dr Johnson displayed a fondness for experiments involving test tubes. Experimental science and inductive methods would, it was believed, make it possible to discover general laws that controlled both the workings of the universe and human conduct. David Hume and his fellow-historians – who would, in due course, include Smollett – were convinced that the study of man's past would reveal the principles of his behaviour; Adam Smith moved on from being, in effect, a pioneer anthropologist and student of linguistics, isolating universals common to all mankind, to the study of man as an economic being. The *Compendium*, which ran to seven volumes, reflected this abstract search for pure principles and uncluttered information by refusing to acknowledge the sources from which it drew its information, and by emphasising its travellers' observations of topography, livestock, native peoples and fauna and flora at the expense of their experiences and personalities; the sense of history which animated the whole enterprise was assumed to include natural history, ethnography and anthropology, as well as political and military history. The first comprehensive collection of its kind, it was, despite its huge length, reprinted in Smollett's lifetime, and spawned innumerable imitations, many of which recycled material selected and shaped by its editor. But it was designed to entertain as well as inform: as Smollett put it in his Preface,

We live in an age of levity and caprice, that can relish little besides works of fancy; nor do we listen to instruction unless it be conveyed to us under the pleasing form of entertainment.

But to mix profit with delight should be the aim of all writers, and the business of every book; and nothing can contribute more to these valuable ends, than a detail of voyages; in which we can travel to the most distant corners of the world without stirring from our closets, choose the most enterprising route, embark with the most agreeable companions, view remote cities and their governments, extend our acquaintance thro' all the nations of the globe, and interest ourselves in a succession of incidents and adventures, that at once improve the mind and delight the imagination.

'I have made some progress with the History of the German Empire,' Smollett told John Moore in the spring of 1754, while at the same time keeping him up to date with his labours on *Don Quixote*, Volume II of Dr Smellie's obstetrical masterpiece, Drummond's travel book and the *Journal Oeconomique*. The 'German Empire' formed a minuscule part of what was, even by the all-inclusive and exhaustive standards of the age, the most monumental project in which Smollett as editor and contributor was ever involved. *The Modern Part of the Universal History* was published in forty-four volumes between 1759 and 1765 – and was itself a mere extension of *An Universal History from the Earliest Account of Time to the Present*, which had begun to appear in print in 1730. Appointed co-editor with Dr John Campbell, Smollett was editorially responsible for nearly a third of the *Modern Part*; he contributed histories of the German Empire, the United Provinces, Denmark and Sweden, was involved with those of Italy, Poland, Lithuania and Russia, and – when one of his compilers defaulted – had to fill up, at short notice, sixteen sheets on Antarctica to enable that particular volume to make its way into print. Samuel Richardson was responsible for printing some volumes, sending Smollett eight sheets on the history of the Hottentots for his expert opinion, and worrying about a Mr Shirley's 'barrenness of style and compilation'. Smollett shared his view of Mr Shirley's work, and, faced with the task of 'filling up a chasm of fifteen or sixteen sheets, with a description of a country which all the art of man cannot spin out to half the number', namely Antarctica, confessed to finding the job beyond him 'unless we throw into this place the discovery and description of the Straits of Magellan, Tierra del Fuego, the Straits of Le Maire, Cape Horn, and an account of the voyages of some navigators who have sailed round it into the South Sea'. Seemingly indefatigable, he urged his fellow-novelist to 'reflect upon this proposal, and favour me with your sentiments on it, that I may proceed accordingly . . .' By the spring of 1760 an increasingly ill and exhausted Smollett had turned his hand to Dutch history. 'As the authors who treat of Sweden cannot be procured, I must either lay the work aside, or proceed to another subject,' he told Richardson, who seemed to be doubling up as publisher and printer, providing Smollett with editorial advice and reading matter as well as supervising his printing works. 'I have pitched upon Holland, and enclose a list of books which I beg may be sent with all expedition, as both I and my amanuensis are idle in the meantime.'

Astonishingly, Smollett had also embarked, in 1755, on his *Complete History of England*, published in four volumes in 1757–58 and comprising over 2,600 quarto pages, and its *Continuation*, published in 1760–61, initially in sixpenny weekly numbers: only here, rather than acting as editor, compiler and occasional contributor, he was writing the whole thing himself. The *Complete History* was – to give its title in full – *Deduced from the Descent of Julius Caesar to the Treaty of Aix La Chapelle 1748. Containing the Transactions of One Thousand Eight Hundred and Three Years*, and the four quarto volumes of the *Continuation* covered the years up to the accession of George III in 1760; a very rare fifth volume, published in 1765, is said to have been suppressed for hinting that the King had suffered a bout of lunacy that year. It is not entirely certain that the elusive fifth volume was written by Smollett: Professor Knapp suspects it is, but others have promoted the cause of one James Guthrie, a Scot who, like Smollett, was charged with being a Tory and a crypto-Jacobite. Despite the accusations levelled by his enemies, Smollett was far from being a committed, let alone a Tory historian. Writing about the Glorious Revolution, he suggested that the royal prerogative had been reduced too little, hardly a High Tory line to take; in his account of the Sacheverel Affair, he attacked the High Church Sacheverel and supported the latitudinarian Benjamin Hoadly; he shared Hume's anti-Catholicism, and was no great admirer of Swift. Although he painted a sympathetic picture of James II dying in exile, he was, in general, harsh about the hapless monarch. 'I can safely say I had no other view in the execution of that work than historical truth, which I have displayed on all occasions to the best of my knowledge without fear of affection,' he told his friend William Huggins:

> I have kept myself independent of all connections which might have affected the candour of my intention. I have flattered no individual; I have cultivated no party. I look upon the historian who espouses a faction, who strains incidents or willfully suppresses any circumstances of importance that may tend to the information of the reader, as the worst of prostitutes. I pique myself on being the only historian of this country who has honesty, temper and courage enough to be wholly impartial and disinterested.

Smollett's impartiality as an historian had been tested to the full in the case of William Huggins, a man of whom he was particularly fond. In the *Complete History*, Smollett had described some of the cruelties perpetrated in the 1720s at the Fleet Prison by its notorious warden Thomas Bambridge, and the 'many inhuman barbarities which had been committed by that ruffian', who had also 'been detected in the most iniquitous scenes of fraud, villainy and extortion'. Unwisely, Bambridge had threatened Sir William Rich with a red-hot poker for a failure to pay his dues, and, when the Baronet fought back, had him shackled and thrown in a dungeon. Rich's friends had the tyrant brought to court, and General James Oglethorpe, the philanthropist and founder of the colony of Georgia, headed an inquiry to look into the running of the prison service. Bambridge had bought the wardenship in 1728 from William Huggins's father, John; and John had been even worse than his deputy and successor. He had himself bought the office from Lord Clarendon for £5,000, on the understanding that his son William would succeed him; and, once installed, he had proved a monster of cruelty and negligence. To recover his outlay, he cut costs and charged extortionate fees to those who were in a position to pay for private accommodation rather than communal cells. The drains were blocked, the roof leaked, the bedding stank and dead bodies were not removed until friends or relatives paid for their release; one unlucky inmate was thrown naked and starving into a shed, appeared in the chapel wrapped in a mattress and covered in feathers, was returned to the shed, and promptly died.

Unlike his old father, William Huggins was a highly civilised man. Far from inheriting the wardenship, he lived in a manor house in Hampshire, wrote the libretto for an oratorio and a translation of *Orlando Furioso*, tried his hand, without success, as a playwright, and sent the occasional haunch of venison to the Smolletts in Chelsea. He was also a friend of Hogarth, and helped him, as a lawyer, in his successful campaign to secure copyright for engravers in their work. Hogarth, in his turn, painted 'my dear warm friend', and if Smollett ever met the painter with whom he had so much in common, it might have been through Huggins. Though doubtless bruised by what had been written about his father, Huggins refused to let it affect their friendship after Smollett, in answer to his mild enquiry, had explained that his findings had been based on General Oglethorpe's parliamentary inquiry. When, in due course, Huggins asked Smollett if he could recommend his play to Garrick, Smollett managed, with admirable sleight of hand, to avoid having to show an unactable piece to the great theatre manager without, at the same time, giving offence to his old friend.

Smollett told John Moore that although 'I am afraid the history will not answer the expectations that seem to be raised among my friends in Scotland', and 'the last volume will, I doubt not, be severely censured by the west country Whigs of Scotland', he had, as far as possible, 'adhered to truth without espousing any faction'. Whatever his intentions, no historian can ever be free of bias, in his selection of material if not in the views expressed. Smollett's *History* has always been ignored or compared unfavourably with that of his friend David Hume. 'I spent much of the day on Smollett's History,' Macaulay once wrote. 'It is exceedingly bad; detestably so. I cannot think what has happened to him. His carelessness, particularity, passion, idle invective, gross ignorance of facts, and crude general theories do not surprise me much. But the style, wherever he tries to be elevated, and wherever he attempts to draw a character, is perfectly nauseous'. Some modern historians, on the other hand, consider it an underrated work, finding his emphasis on individuals rather than abstract movements more congenial in a post-Namierite world, and his style more vivid and incisive than that of his rival, the first part of whose history had been published in 1754. For his part, Smollett disapproved of Hume's 'philosophising', in much the same way as he disapproved of Fielding's moralising, and favoured a brisk narrative with a minimum of commentary: or, as he once put it, 'Nothing is more agreeable to an *English* reader than a battle well told.'

Although Smollett may have been earning between £600 and £800 a year during his time at Monmouth House – far more than most of his contemporaries – money remained in short supply. He continued to be a generous host, he had his portrait painted by Nathaniel Dance and Willem Verelst, and his household included not just his wife, daughter and mother-in-law, but his servants – among them the long-serving Alexander Tolloush and, it may be, the two girls who would accompany the Smolletts to France in 1763. 'I have been last week threatened with writs of arrest, and some tradesmen of Chelsea have been so clamorous that I actually promised to pay them at the beginning of this week,' he told Dr Macaulay in April 1756. The bookseller John Rivington was prepared to advance him £100 against the *Complete History*, but in the meantime, pending the arrival of funds from Jamaica, if the good doctor could possibly help him out . . . Five months later, he was so 'harassed by duns' that he had written nothing for two months. He had empowered Tom Bontein to 'sell our Negroes in the West Indies', and was owed £1,000 from that quarter, but still the bills kept flooding in. 'I have just finished the third volume of my History, and am as sick as ever an alderman was of turtle,' he told Huggins in April 1757. A month later he apologised to John Moore for not having replied sooner, but he had been worn out by 'the hurry and fatigue to which I have been exposed in bringing out my History of England'. The *History* was eventually completed in fourteen months – a monumental task which took a terrible toll on Smollett's health and his social life, for Tolloush was instructed to keep stray visitors at bay and 'deny me to all those with whom I have no express business'.

All four volumes had been published by the early spring of 1758. The opening volume had been dedicated, effusively, to William Pitt, who attributed his belated acknowledgement to 'a long disability from the gout in my right arm'. Although Smollett would soon turn against the 'Great Commoner' as a champion of the mob and spokesman for the mercantile classes, he still admired him for his opposition to expensive and irrelevant Continental alliances, of no value to Britain itself, and entered into solely in the interests of the Electorate of Hanover. Despite the commercial and publishing success of the *History*, its reception was mixed. Reviewing the first three volumes in the *Monthly Review*, Oliver Goldsmith suggested that Smollett did 'not pretend to have discovered any hidden records, or authentic materials that have escaped the notice of former writers; or to have thrown such lights upon contested events, or disputed characters, as to serve to rectify any mistaken opinions mankind may have entertained with respect to either'. His aim had been to produce a straightforward narrative, uncluttered with scholarly references and devoid of what Smollett himself had referred to as 'all *useless disquisition*'. Goldsmith regretted that Smollett had not 'afforded us something more', since 'a moderate interspersion of manly and sensible observations, must have greatly enlivened his work'. But Smollett's style was 'clear, nervous and flowing', and he had a rare ability to evoke the characters he described.

Not all Smollett's readers and reviewers were as well disposed. Reviewing Volume IV in the same magazine a year later, Owen Ruffhead suggested that Smollett's merit was 'rather that of an ingenious novelist than of an accurate historian'. He had taken 'little pains to digest his matter', got things out of order, and had come up with 'a hasty and indigested performance': the whole thing was elegantly and vigorously written, but his 'partiality to the Tory party [was] manifest on every page'. An intemperate clergyman called Thomas Comber devoted 150 pages to his belief that the *Complete History* was a work of papist propaganda, and that Smollett, 'lost to all sense of shame', was intent on slandering the memory of William and Mary; and Lady Mary Wortley Montagu referred in passing to 'my dear Smollett, who, I am sorry to say, disgraces his talent by writing those stupid romances commonly called history'. Horace Walpole,

Smollett in his prime, before illness and overwork had begun to take
their toll. Artist unknown.

The Court of Glasgow University, 1761.

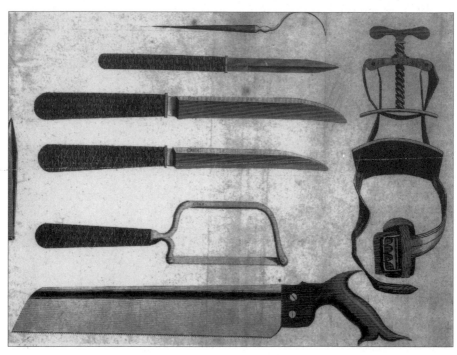

Surgical implements of the kind with which Smollett must have been familiar.

Rowlandson is, of all British artists, the closest in spirit to Smollett; his rendition of an amputation has a suitably Smollettian flavour.

British Men-of-War, *c.*1720–30.

Cartagena under siege: Smollett was infuriated by British naval and military incompetence.

The petulant Admiral Knowles, a veteran of Cartagena and Smollett's implacable enemy.

'Starving Poet and Publisher' by
Rowlandson. For further details,
see the College of Authors scenes
in *Peregrine Pickle*.

'The Distrest Poet' by Hogarth.

James Quin, Garrick's rival and the
Donald Wolfit of his age.

'That little rascal Garrick.'

Smollett's arch-rival, Henry Fielding.

The dapper, diplomatic William Hunter,
surgeon, anatomist and London's most
emollient midwife.

William Hogarth: a self-portrait. His pallet was his trademark, and may have lent its name to the stocky, verbose painter in *Peregrine Pickle*.

John Wilkes and his wife, Mary.

'That devil Wilkes', portrayed by Hogarth at his most diabolical.

The thuggish clergyman-poet Charles Churchill, disguised as a bear by Hogarth: note the lies engraved on his cudgel.

'Englishman at Paris, 1767'. Note the contrast between sturdy John Bull
and the scrawny, effete and priest-ridden French.

'Petit Maitre and his Valet'.
If Smollett is to be believed,
he has in his pockets a comb and a
pair of scissors, ready to attend
to a lady's elaborate coiffure;
Charles Grignion, who engraved
this drawing, was one of the artists
whom Smollett encouraged.

resentful perhaps of Smollett's uncharitable views of his uncle Robert, savaged him in his posthumously published *Memoirs of George II*. Smollett, he declared, 'was a worthless man, and only mentioned here because author of a History of England, of the errors of which posterity ought to be warned'. Writing the *History* had been 'an easy task, as being pilfered from other authors', yet although it had been 'compiled from the libels of the age and the most paltry materials, yet being heightened by personal invectives, strong Jacobitism, and the worst representation of the Duke of Cumberland's conduct in Scotland, its sale was prodigious'. Smollett's fear that Scottish Whigs would disapprove of the *History* reflected, in part, the strong line he had taken, for all his disapproval of 'philosophising', on the Forty-Five and its aftermath, and his enemies were swift to denounce him as a Tory and a Jacobite. 'From an education in a very opposite principle,' Smollett had become a 'declar'd convert to the Stuart family, which he has sufficiently shown in his Complete History', the Reverend Birch informed the Earl of Hardwicke, and William Warburton, the Bishop of Gloucester, declared that 'when Clarendon and Temple wrote history, they little thought the time was so near when a vagabond Scot should write nonsense ten thousand strong'.

'Ten thousand strong' was, as it happened, descriptive rather than hyperbolical, for shortly after the publication of Volume IV the *History* was reissued in eleven octavo volumes, and – more remuneratively – in weekly numbers, costing sixpence each. Publishers anxious to reach a wider and less well-heeled market among the newly literate classes begun to republish and reissue books by selling off 16- or 32-page sections or 'fascicles', wrapped, more often than not, in blue paper, and selling for fourpence or sixpence each. Readers who couldn't afford a new novel or history could buy it in instalments, and, once they had the complete books, either bind up the sections or leave them in their blue wrappers. Fascicle publishing boomed in the second quarter of the century; such enterprises were often financed by a conger of booksellers, printing on average 2,000 or 3,000 copies per weekly issue. In the mid-1730s Knapton's, the booksellers, had a phenomenal success with their translation of Rapin's *History of England*: they were said to have made between £8,000 and £10,000 from their reissue of the work in monthly and then weekly parts, and this may well have inspired James Rivington and James Fletcher to try their luck with Smollett's *History*. They mounted a promotional campaign of a kind familiar to their modern equivalents in the trade. It was said that as well as spending £300 on advertising and £200 on printing a 'very large quantity of proposals', they 'addressed a packet of the proposals to every parish clerk in England, carriage-free, with half-a-crown enclosed, as a compliment, to have them distributed through the pews of the church, which being generally done, the pious people read the papers instead of listening to the sermon, and the result was an extensive demand for the work'. Thirteen thousand copies were printed of each of the first fourteen numbers, and in due course sales reached 20,000 per section. A total of 2,281 reams of blue paper were ordered for the wrappers, and the printers were paid £7,589 5s. for delivering 421,625 copies to the publishers. Parts of the *History* were also serial-ised in the *Public Advertiser*, and in two Scottish newspapers. Although revising his book for fascicle publication must have added to his exhaustion, Smollett is thought to have earned at least £2,000 from the *History* and its *Continuation* – for the *History* alone he was paid three guineas a sheet for writing 332 sheets, plus a further £500 for revisions and corrections. His money worries appeared to be over, and much less was heard, in his letters at least, about creditors and duns and sums overdue from Mr Bontein in Jamaica.

'I like much better your publishing in volumes than in numbers. Tho' this last method has been often practiced, it has somewhat of a quackish air,' Hume told Andrew Millar, adding that, unlike the more commercially minded Smollett, he had no need for engraved front-ispieces either, for 'I do not imagine, because these ornaments have helped the sale of Smollett's history, that mine would be the better for them.' 'I am afraid this extraordinary run upon Dr Smollett has a little hurt your sales: but these things are only temporary,' he wrote to Millar on another occasion; momentarily embattled, he told William Robertson, also making his mark as an historian, 'A Plague take you! Here I sit near the historical summit of Parnassus, immedi-ately under Dr Smollett: and you have the impudence to squeeze your-self by me, and place yourself directly under his feet.' Robertson had not, as yet, met Smollett, and was 'very desirous of his acquaintance'.

Carlyle and the playwright-cum-politician John Home had learned that Smollett came up from Chelsea once a week to visit Forrest's Coffee House, and it was agreed that they would all have dinner there, and effect the introduction. Smollett, according to Carlyle,

> was now become a great man, and being much of a humorist, was not to be put out of his way. Home and Robertson and I met him there, when he had several of his minions about him, to whom he prescribed tasks of translation, compilation, or abridgement, which, after he had seen, he recommended to the booksellers. We dined together, and Smollett was very brilliant. Having to stay all night, that we might spend the evening together, he only begged leave to withdraw for an hour, that he might give audience to his myrmidons; for we insisted that, if his business permitted, it should be in the room where we sat. The Doctor agreed, and the authors were introduced, to the number of five, I think, most of whom were soon dismissed. He kept two, however, to supper, whispering to us that he believed they would amuse us, which they certainly did, for they were curious characters.
>
> We passed a very pleasant and joyful evening. When we broke up, Robertson expressed great surprise at the polished and agreeable manners and the great urbanity of his conversation. He had imagined that a man's manners must bear a likeness to his books, and as Smollett had described so well the characters of ruffians and profligates, that he must, of course, resemble them.

Once again, it seemed, the novelist was being confused with his creations.

All too soon he would be undermined by exhaustion and ill health, but now, in his late thirties, Smollett was at the height of his powers. John Moore remembered that 'The person of Dr Smollett was stout and well-proportioned, his countenance engaging, his manner reserved, with a certain air of dignity that seemed to indicate that he was not unconscious of his powers.' John Anderson, writing some twenty-five years after his subject's death, said of him that

In his person and manners, Smollett was fashioned to prepossess all men in his favour. His figure was graceful and handsome; in his air and manner, there was a dignity that commanded respect, joined with a benignity that inspired affection. With the most polished manners, and the finest address, he possessed a loftiness and elevation of sentiment and character, without pride or haughtiness. His general behaviour bore the genuine stamp of true politeness, the result of an overflowing humanity and goodness of heart. He was a man of upright principles, and of great and extensive benevolence. His conversation was sprightly and agreeable . . .

Such a paragon had his Achilles' heel, however: 'He was occasionally misled by a heated imagination, strong resentments, and the mortification of disappointed hopes, into bitterness and party virulence', and 'the defects in his temperament, natural and habitual, made him unprosperous and unhappy. His sensibility was too ardent; his passions were too easily moved.' Moore noted that 'nothing was more abhorrent to his nature than pertness or intrusion, few things could render him more indignant than a cold reception'; though 'free from vanity', he had a 'considerable share of pride, and great sensibility' and 'could not conceal his contempt of folly, his detestation of fraud, nor refrain from proclaiming his indignation against every instance of oppression'. He was, Moore concluded,

> of an intrepid, independent, imprudent disposition, equally incapable of deceit and adulation, and more disposed to cultivate the acquaintance of those he could serve, than of those who could serve him. What wonder that a man of his character was not, what is called, successful in life!

Smollett the writer and Smollett the medical man still kept in touch, even as his practice gave way to the demands of the literary life. His continuing interest in obstetrics was put to comic effect in the pages of *Peregrine Pickle* which deal with the vexed matter of Mrs Trunnion's phantom pregnancy. Her sudden craving for a fricassee of frogs, flavoured with hairs from the Commodore's beard and followed by huge quantities of pineapple, reflected the familiar yearning by pregnant women for unfamiliar foods, and the notion, prevalent at the time, that women with 'absurd imaginations' could become 'overheated' during pregnancy and bring forth monsters, akin to Mary Tofts and her rabbits. In his novel *The Adventures of George Edwards, a Creole*, published in the same year as *Peregrine Pickle*, 'Sir John' Hill told of a woman who touched a robin redbreast while pregnant, and subsequently gave birth to a red-chested child, and controversy was stirred by *Lucina sine Concibutu*, a satire on curious births. During the 1730s and 1740s experiments were carried out at the Royal College of Physicians on foetuses and pregnant women by James Blondel, Daniel Turner and William Smellie: the notion of 'overheating' was ridiculed, and it was agreed that deformities were caused by factors other than the mother's imagination. Smollett shared to the full the current fascination with the subject, and the scepticism of obstetrical friends like Smellie and William Hunter. As a trainee surgeon in Glasgow, he may have read John Pechey's *Complete Midwife's Practice Enlarged*, required reading at the time and containing a chapter on 'False Conception', and he seems to have been aware of the case of Sarah Last, who, like the hapless Mrs Trunnion, went through all the stages of a normal pregnancy, but to no avail.

For all his interest in obstetrics, and his herculean labours on Smellie's mighty tomes, Smollett's longest contribution to the literature of medicine was devoted to a subject far dearer to his heart. He had a lifelong devotion to, and belief in, the beneficial effects of immersing the body in cold water in general, and sea water in particular, and no doubt he had read and admired Richard Russell of Brighton's *A Dissertation on the Use of Sea Water in the Diseases of the Glands*, published in 1750; but his own *Essay on Water*, published in 1752, was devoted to water at its most unsavoury. Famed for its waters since Roman times, Bath was, by the middle of the century, firmly established as the most fashionable and elegant spa in England. Its population trebled between 1700 and 1765; by the mid-1740s it was receiving some 15,000 visitors a year, and whereas in 1740 it was served by seventeen coaches a week from London, a further six were available by 1757. Seventeenth- and early eighteenth-century

Bath had been a rough and boisterous country town, and Ralph Allen – Pope's 'Man of Bath', and a wealthy local landowner – was determined to attract a better class of visitor. He appointed 'Beau' Nash as Master of Ceremonies, and the dapper Nash banned boots and swords in the assembly rooms, introduced musicians, encouraged the theatre and balls and, on the surface at least, made Bath seem an altogether more reputable spot, far more suitable for sophisticates than for country bumpkins. He also commissioned John Wood and his son to build the butter-coloured Bath stone crescents, squares, streets and circuses that transformed a small Somerset town into one of the most beautiful cities in Europe.

Bath attracted the sick, the hypochondriacal and the pleasure-loving in equal measure, all of whom needed deep pockets or a reliable source of funds. By the 1750s, it cost £130 a year to rent a house on Grand Parade; to rent a terrace house on the west side of Gay Street would set a visitor back by £60 a year – one of the east side was a mere £40 – while a ride in a bath chair would cost all of two shillings, four times as much as a sedan chair. Charles Wesley once described Bath as 'the headquarters of Satan', and in *Roderick Random* and *Peregrine Pickle* Smollett at his most abrasive wrote about the gamblers, fortune-hunters, card-sharpers and predatory, ingratiating doctors who hovered round the rich and the hypochondriacal like so many black-clad vultures. Now he found himself caught up in a vicious and long-drawn-out feud over the properties of Bath water, and the repellent conditions endured by those who came to the city in search of health.

Like many before him, Dr William Oliver – a benign and influential local doctor, best remembered as the alleged inventor of the Bath Oliver biscuit – recommended that his patients should both drink and bathe in the warm and sulphurous Bath water; but neither was likely to prove an agreeable experience. Most of the bathing took place in the early morning, after which visitors would sip the waters, visit coffee-houses to remove the taste, attend a service in the Abbey at noon, ride, shop or stroll all afternoon, and devote the evening to the assembly rooms, the theatre, balls and gambling. Dr Oliver was all too well aware of the overcrowding in the baths. 'The passages out of them are so few that a poor, weak, hysterical creature who cannot bear the bath above ten minutes is often kept in it above half an hour and sometimes much longer, to the great peril of her life, at least to the irreparable damage of her health,' he declared. Both sexes bathed together in the ancient Roman pool, the women swathed in canvas sacking which, once waterlogged, must have weighed a ton. Dr Oliver thought it wrong that those of 'gross habits and unsound viscera, stuffed with full meals and inflamed by spiritous liquors' should immerse themselves alongside others who were 'emaciated, weak and dispirited, worn down by their distemper and easily becoming hectical'. Gorging and heavy drinking were *de rigueur* among many of the bathers: Philip Thicknesse, later to be a severe critic of Smollett's *Travels* and the man who persuaded the young Gainsborough to move from his native Suffolk to try his luck as a portrait painter in fashionable Bath, noted how some patients would swallow a quart of sulphurous water for their health before tucking into a mound of 'Sally Lunns' or hot sponge rolls coated with burned butter, and Dr Oliver observed that faintness, palpitations and apoplexies were all too common among those taking a cure.

The baths were also dirty, uncomfortable and exposed to the elements – matters on which Smollett waxed eloquent in his *Essay* and, more famously, in *Humphry Clinker*. The *Essay on Water* was written in defence of Archibald Cleland, a Scottish doctor who had settled in Bath in 1740. Smollett thought him 'a man of good morals, and uncommon ability', but his 'Proposals' for rendering the baths 'more safe, agreeable, and efficacious' had infuriated the grandees of Bath, including Ralph Allen. A flurry of angry pamphlets was discharged in Cleland's direction, and he was sacked from his job as surgeon and obstetrician at the Bath General Hospital on trumped-up immorality charges; among his detractors was the selfsame William Warburton, the Bishop of Gloucester, who was married to Ralph Allen's niece.

Smollett, who shared Cleland's views about the repulsive conditions on offer, was outraged by the way his fellow-medic had been treated. He may have helped Cleland to get an MD from Aberdeen, so enabling him to practise as a physician, and he belatedly came to his defence in the *Essay on Water*. He began by discussing the various properties of water. Both to drink and to wash in, 'pure water is certainly, of all others, the most salutary beverage, as being the best fitted to mix with all the animal juices, assist the various secretions of the human body, and prevent that rigidity and coalescence of the vessels, which are the immediate causes of old age'. Smollett's passion was for bodily immersion in cold water, which 'communicates a spring to the whole system'. Cold water was ideal for swollen joints and for 'the most sordid and inveterate scrofulous and scorbutic ulcers'; it was also far superior to warm water when it came to unblocking the pores, another subject on which Smollett had strong views. Warm water, on the other hand, was good for asthma, palpitations, 'hypochondriacal and hysterical disorders', and bathing the feet; it had a particular appeal for 'many modern voluptuaries', rendering rigid fibres supple, washing away 'acrid impurities' which clog the pores, and improving the 'velocity' of the blood. Its use, he warned, could lead to the discharge of 'an amazing quantity of foul humours' through the skin. In evidence he cited a German woman who, to ease a pain in her loins, took a warm bath, as a result of which 'gross, *unctuous* matter was found floating upon the water, such as might have been taken off with a spoon'. Sometimes, in Bath itself, the scum that formed on the water 'grew every day more and more *corrosive*, and smelled so foetid, that they were obliged to infuse fresh herbs to correct the noisesome stench'. Warm baths could be recommended to those bitten by a wolf or a mad dog – the poison could be sweated out – and for 'manic disorders, whether of the melancholy or frantic species: both these are owing to a disordered circulation in the brain, occasioned by the thick foul viscocity in the juices . . .' The Negroes of the West Indies made good use of warm-water bathing, adding 'emollient herbs' for extra effect.

Rather more contentious was the vexed matter of whether health-giving properties were inherent in the water itself, or in the minerals it contained. Smollett had no doubts, and made himself unpopular by airing his views. 'I fully believe that efficacy is often ascribed to the *mineral particles*, which properly belong to the *element* itself, exclusive of any foreign assistance,' he pronounced. Much was made of the medical properties of minerals, but as far as Smollett was concerned they merely blocked the pores and formed an unwelcome crust on the surface of the skin. Still more controversial was his support for the embattled Cleland. Although Bath was 'the great hospital of the nation, frequented by almost all the valetudinarians whose lives are of any consequence to the commonwealth', the baths themselves and Cleland's proposals for their improvement had been subjected to the 'supercilious and willful neglect' of the all-powerful Corporation. Under the present arrangements, 'diseased persons of all ages, sexes and conditions are promiscuously admitted into an open bath' without shelter from wind and rain, summer and winter alike. Women bathers were ogled by footmen and assorted idlers; attendants were in short supply; bathers were left too long after bathing in their wet canvas costumes, which became cold and clammy; changing rooms were few, cold and uncomfortable; many bathers were rightly 'disgusted with the nauseating appearance of the filth, which, being washed from the bodies of the bathers, is left sticking to the side of the place'. The savaging of Cleland's plans to make the baths healthier, safer and more comfortable was a disgrace, and his enemies – here he referred to the polemical outpourings of the Bishop of Gloucester – had had 'recourse to the pen of an author as notorious for the servile homage he yields to his patrons, as for the insolence and scurrility with which he treats all the world besides'.

But Smollett was far from done with Bath and its waters. Over the next decade he was to be involved, intermittently, in what was known as the 'sulphur controversy', and in *Humphry Clinker* he would describe, in tones of outrage, the state of the baths and, still worse, the people who frequented them. The 'sulphur controversy' was, in effect, an extension of the seventeenth-century battle between the Galenists, who subscribed to the medieval notion that bodily health depended on the correct balance of the 'humours', and the more modern-minded Paracelsians, who put their faith in chemistry and chemical-based drugs. Smollett was an instinctive 'humourist', as was the disreputable Dr Shebbeare, who claimed in his *New Analysis of the Bristol Waters*, published in 1740, that, despite the prevailing whiff of rotten eggs, there was no evidence of sulphur being present in the waters of either Bath or Bristol. The most influential 'humourist' was Dr Charles Lucas, who was sceptical about the value and the existence of sulphur in spa waters, and suggested that the so-called sulphur at Bath consisted of nothing more than scum and excrement, that the attendants dyed shillings yellow in order to convince credulous bathers that this was caused by the sulphur in the water, and that any beneficial side-effects of bathing were caused by the water alone, which induced the body to discharge poisonous and unwholesome matter, thereby restoring a proper balance of the 'humours'. The 'chemists', whose views were beginning to prevail, were led by a German named Diederich Wessl Linden, who had practised as a physician at the Bristol Hot Wells and at the Welsh spa of Llandrindrod Wells, and by Dr John Rutty, the author of a 700-page book devoted to the salutary effects of sulphur in spa water. Smollett met both Lucas and Rutty when he spent the summer of 1757 in Bath, and despite the views so forcibly expressed in the *Essay on Water*, he seems, for whatever reasons, to have temporarily sided with the 'chemists'. He prepared Rutty's book for press, and then gave it a favourable review in the *Critical Review*, but wrote highly critically of Lucas's *Analysis of Dr Rutty's Methodical Synopsis of Mineral Waters*.

Dr Linden resurfaced in comical if repellent form in the early pages of *Humphry Clinker*. Squire Bramble and his party visit the pump room at Bristol Hot Wells, where the old gentleman complains of the 'stink, occasioned by the vast quantity of mud and slime, which the river leaves at low ebb under the windows of the Pump room', and suggests that 'the exhalations arising from such a nuisance, could not but be prejudicial to the weak lungs of many consumptive patients, who came to drink the water'. Bramble's remarks are overheard by 'the famous Dr L——n, who is come to ply at the Well for patients', and who subjects them to a 'learned investigation of the nature of stink'. A relativist and social anthropologist in the making, Linden tries to convince them that our reactions to particular smells are culturally conditioned, that 'the French were pleased with the putrid effluvia of animal food; and so were the Hottentots in Africa, and the Savages in Greenland; and that the Negroes on the coast of Senegal would not touch fish till it was rotten . . .' He goes on to note 'that every person who pretended to nauseate the smell of another's excretions, snuffed up his own with particular complacency', appeals to the ladies present for support of his views, tells of a recent Duke of Tuscany who so relished the stink of his own excrement that 'he caused the essence of ordure to be extracted, and used as the most delicious perfume', and reveals how he himself 'when he happened to be low-spirited, or fatigued with business, found immediate relief and uncommon satisfaction from hanging over the stale contents of a close-stool, while his servant stirred it about under his nose'. By now 'the company began to hold their noses', but, unabashed, Dr Linden continues in like vein for another two pages at least.

Bath proves as squalid as expected, despite Cleland's 'Proposals' and Smollett's fulminations in the *Essay on Water*. 'The first object that saluted my eye, was a child full of scrophulous ulcers, carried in the arms of one of the guides, under the very noses of the bathers,' Bramble informs Dr Lewis in *Humphry Clinker*. 'I was so shocked by the sight that I retired immediately with indignation and disgust – suppose the matter of these ulcers, floating on the water, comes in contact with my skin, when all the pores are open . . . Good Heaven, the very thought makes my blood run cold!' And if Smollett himself had momentarily reneged on the matter of sulphur, Bramble is an unrepentant 'humourist', convinced that clear water is 'more effectual than any water impregnated with salt and iron; which, being astringent, will certainly contract the pores, and leave a kind of crust upon the surface of the body'. As for drinking the waters, Bramble is sure that there must be some 'regurgitation' from the baths into the pump – in which case, 'what a delicate beverage is every day quaffed by the drinkers; medicated with the sweat and dirt and dandruff; and the abominable discharges of various kinds, from twenty different diseased bodies, parboiling in the kettle below'. To make matters worse, the baths were said to be adjacent to an ancient cemetery, so those rash enough to sample the waters may well 'swallow the strainings of rotten bones and carcasses' as well as the 'decoction of living bodies'. And, as in the *Essay*, Bramble raises the vexatious matter of sedan chairs. Not only does the Corporation stint on arcades to shelter bathers from the elements, but the city's sedan chairs 'stand soaking in the open street, from morning till night, till they become so many boxes of wet leather, for the benefit of the gouty and rheumatic', and 'even the close chairs, contrived for the sick, by standing in the open air, have their linings impregnated, like so many sponges, with the moisture of the atmosphere, and those cases of cold vapour must give a charming check to the perspirations of a patient, piping hot from the bath, with all his pores wide open'.

The baths were bad enough, but the bathers were even worse. The better class of old-fashioned visitor had been driven out by a tidal wave of opulence and vulgarity. 'Every upstart of fortune, harnessed in the trappings of the mode, presents himself at Bath, as in the very focus of observation,' grumbles old Bramble. These rude intruders include

Clerks and factors from the East Indies, loaded with the spoil of plundered provinces; planters, Negro-drivers, and hucksters, from our American plantations, enriched they know not how; agents, commissaries, and contractors, who have fattened, in two successive wars, on the blood of the nation; usurers, brokers, and jobbers of every kind; men of low birth, and no breeding, have found themselves suddenly translated into a state of affluence, unknown to former ages; and no wonder that their brains should be intoxicated with pride, vanity, and presumption. Knowing no other criterion of greatness but the ostentation of wealth, they discharge their affluence without taste or conduct, through every channel of the most extravagance; and all of them hurry to Bath, because here, without any further qualification, they can mingle with the princes and nobles of the land. Even the wives and daughters of low tradesmen, who, like shovel-nosed sharks, prey upon the blubber of those uncouth whales of fortune, are infected with the same rage of displaying their importance; and the slightest indisposition serves them for a pretext to insist upon being conveyed to Bath, where they may hobble country-dances and cotillions among lordlings, squires, counsellors and clergy. These delicate creatures from Bedfordbury, Butcher-row, Crutched-friars, and Botolph-lane, cannot breathe in the gross air of the Lower Town, or conform to the vulgar rules of a common lodging house: the husband, therefore, must provide an entire house, or elegant apartments in the new buildings. Such is the composition of what is called the fashionable company at Bath; where a very inconsiderable proportion of genteel people are lost in a mob of impudent plebeians, who have neither understanding nor judgement, nor the least idea of propriety and decorum; and seem to enjoy nothing so much as an opportunity of insulting their betters.

For a man who was married to a Jamaican heiress and supplemented his income by the occasional sale of a slave to complain about planters and Negro-drivers smacks of un-Smollettian humbuggery, but his wrath overrides such scruples. This 'torrent of folly and extravagance' is a direct result of 'the general tide of luxury, which hath overspread the nation, and swept away all, even the very dregs of the people'. As far as Bramble is concerned, 'it is a subject on which I cannot write with any degree of patience; for the mob is a monster I never could abide, either in its head, tail, midriff, or members; I detest the whole of it, as a mass of ignorance, presumption, malice and brutality.' Although Bramble has some un-Smollettian characteristics, in his views on society he is very much his master's voice. Smollett's apopletic loathing for the new social order was excessive even by the standards of the day, but, like so many English novelists after him, he put the aspirations and the pretensions and the ineptitude of the *nouveaux riches* to good comic effect. His eagerness to blame luxury for all the social evils afflicting his adopted country was shared by others who, panic-stricken and resentful at rapid social change, pined for the stability and tranquillity of an imaginary *ancien régime*. Among the milder manifestations of luxury were the Woods' new buildings in Bath: Bramble seems not to have rated them highly, reserving his greatest scorn for the terrace houses in the Circus, completed in 1758 by John Wood the Younger, who had taken over as the architect in charge of the rebuilding of Bath after his father's death four years earlier. The Circus is now regarded as the apotheosis of urban architecture, but Smollett felt that Wood had indulged a fanciful aesthetic at the expense of practicalities: he thought some kind of colonnade should have been provided to protect those going in and out from the rain, and assumed that all the rooms in the houses must be shaped like wedges of Cheddar cheese, with the thin edges facing forward.

William Hazlitt said of Smollett's third novel, *The Adventures of Ferdinand Count Fathom*, that 'there is more power of writing occasionally shewn in it than in any of his works'. In particular, he went on,

> I need only refer to the fine and bitter irony of the Count's address to the country of his ancestors in landing in England; to the robber scene in the forest, which has never been surpassed; to the Parisian swindler who personates a raw English squire (Western is tame in comparison); and to the story of the seduction in the west of England. It would be difficult to point out, in any author, passages written with more force and mastery than these.

Few modern readers are likely to linger long enough to savour *Count Fathom*'s odd moments of excellence – 'occasionally' is the key word in Hazlitt's critique – but after 800-plus pages of *Peregrine Pickle* it has, at least, the merit of relative brevity. The writing is more abstract, more consciously polished, than in the first two novels, and as such it has a glazed, impenetrable quality: much of the novel is set in France and Central Europe, and although the English chapters have the actuality and tangibility of a world observed and known by the author, their European equivalents read more like a fable or a parable. This sense of *Count Fathom* as a ponderous fairy tale is, perhaps, inherent in the nature of its satanic anti-hero. Count Fathom is, for most of the novel, the embodiment of evil: much influenced by Iago in his dealings with the unsuspecting Renaldo and the innocent Monimia – in his Dedication to the novel Smollett acknowledges his debt to Elizabethan and Restoration drama – he is also the precursor of those vampiric figures in opera cloaks and top hats who were to haunt fog-shrouded London alleyways and vertiginous Transylvanian castles in the horror tales of the nineteenth century. Although, by some implausible miracle of redemption, he becomes the incarnation of goodness in the final pages of the novel, devoting his life to the service of others and resurrected in *Humphry Clinker* as an altruistic and much-loved Yorkshire country doctor, most of his career is given over to the seduction and ruination of innocent maidens and the betrayal of those rash or trusting enough to offer him the hand of friendship. As such, he has much in common with the smooth, devilish seducers who were surfacing, on the other side of the English Channel, in the novels of Laclos and Crébillon *fils*. Fiendishly good-looking, he is the son of an Englishwoman who made her living as a camp-follower to the Duke of Marlborough's armies during the War of the Spanish Succession, combining her work as a prostitute with a lucrative line in stripping the valuables from the bodies of the dead or wounded on the battlefield (the wounded are swiftly dispatched with a dagger carried for the purpose). Nurtured on 'brandy impregnated with gunpowder', young Fathom soon embarks on his career of conscienceless crime. The scenes in which he seduces and abandons unsuspecting and adoring maidens have, at their best, a touch of *Les Liaisons dangereuses*, and there is a good chapter, much acclaimed by literary historians as an early example of the Gothic, a precursor of Monk Lewis and Mrs Radcliffe, in which Fathom finds himself alone and adrift in a haunted wood, seeks refuge in a cottage owned by a wrinkled dame, is offered a room with no lock on the doors, with bars on the windows and a still-warm corpse in the corner, and escapes an identical fate only by changing places with the corpse, which is stabbed afresh when two men burst into the room to polish off their latest victim: but it is only when the English bluster and bully their way on stage that the novel flickers fitfully into life.

Until he visits England and is exposed to the full cunning of the natives – including avaricious lawyers and vindictive landladies in search of a husband – Fathom is rash enough to believe that 'the English were dupes to all the world; and that in points of genius and address, they were no more than noisy braggarts'. Sir Stentor Stiles, whom he encounters in Paris, seems to conform to the stereotype of the English squire as a 'genuine, rich country booby'. 'A person habited in the exact uniform of an English jockey', he cracks his whip and gives voice to huntsmen's halloos in polite Parisian *salons*, where he is regarded as the epitome of the boorish and insular

Anglo-Saxon. He makes no effort to 'jabber your French lingo', boasts that 'a true-born Englishman need not be afeared to show his face, nor his backside neither, with the best Frenchman that ever trod the ground' and, like many English travellers, Smollett among them, takes a dim view of French cooking. 'One can't have a slice of a delicate sirloin, or nice buttock of beef, for love or money,' he complains. 'I could get no eatables upon the road, but what they call Bully, which looks like the flesh of Pharoah's lean kine stewed into rags and tatters.' The buffoonish Sir Stentor turns out to be a con-man, very similar to those encountered by Roderick Random and Strap when they first arrive in London. Fathom is lured into playing dice with Sir Stentor and his sidekick, and although in the early stages of the game Sir Stentor pretends to be an incompetent and irascible loser, feigning fury and hurling his wig in the fire, he gradually ups the stakes and finally strips the Count of every penny.

Despite his treatment at Sir Stentor's hands, and a warning that England is a paradise for adventurers and wide-boys, Fathom is a passionate Anglophile. When, from the French side of the Channel, 'he beheld the white cliffs of Albion, his heart throbbed with all the joy of a beloved son who, after a tedious and fatiguing voyage, reviews the chimneys of his father's house', and once on English soil, he 'could not help snuffing up the British air with marks of infinite satisfaction and relish'. As he trundles in a coach through the Kentish countryside, squeezed between a stout Wapping landlady and a portly Quaker, 'like a thin quarto between two voluminous dictionaries on a bookseller's shelf',

> He perceived between the English and the people among whom he had hitherto lived, such essential difference in customs, appearance, and way of living, as inspired him with high notions of that British freedom, opulence, and convenience, on which he had often heard his mother expatiate. On the road, he feasted his eye-sight with the verdant hills covered with flocks of sheep, the fruitful vales pastured out into cultivated enclosures; the very cattle seemed to profit by the wealth of their masters, being large, sturdy and sleek, and every peasant breathed the insolence of liberty and independence.

He notes, too, the contentious nature of the English, 'that freedom of altercation so happily preserved in this age and country', and the disdain aroused by foreigners, and by the French in particular. 'I suppose you are some poor starv'd journeyman tailor come from France, where you have been learning to cabbage [*sic*], and have not seen a good meal of victuals these seven years; you have been living upon rye-bread and soup maigre,' one of the foreigners present is told, and Fathom himself 'sat in silent astonishment at the manners of his fellow-travellers, which far exceeded the notions he had preconceived of English plainness and rusticity: he found himself a monument of that disregard and contempt, which a stranger never fails to meet with from the inhabitants of this island.' Quite apart from providing a useful if familiar summary of Anglo-Saxon attitudes, Smollett displays an entertaining disregard for chronology. At one point Fathom – then in his twenties, and born in the early years of the century – is hauled before an idle, pipe-puffing, ale-quaffing country JP on suspicion of being Bonnie Prince Charlie, recently escaped from the débâcle of Culloden; and while incarcerated in the King's Bench Prison he encounters Theodore de Neuhoff, the deposed ex-King of Corsica, who was imprisoned in 1749, and may well have met Smollett at some stage.

Far and away the liveliest passages in the novel are those which deal with xenophobia, medical tricks of the trade, and the wily ways of lawyers; the most interesting, perhaps, is Smollett's Dedication, for what it reveals about its author and his views on the novel. Coyly dedicated to 'Doctor S*******', it includes 'as a testimony of my particular friendship and esteem', a rare fragment of Smollettian self-portraiture. 'Know then,' he writes,

> I can despise your pride, while I honour your integrity; and applaud your taste, while I am shocked at your ostentation. I have known you trifling, superficial and obstinate in dispute; meanly jealous and awkwardly reserved; rash and haughty in your resentments; and coarse and lowly in your connexions. I have blushed at the weakness of your conversation, and trembled at the errors of your conduct. Yet, as I own you possess certain good qualities, which over-balance these defects, and

distinguish you on this occasion, as a person for whom I have the most perfect attachment and esteem, you have no cause to complain of the indelicacy with which your faults are reprehended: and as they are chiefly the excesses of a sanguine disposition and looseness of thought, impatient of caution or control; you may, thus stimulated, watch over your own intemperance and infirmity, with redoubled vigilance and consideration, and for the future profit by the severity of my reproof.

Smollett then moves on to tell us what he hopes to have achieved in *Count Fathom*. A novel, he informs us in a rare outburst from a writer not greatly given to abstractions or to analysis of his craft, is

a large diffused picture, comprehending the characters of life, disposed in different groups, and exhibited in various attitudes, for the purposes of an uniform plan, and general occurrence, to which every individual figure is subservient. But this plan cannot be executed with propriety, probability or success, without a principal personage to attract the attention, unite the incidents, unwind the clue of the labyrinth, and at last close the scene by the virtue of his own importance.

Most such 'principal personages' have tended to be 'characters of transcendent worth', but fear is 'the most violent and interesting of all the passions' and

Let me not therefore be condemned for having chosen my principal character from the purlieus of treachery and fraud, when I declare my purpose is to set him up as a beacon for the benefit of the unexperienced and unwary, who from the perusal of these memoirs, may learn to avoid the manifold snares with which they are continually surrounded in the paths of life; while those who hesitate on the brink of iniquity, may be terrified from plunging into that irremeable [*sic*] gulf, by surveying the deplorable fate of FERDINAND Count FATHOM.

Ending one's days as a highly respectable Yorkshire GP may not be the most 'deplorable' of fates, but for all his hard-boiled protestations – 'I look upon mankind to be in a state of nature; a truth which Hobbes has stumbled upon by accident' – Smollett was more than ready to make conventional moral points about the rewards of virtue and the penalties of vice. Contemporary novelists were often seen as sheep or goats: the sheep, keen on the elevation and instruction of their readers, tended to concentrate on exemplary and virtuous characters, to be studied and, ideally, imitated, whereas the goats described life as it was, both good and bad, and left the readers to draw their own conclusions. Smollett was by nature and inclination a goat, but he may well have been riled by the charges of 'lowness' aimed at his first two novels. Like Defoe in *Moll Flanders* and Fielding in *Jonathan Wild*, he aimed to document low life, but to do so in a way that pointed a moral without having to preach. The virtuous characters in *Count Fathom* – the long-suffering Renaldo, Fathom's oft-betrayed childhood friend, and his glutinous girlfriend Monimia – are almost Dickensian in their undiluted goodness, and duly receive their rewards, whereas until his sudden redemption, Fathom has more than a touch of Don Giovanni capering on the brink of hell. An unusual virtuous character, less saccharine than most, is the benign Jew Joshua Manassah, seen by some as a precursor of Riah in *Our Mutual Friend* and introduced, perhaps, to coincide with the controversial Jewish Naturalisation Bill of 1753.

Thackeray once said of Smollett that he 'did not invent much' but drew heavily on his own experiences, and the weakness of *Count Fathom* has been attributed to its relative paucity of direct observation. The Count seems more of an abstraction than a rounded character, but it is possible that he is based on the mysterious Count Saint-Germain, whom Smollett may have met when trying to elicit Lord Chesterfield's support for *The Regicide* in the 1740s.

In the year 1743 or thereabouts there came into England a person who called himself Count St Germain, which he owned was not his name, but would never own what was, nor give any account of himself, nor could it be discovered who he was. He had little or no colour, his hair and beard were extremely black.

He dressed magnificently, had several jewels, large remittances, but made no other figure,

Horace Walpole reported, adding that 'he is called an Italian, a Spaniard, a Pole; a somebody that married a great fortune in Mexico, and ran away with her jewels to Constantinople; a priest, a fiddler, a vast nobleman . . .' He was thought by some to be a French spy; he specialised in the manufacture and sale of luxury goods made from ersatz materials; like Fathom, he was said to have been a brilliant linguist, a traveller, a raconteur, an exquisite violinist and a talented composer; he had strong views on medical matters, and liked to distribute 'rejuvenation water' to his lady friends.

Whatever Count Fathom's pedigree, he failed to impress the reading public: so dismal was his reception that Smollett abandoned novel-writing for the next seven years. 'We are reading Count Fathom, a very indifferent affair,' the blue-stocking Mrs Delaney told her friend Mrs Dewes, not long after the novel appeared in the spring of 1753. Nor was it a money-spinner: William Johnston seems to have paid £120 for the copyright in Fathom, employing William Strahan to print the 1,000 or 1,250 copies standard for a commercially unexceptional novel, and there was a separate Dublin edition. To get away from the whole dispiriting business, Smollett set out for Scotland in June to visit friends and relatives. He went first to see his mother, who was living with his sister Jane and her husband, Alexander Telfer, in Scotstoun in Peeblesshire. According to John Moore, he began by playing a practical joke on the old lady, albeit of a benign, un-Pickle-like kind:

With the connivance of Mrs Telfer, on his arrival, he was introduced to his mother as a gentleman from the West Indies, who was intimately acquainted with her son. The better to support his assumed character, he endeavoured to preserve a very serious countenance, approaching to a frown; but while the old lady's eyes were riveted with a kind of wild and eager stare on his countenance, he could not refrain from smiling: she immediately sprung from her chair, and throwing her arms around his neck, exclaimed, 'Ah, my son! my son! I have found you at last!'

She afterwards told him, that if he had kept his austere look, and continued to *gloom*, he might have escaped detection some time longer; but your old roguish smile, added she, betrayed you at once.

He went on to stay with Alexander Carlyle in Musselburgh, and visited old friends in both Edinburgh and Glasgow. Back in Chelsea, he found himself homesick for Scotland. 'I do not think I could enjoy life with greater relish in any part of the world than in Scotland among you and your friends, and I often amuse my imagination with schemes for attaining that degree of happiness, which, however, is altogether out of my reach,' he told Carlyle on his return; and for all his admiration for Albion in *Count Fathom*,

> I am heartily sick of this land of indifference and phlegm where the finer sensations of the soul are not felt, and felicity is held to consist in stupefying port and overgrown buttocks of beef, where genius is lost, learning undervalued, and taste altogether extinguished, and ignorance prevails to such a degree that one of our Chelsea club asked me if the weather was good when I crossed the sea from Scotland . . .

Before long, no doubt, he settled back into the life of a paterfamilias and hard-working literary man; as he told Moore a year or two later, 'I live in the shade of obscurity, neglecting and neglected, and spend my vacant hours among a set of honest, phlegmatic Englishmen whom I cultivate for their integrity of heart and simplicity of manners . . .' The calm was deceptive, however: he was about to make a move that would place him at the very centre of London literary life, expose him to political in-fighting at its most brutal, and lead, in due course, to his quitting his adopted country, temporarily at first and finally for ever.

6

Critical Matters

Writing to John Moore in the summer of 1756, Smollett told his old friend that he had been brooding on 'a sort of academy of the belles letters, a scheme which will, one day, I hope be put in execution to its utmost extent'. Smollett's dream of an English equivalent to the Académie Française, founded in Paris in 1653 to codify, improve and regulate the French language, was to remain a pipe-dream, intrinsically alien, perhaps, to the pragmatic, bloody-minded spirit of the British; but it was widely shared by many of his contemporaries, and Dr Johnson's *Dictionary* – published the previous year, and the work of one man rather than a committee of dignitaries – had provided a practical manifestation of this near-universal urge. Dryden had pondered the notion late in the seventeenth century; zealous to monitor and standardise usage, grammar and vocabulary, Swift had, in 1712, published his 'Proposals for Correcting, Improving and Ascertaining the English Tongue'.

It was widely agreed that language should be codified and prescribed through grammars and dictionaries; the 'custom' to be followed should be common to all four nations of the British Isles – impenetrable local variations or dialects were frowned upon, in the written if not the spoken word – yet at the same time that of 'the most polish'd speakers . . . residing in the metropolis'. Such authorities would not confine themselves to semantics, however.

Smollett's imaginary academy, a government-sponsored body made up of 'sober and judicious' literary men, would establish a board of critics, 'according to whose censure, all books or authors, should either stand or fall'. Appealing to neo-classical notions of authority and immutable rules carved in stone, Fielding regretted in his *Covent Garden Journal* that 'the constitution of Aristotle, Horace, Longinus and Bossuet, under which the state of criticism so long flourished, has been entirely neglected and the government usurped by a set of fellows, entirely ignorant of all those laws'. Authorities should set the rules and the standards for the theatre and the decorative arts as well as for literature, and the poet William Collins advocated a definitive reviewing journal to be published under the auspices of the Clarendon Press in Oxford.

Such ideas seem, in retrospect, illiberal, censorious and over-prescriptive, but they reflect both the passion for ordering and classifying knowledge, and a fear of the potential anarchy unleashed by the collapse of the old system of court and aristocratic patronage, the rise of the professional author selling his wares in the open market, and the looming presence of the 'common reader', a character whom writers both exploited and disdained. Never, to his partial regret, the recipient of patronage or a government pension, Smollett was the embodiment of the diligent, unsubsidised writer, making his own way through the literary jungle; but, like so many of his contemporaries, he deplored what he saw as the overweening power and influence of booksellers and yearned for some kind of countervailing influence. But, as he wrote in the *Continuation* to his *Complete History of England*, such dreams were allergic to the spirit of the nation: 'No Maecenas appeared among the ministers, and not the least ray of patronage glimmered from the throne', and our native authors were denied 'the protection, countenance and gratification, secured in other countries by the institution of academies, and the liberality of princes.'

If Smollett's earlier dealings with prospective patrons were anything to go by, it was probably just as well. His urge to establish and elevate critical standards, and provide a record of all that was being published, was to take a far more practical form when, in March 1756, he published the first issue of the *Critical Review*, the

Times Literary Supplement of its day, and a magazine that would continue to be published until 1817. As with the Academy, the inspiration for a magazine devoted to new books had come from France, where the *Journal des Scavans* had been founded in 1665. Imitations of the *Journal* had appeared in late seventeenth-century London, designed to keep scholars up to date with listings of new books: Michael de la Roche's *Memoirs of Literature*, published between 1710 and 1717, had included short book reviews, and in the late 1720s John Wilford's *Monthly Catalogue* had provided a complete listing of new books, plus a one-sentence summary of their contents. Less scholarly readers looked out for short and highly selective book reviews in the *London Magazine* and in Edward Cave's hugely successful *Gentleman's Magazine*, which from 1751 provided brief summaries and descriptions as well as listing new titles. But those responsible for writing the reviews were regarded as so many hacks, and in *Tom Jones* Fielding, a not untypical author, warned 'all those critics to mind their own business, and not meddle with affairs or works, which no way concern them: for till they produce the authority by which they are constituted judges, I shall plead their jurisdiction'.

The first magazine to attempt an exhaustive survey of new books was Ralph Griffiths's *Monthly Review*, which was founded in 1749, continued publication until 1845, and was the precursor and rival to Smollett's *Critical Review*. Like so many eighteenth-century book-sellers, Griffiths was a self-made man, and a bit of a bounder. A Welsh Presbyterian, he had been apprenticed to a watchmaker in Shropshire before coming to London in his early twenties. After working in a bookshop on Ludgate Hill, he set up as a bookseller-cum-publisher on his own account, trading under the sign of the Dunciad in Paternoster Row. He wrote a history of the Forty-Five, but it was his publication of John Cleland's *Memoirs of a Woman of Pleasure* – better known as *Fanny Hill* – that brought him both noto-riety and riches. Cleland, a Scot, had written the novel while impris-oned in the Fleet for debt, and sent it to Fenton Griffiths, who passed it on to his brother Ralph; he, in turn, paid Cleland £20 for the copyright, published the novel under the imprint of 'G. Fenton', which didn't prevent him from being prosecuted for obscene and seditious libel, and was said to have made at least £10,000 from *Fanny Hill* in its complete and expurgated forms. Publication coincided with a small earthquake, leading the Bishop of London to wonder whether this had been sent to 'punish bawdy prints, bawdy books, and all other sins, natural or not'.

In May 1749 the *Daily Advertiser* announced the imminent publication of 'a new periodical work', the *Monthly Review*, which would provide 'an historical and critical account with proper abstracts of all the new books published in Great Britain and Ireland'. Like the *Critical Review* a few years later, it aimed to be a journal of record, covering the sciences, medicine, agriculture, geography, economics and philosophy as well as more literary matters such as history, biography, memoirs and travel; it dealt with new fiction, poetry and drama as well as learned works, reviewing as many titles as possible in each issue and reserving shorter notices for what seemed to be less important books. And whereas earlier book reviews had consisted of summaries coupled with extended quotations, the *Monthly* – like the *Critical* – aimed at a more analytical and critical approach. It was not the first to review fiction – Cave had provided summaries of new novels in the *Gentleman's Magazine* – but the fact that the *Monthly*, and then the *Critical*, were prepared to take seriously such a relatively new form did much to establish its literary credentials.

Griffiths printed 1,000 copies of the first issue, eighty pages long and priced at a shilling; by 1752 it was selling 1,250 copies of each monthly issue, and twice that number by 1760. Like the *Critical*, it was bought by individual subscribers and, more importantly, by institutions – universities, book clubs, literary and learned societies, circulating and subscription libraries. Griffiths's editorial team consisted of Cleland, a regular reviewer for the first two years of the magazine's existence, a Dissenting schoolmaster called William Rose, and John Ward, later the Vice-President of the Royal Society. His most eminent editorial assistant was Oliver Goldsmith, then in his late twenties, recently returned from his wanderings in Europe and failing to make his way in the medical world. He was paid £200 a year and provided with board and lodgings above the shop in exchange for editorial work and reviews of plays, poetry, travel books and works of natural history; he was expected to be on call from nine in the morning till two in the afternoon, and eventually moved on after complaining (or so it was said) that Mrs Griffiths interfered with his copy. Griffiths was a more intrusive and controlling editor than Smollett, and Mrs Griffiths seems to have been a bone of contention: Smollett was to ridicule 'the old gentlewoman who directs the *Monthly Review*', and Griffiths was once driven to declare that he could 'with the most sacred truth declare that there never was a single word written for the Review by a female pen' other than that wielded by the 'learned' Miss Carter of Deal.

Although relations between the two magazines were to become highly embattled – matters had not been helped by Griffiths's publication of 'Sir' John Hill's *Lady Frail* and *A Vindication of the Name and Random Peregrinations of the Family of Smallwits* – Smollett wrote his first reviews for the *Monthly*, including one of Cleland's *Memoirs of a Coxcomb*, and learned much from watching its editor at work. Smollett disapproved of Griffiths doubling up as a bookseller and as editor of the *Monthly* – all his publications received favourable notices, often written by the editor himself, and both Cleland and 'Sir' John Hill reviewed their own books in its pages – but seems to have had no compunction about reviewing William Smellie's *Theory and Practice of Midwifery* there, despite having prepared the book for press. As editor of the *Critical Review*, Smollett would prove both more easygoing and more severe than his rival: he allowed his contributors to say what they liked, to disagree among themselves and contradict each other, and more than once he had to apologise for a hurtful review, most notably to Samuel Richardson. Reviewers' own books were invariably praised, as was the custom of the age, but whereas Griffiths cheerfully advertised his own books and those of rival booksellers, Smollett, in his eagerness to keep booksellers at arm's length, refused their advertisements in the early days, and was perfectly happy to carry hostile reviews of works published by R. Baldwin, the bookseller responsible for initial publication of the *Critical*. But the differences between the magazines and their editors were not restricted to matters of editorial scruples. The *Monthly* was more sympathetic to the Dissenting, nonconformist traditions that had their origins in Bunyan and the Puritans of the seventeenth century; it had little time for formal doctrines or the classical traditions, and tended, in matters of politics, religion, science, literature and social and cultural trends, to favour the more liberal, tolerant and experimental end of the spectrum. The *Critical* was more conservative, worried by socially disruptive movements in society and the arts, keen on order and hierarchy, emphasising the weight and the value of authority and the classical tradition.

On the penultimate day of 1755, the *Public Advertiser* carried a notice announcing the forthcoming publication of a new literary review. Temporarily entitled *The Progress or Annals of Literature and the Liberal Arts*, it would not – like some unnamed competitors – be

> patched up by obscure hackney writers, accidentally enlisted in the service of an undistinguishing bookseller, but executed by a set of gentlemen whose characters and capacities have been universally approved and acknowledged by the public: gentlemen, who have long observed with indignation the productions of genius and dullness; wit and impertinence; learning and ignorance, confounded in the chaos of publication; applauded without taste, and condemned without distinction; and have seen the noble art of criticism reduced to a contemptible manufacture subservient to the most sordid views of avarice and interest, and carried on by wretched hirelings, without talent, candour, spirit or circumspection.

It would cover 'theology, metaphysics, physics, medicine, mathematics and the belles lettres' both in the British Isles and overseas, and would give 'an accurate description of every remarkable essay in the practical part of painting, sculpture, and architecture, that may do honour to modern artists of this or any other kingdom'. Its reviewers would be dedicated to 'reviving the true spirit of criticism': with 'no connexions to warp their integrity', the aim of these self-proclaimed 'enemies of dullness' was to 'befriend merit, dignify the liberal arts, and contribute towards the formation of a public taste, which is the best patron of genius and science'. Thwarted of dreams of an academy, a monthly review would do the job by other means.

The first issue was announced for February 1756 publication, but had to be delayed until March – by which time it had been renamed the *Critical Review*. Printed by Archibald Hamilton and published, to begin with, by R. Baldwin at the Rose in Paternoster Row, it was priced at a shilling and, at 96 pages, was some 16 pages longer than the *Monthly* – which immediately added another section to bring itself up to par. Each copy was bound in a dark blue wrapper carrying a table of contents – so setting a style that would last until the days of Cyril Connolly's *Horizon* and John Lehmann's *London Magazine*. Seventeen new books were reviewed, and short notices covered paintings, sculpture and foreign literature; on the last page, the anonymous editor apologised for any errors or lapses of taste, promising if necessary to 'kiss the rod of correction with great humility', and begged for the assistance and advice of 'the learned and ingenious of every denomination' and, in particular, 'the gentlemen of the two universities'. The *Critical*'s reviewers were shouldering grave responsibilities, the editor declared in the second issue, for 'the task of professed critics, who undertake to reform the taste of mankind, is like that of cleansing the Augean stables; they must not only wade through dunghills of dullness, but also be exposed to the stench and sting of all the vermin hatched amidst such heaps of noisesome pollution'.

'The Critical Review is conducted by four gentlemen of approved abilities, and meets with a very favourable reception,' Smollett told John Moore in the summer of 1756. Apart from Smollett himself, the four gentlemen consisted of Dr John Armstrong, the Reverend Thomas Francklin, and the ubiquitous Samuel Derrick. A friend of Wilkes, James Thomson and Charles and Fanny Burney, Armstrong was melancholy, witty, hard-drinking, arrogant and famously idle; Boswell was extremely fond of him, but amazed by his sloth, and a friend once remarked that 'I know not what is the matter with Armstrong, but he seems to have conceived a rooted aversion to the whole human race, except a few friends, which it seems are dead.' Trained as a physician in Edinburgh, he combined intermittent medical practice with literary endeavours. His best-known poem was entitled 'The Art of Preserving Health', and he was the author of *A Synopsis of the History and Cure of Venereal Diseases*; he bore a lasting grudge against Garrick for not staging a play he had written, which David Hume considered to be 'one of the worst pieces' he had ever had the misfortune of reading. He had been, for a time, Physician to the Hospital for Lame, Maimed and Sick Soldiers; while Physician to the Army in Germany he met Henry Fuseli, and effected introductions on the painter's behalf when he eventually moved to England. Smollett seems to have enjoyed a joshing relationship with his sardonic fellow-doctor. Armstrong couldn't understand his friend's liking for the haunches of venison sent up from the country by William Huggins, while Smollett was equally baffled by Armstrong's taste in veal: Smollett once told Wilkes that 'reading dull books and writing dull commentaries' was 'a task almost as disagreeable as dining with our friend Armstrong, when the wind blows from the east, on a loin of veal roasted with butter sauce'. Alexander Carlyle recalled a convivial dinner party in the City, attended by, among others, Smollett, William Robertson, John Home and Dr Blair the celebrated preacher, and how

> Smollett had given Armstrong a staggering blow at the begin-ning of dinner, by asking him some questions about his nose which was still patched on account of his having run it through the side-glass of his chariot when somebody came up to speak to him. Armstrong was naturally glumphy [*sic*], and this I was afraid would have silenced him all day. But he knew that Smollett loved and respected him, and soon recovered his good humour and became brilliant. Had not Smollett called him familiarly John, soon after his joke on his nose, he might have been silenced for the day.

But for all their mutual affection, Armstrong left the *Critical Review* after a year or two, worn out, no doubt, by his labours.

Thomas Francklin, on the other hand, was to remain with the review for a good twenty years. A playwright, a clergyman, a don and a translator of Sophocles, he bridged the gap between Grub Street and academia: his father had printed the *Craftsman*, which had hounded Walpole so mercilessly in the 1720s and 1730s; he himself was a Fellow of Trinity College, Cambridge, and the Professor of Greek at the university, and kept an editorial eye on books of a religious or theological bent. He also co-edited, with Smollett, an

English translation of the complete works of Voltaire, published in thirty-five volumes between 1761 and 1765, with a thirty-sixth bringing up the rear in 1769. Francklin specialised in translating Voltaire's dramatic works and the poetry, while Smollett – who probably combined some translating with overall editorial supervision – concentrated on the history and philosophy: he had translated 'Micromegas' in 1752, and may well have been responsible for *Details of the Crusades* and *A New Plan for the History of the Human Mind* as well. Smollett admired Voltaire, but was more than ready to point out his mistakes and tick him off at times as 'frivolous', 'unsatisfactory', 'invidious and unjust'. His running commentary in the accompanying editorial notes irritated William Kenrick in the *Monthly Review*: he deplored Smollett and Francklin as 'unknown and desperate bravoes' who had 'mangled' Voltaire's work, and described Smollett as 'a carping hypocrite, who with the strength of a boy would correct the labours of Hercules'.

Samuel Derrick, the fourth gentleman, was Grub Street incarnate. When Dr Johnson was asked whether Derrick or Christopher Smart was the better poet, he famously replied 'Sir, there is no settling the point of precedency between a louse and a flea' – displaying as he did so an uncharacteristic disloyalty towards his old friend Smart, a fellow-inhabitant of Grub Street who 'shewed the disturbance of his mind, by falling upon his knees, and saying his prayers in the street, or any other unusual place', but should not, Johnson once told Dr Burney, be locked away in the 'mad-house' since 'his infirmities were not noxious to society': he insisted on praying with him, for 'I'd as lief pray with Kit Smart as anyone else. Another charge was, that he did not love clean linen; and I have no passion for it.' Although he had been apprenticed a linen draper in his native Dublin, it seems unlikely that Derrick had enjoyed clean linen either after his arrival in London in 1751; he slept, as vagrants often did, on cold frames or in the streets before living for a time with the Smolletts in Chelsea, and must have been a regular at Smollett's Sunday lunches for assorted hacks. 'A little, lank Hibernian poet,' in Smollett's words, he was Boswell's 'first tutor in the ways of London, both literary and sportive': Boswell later confessed that 'I unluckily got acquainted with this creature when I was first in London, and after I found him to be a little blackguard pimping dog, I did not know how to get rid of him.' Though happy to use him as an intermediary when dealing with affronted authors, Richardson among them, Smollett seems to have been equally embarrassed by, and apologetic for, his association with Derrick. 'The little Irishman about whom you express some curiosity was my amanuensis, and has been occasionally employed as a trash reader for the Critical Review,' he told Moore, adding that 'you are not to number him among my companions, nor indeed does his character deserve any further discussion'. In 1763 he succeeded Beau Nash as Master of Ceremonies at Bath, and Dr Johnson observed that 'his being a literary man has got him all he has. It has made him king of Bath.' Like Quin, the old ham actor, he resurfaces in the Bath scenes in *Humphry Clinker*. Squire Bramble's niece Lydia, who doesn't share her uncle's dyspeptic view of Bath and its patrons, and is anyway inclined to think the best of those she encounters, describes him as 'a pretty little gentleman, so sweet, so fine, so civil, and polite, that in our country he might pass for the prince of Wales; then he talks so charmingly, both in verse and prose, that you would be delighted to hear him discourse; for you must know he is a great writer, and has got five tragedies ready for the stage . . .' Not long afterwards, the Master of Ceremonies tries to discipline Tabitha Bramble's bad-tempered dog, but it 'seemed to despise his authority, and displaying a formidable case of long, white, sharp teeth, kept the puny monarch at bay'.

Among those also involved with the *Critical* were Patrick Murdoch, a graduate of Edinburgh University, Fellow of the Royal Society, mathematician, clergyman, and the author of a life of James Thomson, who had died in 1748; and Oliver Goldsmith, a regular reviewer after his falling out with Ralph Griffiths and his wife, who had threatened to take him to court after a suit they had lent him had been spotted in a pawnshop window. Rather than pay him £2 a week, as Griffiths had done, Smollett paid him for copy provided at the going rate of two guineas a sheet; during his time at the *Critical*, he specialised in *belles-lettres*, leaving in 1759 to set up his own short-lived periodical, the *Bee*.

Of the 'four gentlemen', Smollett was far and away the most diligent and influential. Most of the real work of putting the magazine together was done by Smollett and his printer, Archibald Hamilton. A Scot who had left Edinburgh after the Porteous Riots of 1736, Hamilton had worked for the printer William Strahan, who may have introduced him to Smollett; like Strahan, he liked to combine printing with a certain amount of publishing, while keeping his name off the title page. Once on his own, he made enough money to be able to buy himself a coach: Dr Johnson approved, on the grounds that 'The sooner that a man begins to enjoy his wealth the better.' Hamilton and Smollett worked closely together, shunting between Chelsea and his print-shop in Chancery Lane with copy and proofs, and meeting once a week at Forrest's Coffee House in Charing Cross. A huge and convivial figure – a contemporary once described him as 'Tremendous Hamilton! of giant strength/ With crab-tree staff full twice two yards in length' – Hamilton was responsible for copy-editing, providing proofs, dealing with papermakers and supervising the production and printing of the magazine; Smollett dealt with contributors, and looked after the literary side of things. Much of the material was contributed by Smollett himself: he wrote some seventy reviews – about a third of the total text – for the first year's issues, and although he was unable, and unwilling, to keep up such an outflow, he probably contributed some 250 reviews, all unsigned, during his time with the *Critical*. But that was only part of the job. It was up to him to find contributors, cut and edit their reviews, make sure copy got to Hamilton in time, decide whether a particular book merited a long or a short review, make sure that proofs were corrected and returned quickly enough for the type to be distributed and re-used for the next sheet to be printed, and – since booksellers appear to have been lamentably slow in providing review copies – beg, borrow or even buy the books needed for review.

Easygoing as an editor, Smollett was to find himself increasingly irritated and embattled when caught in the cross-fire between reviewer and outraged author, and still more so since his enemies in the literary world were more than happy to see him take the blame. 'I was extremely concerned to find myself suspected of a silly, mean insinuation against Mr Richardson's writings, which appeared some time ago in the Critical Review, and I desired my friend Mr Millar to assure you in my name that it was inserted without my privity or concurrence,' he assured Samuel Richardson after the great novelist had been charged with long-windedness; he added that he had never once spoken of him or his writings with disrespect, but thought of him only with 'admiration and applause'.

As in the *Monthly*, the reviews followed the contemporary (and very sensible) fashion of quoting at length from the work under review, so allowing the reader to make up his own mind about the quality of the writing, and the mind behind it. For his own part, Smollett was a brutal reviewer at times. In the first year of publication he ridiculed Richard Rolt's *A New and Accurate History of South America* for suggesting that gold deposits in tropical countries were generated by the heat of the sun: the fact that historians like Rolt were a national disgrace – 'by their presumptuous ignorance they depreciate and degrade the character of their country' – was no bar to Smollett's pillaging their works for his contributions to the *Universal History*. At a more elevated level, he retained his belief in the *Critical's* importance in defining and maintaining literary rules and standards. His reviewers must learn 'to discriminate between personal and literary reputation; to distinguish the forced productions of necessity from the spontaneous growth of genius', and to see themselves as guides and arbiters: 'the regions of taste can be travelled only by a few,' he declared, and an idle, gullible and ignorant reading public had to be both protected and advised.

The best works, Smollett believed, conformed to the Horatian ideal of *utile et dulce*, in that they combined instruction with entertainment. Works that adhered to neo-classical rules were preferred to anything with a whiff of the Romantic, the disorderly or the subversive: fashions for the Gothic, for *chinoiserie*, for Rousseauesque notions of Romantic primitivism and the noble savage were abominated as disruptive of literary standards and the institutions of society by *Critical* reviewers – who included, at various times, David Hume, Dr Johnson, William Robertson, Alexander Carlyle, William Hunter and, possibly, Adam Smith and Samuel Richardson. Smollett himself probably reviewed more books about science and medicine than about any other subjects. He approved of practical science, giving favourable reviews to *Experiments on Bleaching* (a work reviewed elsewhere by Dr Johnson) and *The Manner of Securing Buildings from*

Fire; he resented the assumption that only Oxford and Cambridge were equipped to impart scientific knowledge, disapproved of experiments on animals, enjoyed scientific debates and controversies, was eager to denounce quacks and charlatans, gave his views on books about archaeology, geology, chemistry and physics, and displayed his conservative credentails in a dispute with Joseph Wharton:

> We think the author of the essay mistaken when he asserts that the sciences cannot exist but in a republic. The assertion savours too much of a wild spirit of democratic enthusiasm, which some people have imbibed from the writings of the Greeks . . . The sciences will always flourish where merit is encouraged; and this is more generally the case under an absolute monarchy, than in a republic.

Since no contributions were signed, it is impossible to know exactly who wrote what, but Smollett was widely assumed to be the author of the *Critical's ex cathedra* pronouncements and anathemas. Poetry was preferred in which 'the style is chaste and animated, the language pure, the sentiments grave and sublime'. Macpherson's best-selling bardic poem *Ossian*, originally described as a translation from the ancient Gaelic, enthusiastically promoted by John Home, but later revealed to be a contemporary concoction, was, for a time, thought superior to Homer and Virgil; Shakespeare, though highly regarded, was criticised for his lack of learning, his 'absurdities', his 'confusion' of tragedy and comedy, and his general failure to observe the rules. As far as fiction was concerned, Smollett seems to have been chastened by the attacks on his first two novels as 'low' examples of the genre. Not only should the novelist eschew 'wild imagination, little judgement, no probability', but 'the one great aim of novel writers ought to be, to inculcate sentiments of virtue and honour, and to inspire an abhorrence of vice and immorality'. Like Richardson and Dr Johnson, the *Critical* had come to believe that novels should 'serve as lectures of conduct, and introductions into life', since they 'convey the knowledge of vice and virtue with more efficacy than axioms and definitions'. They should exhibit exemplary characters, 'the highest and purest that humanity can reach' –

so debarring, on the spot, the frightful Peregrine Pickle with his perforated chamber-pot and hideous practical jokes. It was the duty of fiction reviewers to 'exhibit a succinct plan of every performance; to point out the most striking beauties and glaring defects; to illustrate those remarks with proper quotations; and to convey those remarks in such a manner, as might conduce to the entertainment of the public'. As a definition of the reviewer's job, it could hardly be bettered.

And, of course, Smollett the thwarted academician kept a beady eye on the use and abuse of language. 'Even our public orators, and authors, who ought to be her guardians, improvers, and refiners, are, from their negligence, likely to prove her corrupters,' he wrote, and it was up to *Critical* reviewers to watch out for grammatical howlers, the misuse of words, unseemly Gallicisms, and unwelcome neologisms like 'adroitly', 'insurgents', 'tramp' and 'abandonment'. Many of those associated with the *Critical* were, like its editor, Scots; and the Scots were both the worst offenders, and the best equipped to police the language. As the *Critical* declared in its opening year, 'every idle Scotchman who cannot, or will not, earn his bread by the employment to which he was brought up, commences author, and undertakes to translate books into a language of which he is entirely ignorant'; on the other hand, as David Hume once noted, 'a Scotsman who, by care and attention, has corrected all the vices of expression incident to his country, is the best critic whom one could have recourse to'. Hume, like Smollett, was desperately anxious to purge his writing and, if possible, his speech of 'those vicious forms of speech which are denominated Scotticisms'. In an appendix to his *Political Discourses*, published in 1752, he printed a list of Scotticisms with their English equivalents: his mortification was uncalled for, since in many cases – 'friends and acquaintances' for 'friends and acquaintance', 'nothing else' for 'no other thing', 'in the long run' for 'at long run' – the rude intruders from the north have long outlived their southern siblings, in much the same way as many of the Scottish words anathematised in the *Critical Review* ('succumb', 'adduce', 'phenomenon', 'rescind') and stigmatised in Dr Johnson's *Dictionary* ('giggle', 'hopeful', 'incarcerate', 'missive', 'placate', along with 'auld' and 'dirk') quickly joined the mainstream of the language.

Boswell, who tended to shun the company of his fellow-Scots in London, noted that 'although an Englishman often does not understand a Scot, it is rare that a Scot has trouble in understanding what an Englishman says'. The neurotic anxiety on the part of so many educated Scots on both sides of the Border to dilute or abandon their linguistic inheritance, both written and spoken, reflected a tendency, still current, to impose a London-based culture on a Britain that was now united politically as well as geographically, and a desire on the part of even the proudest Scots to be seen as Britons, and not be discriminated against or misunderstood because of their accents, or regarded as uncouth or barbarous provincials. Once behind his writing-desk, a North Briton took particular care to write an English that was free from the vulgarities and parochialisms allegedly inherent in regional or dialect forms of speech, and indistinguishable from that written in London and the ancient universities.

As Smollett would have discovered on his visit home, the eagerness with which some of his contemporaries sought to replace battlemented halls with Adam mansions, and matted beards with periwigs, was matched by the inclination to disown a past which William Robertson saw as representative of barbarism and religious fanaticism, and play down the Irish and Gaelic contribution to their country's history and culture. Sir John Clerk refused to accept that the Scots had originally come over from Ireland, and insisted that even the aboriginal inhabitants of the Highlands and islands had spoken a form of Anglo-Saxon; in the Lowlands, where the Gaelic tradition was far more diluted, Scots, or Lallands, was demoted or even obliterated as a written language, while surviving in spoken form. Smollett's Edinburgh friends – Carlyle, Hugh Blair, William Wilkie, William Robertson – identified themselves strongly with the London regime, and their eagerness to speak and write London or southern English coincided with the contemporary urge to standardise and codify the language. David Hume, who never lost his strong Scots accent, confessed that he and others like him remained 'unhappy in our accent and pronunciation', for 'notwithstanding all the pains I have taken in the study of the English language, I am still jealous of my pen. As to my tongue, you have seen that I regard it as totally desperate and irreclaimable.' He confessed, too, that those Scots who tried too hard were liable to end up feeling *déraciné*, unable, like him, to decide whether to settle in Edinburgh, Paris or London: 'few Scotsmen, that have had an English education, have ever settled cordially in their own country, and they have been commonly lost ever after to their friends'. At the height of the Scottish Enlightenment, when Voltaire had announced that 'It is to Scotland that we look for our idea of civilisation', and even Horace Walpole conceded that 'Scotland is the most accomplished nation in Europe', feelings of unease and inferiority persisted. 'At a time when we have lost our princes, our parliament, our independent government . . . and speak a very corrupt dialect of the tongue which we make use of, is it not strange, I say, that we should be the people most distinguished for literature in Europe?' Hume asked.

It was indeed, and in an effort to sort out the spoken language at least, the Irish actor Thomas Sheridan, father to the playwright, came to Edinburgh in 1761 to give a series of lectures on proper pronunciation to the city's Select Society, which had earlier lamented the fact that 'gentlemen educated in Scotland have long been sensible of the disadvantage under which they labour from their imperfect knowledge of the English tongue, and the impropriety with which they speak it'. Boswell, who advised his compatriots 'not to aim at absolute perfection in this respect', since 'a studied and factitious pronunciation, which requires perpetual attention and imposes perpetual restraint, is exceedingly disgusting', noted that, after attending Sheridan's course, the lawyer Alexander Wedderburn 'got rid of the coarse part of his Scottish accent, retaining only as much of the "native woodnote wild" as to mark his country; which, if any Scotchman should affect to forget, I should heartily despise him'. Roderick Random, on the other hand, has no trace of a Scots accent, and his creator was adamant about excising any hints of the same from the pristine pages of the *Critical Review*.

And yet, despite the best efforts of Smollett and his kind, Scottophobia was as rampant as ever, and Smollett was inevitably accused of running the *Critical Review* as a self-regarding and self-serving Scottish cabal. One Joseph Reed, whose book had been mauled in its pages, claimed that the review was run by 'a certain Caledonian quack, by the courtesy of England called a Doctor of

Physic', while an anonymous pamphleteer described Smollett as 'a Scotch adventurer in wit and physic, who hacks at *random* the reputation of his betters'. The malign, ubiquitous John Shebbeare savaged the review in his essay, 'The Occasional Critic, or the Decrees of the Scotch Tribunal in the Critical Rejudged', claiming that Smollett was prejudiced in favour of Scottish authors and gave them good reviews in return for 'very small gratuities', and comparing the *Critical* to an Edinburgh lavatory, the stench of which is 'very offensive to all gentlemen'. In reply, the *Critical* claimed, misleadingly, that 'of the five persons engaged in writing [it], only one is a native of Scotland', and, eager to distance itself from any hint of corruption, offered fifty guineas to anyone who could provide evidence that it was controlled or even swayed by the booksellers. But still the attacks continued.

> Scot with Scot, in damned close intrigue
> Against the Commonwealth of letters league

wrote the brutish clergyman poet and friend of Wilkes, Charles Churchill, despite the fact that his own early verse had been favourably reviewed in the *Critical*. Still worse doggerel was supplied by the anonymous author of 'Queries to the Critical Reviewers', published in 1763, the year in which an embattled and exhausted Smollett finally decided that enough was enough, and gave up the editorship:

> Ye judging Caledonian pedlars
>   That to a scribbling world give law
> Laid up, engaretted, like medlars,
>   Ripening to rottenness in straw
>
> Why d'ye suppose that the sublime
>   Should only rant beneath Scotch bonnets?
> Why humour, wit, poetic rhyme
>   Be only found in Scottish sonnets?

'The authors of the C. Review have been insulted and abused as a *Scotch Tribunal*,' Smollett told John Moore, adding that 'the truth is that there is no author so wretched but he will meet with countenance in England if he attacks our nation in any shape. You cannot conceive the jealousy that prevails against us. Nevertheless, it is better to be envied than despised.'

One 'wretched' author more than happy to savage Smollett and the *Critical* was Dr James Grainger, who had been a contemporary of Goldsmith in the medical school at Edinburgh University, and was a regular contributor to the *Monthly Review*. Grainger had already irritated Smollett by attacking William Hunter in the *Monthly*; Smollett sprang to his friend's defence in the *Critical*, and this in turn provoked a pamphlet, paid for by Griffiths and entitled *A Letter to the Author of the Critical Review*, in which Grainger charged its editor with lying, ignorance and libel. 'I thank you for all the kindness to me, and particularly for the last instance of your warm friendship: and I'm sorry that it must occasion some further trouble,' Hunter wrote to his old friend.

> That part of the letter that relates to yourself, I hope, will be flea'd and broil'd alive; for it is damn'd impertinent. He pretends it was the writer, not the man, that stuck with him. Your friends and mine say, they think you can, from your own knowledge, contradict him in this. I suppose you know that he was some time (about twelve months, as I have been told) out of his senses, and confined at Edinburgh . . .

Answering like with like in the *Critical*, Smollett compared Grainger to a cur, a reptile and a grub, and urged him to

> Endeavour to acquire a more perfect knowledge of your own importance. Confine yourself within your own sphere. Let not your vanity and self-conceit provoke you to deeds above your prowess. Let not the acrimony and gall of your disposition, stimulate you to kick against the pricks. The gentleman against whom you level your leaden arrows, is malice-proof.

Hunter was duly grateful, and suggested a meeting. 'Pray are you to be in town in a day or two?' he wondered. 'Could not you and Mrs

Smollett etc dine with us some day soon & I would send the chariot for you & with you?' At some point Smollett and Hunter may have had some kind of falling-out: a year after Smollett had rushed to his friend's defence, in the summer of 1758, Hunter referred to the matter in a letter to William Cullen, and to other angry rebuttals by Smollett on his behalf:

> Smollett I know not what to say of. He has great virtues, and has a turn for the warmest friendships. I have seen very little of him for some years. He is easily hurt, and is very ready to take prejudices. There had been a great shyness between him and me, which his very kind behaviour to me when I was attacked by Douglass, Pott and Monro, has as yet scarcely conquered . . .

But Grainger was far from done with Smollett and the *Critical Review*, and when his translation of the Elegies of Tibullus was shredded in its pages, he wrote to his fellow-translator, Bishop Percy of *Reliques* fame, to say that his vengeance would be terrible. Smollett, he told the Bishop, 'has a personal pique to me which upon this occasion has betrayed him into many false criticisms, delivered in very illiberal expressions'. His friends were urging him to 'enter the lists' with his 'unmannerly' opponent and administer a 'drubbing'. Perhaps the most irritating ingredient of Grainger's 'A Letter to Tobias Smollett MD Occasioned by his Criticism upon a Translation of Tibullus' was his deliberate reference to his enemy as 'Toby'; he also, for the first time, explicitly named Smollett as editor of the *Critical*. The *Critical*'s riposte, possibly written by Goldsmith, suggested that Grainger was one of those sponging hacks who soaked up Smollett's hospitality on Sundays, and then abused him behind his back:

> That Dr Smollett does keep house, and lives like a gentleman, divers authors of the age can testify, and among the rest Dr James Grainger, who has been hospitably treated at his table . . . All those who are acquainted with Dr Smollett know, that for every dinner he ever received, he has given fifty at least.

'What cannot venison do?' Grainger wondered in public after learning of William Huggins's gift of venison to the Smolletts – so intimating that the editor of the *Critical* was a soft touch when it came to printing a favourable review of his friend's translation of *Orlando Furioso*.

Never the man to mince his words, Smollett had described Grainger as 'an obscure hireling' who worked 'under the inspection and correction of an illiterate bookseller', compared with whom the editor of the *Critical* 'lived like a gentleman'. Warming to his theme, unapologetic about repeating himself and eager to take a swipe at the opposition, Smollett suggested elsewhere that, unlike the *Monthly*, his own review was not 'written by a pack of obscure hirelings, under the restraint of a bookseller and his wife, who presume to revise, alter, and amend the articles occasionally. The principal writers of the Critical Review are unconnected with book-sellers, unawed by old women, and independent of each other.' Griffiths, stung by the charges, retaliated in kind: the *Monthly*, he claimed, was 'not written by physicians without a practice, authors without learning, men without decency, gentlemen without manners, and critics without judgement'. Relations between the two month-lies deteriorated further when, in 1757, the *Critical*'s reviewers were slated in a pamphlet entitled *The Occasional Critic*. Smollett retali-ated with an unsigned letter in the *Critical* in which he assumed that Mrs Griffiths wore the trousers at the rival establishment, and reminded her that 'though we never visited your garrets, we know what sort of doctors and authors you employ as journeymen in your manufacture'. Another anonymous pamphlet, aptly entitled *The Battle of the Reviews*, referred to Smollett as 'Sawney MacSmallhead', a man 'quite tarnished by his vanity; a vanity always fulsome, and always odious'. 'Sawney' was an unflattering nickname applied to Scotsmen in general; the ponderous jokes about 'MacSmallhead' suggest the work of the poisonous 'Sir John' Hill, who had earlier cracked jokes about 'Mr Smallhead' in his 'Inspector' column.

Grub Street warfare quickly assumes a leaden, dated quality, and a little goes a very long way. Behind the front line, sales of the *Critical* slowly inched ahead, eventually settling at around 2,000–2,500 a month. Subscribers, individual or institutional, were to be found in Europe, India and North America as well as in the British Isles; wholesalers and distributors were entitled to a discount of 25 per cent. The *Critical* claimed to be quicker off the mark than the *Monthly* when it came to reviewing new books: Dr Johnson – whose own short-lived *Literary Magazine* was also announced in December 1755, and aimed to cover all the new books, rescue crit-icism from the booksellers, and be written by independent 'gentlemen' – once told George III, who had asked him which was the better of the two reviews, that 'the *Monthly Review* was done with most care, the *Critical* upon the best principles'. Later, after Smollett's death, he expanded on the matter:

> The Monthly Reviewers are not Deists; but they are Christians with as little Christianity as may be; and are for pulling down all establishments. The Critical Reviewers are for supporting the constitution, both in Church and State. The Critical Reviewers, I believe, often review without reading the books through; but lay hold of a topic, and write chiefly from their own minds. The Monthly Reviewers are duller men, and are glad to read the books through.

Whereas Johnson's *Literary Magazine* survived for a mere three years – he soon lost interest, and it became more political and less literary after his departure – the *Critical* began, very slowly, to pay its way in the world. 'Smollett imagines that he and I may both make fortunes by this project of his: I'm afraid he is too sanguine, but if it should turn out according to his hopes, farewell physic and all its cares for me and welcome dear tranquillity,' the indolent Armstrong told Wilkes two months before the *Critical* was launched. To edit a literary magazine and make a living from it is the most alluring of pipe dreams: Smollett may have given his services free for the first year or two, and such funds as were available were depleted still further by the heavy initial costs of advertising in the London, Scottish and provincial papers, and by the free distribution of the first issue. Smollett probably began to make some money from the *Critical* in 1762, by which time, as he told Moore, 'the laborious part of authorship I have long resigned. My constitution will no longer allow me to toil as formerly.' His health, never strong, began to replace money worries as the leitmotif of his letters, and was worsened by an apparent inability to turn work down, however detrimental its effects on his well-being and his family life; and for all the vigour and apparent insouciance of his adversarial ripostes, the viciousness and ingratitude of Grub Street life began to take its toll. His brief and ineffectual foray into politics, and his feud with his former friend, John Wilkes, were to prove the breaking-point; in the meantime, as he told John Moore in the autumn of 1758,

> I am equally averse to the praise and censure that belong to other men. Indeed, I am sick of both and wish to God my circumstances would allow me to consign my pen to oblivion. I really believe in my conscience that mankind grows every day more and more malicious. I have taken some pains to live like an honest, inoffensive man; I will venture to say that nothing base or dishonourable can be justly charged upon my character. Yet I am daily persecuted by the most malicious slanders merely because I have written with some success.

To a correspondent in Jamaica he complained that

> If I go on writing as I have proceeded for some years, my hand will be paralytic, and my brain dried to a snuff. I would not wish my greatest enemy a greater curse than the occupation of an author, in which capacity I have toiled myself into an habitual asthma, and been baited like a bear by all the hounds of Grub Street . . . I have been abused, reviled, and calumniated for satires I never saw; I have been censured for absurdities of which I could not possibly be guilty.

'My constitution,' he went on, 'is quite broken. Since last May I have hardly enjoyed one day of health. I am so subject to colds and rheums that I dare hardly stir from my own house, and shall be obliged to give up all the pleasures of society, at least those of tavern society, to which you know I have always been addicted.' All was not well behind his increasingly urbane façade. As John Moore later wrote of his friend in his capacity as editor, 'However adequate his taste and judgement in literary matters may have been for such an undertaking, it certainly was not suitable to a man of his temper and acute sensibility, as it exposed him to continual attacks from authors whose performances were censured, or, in their opinion, not sufficiently praised in the Review.' On the assumption, perhaps, that troubles never come singly, Smollett burdened himself still further by starting yet another magazine; and, at the end of that same year, he was to find himself in prison for libelling an irascible ghost from his past.

'At present I am so enveloped in a variety of perplexing schemes and deliberations that I have neither time to consider, nor leisure to explain, my sentiments or the manner in which the new magazine is to be executed and improved,' Smollett told William Huggins in February 1760. A mass of poems and essays had been submitted, but 'If you have any detached pieces which you think will gratify the general taste of magazine readers, we shall receive them with all due acknowledgement.' Three months later he was writing on similar lines to Samuel Richardson, wondering whether the great man could 'favour our magazine with any loose essay lying by you which you do not intend for another sort of publication'.

The use of the world 'magazine' in both letters was enough to suggest that he was not referring to the *Critical Review*. Magazines and periodicals were shorter and, at sixpence each, cheaper than the more heavyweight reviews; they were, by definition, 'miscellanies', happy to snap up trifles that happened to be languishing on the desks of eminent authors. Published by John Newbery, printed by Archibald Hamilton, edited by Tobias Smollett and boasting a royal licence, the *British Magazine*, subtitled 'The Monthly Miscellany for Ladies and Gentlemen', was designed to make money and since, unlike Goldsmith's hapless *Bee*, it survived for seven years and notched up sales of some 3,000 per issue, it may well have eased the Smollett finances, already boosted by the phenomenal success of the *Complete History of England*. The first issue was devoted, warmly, to William Pitt, whose 'incorruptible integrity' and brilliance as a war leader were singled out for special praise. Smollett insisted on retaining the copyright in the magazine and its contents, which included a familiar mixture of articles, fables, poems, stories and telegraphic book reviews (*The Life and Adventures of an Animal* was dismissed as 'Very dull, and very obscene'). He also contributed several anonymous poems, including 'Ode to Sleep', 'Ode to Mirth' and 'Ode to Blue-eyed Ann', composed for his wife:

> When the rough north forgets to howl,
> And ocean's billows cease to roll:
> When Lybian sands are bound in frost,
> And cold to Nova Zembla's lost;
> When heav'nly bodies cease to move,
> My blue-eyed Ann I'll cease to love.
>
> No more shall flowers the meads adorn,
> Nor sweetness deck the rosy thorn,
> Nor swelling buds proclaim the spring,
> Nor parching heats the dog-star bring,
> Nor laughing lilies paint the grove,
> When blue-eyed Ann I cease to love.
>
> No more shall joy in hope be found,
> Nor pleasures dance their frolic round,
> Nor love's light god inhabit earth,
> Nor beauty give the passion birth,
> Nor heart to summer sunshine cleave,
> When blue-eyed Nanny I deceive.
>
> When rolling seasons cease to change,
> Inconstancy forgets to range;
> When lavish May no more shall bloom,
> Nor gardens yield a rich perfume;
> When nature from her sphere shall start,
> I'll tear my Nanny from my heart.

Smollett's helpers on the new magazine included Samuel Derrick, some of whose verses were published there, and Oliver Goldsmith, who contributed stories, oriental fables, political satire and literary criticism: his oriental tale, 'Omrah', appeared in the first issue, while 'The History of Miss Stanton' provided the germ for what became *The Vicar of Wakefield*. Samuel Richardson seems to have reacted favourably – 'When I first heard that an author of distinguished abilities had submitted himself to the task of furnishing out a new magazine, it gave me great pleasure,' he told Smollett – and Dr Johnson graciously consented to the reprinting of his 'Idler' essay on 'The Bravery of English Common Soldiers'. Smollett and Johnson were alike in their addiction to the literary life and in their conservative cast of mind, but disagreed on such contentious issues as luxury, the merchant classes and booksellers, whom Johnson considered to be 'generous, liberal-minded men'. Fresh from compiling his *Dictionary*, he may have taken a dim view of Smollett's plans for an academy of letters, and he may have resented his possible portrayal as the President of the College of Authors in *Peregrine Pickle*; he was a friend of the irascible Grainger, and seems not to have been best pleased by the *Critical's* review of his own *Rasselas*, sending the printer – though not the editor – a 'petulant card' to that effect; but although the two men would never be close, they probably liked and respected one another. Johnson warned Smollett, when writing his *Complete History of England*, not to rely too much on the parliamentary reports he had written, as a young man, for Cave's *Gentleman's Magazine*, on the grounds that he had made up a great deal of them; and in the spring of 1759, nine months before the appearance of the *British Magazine*, Smollett made a much-valued intervention on Johnson's behalf, during the course of which he bestowed upon him one of the epithets by which he is best remembered. 'I am again your petitioner on behalf of that great Cham of literature, Samuel Johnson,' he wrote to Wilkes, the MP for Aylesbury and a man with good political connections, not least on the Admiralty Board:

> His black servant, whose name is Francis Barber, has been pressed on board the Stag frigate, Capt. Angel, and our lexi-cographer is in great distress. He says the boy is a sickly lad of a delicate frame, and particularly subject to a malady in his

throat which renders him very unfit for his majesty's service. You know what matter of animosity the said Johnson has against you, and I dare say you desire no other opportunity of resenting it than that of laying him under an obligation . . .

Wilkes had a word in the right ears, and Francis Barber was restored to Dr Johnson's service. One of the most touching, and celebrated, scenes in Boswell's *Life* describes the meeting, engineered by Boswell, between Wilkes and Johnson, who had always regarded the former editor of the *North Briton* as the worst kind of demagogue and sub-versive influence; but by then Smollett was dead, and his own close friendship with Wilkes had long before evaporated in acrimony and public abuse. In the meantime, however, he wrote to his raffish friend to say that 'Your generosity with respect to Johnson shall be the theme of our applause and thanksgiving.'

Poems excepted, Smollett contributed a multi-part 'History of Canada' to the *British Magazine*, but the whole venture was best remembered for – and may well have been created for – the serial-isation, in twenty-five monthly chapters, of his new novel, *The Life and Adventures of Sir Launcelot Greaves*. For many years it was claimed, erroneously, that *Launcelot Greaves* was the first novel to be seri-alised in a magazine in this country. Magazines had been publishing fiction, ranging from 100-word fables to full-length stories of 5,000 words or more, since the seventeenth century; *Robinson Crusoe* was serialised in the *Original London Post*, but only after publication in volume form, and abridged versions of both *Rasselas* and *Candide* were published in London magazines. *Launcelot Greaves* differed from its predecessors in that it first appeared in serial form, and Smollett, too busy to take the time needed to write a new novel in one fell swoop, anticipated Dickens, Trollope and Thackeray by writing the novel as he went along, making sure that each chapter ended, in principle at least, on a suitably cliff-hanging note. In his *Lives of the Novelists*, Sir Walter Scott claimed that Smollett wrote part of the novel, 'with very little premeditation', while staying with George Home in Berwickshire, and that 'when post-time drew near, he used to retire for half an hour, to prepare the necessary quantity of copy, which he never gave himself the trouble to correct, or even to read over'. Scott may have been instinctively right about Smollett's casual approach, but since George Home was only twenty at the time, it is unlikely that he was Smollett's host: but Smollett did make a trip to Scotland in 1760, staying with Alexander Telfer and being made a Burgess and Guild Brother of the City of Edinburgh.

Although it has elements of satire which may be of interest to historians of the period – an account of a country election, not dissimilar to the Eatanswill election in *The Pickwick Papers*; strong views on the general undesirability of private lunatic asylums, and the conditions endured by inmates; an insight, based on Smollett's own experiences, of life in the King's Bench Prison; familiar Smollettian swipes at doctors, lawyers and Grub Street hacks – *Launcelot Greaves* is so feeble, and so dull, that no sensible modern reader will pluck it from the shelves. There was, at the time, a mild fashion for Quixotic novels, among them Charlotte Lennox's *Female Quixote* and Richard Graves's *Spiritual Quixote*, and Sir Launcelot is a noble-minded but faintly half-witted young man who, clad in a suit of rusty armour and accompanied by his Sancho Panza-like retainer, Crabshaw, rides about England on his steed Bronzomarte, putting the world to rights and pining for the fair Aurelia. Among those encountered between Newark and London are Captain Crowe, the last of Smollett's good-hearted nautical windbags; the corrupt and repellent local JP, Mr Gobble, thought by some to be based on Ralph Griffiths on account of his overweening wife; Tom Clarke, a young lawyer 'whose goodness of heart even the exercise of his profession had not been able to corrupt', whose well-meaning, strangulated efforts to use long and important-sounding words give Smollett a welcome opportunity to ridicule the incomprehensibility and pomposity of legal jargon, and lament the debasement of language; and the misanthrope Ferret, based on his old enemy John Shebbeare, whose 'eyes were small and red, and so deep set in the sockets, that each appeared like the unextinguished snuff of a farthing candle, beaming through the horn of a dark lanthorn'. It is a memorable image in an unmemorable book, and for all his loathing of Shebbeare, Smollett used Ferret to articulate political views which he shared with his old enemy. In a series of 'Letters to the People of England', Shebbeare – like Ferret – attacked the policies which Smollett's erstwhile hero, William Pitt, had earlier denounced but now, as a loyal member of the government, assiduously promoted during the course of the Seven Years War: the setting up of a militia or territorial army, the use of Hessian and Hanoverian mercenaries in the British army, higher taxes, a bloated national debt, excessive deference to the interests of the Electorate of Hanover, and an alliance with Frederick the Great. After Shebbeare had attacked the House of Hanover with particular venom in his Sixth Letter, a general warrant was issued for his arrest, together with the printer and publisher. Shebbeare was found guilty of seditious libel, fined £5, and sent to prison for three years. He was also ordered to stand in the pillory at Charing Cross. One of the under-sheriffs was a good friend of the arch-hack: Shebbeare arrived at Charing Cross in a smart coach instead of a prison cart, and, rather than crouch, he was allowed to stand upright in the pillory while an Irishman in livery held an umbrella over his head to shield him from the rain. After half an hour in the stocks he was driven back to the King's Bench Prison, where he resumed work on his *History of the Sumatrans*.

Although the *Critical Review* was suitably polite about its editor's latest work, the *Monthly* thought it 'unworthy the pen of Dr Smollett'. Rather more complimentary was Goldsmith's account in the *Public Ledger* of February 1760 of a 'wow-wow' or gathering in a country pub, at which

> An Oxford scholar, led there by curiosity, pulled a new magazine out of his pocket, in which he said there were some pieces extremely curious, and that deserved their attention. He then read the adventures of Sir Launcelot Greaves to the entire satisfaction of the audience, which being finished, he threw the pamphlet on the table: that piece, gentlemen, says he, is written in the very spirit and manner of Cervantes, there is a great knowledge of human nature, and evident marks of the master in almost every sentence; and from the plan, the humour, and the execution, I can venture to say that it comes from the pen of ingenious Dr———. Everyone was pleased with the performance, and I was particularly gratified in hearing

all the sensible part of the company give orders for the *British Magazine*.

As a puff for the novel and the *British Magazine* it could not have been bettered.

Some six months before Sir Launcelot began to creak his way through the pages of the *British Magazine*, the Seven Years War had intruded on Smollett's professional and domestic life in the unwelcome form of a libel writ, issued by a litigious and irascible admiral incensed by a review in the *Critical*. This was not the first time an admiral had engaged Smollett's interest. In June 1756, when the *Critical* was in its infancy, and the war, then in its early stages, seemed to consist of a series of disasters, the hapless Admiral Byng had failed to relieve St Philip's Fort in Minorca, which was under siege by superior French forces, and was eventually captured by them. Anson, the First Lord of the Admiralty, concentrated his energies on guarding the Channel against the French, and was not prepared to send warships to Byng's assistance. Desperate to divert blame from their inept handling of the war, the Newcastle administration prompted ministerial hacks and pamphleteers to whip up a frenzy of indignation against the unhappy admiral: as Smollett observed in his *Continuation* to his *Complete History of England*, Byng 'had never met with any occasion to signalize his courage', but 'agents were employed to vilify his person in all public places of vulgar resort; and mobs were hired in different parts of the capital to hang and burn him in effigy'. Byng was court-martialled and condemned to death – according to Smollett, he displayed 'the most cheerful composure' at his trial – and although Newcastle had by then passed the conduct of the war on to Pitt, who was to prosecute it in a far more forceful manner in his capacity as Secretary of State for the Southern Department, the new administration decided not to exercise leniency. Voltaire famously remarked that Byng had been executed '*pour encourager les autres*', and both Dr Johnson and Smollett felt that he had been used as a scapegoat. 'Tho' I never dabble in politics, I cannot help saying that there seems to have been no treachery in delivering up St Philip's fort, nor even in the scandalous affair with the French fleet, which was owing to the personal timidity of our admiral, who is at present the object of public detestation,' Smollett told John Moore. 'Indeed,' he continued, revealing his obsessive fear and hatred of mob hysteria, 'the people seem to be in a ferment, and there are not wanting rascally incendiaries to inflame their discontent so that in a populace less phlegmatic the consequence would in all probability be very mischievous . . .'

Pitt's great wartime achievements were in India, Canada and the West Indies, where he immeasurably expanded the British Empire at the expense of the French; but even under his leadership, European operations tended to go adrift. In the summer of 1757, Britain's most important ally on the Continent, Frederick II of Prussia, later known as 'the Great', put pressure on the British government to land troops on the coast of France, in the hope that this would lead to a lightening of French pressure on his own beleaguered forces. The alliance with Frederick was not universally popular in Britain, but British troops in Germany under the command of the Duke of Cumberland would also be the beneficiaries of a 'second front'. A year or two earlier, Robert Clerk, an officer in the Engineers, had called in at Rochefort, on the north-west coast of France, on his way home from Gibraltar, and he now suggested to those in authority that this might be the ideal place in which to mount a combined naval and military operation. George II approved the idea, and appointed Sir John Mordaunt, Henry Conway and Edward Cornwallis to joint command. Anson put Sir Edward Hawke in charge of the naval side of the business, with Admirals Knowles and Broderick lending support. Joseph Thiérry, a French Protestant and a former pilot in the French navy, provided a detailed account of the approaches to Rochefort, with particular emphasis on the difficulties of navigating the River Charante, the fortifications bristling on the isle of Aix, and the possibility of landing troops on Fort Fouras, opposite Aix: both Clerk and Thiérry stressed the importance of speed in attack, and recommended the use of scaling ladders. At a ministerial meeting attended by Pitt, Newcastle and Admiral Knowles, it was decided to press ahead; and after some delay in leaving harbour at Cowes, the fleet made its way across the Channel. The island of Aix was captured, but Fort Fouras, which guarded the approach to Rochefort, proved impregnable; a storm blew up, the admirals decided to abandon the attempt, and the fleet limped back to Spithead. It had been an expensive and humiliating failure, and although Sir John Mordaunt was acquitted at his court-martial, those involved were exposed to public obloquy; the most thin-skinned of them all was Smollett's old acquaintance, Vice-Admiral Charles Knowles, who, alone of the naval men involved, had been reprimanded by the Commission of Inquiry.

Knowles had done very well for himself in the years since Cartagena. In 1746 he was appointed Governor of Louisbourg, recently taken from the French; the following year he was made a rear-admiral, and Commander-in-Chief in Jamaica. A splenetic character, with the retroussé nose of a petulant pug, he was contentious and controversial, and not averse to litigation. Several captains who had served under him in Jamaica accused him of having given 'great advantage to the enemy by engaging in a straggling line and late in the day, when he might have attacked much earlier' during an abortive engagement with a Spanish fleet, and of having then 'transmitted a false and injurious account' of the proceedings to the Admiralty; he in turn accused his captains of 'bashfulness, to give it no harsher term'. Knowles and the upstart captains were court-martialled; Knowles was reprimanded, and a flurry of duels followed, in the course of which a Captain Holmes exchanged shots with the furious admiral. In 1752 Knowles started a four-year term as Governor of Jamaica; he offended the locals by insisting on the supreme jurisdiction of the Westminster Parliament, and by moving the seat of government from Spanish Town to Kingston.

Outraged by his public humiliation after the Rochefort fiasco, Knowles sought to defend himself in a thirty-page pamphlet entitled *A Genuine Account of the Late Great Expedition*. Fort Fouras, he claimed, was inaccessible by sea, so his failure to take it was irrelevant; nor could he understand why he had been singled out for blame by the Commission of Inquiry. 'Hard indeed is my fate,' he complained, and this 'after forty-one years constant and faithful service to the Navy'. Smollett reviewed his pamphlet in the *Critical Review*, and decided to deliver a broadside.

'If Vice-Admiral K——s had recollected a certain unsavoury proverb, perhaps he would have saved himself the trouble of stirring up the remembrance of a dirty expedition, which has stunk so abominably in the nostrils of the nation; he might likewise have been more cautious of disturbing the quiet in which his own character was suffered to rust,' he declared. After comparing the Admiral to a cat which always manages to land on its feet, he became *ad hominem* in the most virulent eighteenth-century manner. 'We have heard of a man who, without birth, interest, or fortune, has raised himself from the lowest paths of life to an eminent rank in the service; and if all his friends were put in the strappado, they could not define the quality or qualities to which he had owed his elevation,' he wrote. It seemed unlikely that the Admiral had any friends, but friendless or not, 'for a series of years he has been enabled to sacrifice the blood, the treasure, and the honour of his country to his own ridiculous projects'. Knowles was, Smollett concluded, 'an admiral without conduct, an engineer without knowledge, an officer without resolution, and man without veracity'. 'An ignorant, assuming, officious, fribbling pretender; conceited as a peacock, obstinate as a mule, and mischievous as a monkey', the Admiral had 'played the tyrant with his inferiors, the incendiary among his equals, and commanded a sq——n occasionally for twenty years, without having ever established his reputation in the article of personal courage'. Knowles, he concluded, 'needs not be surprised at his being laid aside after forty years constant and faithful service'.

According to a memoir of Knowles written some forty years after the event, the Admiral summoned Smollett, and asked how he had offended him; Smollett apologised, and nothing more would have been said had Knowles not been urged on by Smollett's old antagonist in court, Alexander Hume Campbell, and his fellow-Scot William Murray, first Earl of Mansfield, the Chief Justice of the King's Bench and the man for whom Robert Adam had designed Kenwood House, on the edge of Hampstead Heath: Hume Campbell, by now the Lord Register of Scotland, died in his house in Curzon Street in the summer of 1760, no doubt to Smollett's great relief. Given Knowles's prickly demeanour and litigious nature, this meeting seems unlikely, and, a mere ten days after he had written to Wilkes on behalf of Francis Barber, Smollett was once again begging a favour from his friend. 'It is not, I believe, unknown to you that Admiral Knowles has taken exception at a paragraph in the Critical Review of last May and commenced a prosecution against the printer,' he told Wilkes in March 1759. Various friends of Smollett's had promised to have a word with the offended sea-dog, and if Wilkes could weigh in as well, that might tip the balance: but 'if the affair cannot be compromised, we intend to kick up a dust and die hard'. If the 'foolish admiral' had any regard for his own interests, he would surely withdraw. A month later, Smollett thanked Wilkes for 'the pains you have taken to pacify our incensed admiral, who is, it seems, determined to proceed to trial'. By October, matters were looking worse. 'K—— and his friends talk of nothing but heavy fines and imprisonment': would it be possible, Smollett wondered, to obtain from the Attorney-General a writ of *nolle prosequi*, whereby the plaintiff would withdraw all or part of his suit, while retaining the right to obtain any damages he might have sustained as a result of the libel? If so, would Wilkes be able to intervene with Pitt on his behalf?

Deemed a disruption of the peace, Smollett's libel was a criminal rather than a civil case, and there was no way in which he could escape prosecution. Ordered by the Sheriff of Middlesex to 'have his body before us at Westminster', he was brought to trial before Lord Mansfield, a former Solicitor-General and Attorney-General who had been appointed Chief Justice of the King's Bench in 1756, and would remain *in situ* until 1788. Smollett's case was heard in November 1760, in the grand if daunting medieval setting of Westminster Hall, where the Jacobite peers had been tried and condemned after the Forty-Five. Knowles had taken out an action for seditious libel against both the printer of the *Critical Review* and the theoretically anonymous author of the offending piece, but had declared himself ready to abandon his case against Archibald Hamilton if he would disclose the reviewer's name. Smollett had instructed his counsel to take up this offer, since 'my humanity and friendship were interested for the printer whom I had unwillingly involved in trouble, and I thought I could not in conscience do too much for his indemnification'. Hamilton had, in fact, already gone on trial, but was acquitted when Smollett stepped forward to shoulder the blame; and now the author of the piece was left alone to face the charges. Smollett wrote Lord Mansfield a long 'letter of appeal', explaining that he had never intended to show any contempt of court, and that he was more than ready to pay the Admiral's costs: this may have been read out in court by Smollett or his lawyer, and had a mitigating effect in the opinion of the great jurist Sir William Blackstone, the first Vinerian Professor of English Law at Oxford, a future Solicitor-General, and the author of the vast and definitive *Commentaries on the Laws of England*.

'I beg to be indulged with a few words in justification of some parts of my conduct which I apprehend have been misrepresented and misunderstood,' Smollett told his fellow-Scot, now best remembered as the father of commercial law. He may well have appeared before Mansfield earlier in the year, since he apologised for his unwonted and seemingly disrespectful silence ever since, but 'My being produced in the character of a delinquent before such an awful tribunal had such an effect upon my spirits that I was really deprived of the power of utterance.' After Knowles had withdrawn his case against Hamilton, Smollett had found himself 'suddenly ordered to appear in court so contrary to my expectation so much against my will that I was never so surprised and mortified in the whole course of my life'. Quite why he should have been so thrown remains unclear, but 'far from being in a condition to shew any contempt for the law or the prosecutor on that occasion I was for some minutes so discomposed that all my faculties were suspended'. Not only had he paid 'a considerable sum of money' towards the Admiral's costs, but – and this must have been a doubly bitter pill to swallow – he had asked Knowles's pardon 'in the terms dictated by his own friend the Lord Register'.

For all his eloquence, Smollett was fined £100, sentenced to three months in the King's Bench Prison, and bound over to keep the peace for seven years, paying over £500 as security for his good behaviour. Smollett was to take revenge on Knowles in *The Adventures of an Atom*, published after the seven years had lapsed; and the whole unhappy business merely confirmed him in his low opinion of the law. 'What can be more repugnant to the principles of justice than the undistinguishing institution which decrees the same penalty against the felon who robs his neighbour of five shillings, and the execrable homicide who murders his benefactors?' he wrote in his *Complete History of England*; it would be wiser, perhaps, to trust in a benevolent aristocrat like Launcelot Greaves, who could 'act as a coadjutor to the law, and even to remedy evils which the law cannot reach; to detect fraud and treason, abase insolence, mortify pride, discourage slander, disgrace immodesty, and stigmatize ingratitude'. In the meantime, the Dublin publisher George Faulkner told Samuel Derrick, 'The Press hath received a fatal wound through the sides of Dr Smollett . . .'

Smollett spent eleven weeks in the King's Bench Prison, which had been built only two years earlier in St George's Fields, a mile or so south of Westminster. Surrounded by a thirty-foot wall, it contained comfortable quarters for better-off prisoners like Smollett. According to *Launcelot Greaves*, chapters of which were written there, it

> appears like a neat little regular town, consisting of one street, surrounded by a very high wall, including an open piece of ground which may be termed a garden, where the prisoners take the air, and amuse themselves with a variety of diversions. Except the entrance, where the turnkeys keep watch and ward, there is nothing in the place that looks like a jail, or bears the least colour of restraint . . . Here are butchers-stands, chandlers-shops, a surgery, a tap-house well frequented, and a public kitchen in which provisions are dressed for all the prisoners, at the expense of the publican. Here the voice of misery never complains, and, indeed, little else is to be heard but the sounds of mirth and jollity. At the farther end of the street, on the right hand, is a little paved court leading to a separate building, consisting of twelve large apartments, called state-rooms, well furnished, and fitted up for the reception of the better sort of crown-prisoners; and on the other side of the street, facing a separate division of ground, called the common side, is a range of rooms occupied by prisoners of the lowest order, who share the profits of a begging-box, and are maintained by this practice, and some established funds of charity.

Not all reports on life in the King's Bench were as favourable. In a pamphlet devoted to the incarceration there of the irascible Philip

Thicknesse, also in for a libel, Francis Vernon, the Admiral's nephew, said that he had heard

> an account so very opposite to that given by a celebrated author, in the adventure of Launcelot Greaves, that I cannot avoid embracing this occasion to express my surprise, that a man, who, if I mistake not, was himself a prisoner there, should have drawn a picture so very unlike the original. For, though there is a large, handsome, airy house, for the better sort of prisoners, called the State House, the upper part of which commands a fine prospect; yet the avenues to it are characteristic enough of a gaol, and exhibit so many sons and daughters of woe, that a man must be void of all the sensible and susceptible emotions, of humanity and benevolence, who can eat, drink, and sleep, with any degree of content, amidst such a multitude of unfortunate people on one side, and such a banditti of reprobates on the other.

Vernon's account certainly seems the more plausible, but if he had read *Roderick Random* he may well have been prejudiced against Smollett on his uncle's account.

The fact that Shebbeare was a fellow-prisoner can hardly have cheered Smollett's spirits; altogether more welcome were visits from Garrick, Wilkes, Dr Macaulay, William Hunter, Archibald Hamilton and the indolent John Armstrong. When Smollett was released, he found waiting for him in Chelsea a letter from the warm-hearted Huggins, hoping that 'this finds my inestimable friend at his own fireside surrounded by his enraptured family'. 'I have not been so deeply affected these many years as I was when I received your last favour,' Smollett replied, adding that 'even my eyes overflow, with tenderness, when I now review the contents'. Huggins may well have offered the Smolletts the use of a suite of rooms at Headly Park, his country house in Hampshire; but he himself was unwell, and Smollett felt unable to take up the offer. Smollett told his good friend that the 'bells of Chelsea' had rung out to celebrate his deliverance. 'I can safely say that I never was more affected by the loss of the nearest relation than I should be upon losing Mr Huggins whom I have ever loved with the most cordial affection,' Smollett told Huggins's son-in-law, Sir Thomas Gatehouse, the man responsible for the pealing of bells; and Huggins's death in July 1761 deprived him of one who was, in epistolary terms at least, among his closest and dearest friends.

Smollett was barely forty, but already his life had a valedictory note. A year after Huggins's death, Boswell reported of him that 'he writes very little in the Critical Review'. He was, indeed, severing the connection, but, much to his irritation, it was assumed for many years to come that he was still actively involved, both editorially and as a writer. As late as December 1766, three years after he had cut all ties with his creation, its editors had to assure their readers that Smollett had 'not, for several years now, had the least concern with the Critical Review', even though 'we have lately seen the doctor abused in several publications, on the supposition of his still being concerned in the review'. By now his health was fading fast, and his appetite for the fray was no longer as sharp as before: but Smollett the polemicist, the man who had once declared that he never dabbled in politics, was about to become involved in one of the most vicious political feuds of the century, losing in the process a man he had thought of as a close friend and adviser, and very much a kindred spirit.

7

Rearguard Action

'The early part of the eighteenth century has something of the glamour of Arcadia,' the historian Dorothy George once wrote. 'We think of it as the last age of the old England, of solid, stable, rural England: the last age before invention, the machine, and the factory made the country industrial instead of merely agricultural.' Although the Industrial Revolution was in its infancy, Smollett's England was in a state of rapid and unsettling change, in transition from a rural society based on land and agriculture to an urban society based on banking and commerce; and no one regretted the change more bitterly, or more uncompromisingly, than Smollett himself – so much so that he seems, at times, like an eighteenth-century Evelyn Waugh, apoplectic with rage at the antics of the *nouveaux riches*, dreaming of a vanished Eden in which all was 'decorum, order and subordination', yet nimble at exploiting the professional opportunities offered by the new order. As an over-busy and influential literary man, he needed to live and work in London. Like many Londoners, native or adopted, he grumbled incessantly about its size, noise, dirt, impersonality and general incivility; as a novelist, he made sure that his heroes eventually escaped the vicious, predatory and corrupt life of the capital to settle down as well-heeled and well-regarded country gentlemen, surrounded by grateful tenantry and, as men of the world who had been tempered and enlightened by their experiences and

199

misfortunes, well aware of the responsibilities and the privileges that went with their position. City-dwelling writers have often tended to idealise and romanticise country life of the ordered and hierarchical variety, and Smollett is in a familiar line.

Though businesslike in his dealings with publishers and in the running of his various publications, Smollett, like all too many literary men, despised and disdained the world of trade. In this he differed sharply from Dr Johnson, who famously observed that 'There are few ways in which a man can be more innocently employed than in getting money', and declared that 'an English merchant is a new species of gentleman'. Smollett, for his part, announced that commerce was 'a subject quite foreign to my taste and understanding'; and in *The Present State of All Nations*, a survey of Britain which he compiled and partly wrote in the late 1760s, he took pains, when ranking classes in order of merit and importance, to place upstart merchants and traders low down in the pile, following at a defer-ential distance behind the nobility, gentlemen and the John-Bull-like figure of the yeoman.

Smollett's veneration of the country gentleman was theoretical and nostalgic: he had little direct experience of the English variety, and was far too taken up with his literary endeavours to enjoy more than the very occasional foray into the countryside, but the ideal of the gentleman meant much to him. In his platonic form, the English gentleman was the natural and perfect legislator, and the linchpin of society. The possessor of rolling acres, he had the inde-pendence that wealth bestows and was impervious to corruption and contemptuous of faction, two of the evils that Smollett most abhorred; as, in theory at least, an educated man, he had time and leisure to ponder the public good, and was in a position to take a detached, all-round view of the national good. Whereas traders and speculators and stock-jobbers and merchants and bankers and all the other vulgar, pushy *nouveaux riches* who had made vast fortunes out of the Wars of the Spanish and Austrian Successions, and contributed to the fevered madness of the South Sea Bubble, had a partial, selfish view of society, the country gentleman alone could see it as a whole. The aristocracy, as Roderick Random, Peregrine Pickle and Smollett himself had discovered to their cost, were

corrupt, venal and untrustworthy, and more than happy to inter-
marry and consort with the new 'moneyed interest': only the
gentleman, untainted by ambition, incorruptible and above faction
and party, could understand how varied and complex society was,
and judge its best interests accordingly.

Such views were shared not just by Tory squires, but by the Country
Whigs, who felt that the 'true' or 'old' Whig cause had been sullied
and betrayed by the 'junto' or Whig oligarchy and its retinue of
placemen and courtiers; disdaining the slogans of party, the old guard
constituted, however loosely, the 'patriot' or 'Country party', the
grouping with whom Smollett had most in common. They had, in
the early years of the century, relished the *Craftsman*'s savaging of
Walpole, the quintessence of all they loathed; drawing succour from
the past, they idealised Cato the Younger as a disinterested patriot
who had committed suicide rather than endure life under the Caesars.
Cato resurfaced in Joseph Addison's play of that name and in the
popular and influential *Cato's Letters* by John Trenchard and Thomas
Gordon, published between 1720 and 1724 and reprinted throughout
the century on both sides of the Atlantic. Land, not commerce, was
the true source of wealth and status. In *The Idea of a Patriot King*,
published in 1738, Lord Bolingbroke had declared that 'the landed
men are the true owners of our political vessel; the moneyed men,
as such, are no more than passengers in it'; the 'patriot king' himself,
or so it was hoped, could be found in the person of Frederick, Prince
of Wales, whose London base, Leicester House, was the informal
headquarters of opposition to the oligarchy. For those who, like
Smollett, feared and dreaded social change and clung to the status
quo, the ideal was to be found in the *Spectator*'s Sir Roger de Coverley:
a just and exemplary JP, the 'best master in the world', kind to
tenants and servants alike, he was, with his sense of *noblesse oblige*,
the embodiment of the benevolent 'patriarch', and the polar opposite of those upstart 'patricians' who had made their piles in dubious
ways and bought their country estates off the peg. Patriarchs and
patricians alike agreed with Bolingbroke's distinction between 'the
few designed to govern' and 'the multitude designed to obey': quite
who should make up the few was a matter of debate.

Though widespread throughout the first half of the century, such

views were passing out of fashion by the 1750s, and could hardly fail
to bring Smollett into conflict with the rapidly changing spirit of
the age. During the late seventeenth century those economists who
emphasised the economic and social benefits of competition, enterprise, freedom from governmental and institutional restraints – what
would now be called the 'free market' – began to prevail over the
mercantilists, with their belief in order, stability and governmental
supervision. Smollett's fellow-Scots, most notably Adam Smith, were
promoting the idea of specialisation, of the division of labour, of
society as a machine in which all partial or 'factional' interests had
their parts to play and were both competitive and complementary.
In his *Fable of the Bees*, published in 1723 and subtitled 'Private
Vices, Publick Benefits', Bernard de Mandeville suggested that the
greed, selfishness, vanity and envy of the individual could, and often
did, contribute to the good of society, that 'private vices' led to
'public benefits', that the creation of wealth by the few would
inevitably benefit the many by creating work and spreading money
through the body politic. In the age of the consumer – to use un-
Mandevillean language – emulation of those richer than oneself, and
the pursuit of the fashionable and the ephemeral, led to a situation
in which

> every part was full of Vice,
> Yet the whole mass a Paradise.

The prodigal and the wastrel could well prove 'a blessing to the
whole society' – as, indeed, could prostitutes and highwaymen – in
that they stimulated demand and encouraged the circulation of
money; whereas frugality and providence, so admired by the old
order, had a constipating and negative effect. Not surprisingly,
Mandeville was regarded as the Antichrist by some, including John
Wesley, and compared in his wickedness and cynicism to Machiavelli
and Hobbes; in France, the *Fable* was burned by the common
hangman, along with an effigy of its author.

Though hard-boiled and unflinching in his view of most aspects
of human nature, Smollett had no use for such disruptive and
newfangled notions; and if there was one subject which rendered

him incandescent with rage it was the related matter of 'luxury'. Luxury was particularly associated with the mercantile *nouveaux riches*, but its manifestations and its influence were ubiquitous; it was, he believed, responsible for every known social evil, from rank insubordination, indolence, effeminacy, social unrest, rioting in the streets and what Goldsmith described as 'a universal degeneracy in manners' to vulgarity, tea-drinking, shoddy workmanship, fraud and over-pricing. (In his influential tract of 1752, *Estimate of the Manners and Principles of the Times*, John Brown added to the list cowardice, hypochondria, suicide, self-promoting vicars and the staging by theatre managers of opera and pantomime rather than Shakespeare.) Once again, Smollett was more intransigent than most; and, once again, he was increasingly at variance with the spirit of the age. For reactionaries like Smollett, Ancient Rome served as a dreadful warning. Luxury, or so they believed, had been directly responsible for the disastrous deterioration whereby the austere, high-minded, public-spirited republican virtues most famously embodied in Cincinnatus gave way to the 'indigence and effeminacy' which, according to the *Craftsman*, prompted the degeneration and collapse, both moral and political, of the luxury-loving Empire. Whereas the Stoics had preached simplicity, thrift, sobriety and self-denial, luxury-lovers were, by definition, addicted to the unnecessary; lacking moral discipline, and enfeebled by their appetites, they had become the slaves of mere objects. Luxury appealed to the baser instincts; it was irrational and disorderly, and dissolved both hierarchy and the bonds that tied men together. It was also an urban vice, and more than once Rome had been rescued from itself by a simple, uncorrupted landowner or farmer. Socrates had derided the luxury-lover as 'a man of mere appetite . . . a creature of impulse and passion unable to distinguish necessary from unnecessary desires', and his views had been shared by Catullus, Livy and Tacitus.

Nor were the ill effects of luxury confined to the aristocracy and the ever-expanding middle classes. In his *Enquiry into the Cause of the Late Increase of Robbers*, published in 1751, Fielding noted how 'the vast torrent of luxury which of late years hath poured itself into this nation' had 'almost totally changed the manners, custom and habits of the people, most especially of the lower sort . . . The narrowness of their fortune is changed into wealth; the simplicity of their manners is changed into craft, their frugality into luxury, their humility into pride, and their subjugation into equality.' Prices were low, including that of corn, and although most wages were extremely modest, and the gulf between the few and the many dizzyingly wide, there was more disposable income to spend at all levels of society. Smollett, who fretted dreadfully about the effect luxury was having on the inherently idle and dissolute lower orders, and disapproved of the fashionable notion that higher wages all round had a beneficial effect by stimulating the economy, must have agreed wholeheartedly with his fellow-novelist's diagnosis of the way in which luxury

> reaches to the very dregs of the people, who aspiring still to a degree beyond that which belongs to them, and not being able by the fruits of honest labour to support the state which they affect, they disdain the wages to which their industry would entitle them; and abandoning themselves to idleness, the more simple and poor-spirited betake themselves to a state of starving and beggary, while those of more art and courage become thieves, sharpers and robbers.

According to Smollett's *Complete History*, the years that followed the Peace of Aix-la-Chapelle had been marked by 'an irresistible tide of luxury and excess', which had 'flowed through all degrees of the people, breaking down all the mounds [sic] of civil polity and opening the way for license and immorality. The highways were infested with rapine and assassination; the cities teemed with the votaries of lewdness, intemperance and profligacy.' His fear and loathing of the mob merged with his hatred of luxury, and, in his own mind at least, gin-drinking, cock-fighting, bear-baiting, homosexuality and rioting were all manifestations of luxury. As for the dreaded *nouveaux riches*, 'Intoxicated by the flow of wealth, they affected to rival the luxury and magnificence of their superiors,' he observed in the *Complete History*. 'They laid aside all decorum; became lewd, insolent, intemperate and riotous. All principles and even decency was gradually abolished . . .'

But Smollett's views on luxury were far from universal. Even Goldsmith, who had memorably castigated the effect of luxury on English country life in *The Deserted Village*, was moved to declare in *The Citizen of the World* that 'those philosophers who declaim against luxury have little understanding of its benefits; they seem insensible, that to luxury we owe not only the greatest part of our knowledge, but even of our virtue.' Earlier in the century, Daniel Defoe had exalted the diligent, ingenious middle classes at the expense of the weak and idle aristocracy; in more recent times, Dr Johnson was a keen believer in the social benefits of luxury. 'You cannot spend on luxury without doing good to the poor. Nay, you do more good to them by spending it in luxury than by giving it; for by spending it in luxury you make them exert industry, whereas by giving it you keep them idle,' he declared; while on another occasion he announced that 'Luxury, so far as it reaches the poor, will do good to the race of people; it will strengthen and multiply them. Sir, no nation was ever hurt by luxury . . .' Mandeville had shrewdly suggested that his critics didn't necessarily object to wealth as such, but resented it falling into the hands of their social inferiors; David Hume, who differentiated between 'innocent' and 'vicious' luxury, pointed out that whereas Smollett regarded city life and luxury as conjoined evils, he associated both with wealth, knowledge, liberal attitudes, discipline, industry and a humane and sympathetic cast of mind.

Like the Country Whigs and the disaffected country gentlemen whom he saw as kindred spirits, Smollett abominated equally the self-perpetuating ruling oligarchy of aristocratic Court Whigs and the new money associated with trade and the City of London. In *The Idea of a Patriot King*, Bolingbroke had accused Walpole of system-atically undermining the liberties of England through corruption, and by using pensions, 'places' (jobs for the boys) and government funds to buy votes and support. The Country party believed that the Court Whigs had employed corruption – itself invariably associated with luxury – to undermine and subvert the Constitution and the balance of power, prevailing in theory since the Glorious Revolution of 1688, between the King, the Lords and the Commons. 'The scenes of corruption, perjury, riot and intemperance, which every election for a member of parliament had lately produced, were now grown so infamously open and intolerable . . . that the fundamentals of the constitution seemed to shake, and the very essence of parliament to be in danger,' Smollett recorded in the *Continuation* to his *Complete History*. Corruption would lead to the loss of individual, and then national, liberty, and the reimposition of arbitrary rule by the King: the antithesis of the placemen – and of the hack politicians standing for election in *Sir Launcelot Greaves* – was an independent country squire like Matthew Bramble, who, in an earlier incarnation as MP for Dymkymraig, 'never voted with the ministry but three times, when my conscience told me I was in the right'.

Concern about the corrupting effects of luxury reached a climax during the Seven Years War, to the extent that a correspondent in the *London Magazine* worried that it threatened 'the undermining of our constitution and the downfall of our state'. Both the Court Whigs and the moneyed interest were in favour of the war, still more so after Pitt had taken charge, moving its focus from Europe to North America, the Caribbean and India. Though loyal, for the most part, to the House of Hanover, the country gentlemen were far from enthusiastic. Shebbeare had given voice to their opinions in his 'Letters to the People of England', but although he increasingly came round to the views of his old adversary, Smollett continued to support the war until 1760. He attacked the 'Letters' in the *Critical Review*, ridiculing their author as 'a quack in politics, an enemy to his king and country, and a desperate incendiary [who had] endeavoured to raise a ferment in the nation'; and in his dedication to Pitt of the first issue of the *British Magazine*, published in January 1760, he told the great war leader and orator that 'We admire that resolution and conduct which you have so conspicuously exerted, amidst the tempests of war and the turmoils of government: but we wish to see you adorned with the garlands of peace, diffusing the blessings of domestic tranquillity.' Early in 1760, the *Critical* attacked a pamphlet on *The Necessity of Putting an Immediate End to the War*, and Smollett seemed keen to expel the French from as much of North America as possible; but as the year wore on, he became less well disposed, and in November the *Critical* heaped praise on Israel Maudit's *Considerations on the Present German War*, which condemned the campaign in Europe.

Although the *Critical Review* continued to review new pamphlets on social and political issues, taking an illiberal and Scrooge-like line on such matters as working men's wages and tending to ignore those of a more lenient or enlightened bent, Smollett was wary of lambasting politicians after the Knowles affair. For the time being at least, he kept to himself his thoughts about the Duke of Newcastle, the long-serving and seemingly indestructible embodiment of the corrupt Whig oligarchy. Named by Smollett 'the father of corruption', 'this ridiculous ape, this venal drudge' and 'an old pilot conveyed through the streets on an ass, his face turned towards the tail', Newcastle combined personal absurdity with professional ruthlessness and managerial competence: he was mocked for his incessant, inconsequential chattering and his hypochondria – he had a phobia about unaired beds, and at George II's funeral he insisted on standing on the train of the Duke of Cumberland's velvet robe for fear of catching a chill from the flagstones in the Abbey – and two of the most comical scenes in *Humphry Clinker* describe encounters between Bramble, Jery Melford and the blithering duke. In his novel *Lydia*, Shebbeare, pre-empting Smollett's masterly evocation of Newcastle's social style and manner of speech, described him as a man 'undignified by nature, whiffling, inconstant, whose words, hurried out like water from an inverted bottle, included nothing to be understood, ever beginning, never closing one sentence, rambling from man to man, from one half-thought to another . . .'

The fact that Pitt's letter thanking him for the dedication to the *Complete History* was found among Smollett's papers after his death suggests that although 'the Great Commoner' fell from grace and, like Newcastle, was mercilessly savaged in print by his erstwhile admirer, the early fondness never entirely evaporated. When, in 1757, Pitt replaced Newcastle as the most powerful figure in the administration, Smollett had high hopes that he would break with the Court Whigs and repudiate the alliance with Frederick the Great. The *Monitor* had exalted him as a combination of Cato and Cincinnatus – for all his theatricality and neuroses, it is hard to imagine the gout-ridden war leader falling on his sword, or austerely tilling the soil – but for his admirers in the Country party Pitt turned out to be a broken reed, and his closeness to the City of London, as well as his readiness to play to the gallery, metamorphosed him into 'the grand pensionary, that weathercock of patriotism that veers about in every point of the compass, and still feels the wind of popularity in his tail'. But whatever his demerits, as a war leader he was in a different league from Newcastle.

After a wobbly start, epitomised by the Byng court-martial and the Rochefort fiasco, the war began to go well for Britain and her allies. Still subsidised from London, Frederick the Great defeated the French, the Austrians and the Russians; the French Mediterranean fleet was worsted off the Portuguese coast at Lagos, and Admiral Hawke destroyed its Brest equivalent at Quiberon Bay; and French overseas colonies were captured and annexed. In North America, Amherst took Louisbourg, Fort Duquesne (later renamed Pittsburgh after the leader at home), Niagara and Ticonderoga; Wolfe captured Quebec, dying gloriously in the battle, and Amherst's taking of Montreal marked the end of French power in Canada. Clive ousted the French from Bengal, and Eyre Coote took Pondicherry, so establishing British pre-eminence in the Indian subcontinent; in the Caribbean, the riches of Guadeloupe and, later, of Martinique were snatched from the French. None of this was of immediate concern to Smollett, but the anxiety of Pitt's successor and the new King to bring the war to an end was to plunge him into the maelstrom of politics, reanimating his hatred of the moneyed interest and leaving him ill, exhausted and demoralised.

Opposition to the Court Whigs received a nasty blow in 1751 with the unexpected death of the charasmatic Frederick, Prince of Wales; but Leicester House remained a nucleus of opposition, based on the future George III and his Scottish tutor, Lord Bute, with whom he was said to be besotted. Bute was good-looking, charming and ineffectual; a nephew of the omnipotent Duke of Argyll, he had, like so many post-Union grandees, been educated in England, and was married to the daughter of the gossipy Lady Mary Wortley Montagu. He was also very close – too close, in the opinion of the scandalmongering anti-Scots brigade – to Frederick's widow, the Dowager Princess Augusta, who looked to him for help and advice after the death of her husband. Bute's private secretary was Smollett's old Edinburgh acquaintance, the clergyman-playwright John Home.

Handsome, vivacious, well-intentioned and, according to Alexander Carlyle, lacking any shred of wit or humour, Home was a man on the make; he was a master of flattery, and life had improved no end since he had first come to London with the manuscript of *Agis* rolled up in his pocket. *Douglas*, once rejected by Garrick, had enjoyed a huge success in Edinburgh and London – 'Whaur's your Wullie Shakespeare noo?' an over-charged member of the audience had cried out at the Edinburgh première – and Garrick had agreed to take the lead in the once-spurned *Agis*: Carlyle had sat up all night to review it for the *Critical*, and was 'obliged to give it to the press blotted and underlined – but they are accustomed to decipher the most difficult hands'. When Carlyle met Home in London in 1758, the assiduous flatterer was already 'entirely at the command of Lord Bute, whose nod made him break every engagement'; three years later, by which time Bute had been appointed Groom of the Stole, Secretary of State to the Northern Department and finally First Lord of the Treasury – the equivalent of the modern Prime Minister – Home 'might really have been said to have been the second man in the kingdom while Bute remained in power'. Home arranged for Carlyle and Robert Adam to meet Bute: their dry and cold reception infuriated the ambitious young architect ('What! had he been presented to all the princes of Italy and France, and most graciously received, to come and be treated with such distance and pride by the youngest earl but one in all Scotland?'), but when Carlyle met the Earl out riding in Hyde Park, he formed a better opinion: 'I believe he was a very worthy and virtuous man – a man of taste, and a good *belles lettres* scholar, and that he trained up the prince in true patriotic principles and a love of the constitution, though his own mind was of the Tory cast, with a partiality to the house of Stuart, of whom he believed he was descended.'

Despite their unfortunate first encounter, Robert Adam was more than happy to accept the patronage of Bute, as well as of other Scots like Lord Mansfield, so fuelling the popular belief that, as Wilkes put it, 'no Scot ever exerted himself but for a fellow-Scot', and that the freemasonry of Scots in England lent weight to those, like Dr Johnson, who were 'particularly prejudiced against the Scots' on the grounds that 'their success in England rather exceeded the due proportion of their real merit'. Hostility to the Scots was to plumb new depths after the accession of the twenty-two-year-old George III in 1760. The old king – who, according to Smollett's *Complete History*, had, on the day of his death, 'risen at his usual hour, drank his chocolate, and enquired about the wind, as anxious for the foreign mails' before finally collapsing – had spoken English with a German accent, and thought of himself as a German prince; his grandson may have declared, in his first address to Parliament, that he 'gloried in the name of Briton', and described Hanover as 'that horrid protectorate', but he was also devoted to Bute, whose family name of Stuart led his enemies to assume that he yearned to reinstate an absolute monarchy. To the fury of Pitt and the City interests, the King shared his old tutor's anxiety to bring 'this bloody and expensive war' to a speedy conclusion. At the end of 1761 Pitt resigned after the Cabinet had rejected his plan for a pre-emptive strike against Spain and its treasure fleets, based on a rumour that the Spaniards were about to ally themselves with the French: to the disapproval of many of his admirers, he took himself off to the Lords as the Earl of Chatham, and Lord Bute was made First Lord of the Treasury. Alarmed by the cost and apparent unpopularity of the war – taxes had risen again, and an increase in the price of beer had provoked rioting in London – the new administration was happy to make concessions to the French in order to negotiate a peace. The City merchants, who had done well out of the war, argued that the British had every right to expand their empire at the expense of the French, and were horrified by rumours that Bute was planning not only to return Cuba and the Philippines to Spain – which had, as Pitt predicted, allied itself with France – but to restore Guadeloupe and Martinique to France. The English, Smollett suggested in the *Critical Review*, 'are become intoxicated with conquest, and woe be to any minister who should return any of those conquests at a peace, except for a valuable consideration'. On their way to a City dinner arranged to thank Pitt for his services, the great war leader and his cousin Lord Temple, who had resigned at the same time as Lord Privy Seal, were loudly cheered, while the King and the peace-mongering Bute were hissed and booed.

The scene was being set for vicious political warfare, and the Scots were the scapegoats. Dr Johnson told his friend Joseph Baretti that the new king 'has been long in the hands of the Scots, and has already favoured them more than the English will contentedly endure', but if the Great Cham is, in retrospect, the most celebrated Scottophobe of all – 'That, Sir, I find, is what a very great deal of your countrymen cannot help,' he famously remarked when, at their first meeting, Boswell apologised for his nationality – his views were all too common. The Scots were seen as both poverty-stricken and predatory. Supposedly ill at ease in breeches, they were associated with bare buttocks and lice: according to Sir Charles Hanbury Williams, the Scots after the Forty-Five ran home to 'beggary, oatmeal and itch', and cartoonists liked to portray scrawny, ill-kempt Scots in kilts scratching themselves against 'scrubbing posts'. At the same time, they were thought to be over-ambitious and, once south of the Border, intent on taking the best jobs for themselves and their cronies. 'They send us whole cargoes of their staple commodity, half-bred doctors and surgeons to poison and destroy us,' a contemporary remarked of Smollett and his kind; but, doctors apart, Scots were making their mark in other areas of life as well. Unionist Scots may have been affronted when, from fear that their fellow-citizens were still crypto-Jacobites at heart, Pitt's Militia Bill of 1757, creating a home defence force, was not extended north of the Border, yet within a few years of the Forty-Five one officer in four in the British army was a Scot. Six Highland regiments had been recruited for the Seven Years War, serving with distinction in North America. Pitt, or so it was said, had remarked that ''Tis no pity if they fall', and when, at the height of the anti-Bute agitation, two Highland officers attended Covent Garden they were greeted with cries of 'No Scots! No Scots! Out with them!' and a deluge of apples. 'Damn you rascals!' fulminated a furious Boswell, who was in the theatre that evening. 'I hated the English; I wished from my soul that the Union was broke, and that we might give them another battle of Bannockburn.' 'Can you seriously talk of my continuing an Englishman,' David Hume asked his fellow-Scot, Sir Gilbert Elliot, a member of the Navy Board with whom Wilkes had earlier intervened on behalf of Francis Barber. 'Am I, or you, an Englishman? Do they not treat with derision our pretensions to that name?' Boswell might, in calmer, more ingratiating moments, feel that he 'should not keep too much time with Scotch people, because I am kept from acquiring propriety in English speaking', but Hume was only too well aware that 'Scotsmen are hated, superstition and ignorance gain ground daily', and that 'some hate me because I am not a Whig, some because I am not a Christian, and all because I am a Scotsman'.

Like Africans and West Indians today, the Scots were widely attributed with alarming sexual potency: Bute himself was rumoured to have enjoyed a torrid affair with the Dowager Princess, and derisive crowds semaphored their understanding of the situation by carrying a boot and a petticoat, suitably juxtaposed. Whatever his involvement with the Princess, Bute was a manipulator of the polemical press, and was keen to employ pamphleteers and political journalists to make the ministry's case, not least as far as the peace negotiations were concerned. Shebbeare was enlisted in his cause, as was Caleb Whitefoord, a wine merchant, literary gent and Fellow of the Royal Society, but far and away his most eminent recruit was Tobias Smollett. Some eight years later Smollett referred, in a letter to Whitefoord, to the 'absurd stoicism of Lord Bute, who set himself up as a pillory to be pelted by all the blackguards of England'; in the meantime, though, he hurried to the aid of his compatriot, and his embattled royal master. Two Scottish MPs, Alexander Wedderburn and Sir Harry Erskine, may have suggested him to Bute as the best man to write and edit a weekly paper which would defend the ministry and the peace negotiations. Carrying on its masthead the royal coat of arms, and dedicated to 'plucking the mask of patriotism from the front of faction', the *Briton* ran to between four and six pages: the first issue appeared four days after Bute took office in May 1762, and the last in the following February, two days after the signing of the Peace of Paris and the resignation of the embattled First Lord. Its sales were absurdly modest, some 250 copies per issue, it had no impact other than goading into existence a far more effective, scabrous and notorious rival publication, and it took a terrible toll on its editor's health and reputation: as John Moore remembered, 'Dr Smollett was not formed with that insensibility and coolness that is necessary for political altercation. The *Briton* was not so favourably received as his former writings had been, and he had reason to regret that he ever became a party writer, by which he lost some of his old friends, and acquired but very cold-hearted new ones in their stead.'

Smollett's lack of political acumen was all too obvious. Like many literary men, he was both inconsistent and out of his depth when it came to the practicalities of everyday politics. Challenged to list the achievements of Bute's ministry, he pointed to the capture of Martinique – to which his opponents responded that he had recently approved Bute's condemnation of further conquests from the French, and that in taking the island he was merely completing a job started by Pitt. Editing a paper hostile to Pitt and the City was a quixotic venture as far as London readers were concerned, and his attempts to drive a wedge between the Whig grandees and the moneyed interest proved as futile as ever. And Bute proved an ineffectual and disloyal patron, failing to provide his champion with the details he needed to defend the peace negotiations until they were made public in November 1762. 'If it be imputed to me as a crime that I have blamed some parts of Mr P——'s ministerial conduct, I plead guilty to the charge,' Smollett told the *Gazetteer and London Daily Advertiser* in October 1762, in reply to an accusation of 'venality and inconsistency' as editor of the *Briton* in his pronouncements on Pitt:

> I inscribed the first part of my history to that gentleman as the most distinguished patriot of the day, who excelled all his contemporaries in the powers of elocution, and exerted those powers in the service of his country; in stigmatizing a weak and corrupt administration, and particularly in exposing and opposing the absurdity and pernicious tendency of those German connections, which that administration had formed.
>
> Though Mr P—— as a M—— afterwards adopted those very principles against which he had so long and so strenuously declaimed, I was surely under no obligation to follow his example; to renounce the maxims which I had always avowed, and violate my conscience out of respect to his character. I thought it my duty to sacrifice every personal consideration to historical truth; and therefore . . . I freely censured some particulars of his conduct.

Far and away the most painful falling-out was with John Wilkes, whose weekly paper, the *North Briton*, was founded to counteract Smollett's ineffectual *Briton*: it rapidly outsold its enfeebled rival, notching up weekly sales of 2,000 copies, and although Wilkes had intended to limit its life to a handful of issues it soon built up a momentum of its own. A raffish, insouciant, buccaneering character, the MP for Aylesbury since 1757, Wilkes straddled the worlds of politics and journalism; although he proved a poor speaker in the House of Commons, he was a natural journalist for whom 'Delicacy is not the thing. Strength and force are requisite.' As Dr Johnson later learned, he was the best of company: declining an invitation to visit him at home in Aylesbury, Smollett once assured him that 'I am sure I should there find much more agreeable company, and much better cheer, than ever Plato, or at least than ever his master Socrates knew; nor, at your table, should I have any reason to complain that the *sal atticum* [i.e. wit] was lacking.' 'I scarce ever met with a better companion,' declared Edward Gibbon, who came across Wilkes in 1762 when, as Colonel of the Buckinghamshire Militia, he was guarding a group of French prisoners-of-war: 'He has inexhaustible spirits, infinite wit and humour, and a great deal of knowledge; but a thorough profligate in principle as well as practice; his character is infamous, his life stained with every vice, and his conversation full of blasphemy and bawdy.'

The son of a London distiller, cross-eyed and no beauty, Wilkes was famed as a ladies' man – he once boasted that he could talk away his face in half an hour – and had been an enthusiastic member of Sir Francis Dashwood's notorious Hellfire Club, the members of which dubbed themselves the Medmenham Monks and amused themselves with old-fashioned orgies involving flagellation, naked girls stretched out on altars and a touch of black magic: Wilkes once enlivened the proceedings by unleashing a monkey, disguised as a devil with horns and a scarlet cloak. At the age of twenty he had married a frumpish woman many years his senior: although he and his wife soon went their separate ways, he remained touchingly devoted to his daughter Polly, Elizabeth Smollett's schoolfriend in Chelsea.

A natural sympathiser with the views of the Country party and those opposed to the Whig oligarchs, Wilkes saw himself, in his editorial and journalistic roles, as the great champion of embattled liberties, and of the freedom of the press in particular: 'The *liberty of the press* is the birthright of a BRITON, and is justly esteemed the firmest bulwark of the liberties of this country,' he decreed in the opening issue of the *North Briton*. Smollett would not have disapproved such views, but Wilkes's diatribes against the Scots were to drive a wedge between them. As a young man, Wilkes had studied at Leyden University. Alexander Carlyle was a fellow-student, and remembered him as 'a sprightly, entertaining fellow', whose 'ugly countenance in early youth was very striking': even then 'he showed something of the daring profligacy, for which he was afterwards notorious'. His closest friend at Leyden was a Scot, 'Immateriality' Baxter, and, according to Carlyle, 'the people of that nation were always Wilkes's favourites till 1763 . . . when he became a violent party-writer, and wished to raise his fame and fortune on the ruin of Lord Bute'. John Moore confirmed Carlyle's version of events. 'So far from showing any of that acrimony which he afterwards affected to show against the Scotch, Mr Wilkes had hitherto manifested rather a partiality for their acquaintance,' he recalled, adding that 'the dislike he afterwards expressed against North Britons was artificial, and assumed for political motives'. Wilkes's later dislike may also have been prompted by a rather hopeless assassination attempt involving a mad Scots marine discovered lurking near his room with a penknife.

'I hear Dr Armstrong has sent you a most violent renunciation of Wilkes's friendship,' David Hume told Andrew Millar. 'Wilkes is indeed very blameable in indulging himself so much in national reflections, which are low, vulgar and ungenerous, and come with a bad grace from him, who conversed so much with my countrymen.' Like Smollett, John Armstrong had been fond of Wilkes, but his former friend's Scottophobe tirades in the *North Briton* – edited and mostly written by Wilkes, funded by Lord Temple, and available to the reading public a week after the first issue of the *Briton* – made further friendship out of the question. Wilkes's activities had 'forever deprived me of the pleasure of your conversation. For I cannot with honour or decency associate myself with one who has distinguished himself by abusing my country.' As late as March 1762 Smollett was still on good terms with Wilkes, assuring him that 'My warmest regard, affection and detachment you have long ago secured', and that 'when I presume to differ from you in any point of opinion, I shall always do it with diffidence and deference': he had been unwell for the past three months, but he hoped 'soon to be in a condition to pay my respects to Mr Wilkes in person'. The *North Briton* put an end to all that. Wilkes himself would almost certainly have accused Armstrong and Smollett of over-reacting or lacking a sense of humour: as Moore put it, 'that political game he indulged in as sport, they considered as a mortal offence, and could not bear without the fiercest indignation'. Not all Scots were as outraged as Smollett. Boswell, who had first spotted Wilkes dining at the Sublime Society of Beefsteaks with the renegade clergyman-poet Charles Churchill and the debauched Lord Sandwich under a sign reading 'Beef and Liberty', sent copies of the *North Briton* to the Edinburgh actor West Digges, who was 'very grateful to me', and he often dined in the City on publication day in order to pick up a copy fresh from the printers at four o'clock that afternoon, paying 2½d. for the privilege; if not, 'I have it sent to me regularly by the Penny Post, and read it with vast relish'. English readers, it goes without saying, also read it with relish. 'The *North Briton* proceeded with an acrimony, a spirit, and a licentiousness unheard of before even in this country,' Horace Walpole remembered in later years. 'The highest names, whether of statesmen or magistrates, were printed at length, and the insinuations went still higher.'

Supposedly written, in the first few issues at least, by a North Briton, Wilkes's notorious weekly muscled its way on to the streets in June 1762. 'My only patron is the public, to which I will ever make my appeal, and hold it sacred,' declared Wilkes. Since the public, then as now, preferred flamboyant hyperbole to sober truth, he confessed that his journalistic technique was to 'Give me a grain of truth, and I will mix it up with a great deal of falsehood so that no chemist will ever be able to separate them.' His sub-editor and his assistant editor, Charles Churchill and Robert Lloyd, had belonged to a group of young satirical writers that had also included Bonnell Thornton and the half-crazed Christopher Smart. Hogarth was, for a time, friendly with the group, but fell out with Wilkes and Churchill over the *North Briton*. Wilkes ridiculed Hogarth's links with the court after his official post as Serjeant Painter was renewed, suggesting in the *North Briton* 'the term means what is vulgarly called a housepainter'. After the publication of a print by Paul Sandby showing Churchill carrying a bucket of water labelled 'North Briton' in order to help Pitt and others douse a blaze in St James's Palace started by Bute, 'Smallwit' and other Scots, Hogarth turned his pen against his former friends. He savaged Wilkes, Churchill, Pitt and Temple in his prints; *Wilkes and Liberty*, one of his most famous, depicts the great demagogue as a leering, cross-eyed devil, the wings of whose wig double up like horns, while *The Bruiser* shows the 'Baccanalian priest' Charles Churchill, a massive, boorish figure with tree-trunk legs and arms to match, as an overweight bear in a white ecclesiastical tie, clutching a foaming quart of beer in one hand and embracing with the other a vast cudgel, on the sawn-off stumps of which is written the word 'lye', and the relevant number of the *North Briton*.

Churchill, for his part, denounced Dr Johnson, Smollett, Arthur Murphy and other supporters of Bute as 'vile pensioners of state'. Unlike Smollett, Johnson had accepted a pension as a 'reward for literary merit', and had called on the First Lord to thank him in person: anxious not to be accused of enlisting the great man as a party propagandist, Bute assured him that the pension had not been 'given you for anything you are to do, but for what you have done'; his friend Arthur Murphy had been enlisted to edit the *Auditor*, which took a similar line to the *Briton*, and was equally ineffectual. A talented literary thug, Churchill had made a good deal of money from his anonymous poem *The Rosciad*, in which he mocked the pretensions and inadequacies of the theatrical world. It had been unkindly reviewed in the *Critical Review*: Smollett, only recently released from the King's Bench Prison, and wrongly assuming that Garrick's friend George Colman was its author, had written one of his self-exculpatory letters to Garrick to the effect that he might have toned down the review had he read it before it went to press. Churchill had already taken umbrage; nor was he mollified when, reviewing his 'Prophecy of Famine', the *Critical* declared that its author would probably 'be one day ranked among the first poets of the nation', despite the fact that it referred to the Scots as 'nature's bastards' and 'the refuse of mankind'.

> Conscious of guilt, and fearful of the light,
> They lurk enshrouded in the veil of night;
> Safe from detection, seize the unwary prey,
> And stab, like bravoes, all who come their way

he wrote of *Critical* reviewers in general, while of their editor he declared

> How do I laugh, when Publius, hoary grown,
> In zeal for Scotland's welfare, and his own,
> By slow degrees, and course of office, drawn
> In mood and figure at the helm to yawn,
> Too mean (the worst of curses heaven can send)
> To have a foe; too proud to have a friend;
> Erring by form, which blockheads sacred hold,
> Ne'er making new faults, and ne'er mending old . . .

'Reason could never believe that a Scot was fit to have management of English affairs,' Wilkes declared in the *North Briton*, and by savaging the Scots he hoped to bring Bute and his ministry into such disrepute that they would have no alternative but to resign. He not only ridiculed Bute in person, making much of his alleged affair with the Dowager Princess through endless analogies with Edward II's wife and her lover, Mortimer, but, more seriously, suggested that, with the young and susceptible King, he was planning to extend the royal prerogative and, in due course, restore Stuart absolutism and impose an 'eleven years tyranny'. Smollett tried in vain to counter such notions in the *Briton*, hailing Bute as 'the patriot minister, the minister of the people', playing upon his own Whig credentials ('If you are Whigs, you need fear nothing from me, for I profess myself one in the true sense of the word'), and suggesting that 'the present administration is the only one I ever remember to have proceeded upon true and genuine Whig principles: for they allow the crown its due prerogatives, and their subjects their just liberties, and they admit into places of trust, without discrimination, every man of ability who is loyal to his king and country . . .' But Wilkes's anti-Scottish diatribes caught the mood of the moment far more effectively. The first issue of the *North Briton* announced the passing of 'Mr John Bull, a very worthy, plain, honest old gentleman of Saxon descent' who had choked to death 'by inadvertently swallowing a thistle, which he had placed by way of ornament on top of his salad'. The Scots were notorious for their 'declared enmity to England', and as a result 'the very name of Scot' was 'hateful to every true Englishman'. In August the paper provided its readers with 'the perfect description of the people and country of Scotland':

> Their beasts be generally small, women only excepted, of which sort there are none greater in the world. There is a great store of fowl, too, as foul houses, foul sheets, foul linen, foul trenchers and napkins . . . Pride is the only thing bred in their bones, and their flesh naturally abhors cleanliness: their breath commonly stinks of pottage, their linen of p–ss, their hands of pigs' t——ds, their body of sweat.

With such views being voiced by the literate classes in London, it was hardly surprising that Matthew Bramble and party, travelling north, should find that 'From Doncaster onwards, all the windows of all the inns are scrawled with doggerel rhymes, in abuse of the Scotch nation.'

But although Pitt and Temple welcomed Wilkes's support on some issues – the peace negotiations, and Bute's new excise taxes – they were increasingly embarrassed by, and out of sympathy with, his 'levelling' ideas, his attacks on the royal prerogative and the King's right to choose his own ministers, and his growing reliance on the support of the mob. Temple disapproved of the *North Briton*'s attacks on the Scots, and its libellous claims about Bute's royal love affair; Lord Talbot fought a duel with Wilkes after the *North Briton* had mocked his behaviour as Lord Steward at the coronation of George III; most famously of all, the 'authors, printers and publishers of a seditious and treasonable paper' were arrested under the terms of a general warrant and charged with seditious libel after publication of No. 45 of the *North Briton*, in which Wilkes attacked Bute's handling of the peace negotiations, severely criticised the King's speech at the opening of Parliament, and expressed the disloyal hope that the monarch would not sully St Paul's by attending a thanksgiving service there. Although Bute had resigned before the publication of No. 45, Grenville's new administration was determined to take a tough line. Lord Halifax, the Secretary of State, signed a general warrant for the arrest of those involved in its publication. Despite pleading parliamentary privilege, Wilkes was slapped in the Tower, and the offending issue was ordered to be burned by the public hangman; Churchill, also indicted, turned up just as Wilkes was being led away, took the hint when his friend pointedly addressed him as 'Mr Thompson', and hurriedly fled abroad. Wilkes took out a writ of habeas corpus, which was heard at the Court of Common Pleas by Chief Justice Pratt, a friend of Pitt and Temple, rather than by the Scot Lord Mansfield at the King's Bench: he pleaded his case as the champion of 'all the middling and inferior set of people, who stand most in need of protection', and as a man whose case would determine 'whether English liberty shall be a reality or a shadow'. Wilkes's claim to be a doughty defender of press freedom was amply vindicated, but although he was loudly supported by tradesmen's clubs, and by publicans and brewers – Nicholson Calvert, MP, whose beer Smollett served up to the hacks at Sunday lunch, was an ardent Wilkesite – he was viewed askance by the influential and well-established booksellers and printers who made up the Chapter Coffee House, Strahan, Andrew Millar and Thomas Cadell among them: Millar had refused to publish the *North Briton*, and Wilkes's old drinking chum, John Almon, was among the few booksellers to lend him support. But conservatives and radicals alike ran the risk of being indicted by the state on a charge of seditious libel: the Attorney-General could, in such cases, use catch-all general warrants to arrest those responsible, and printers and booksellers could find themselves being locked up without trial while a judge decided whether the offending material was libellous or not. Wilkes took out actions against the government officials who had arrested those involved in the publication of No. 45 of the *North Briton*, and was awarded £1,000 in damages; and although the Wilkes affair was not, as was often claimed, the immediate cause of general warrants being condemned by Lord Chief Justice Camden in 1765 as 'contrary to law', it certainly contributed to their demise – much to the relief of all shades of opinion in the world of printing and publishing.

But Wilkes's troubles were far from over. While he was in the Tower, his house in Great George Street was ransacked in search of incriminating material, and the authorities claimed to have unearthed an obscene poem by Wilkes called 'The Essay on Woman'. Although a mere twelve copies had been printed for private enjoyment, he was found guilty of publishing an obscene libel, and of seditious libel too, in that he had reprinted in volume form the complete run of the *North Briton*, including the contentious No. 45. Among the humbugs who led the prosecution on the ministry's behalf was his old companion from the Hellfire Club, the Earl of Sandwich, a notorious rake best remembered for lending his name to the sandwich, and for provoking a fine shaft of Wilkesite wit: when he told his former friend that he would die on the gallows or of the pox, Wilkes shot back with 'That depends, my lord, on whether I embrace your principles or your mistress.' Now posing as the Secretary of State, Sandwich – who had been outraged to find himself cruelly lampooned in papers found in Wilkes's house – spread rumours that Smollett's old adversary William Warburton, the Bishop of Gloucester, had been grossly libelled by claims that he had provided the notes that accompanied the 'Essay on Woman'. Warburton denounced Wilkes as being worse than Satan; from the other side of the fence, Lord Le Despencer, another veteran of the Hellfire Club, declared after listening to Sandwich in full flight in the House of Lords that he had never heard the Devil preach before. Wilkes was found guilty on both counts, but after being wounded in a duel, he failed to turn up to receive his sentence. With the London mob bawling its support for 'Wilkes and Liberty' outside Westminster Hall, he was expelled from the House of Commons. Declared an outlaw, he withdrew, for a time, from the stage of British politics. Polly was in Paris, learning French and *savoir-faire*; Wilkes hoped to seduce her chaperone, Madame Carpentier, so providing another excuse for temporary exile.

Bute had resigned and the *Briton* had ceased publication before

Wilkes's arrest and subsequent flight, but although the *Critical* had been uneasy about the government prosecuting Wilkes, believing this would merely inflame his popular support, Smollett must have viewed his former friend's activities with abhorrence. The malicious Reverend Birch affected outrage that Smollett should have described Wilkes as 'a monster in person': such, he assured Lord Hardwicke, was 'the return Mr Wilkes receives', despite having 'spoken formerly to me of Dr Smollett as a most good-natured, agreeable man'. Such fondness as Smollett may once have felt had rapidly evaporated. Wilkes was, Jery Melford suggested in *Humphry Clinker*, a man 'without a drop of red blood in his veins', but 'rancour enough in his heart to inoculate and infect a whole nation'. Writing in the *Briton*, Smollett had described Wilkes as 'a venal fool, as void of principle as of talent, who, like a mercenary Swiss, would draw his pen on either side of any dispute as he happened to be listed, without the least regard to the merits of the case in which he embarks'. He abominated the innuendoes about Bute and the Dowager Princess, and although he had never shown any particular fondness for the House of Hanover, he became, as editor of the *Briton* at least, a fervent monarchist. In the *Continuation* to his *Complete History* he described how the young George III had come to the throne 'determined to favour and protect all his subjects equally, without any other distinction than that of merit', and in No. 18 of the *Briton* he urged his fellow-citizens to 'depend upon the paternal affection of a virtuous sovereign, who can have no views distinct from the interest and happiness of his people': like the idealised country gentleman, he would be above both faction and corruption. He ridiculed Wilkes as Jahia Ben Israil Ginn, a goggle-eyed monster who maligns his benevolent caliph, unleashing 'a torrent of the foulest slander and abuse, poured upon the character of a prince, who deserves to be the darling of his people; upon the character of a minister, whose conduct has defied the severest scrutiny of malice'.

Even more offensive was Wilkes's wooing of the mob. Smollett derided the notion – subscribed to by no practising politicians of his day, and by only a handful of theoreticians – that all men are 'equally free', and had 'an equal right to intermeddle in the administration of public affairs; a principle subversive of all government, magistracy and subordination; a principle destructive of all industry and national quiet, as well as repugnant to every fundamental maxim of society'. Wilkes's supporters were '*canaille*, forlorn grubs and gazetteers, desperate gamblers, tradesmen thrice bankrupt, prentices to journeymen, understrappers to porters, hungry pettifoggers, bailiffs' followers, discarded draymen, hostlers out of place, and felons returned from transportation. These are the people who proclaim themselves freeborn Englishmen.' For Smollett, the English were not 'the base, unthinking rabble of the metropolis, without principle, sentiment or understanding', but 'the honest, the sober, the thriving sons of industry, who have an interest in the country they inhabit', and to invoke the rabble was 'the last resource of a gasping faction'. There was no question of the rabble being given the vote – that, as Smollett observed, was reserved for those 'with an interest in the country they inhabit' – but Smollett dreaded the disruptive and violent potential of the mob, and hated the fact that even in so partial a democracy, politicians had to pander to it. 'When I see a man of birth, education and fortune put himself on a level with the dregs of the people, mingle with low mechanics, feed with them at the same board . . . I cannot help despising him as a man of the vilest prostitution,' Squire Bramble declared, probably with Pitt in mind; elsewhere he remarked that he knew 'nothing so abject as the behaviour of a man canvassing for a seat in Parliament', the 'mean prostration' of which had 'contributed in a great measure to raise that spirit of insolence among the vulgar, which, like the devil, will be found very difficult to lay'.

But compared with Pitt's allies in the City and the 'moneyed interest', the man described by the King as 'that devil Wilkes' was an ephemeral and minor irritant. The merchant classes and the City men embodied and promoted the cardinal sin of luxury: as the *Critical* once put it, they included 'contractors, stock-jobbers and brokers, the lowest and vilest of mankind, utterly destitute of taste, knowledge or liberality'. Smollett's loathing was both nostalgic and prophetic: looking back to an imaginary rustic Arcadia of order, stability and *noblesse oblige*; looking ahead to nineteenth-century denunciations, by poets, novelists and political philosophers, of the cash nexus and capitalism at its most ruthless, crushing and impersonal – and, less engagingly, to the etiolated disdain displayed by so many modern writers and academics towards the business and commercial worlds.

With brokers and bankers and East India men buying country estates and intermarrying with the aristocracy, the City was rapidly emerging as a political as well as an economic force; and the Seven Years War, during which fortunes had been made, had hastened the process. The City grandees – the Governors and Directors of the Bank of England, the Court of Aldermen, the Common Council and, below them, the Liverymen and Freemen of the City of London – were proud of their independence of both Whitehall and St James's Palace. Some, like William Beckford, were rich and well connected, but many of the 7,000 or so Liverymen of the City Companies were artisans, shopkeepers and small traders, a lower middle-class electorate who shared the same background as Wilkes and formed the power base of the Wilkesite movement. Rich and not-so-rich alike resented the ways in which the landed interest still controlled so much of commercial policy; they campaigned for free trade and lower taxes, sought a (marginally) wider franchise, dreamed of reducing the political clout of the Whig oligarchs of the Newcastle school, and favoured shorter parliaments and the elimination of rotten boroughs as nuclei of aristocratic power. William Beckford, the Lord Mayor at the time of Bute's travails and Pitt's chief lieutenant in the City, had fought for political reform, and founded the *Monitor* to campaign alongside the *North Briton*. He may or may not have read Smollett's diatribes against the City, but one member of the mercantile order took the time to answer back. 'Could any poor creature write such stuff unless one lately eloped from Bedlam?' wondered William Temple, a Trowbridge merchant, in the pages of the *North Briton*. 'The merchants of London, in their collective capacity, possess more honest, useful political knowledge, and understand more of the true interests of their country, than all the ministers of state ever discovered.'

Smollett was not a recent inmate of Bedlam, but he was, in terms of health, something of a 'poor creature', suffering from persistent asthma, hacking coughs and what may have been the early stages of TB; nor had matters been improved by years of overwork, and the nervous and emotional strain of doing battle with literary and political foes. 'I have had a return of my asthma in consequence of catching fresh cold,' he had told Dr Macaulay in October 1759, at the same time assuring Wilkes, who was then helping him over the Knowles affair, that 'I am still an invalid, otherwise I would wait on you in person.' 'I perceive myself going down hill apace, and promise myself but a few years of enjoyment,' he complained to another friend. 'To tell you a secret, my constitution is quite broken. Since last May, I have hardly enjoyed one day of health. I am so subject to colds and rheums that I hardly dare stir from my own house . . .' A couple of years later, on one of his rare forays out of London, he suffered so bad an attack of asthma in Farnham that 'I really began to think seriously of suffocation.' Ill health alone, he told Garrick, deprived him of 'the unspeakable enjoyment I should sometimes derive from your private conversation as well as from the public exertion of your talents'. Writing to John Moore in the summer of 1762, he reported that although the asthma was holding off, 'I am extremely emaciated, and am afflicted with a tickling catarrh, and cough all night without ceasing.'

'I believe I might retrieve my constitution by a determined course of exercise and the cold bath,' he told his old friend. As a devotee of cold water, and sea water in particular, he visited Dover that summer, 'with a view to bathe in the sea' and do some riding, but 'immediately after my arrival, the weather broke, my asthma returned, my flesh fell away, and my spirits failed, so that I returned very disconsolate, and almost despairing of relief'. He was barely forty, but 'I am now so thin that you would hardly know me. My face is shrivelled up by the asthma like an ill-dried pippin, and my legs are as thick at the ankle as at the calf.' That autumn he set out again in search of health. 'Smollett is, I hear, on his last legs in Bath, his disease being an inveterate asthma, nor will he long continue to disturb the public or injure private character,' gloated the charitable Reverend Birch. Writing to William Hunter, Smollett reported that he had travelled across country from Southampton to Bath, calling in *en route* at Headly Park to visit the family of William Huggins. 'My health was so indifferent during the whole journey that I was obliged to get out of bed every night and sit for two hours until the difficulty of breathing abated,' he informed his fellow-medic, yet

> since my arrival in Bath I have, in spite of a fresh cold, slept
> very well, without any interruption from the asthma. I drink
> moderately of the water, ride out every day on the Downs, eat
> like a horse, and if I could recover a little flesh I should think
> myself already cured; but the truth is I am thinner than when
> I last saw you, and begin to be afraid of looking in the glass of
> a morning . . .

Despite his professional scepticism, and his loudly expressed views on the matter,

> I can feel a very sensible effect from the waters. I have no
> sooner drunk a large glass of them hot from the pump than my
> face, my hands, and feet begin to glow; and this sensation is
> succeeded by an itching and tingling all over the surface of my
> body, resembling what is called the prickly heat in the West
> Indies. I think I can plainly perceive these mineral waters
> opening up the obstructed capillaries, and restoring the perspi-
> ration which in the extremities had been in a great measure
> lost . . .

'I am much affected by the last mark of your friendship which I received on the day before I set out on my journey, and I hope you will give me leave to enjoy it in my own way,' he told Hunter. Despite the success of the *Complete History*, money worries still hovered: his old friend had sent him £50, which Smollett assumed to be a loan but Hunter saw as a gift, scribbling on the back of Smollett's promissory note instructions to his executors not to ask for the money back, 'because I sent the money to him as a present, never meaning to take it again'.

Smollett's poor health was aggravated by his static, sedentary existence. Hours spent on close editorial work and endless reading had, he told Richardson, taken their toll on his eyesight; for most of the time he was emotionally and physically drained. Writing to William

Huggins in those halcyon days when editorship of the *Critical Review* alone enabled 'the lowest reptile to asperse my morals as a man, and impeach my reputation as a writer', he had wondered why

> a man who can live in ease and tranquillity, exercising the virtues of benevolence, and fulfilling all the duties of social life, [should] torment himself with troubles over schemes of literary ambition, embark on a whiffling lottery of public praise, containing a thousand mortifying blanks for a prize of little value, and expose himself to the torrent of opposition swelled by the different streams of satire, ridicule and misrepresenta-tion . . . I long eagerly for some quiet, obscure retreat, where, as from a safe and happy harbour, I may look back with self gratulation upon that stormy sea of criticism in which my little bark has been so long and so violently tossed and afflicted.

Since then his little bark had been pummelled by far rougher waves; nor was there any letting up of his other literary endeavours. He was still involved, marginally, with the *Critical*, and with the *British Magazine*; the translation of Voltaire inched its way forward; and, in the spring of 1761, he had contemplated writing a history of Ireland, and may have visited Dublin that summer to look into the possi-bilities. Smollett was, one Charles O'Conor told a Dublin acquain-tance, 'a man of very considerable historical abilities, and should he attempt writing our history, we should exert ourselves from all quar-ters to supply him with proper materials'. George Faulkner, the Dublin printer, told Samuel Derrick that he had dined with the prospective author at 'Salter's at Chelsea' to discuss his plan, but in the end ill health forced Smollett to withdraw.

He dreamed of warmer climes, and an easier life; and, to facili-tate matters, he approached the bustling flatterer John Home, still active as Lord Bute's private secretary. 'My flesh begins to waste, and I begin to think the best chance I have for recovery will be a removal into a warmer climate,' he wrote in December 1762. The pension he had applied for, or been promised, as a reward for his work on the *Briton* had never materialised, but perhaps he could instead take up 'some moderate consulship abroad, the salary of which would enable me to live in comfort'. Three years earlier he had enquired about a consulship in Madrid – he felt qualified by his knowledge of the language – but nothing had come of it; more recently he had been offered Nice, but the salary was inadequate to support his family. An application to be appointed Physician to the British Army in Portugal had come to nothing, even though the Secretary of War, Charles Townshend, had 'professed great friendship and assured me that I might command his best offices'; Madrid had become vacant again, but should he be considered 'unworthy of filling the office', the Earl might consider him for Marseilles, the climate of which would suit his constitution. All proved fruitless – John Moore attributed this to the fact that 'Dr Smollett never spanielled ministers; he could not endure the insolence of office, or stoop to cultivate the favour of any person on account of his power' – and future attempts were similarly doomed. He was turned down for Nice and Livorno, and by then he had given vent to his views on the Niçois in *Travels through France and Italy*: Lord Shelburne dared not put his name forward for fear that 'the people would rise upon him and stone him in the streets on his first appearance'. In the meantime, Smollett assured a correspondent that 'I have neither pension nor place, nor am I of that disposition which can stoop to solicit either. I have always piqued myself on my independency, and I trust to God I shall preserve it to my dying day.'

Writing to John Moore in the summer of 1762, Smollett thanked his friend for his 'professions of concern about my health and fortune'. 'With respect to the last,' he went on,

> I have no cause to complain for want of encouragement. The public has always been a liberal patron to me since I commenced author. My difficulties have arisen from my own indiscretion; from a warm temper easily provoked to rashness; from a want of courage to refuse what I could not grant without doing injustice to my own family; from indolence, bashfulness and want of economy. I am sensible of all my weaknesses. I have suffered by them severely, but I have not vigour of mind sufficient to reform, and so must go on at the old rate to the end of the chapter.

Smollett's rueful self-analysis suggests that his family may have suffered from his remorseless addiction to work, and the freelance's inability to turn work down; but he could hardly blame himself for what was, in personal terms, the greatest tragedy of his life: the death of his only child.

Elizabeth Smollett was attended in her last illness by Alexander Carlyle's brother-in-law, Thomas Dickson, a doctor at the London Hospital, and died on 3 April 1763 at the age of fifteen, possibly of consumption; she was buried alongside her grandmother in Chelsea Old Church. In a letter to Alexander Reid, a surgeon at the Royal Hospital in Chelsea specialising in smallpox inoculation and a member of the Sublime Society of Beefsteaks and of the Chelsea Bowling Green Society, Smollett hoped that Reid and his wife would 'never feel the pangs of that unspeakable grief which the loss of a beloved child inspires'. Chelsea, he went on, would always remain to him 'a second native place, notwithstanding the irreparable misfortunes which happened to me while I resided in it. I mean the loss of my health, and of that which was dearer to me than health itself, my darling child, whom I cannot yet remember with any degree of composure.' Overwhelmed by 'unutterable sorrow', the Smolletts decided to pack up their Chelsea house, leave London and the literary life, and take themselves abroad for a time. Writing to thank William Hunter for the 'manifold instances' of his friendship, Smollett said he hoped that, should they never return, the possessions they left behind would be sufficient, if sold, to discharge any remaining debts, and that his sole ambition now was that of 'dying with the character of an honest man'. Life, it seemed, had proved too great a burden, and had little more to offer; yet his two greatest works still lay before him, without which he might barely be remembered.

8

End of the Road

Published in 1766, the year after he returned from a two-year absence, Smollett's *Travels through France and Italy* is a curmudgeonly master-piece, replete with bedbugs, filthy habits, sullen, extortionate land-lords, idolatrous priests, garlic-flavoured food and all the other horrors associated with life in Latin Europe. It is one of the most colourful, opinionated and informative of all travel books, yet it is unlikely that Smollett had such a work in mind when he set out on his adventures in June 1763. He travelled south in the hope that the warm, balmy air would somehow improve his ruined lungs, and help him and his wife to recover from the death of their daughter:

> My wife earnestly begged I would convey her from a country where every object served to nourish her grief: I was in hopes that a succession of new scenes would engage her attention, and gradually call off her mind from a series of painful reflec-tions; and I imagined the change of air, and a journey of near a thousand miles, would have a happy effect upon my own constitution.

'Traduced by malice, persecuted by faction, abandoned by false patrons, and overwhelmed by the sense of a domestic tragedy', he had, perhaps for ever, abandoned England as a 'scene of illiberal dispute, and incredible infatuation, where a few worthless incendiaries had, by dint of perfidious calumnies and atrocious abuse, kindled up a flame which threatened all the horrors of civil dissension'.

The Peace of Paris, signed in February 1766, had unleashed a torrent of English tourists, and the Smolletts were soon among them, trundling down the Dover road together with Tolloush, their manservant, and two young women – Ann Curry, a Newcastle girl, and Mrs Leaver's other granddaughter, Frances Lassells. But none loomed so large in Smollett's mind as his crates of books, which he needed to consult while revising the *Universal History* and completing the *Continuation* to his *Complete History of England*, and without which Mrs Smollett, who read no French, would be deprived of reading matter. Among those which Mrs Smollett could look forward to were the *Universal History* (58 volumes), the *Works of Voltaire* (the 25 volumes published so far), complete sets of the *Critical Review* and the *British Magazine*, the works of Shakespeare, Homer, Sophocles, Tibullus, Virgil, Horace and Juvenal, the comedies of Congreve, as well as Greek, Latin, French, Italian and Spanish dictionaries, her husband's collected novels and the *Complete History of England* (eight octavo volumes). When, on arrival at Boulogne, it turned out that his books had been intercepted by the customs and sent on for examination in Amiens, lest they 'contain something to the prejudice of the state, and of the Catholic religion', Smollett raced into action, firing off letters to the British ambassador, Lord Hertford, begging him to intervene with the authorities in Paris, and to Lady Douglas, a distant relative who happened to be in the French capital at the time. Once the books had been restored via the Intendant of Picardy, the Smolletts settled down to a three-month sojourn in Boulogne-sur-mer, paying three guineas a month for 'four bed-chambers on the first floor, a large parlour below', a kitchen and a cellar.

Although he claimed, in the *Travels*, that he had nothing against the French, that he respected them for their achievements in the arts and the sciences, for their gallantry and valour, and for that 'generous humanity which they exercise towards their enemies, even amidst the horrors of war', Smollett – like many of his contemporaries – took a fairly dim view of the people who lived on the far side of the English Channel. It was widely agreed that they were clever, dashing and stylish, but they were also – and here Smollett did much to reinforce a stereotype that was to persist well into the twentieth century, not least among the Germans – an essentially lightweight people: vain, frivolous and grubby, far more concerned with external show than with matters of real substance. 'The French are, generally speaking, very curious, confident, inquisitive, credulous, facetious, rather witty than wise, eternal babblers – in a word, they are at all times what an Englishman is when he's half-drunk,' an English traveller observed at the beginning of the eighteenth century, and Smollett would not have disagreed. The French might think themselves the 'richest, the bravest, the happiest, and the most powerful nation under the sun', but for Smollett they were a 'volatile, giddy, unthinking people', whose 'ruling passion' was vanity. It was when he reached Paris – then, as now, exciting a resentful awe among the English, and the spirit of competition: Parisians were better dressed but less well fed, London houses were more modest but more comfortable – that he gave full vent to his notion of the French as a race of preening coxcombs. In the meantime, he noted of the Boulogne locals that they were hard-featured, and that their brownish hue was attributable to their reluctance to wash or eat meat: their skin was desiccated and deprived of health-giving animal oils, and their pores were blocked with dirt, making it impossible for them to sweat in a free and salubrious way.

Nowadays we take it for granted that the English are scruffier than the French, and that nothing works on this side of the Channel: but until the 1950s at least, the opposite was held to be true, and Smollett was among those responsible for this view. French lavatories were infamous, and for all his fictional enthusiasm for lavatorial matters, he professed himself appalled. 'They are utter strangers to what we call common decency, and I could give you some high-flavoured instances, at which a native of Edinburgh would stop his nose,' he declared. Drawing on his experience of the Boulogne *noblesse* – a 'vain, proud, poor and slothful' crew – he could point to a lady who, lavatory-bound, was 'handed to the house of office by her admirer, who stood at the door, and entertained her with *bons mots* all the time she was within'; before long, he prophesied, 'a conveniency will be placed behind every chair in company, with a proper provision of waste paper, that individuals may make themselves easy without parting company'. Smollett famously loathed French food – 'I hate the French cookery, and abominate garlic' – and matters were made worse by the unwholesome way in which they took snuff while eating, plunging their fingers into the snuff box, up their noses and into the *ragoût* on the table, and by a tendency to swill water around their putrid gums before discharging it in front of the assembled company. Doors and windows never shut properly, locks and latches failed to work, and the chimneys smoked and let in the rain.

French religion, unlike French drains, afforded a 'perpetual comedy'. That those with piles should have their own patron saint in the form of St Haemorrhoisa was all too appropriate for a people too frivolous to have been subjected to the Reformation; he likened Roman Catholicism to comedy and the Calvinism of his native land to tragedy, in that 'the first amuses the senses, and excites ideas of mirth and good humour; the other, like tragedy, deals in the passions of terror and pity'. French religious devotees were, by definition, hypocrites; the cult of the Virgin must surely have originated in France, since the French 'pique themselves on their gallantry to the fair sex'; as for the statues in their churches, 'their attitudes are affected, unnatural and desultory, and their draperies fantastic; or, as one of our English artists expressed himself, *they are all of a flutter*'.

'Every thing is done in a clumsy and slovenly manner, which is very disagreeable and even shocking to those who have been accustomed to English neatness; and there is a total want of delicacy in the manners of the people. They are generally civil, but have no sentiment, and their ignorance and superstition put me out of all patience,' Smollett told Alexander Reid, yet for all his complaints he seems to have enjoyed life in Boulogne. Best of all was swimming in the Channel. 'By a daily repetition of the bath, I have diminished my cough, strengthened my body, and recovered my spirits,' he noted; and although he informed William Hunter that he had been out of action for a fortnight with a 'severe cold which has handled me so severely, and reduced me so much that I now perceive the state of my health becomes a very serious affair', three weeks of sea-bathing had brought 'such benefit as almost transcends belief'. The streets of the lower town, unfairly compared with Wapping, were 'broad and clean and well-paved, and the houses very commodious. I would never desire to live in a more agreeable place if my health did not require a milder climate,' he told Hunter: but it was time to push on towards the south, and to Nice, where 'the cheapness of living will in a little time make amends for the extraordinary expense of the journey' as well as, with luck, improving his health.

The Smolletts made their way from Boulogne to Paris in a *berline*, a large coach drawn by four horses, and manned by two postilions and an *avant courier*, who galloped ahead to make sure that a fresh team of horses was waiting at the next post-house. Contemporaries disagreed over whether French or English roads were better, and which nation effected a swifter change at post-houses: almost all agreed in grumbling about French inns, which were said to be swarming with bedbugs, particularly in the blankets and the tapestries on the walls; dishonest landlords and uncarpeted stone floors also came in for censure. Quite forgetting the poor accommodation endured on the Dover road, where 'the chambers are in general cold and comfortless, the beds paultry, the cookery execrable, the wine poison, the attendance bad, the publicans insolent, and the bills extortion', Smollett found little to praise in their French equivalents, though still worse awaited him in Italy. 'One finds nothing but dirt and imposition,' he grumbled: the landlords and staff of the *auberges* between Boulogne and Paris made no effort to welcome or help travellers, who were 'served with the most mortifying indifference, at the same time they are laying schemes for fleecing you of your money'.

In Paris, the Smolletts took rooms in the Hôtel Montmorency, in the Faubourg St-Germain. Smollett splashed out and hired a carriage, in which they inspected the Tuileries, the Louvre, Les Invalides, the Luxembourg Gardens and Versailles ('a dismal habitation', the apartments of which were 'dark, ill-furnished, dirty and unprincely'). The natural indolence of the French, Smollett decided, was exacerbated by an excess of public holidays: three 'lusty hussies' in the apartment opposite did nothing all day but eat grapes, comb their hair and gawp at the passers-by, and made no effort to make the beds or clean the rooms. The vanity and frivolity of the Parisians were all too obvious. France, Smollett decreed, was 'the general reservoir from which all the absurdities of false taste, luxury, and extravagance have overflowed the different states and kingdoms of Europe'. Although 'human affectation' was carried to the 'farthest point of folly in extravagance' in the 'primed and painted' faces of the women – he particularly objected to their addiction to rouge, and to false hair which resembled 'the woolly heads of the Guinea Negroes' – French men were even more 'ridiculous and insignificant' than the women: indeed, 'of all the coxcombs on the earth, a French *petit maître* is the most impertinent'. *Petits maîtres* had an electrifying effect on bluff, plain-speaking, commonsensical Britons, who regarded them as preening, undersized runts who lived in poverty but spent their all on clothes and wigs and make-up, strutting about in society by day and living in squalor when not on public display. Even more absurd than the French attempt at hunting – according to Smollett, this involved smartly dressed men in wigs taking pot-shots at hares from behind trees – was the way in which the men, especially those of the *petit maître* variety, spent long hours lurking round ladies' bedrooms, advising them on what to wear, helping with their elaborate hair-styles, and whipping out a comb and a pair of scissors at the slightest provocation. The French, he decided, 'have a most ridiculous fondness for their hair, and this I believe they inherit from their remote ancestors'. All classes – the slothful, useless *noblesse*, the bourgeois, the ground-down peasantry – wore their hair long: because of their modest size, this gave them 'no small resemblance to large baboons walking upright'.

Although French men liked nothing more than paying compliments to women, 'their hearts are not susceptible of deep impressions', and of all people they were 'the least capable of feeling for the distresses of their fellow-creatures'. Left to his own devices, a Frenchman would invariably try to seduce a wife or a daughter in the name of gallantry; with his taste for intrusive, impertinent questions, he was the embodiment of levity, and 'if a Frenchman is capable of true friendship, it must certainly be the most disagreeable present he can make to a man of true English character'. When it came to matters of dress, the French were, as a matter of course, superior to the plain, provincial-looking English, who were invariably so awestruck by French style and sophistication that instead of taking pride in their own mode of dress, they tried to dress like the natives within hours of arrival in Paris. Even Dr Johnson bought white stockings, a new wig and a hat for his single visit to the French capital, and Smollett lamented the tendency of his countrymen to emulate French 'frippery', wishing that they 'had anti-gallican spirit enough to produce themselves in their own genuine English dress'. To make matters worse, French card-sharpers, of both sexes, preyed on the British, 'who are supposed to be full of money, rash, incautious and utterly ignorant of play'.

From Paris, the Smolletts moved on to Lyon, via Dijon: Smollett hired a coach, six horses and a postilion, and laid in a supply of provisions rather than face the horrors of French cuisine. Encountering what he assumed to be a *petit maître* on the way, he was extremely short with him, and was horrified to learn that he was a nobleman: he worried that his behaviour would 'confirm that national reproach of bluntness, and ill breeding, under which we live in this country', and that with his 'grey mourning frock under a wide great coat, bob wig without powder, large laced hat, and meagre, wrinkled, discontented countenance' he must have cut an uncouth figure. Many travellers made their way down the Rhône valley by barge or *diligence par eau*, their carriages lashed firmly to the deck, but Smollett decided to stick to the road instead. As they made their way south from Lyon, they were warned of robbers, so Tolloush was ordered to brandish a loaded blunderbuss; it was much admired by the peasantry, who scattered like sheep when it was fired in the air for demonstration purposes. Smollett was revolted by the pervading whiff of garlic and the southern habit of eating thrushes and other small birds; in Nîmes he admired the Roman baths, but was shocked to find two 'dirty hags' washing their children's clothes therein.

From there they travelled on to Montpellier, a small university town with a large population of English residents, where Smollett planned to consult the celebrated Dr Fizès about his lungs. It rained for a week, and, he told William Hunter, 'this change of the atmosphere relaxed me to such a degree that all my complaints returned together with a most uncomfortable dejection of spirits'. It was widely assumed that moist air and melancholy went together, and this partly explained why the English were so prone to melancholia: a damp climate made the blood 'viscid', and diluted the animal spirits. Cheyne and other influential physicians had also attributed melancholy to a relaxation of the nerves and the fibres, which lost tone and elasticity as a result; in *The English Malady*, Cheyne suggested that a sedentary and solitary life worsened the condition, and recommended travel, reading and company as possible antidotes. The bodily 'fibres' and 'juices' had to be kept healthy and in balance, and the fibres 'loose' and 'elastic' enough to allow the juices to flow freely. One of the penalties of luxury was that the upper classes in particular took far less exercise than they needed: exercise built up the fibres, promoted circulation and perspiration, and kept the juices in a fluid state, 'their viscidity broken and dissolved', and sedentary folk needed to keep active in order to give 'their solid parts a more firm and lasting tone'.

Smollett shared such ideas to the full, and while on his travels he also subscribed to Cheyne's belief in the importance of eating plenty of chicken and white meat. He was less impressed by Dr Fizès, both as man and diagnostician. The celebrated doctor turned out to be 'an old sordid scoundrel, and an old woman into the bargain', and his eyes 'sparkled at the sight of the fee'. He prescribed '*bouillons* of land tortoise', opiates, and a 'course of goats' milk', but, to Smollett's annoyance, made no mention of exercise: later in his journey, when he had taken to swimming in the Mediterranean, he wrote that 'as my disorder at first arose from a sedentary life, producing a relaxation of the fibres, which naturally brought on a listlessness, indolence and dejection of the spirits, I am convinced that this hard exercise of mind and body co-operated with the change of air and objects to brace up the relaxed constitution.'

Another of Dr Fizès's unsatisfied patients was Smollett's fellow-novelist and fellow-consumptive, Laurence Sterne, who had also travelled with his wife to the South of France in search of health. The Smolletts and the Sternes met several times in Montpellier, and Sterne later provided some brief but unflattering glimpses of Smollett in his own, very different, account of his travels in France.

A *Sentimental Journey* was published in 1768, two years after *Travels through France and Italy*, achieving a fame and popularity far outstripping its blunter, less fanciful and less poetical rival: as John Moore put it, 'After Sterne's sarcasm appeared, many who had admired and praised [the *Travels*] now condemned them as void of taste, and some who had relished them chiefly on account of their high-coloured painting of certain customs among the French and Italians, now censured them as illiberal and full of national reflections.' Sterne portrayed Smollett as 'Smelfungus', the quintessential bad-tempered, prejudiced, grumbling Briton abroad. 'I pity the man who can travel from *Dan* to *Beersheba*, and cry, 'Tis all barren – And so it is; and so is all the world to him who will not cultivate the fruit it offers,' he wrote, noting how 'The learned SMELFUNGUS travelled from Boulogne to Paris – from Paris to Rome – and so on – but he set out with the spleen and jaundice, and every object he pass'd by was discoloured or distorted – He wrote an account of them, but 'twas nothing but the account of his miserable feelings.' Sterne had, in fact, complained quite as much as Smollett about the heat and the dirt and the verminous inns, and when they met in Montpellier he seemed less reconciled to French life than his fellow-sufferer. Undaunted, Sterne went on to say how, in Rome,

I met Smelfungus in the grand portico of the Pantheon – he was just coming out of it – *'Tis nothing but a huge cock-pit*, said he – I wish you had said nothing worse of the Venus of Medicis, replied I – for in passing through Florence, I had heard that he had fallen foul upon the goddess, and used her worse than a common strumpet, without the least provocation in nature

and how

I popp'd upon Smelfungus again at Turin, in his return home; and a sad tale of sorrowful adventures he had to tell, 'wherein he spoke of moving accidents by flood and field, and of the cannibals which each other eat: the Anthropophagi' he had been flea'd alive, and bedevil'd, and used worse than St Bartholomew, at every stage he had come at –

– I'll tell it, cried Smelfungus, to the world. You had better tell it, said I, to your physician.

Smollett had indeed been disappointed by the Pantheon, and, in defiance of contemporary taste, was critical of the Venus de Medicis ('I cannot help thinking that there is no beauty in the features of Venus; and that the attitude is awkward and out of character'): but he was far better informed about art and architecture, and far less of the philistine, than Sterne would have us believe; nor had any further encounters between the two men taken place, since he had left Italy some time before Sterne's arrival there. (Sterne's other xenophobe abroad, 'Mundungus', was Samuel Sharp, whose *Letters from Italy* was published in 1766. Sharp was scathing about the straw on the beds in Italian inns, the filthy sheets and the shortage of curtains, and regretted the near-universal absence of 'that cleanly and most useful invention, a privy: so that what should be collected and buried in oblivion, is forever under your nose and eyes.' 'I heartily pity them,' Sterne wrote of both men: 'they have brought up no faculties for this work; and was the happiest mansion in heaven to be allotted to Smelfungus and Mundungus, they would be so far from being happy, that the souls of Smelfungus and Mundungus would do penance there to all eternity.')

In mid-September the Smolletts set out from Montpellier to Nîmes, where they found a lavatory in a 'most shocking condition': the locals deliberately misaimed and 'left their offerings on the floor', so displaying 'a degree of beastliness, which would appear detestable even in the capital of North Britain'. In Nice, where they spent the next ten months, the Smolletts rented

a ground floor paved with brick, consisting of a kitchen, two large halls, a couple of good rooms with chimneys, three large closets that serve for bed-chambers and dressing-rooms, a butler's room, and three apartments for servants, lumber or stores, to which we ascend by narrow wooden stairs. I have likewise two small gardens, well-stocked with oranges, lemons, peaches, figs, grapes, corinths, salad, and pot-herbs. It is supplied with a draw-well of good water, and there is another in the vestibule, which is cool, large and magnificent.

He liked the climate, the scenery, the flowers, the fruit and even the food so much that

> When I stand upon the rampart, and look round me, I can scarce help thinking myself enchanted. The small extent of country which I see, is all cultivated like a garden. Indeed, the plain presents nothing but gardens, full of green trees loaded with oranges, lemons, citrons, and bergamots, which make a delightful appearance. If you examine them more nearly, you will find plantations of green peas ready to gather; all sorts of sallading, and pot-herbs, in perfection; and plats of roses, carnations, ranunculas, anemones, and daffodils, blowing in full glory, with such beauty, vigour, and perfume, as no flower in England ever exhibited.

As ever, this earthly paradise was blighted by the residents. The Smolletts' maids were 'slovenly, slothful and unconscionable cheats'; the shopkeepers were 'poor, greedy and over-reaching'; neither industry nor commerce could flourish because 'the natives themselves are in general such dirty knaves, that no foreigners will trust them in the way of trade'. The artisans were 'very lazy, very needy, very awkward, and void of all ingenuity', while the working classes were 'diminutive, meagre, withered, dirty, and half-naked'. The swarthy-looking women were pot-bellied as a result of 'the great quantity of vegetable trash which they eat'; the churches were sanctuaries for criminals – though murder seemed unknown, thieves and beggars abounded – and 'superstition reigns under the darkest shades of ignorance and prejudice'. Smollett was appalled by the plight of the Sardinian galley-slaves, and by the use of the strappado; cultural life seemed non-existent; time and money were wasted on religious festivals. Drawing on his years of experience as a compiler, editor and collector of curious facts, Smollett thought of writing a 'complete natural history' of Nice, but he had 'neither health, strength nor opportunity' to do so. All the same, he made careful notes of every-thing he saw, from the silk industry and the making of olive oil to the use of human excrement as manure: this, he noted, was assessed by taste and flavour, and 'the jakes of a Protestant family, who eat *gras* every day, bears a much higher price than the privy of a good Catholic, who lives *maigre* one half of the year. The vaults belonging to the convent of Minims are not worth emptying.' And to William Hunter he reported that the Niçois had the strongest and whitest teeth he had ever seen; bearing his friend's anatomical collection in mind, 'I wish I could send you a head, but I am afraid I shall find no opportunity.'

Smollett caused amazement among the natives when, in May, he began to swim regularly in the Mediterranean; his house was a mile or so from the sea, and he was taken to and fro in a sedan chair. Monitoring his health as closely as ever, he noted that the high salt levels in the air affected the 'scorbutical eruption on my right hand, which diminishes and increases according to the state of my health'. Such air 'should have no bad effect on a moist, phlegmatic consti-tution such as mine; and yet, it must be owned, I have been visibly wasting since I came hither'. Even so, 'I have breathed more freely than for some years, and my spirits have been more alert.' Very much the Briton abroad, he kept a keen eye on the weather, and at the end of his *Travels* he printed a day-by-day 'Register of the Weather', giving details of temperature, wind direction and rainfall for the entire period they were in Nice.

Smollett had always planned to visit Italy, the classical remains of which formed the climax of an educated man's Grand Tour, and for some time he had been busying himself learning Italian. Nice was part of the Kingdom of Sardinia, and the roads were inferior to those in France: Monaco, to the east, could only be reached, in great discomfort, on a donkey; to the east of Monaco the Ligurian moun-tains swept steeply down to the sea, making road travel between there and Genoa impossible until Napoleon built the Corniche or coastal road early in the next century. John Armstrong wrote recom-mending a sea voyage as preferable to taking a mule or sedan chairs over the mountains (carriages were sometimes dismantled, carried through the mountains on mules, and reassembled on the other side).

The most familiar type of boat was the felucca, rowed by ten or twelve oarsmen and large enough to carry a post-chaise, but the Smolletts opted instead for a gondola, 'rowed by four men, and steered by the patron'. Smollett's steering apart, they ran the risk of storms, Barbary pirates, contrary winds and oarsmen who, according to innumerable English travellers, made for the nearest port at the merest suspicion of rough weather; but although the ladies in the party, now reduced to Mrs Smollett and Miss Curry, were seasick, the Italian oarsmen proved less craven than reported, singing vigorously as they plied the oars, and good progress was made.

Disembarked at St Remo, they stayed in what they were assured was the best *auberge* on the Genoese Riviera. It was, Smollett declared, 'so dirty and miserable, that it would disgrace the worst hedge ale-house in England'; the walls were hung with cobwebs, and 'I believe the brick floor had not been swept for half a century.' The inn at Noli, further round the coast, was even more horrific, and the bedbugs so pestilential that Smollett abandoned his bed and slept on a chest instead. Italian inns may have been even worse than the French, but after inspecting the churches and palaces of Genoa Smollett applauded the Italians for spending their money on public buildings rather than, like the French, on 'tawdry' clothes and inedible meals. The party then travelled on by gondola to Lerici, where they were nearly poisoned in an inn run by a butcher and reeking of recently slaughtered animals. In Siena they stayed in an inn which 'stunk like a privy'; Smollett, in Pooter-like vein, did battle with a recalcitrant ostler, and 'would have caned him heartily' had he not taken to his heels. Although he had been much taken with Pisa, the solitude and quiet of which 'would with me be a strong motive to choose it as a place of retirement', he found little to enjoy as they made their way south via Florence and the dreary Campania.

Like any good antiquarian, or the modish 'connoisseurs' whom he viewed with a jaundiced eye, Smollett was eager to inspect 'the originals of many pictures and statues, which I had admired in prints and descriptions', but Rome itself left much to be desired. Compared to the Thames, the Tiber was 'no more than an inconsiderable stream, foul, deep and rapid', and its bridges were as nothing to Westminster or that in construction at Blackfriars. Despite the profusion of fountains, the streets and even the palaces were 'disgraced with filth', and the corridors and staircases of the most elegant and grandiose buildings turned out to be 'depositories of nastiness'. The Circus Maximus seemed pitifully small after St James's Park, and he ridiculed the naval battles staged by the Ancient Romans on artificial lakes the size of the Serpentine, claiming with John Bullish glee that 'half a dozen English frigates would have been able to defeat both the contending fleets at the famous Battle of Actium'. The Ancient Romans, he decided, had been a 'frowzy' and a 'barbarous' people, whose fibres had been fatally weakened by their addiction to warm baths, 'a point of luxury borrowed from the effeminate Asiatics'. And it was impossible to find the kind of garden that appealed to an Englishman, for although the Italians understood the 'excellencies of art', they had no idea of the 'beauties of nature'.

Nor did all Italian art come up to scratch. The Sistine Chapel was far too busy for its own or the viewer's good: like 'a number of people talking all at once', it was fine in parts but, taken as a whole, 'a mere mob, without subordination, keeping or repose'. And were he the owner of Raphael's *Transfiguration*, he would have sawn it in two for better effect. Such heretical views were put forward with a certain diffidence: 'I do not set up for a judge in these matters, and very likely I may incur the ridicule of the virtuosi for the remarks I have made: but I am used to speak my mind freely on all subjects that fall under the cognisance of my senses . . .' One subject on which he had no hesitation in speaking about was the art associated with the Catholic Church. The altar in St Peter's was 'a heap of puerile finery'; he disapproved dreadfully of Michelangelo's sculpture of the dead Christ lying in his mother's lap ('The figure of Christ is as much emaciated, as if he had died of a consumption: besides, there is something indelicate, not to say indecent, in the attitude and design of a man's body, stark naked, lying upon the knees of a woman'). He abominated such 'implements of popish superstition' as relics, and the 'nauseous repetition of the figure on the cross, which is itself a very mean and disagreeable object, only fit for the prisons of condemned criminals'; paintings of martyrdoms should have been discouraged, since they 'can only serve to fill the mind with gloomy ideas, and encourage a spirit of religious fanaticism'.

By expressing such views, John Moore declared, Smollett 'exposed himself to the reprehension of the whole class of connoisseurs, the real as well as the far more numerous body of pretenders to that science'. Smollett was almost certainly indifferent to the disdain of connoisseurs, the majority of whom he ridiculed as affected and ignorant poseurs with money to burn and a credulous readiness to be cheated by unscrupulous dealers:

I have seen in different parts of Italy, a number of raw boys, whom Britain seemed to have poured forth on purpose to bring her national character into contempt: ignorant, petulant, rash, and profligate, without any knowledge or experience of their own, without any director to improve their understanding, or superintend their conduct. One engages in play with an infamous gamester, and is stripped perhaps in the very first partie: another is poxed and pillaged by an ancient cantatrice: a third is bubbled by a knavish antiquarian: and a fourth is laid under contribution by a dealer in pictures . . .

Not only was Smollett better informed about the visual arts than his critics assumed, but, as in his unorthodox opinions about the then much admired Venus de Medicis, often ahead of his time as well. As editor of the *Critical Review*, he had made a point of writing about artists as well as writers, and had shown himself to be knowledgeable about both the techniques employed by painters and engravers, and the market for their work. In the *Present State of All Nations* he would declare that 'England affords a great variety of geniuses in all the liberal arts, except in the sublime parts of painting. Portraits, it must be owned, are tolerably well executed, and drawing is well understood: but the spirit of invention, the grand composition, the enthusiasm of the art, seem wanting in this climate . . .' That may have been so, but as an editor he had been eager to encourage the development of a national art, and had taken pains to encourage British artists. He had been among the first to review a Reynolds painting; in 1756 he inspected, and then wrote about, Hogarth's altar triptych before its removal to St Mary Redcliffe in Bristol, and later wrote of its creator that, in less devotional vein, he was 'an inimitable original with respect to invention, humour and expression'. His thwarted aspirations for a literary academy found partial expression in his support for the Society for the Encouragement of Arts, Manufacture and Commerce and the Society of Artists, founded in 1754 by William Shipley; like Hogarth's St Martin's Lane Academy, which had been attended by Gainsborough and Allen Ramsay, such bodies were devoted to the encouragement of British art, and culminated in the foundation in 1768 of William Chambers's Royal Academy, the realisation of Robert Foulis's dream of a public institution devoted to the training and display of artists, painters and sculptors. Smollett had made a point of writing about those artists associated with the Society of Artists, including Reynolds, Richard Wilson and the sculptor Joseph Wilton, and he had encouraged Francis Hayman to provide illustrations of Caractacus, some Druids and the Battle of Hastings for the *Complete History*, as well as for *Don Quixote* and the fourth edition of *Roderick Random*. For all his suspicion of commerce, he had taken a particular interest in the ways in which art could be reproduced and thereby shown to a wider public, to the benefit of viewers and artists alike. Many of the most popular and widely used engravers, like Grignion and Ravenet, were French, but he encouraged British talent in the form of Robert Strange, a Scot and a friend of William Hunter, who engraved five portraits for the *Complete History*, and Thomas Frye, one of the pioneers of the new technique of mezzotint, and urged his readers to buy their work; he wrote about the influential print-dealer John Boydell, who in 1763 earned himself some £2,000 from the sale of 8,000 copies of an engraving of Richard Wilson's *Niobe*. Sterne's mockery of 'Smelfungus' may have amused and delighted the connoisseurs, but it could well be that Smollett's knowledge and appreciation far outstripped his own.

With Rome and its antiquities out of the way, the party headed north to Florence. The inns were so dire that Smollett reckoned 'a common prisoner in the Marshalsea or King's Bench is more cleanly and commodiously lodged'. At Terni there was no glass in the window, vermin swarmed everywhere, and the food was repulsive; Smollett, driven to despair, almost resorted to 'manual correction', but had he done so, or refused to pay the bill, the landlord might have withheld fresh horses. 'Of all the people I know, the Italians are the most villainously rapacious,' Smollett decided. In what may have been the worst inn of all, the bedclothes were 'filthy enough to turn the stomach of a muleteer', so much so that Smollett slept wrapped up in his greatcoat, while the 'victuals' were 'cooked in such a manner, that even a Hottentot could not have beheld them without loathing'.

As they pushed north, past Perugia and Lake Trasimene, the journey became still more hellish. Smollett developed whooping cough; the roads were so rough and, at times, so steep that they often had to climb out of the carriage and walk; one of the wheels flew off, causing a maddening delay. Matters reached a climax outside the walls of Florence. It was late in the evening and sheeting with rain, and only two of the city gates were open. Smollett and his wife had to abandon their carriage and make a three-mile circuit of the city in search of an entrance, sloshing through mud that often came up to their thighs. Smollett, who was wearing his greatcoat, was lashing with sweat; he had to support Mrs Smollett, 'a delicate creature, who had scarce ever walked a mile in her life' and 'wept in silence, half dead with terror and fatigue'. Earlier in the evening, Smollett had vented some of his frustration on an uncooperative driver – 'I told him he was an impertinent rascal, and as he still hesitated, I collared him with one hand, and shook my cane over his head with the other' – and when, the following morning, they were joined by their fellow-travellers, and their luggage had been safely loaded on to the carriage, they found themselves, for all their travails, 'well refreshed, and in good spirits'.

From Florence they made their way back to Lerici, where they hired a felucca that would take them, in stages, back to Nice: Smollett deliberately chose one under the command of a Latin-speaking Spaniard rather than an Italian, since 'by this time, I had imbibed a strong prejudice against the common people of that country'. Italian innkeepers did their worst to the end. In the suitably named Finale, just beyond Genoa, the beds were 'so shockingly nasty' as to be unusable, the innkeeper a 'murderous assassin' and the waiter 'stark-staring mad'; when presented with an outrageous bill, Smollett, 'incensed by the rascal's presumption', told him he would be lucky to get half that amount, and 'a good beating into the bargain'. The landlord proving obdurate, Smollett appeared before him 'with my sword in one hand and my cane in the other': mine host was reduced to a 'pale and staring' shadow of his former self, and it was agreed that his prickly guest could pay whatever he saw fit. Porto Mauritio proved even worse: the room next to the Smolletts was occupied by a girl with smallpox, who smelt so strong 'as to perfume the whole house'. They travelled on to San Remo by mule, the ladies sitting astride their steeds, and from there they rejoined their felucca for the short journey back to Nice.

The combination of irritation and enforced exercise left him feeling fitter and stronger than before – so much so that, not long after their return, Smollett and a servant travelled by mule over the mountains to Turin. Smollett fired his pistol at two men who might have been bandits, they encountered a countess in a sedan chair carried by six men, they sledged downhill on the Italian side, and they met up with a grubby, pipe-smoking, hook-nosed marquis whose legs were so long that they almost scraped the ground to either side of his mule: his boots were so filthy, so huge and so waterlogged that he found it impossible to take them off, and could only be prised out of them by means of a rope round the heel and assorted villagers tugging at the other end.

By now it was time to return to England, and after a last-minute row with their landlord the Smolletts packed up and made their way back through Provence. Melting snow made the roads impassable, so they took a boat to Antibes. After pausing in Aix, where Smollett drank the waters and noted the disappearance of the scorbutic 'tetter' from his hand, they trundled up the Rhône valley to Lyon, Dijon, Paris, and so home. As a result, perhaps, of his Italian experiences, Smollett seemed better disposed to the French, and more concerned about social inequalities and the sufferings of the peasantry than with the preening of *petits maîtres*. Years after his death, Smollett was said by some to have been the author of a celebrated 'Prophecy', addressed to an unidentified clerical friend in Northumberland, in which the writer, feeling 'the chill hand of death gradually stealing over me', and uneasily aware of various calamities 'which I foresee, but shall never live to experience', forecast the end of colonisation by European states, the revolt of the American colonies ('republicans to a man'), and revolution in France, where it seemed impossible that 'the present despotic system can, at any rate, continue *more than twenty years longer*'. Whether or not Smollett was the author, he thought it unlikely that life could continue unchanged in France. Pondering the vexed issue of whether the English or the French were more highly taxed, he wrote, in language reminiscent of *Peregrine Pickle*,

> When I, therefore, see the country of England smiling with cultivation; the grounds exhibiting all the perfection of agriculture, parcelled out into beautiful enclosures, corn fields, hay and pasture, woodland and common; when I see her meadows well stocked with black cattle; her downs covered with sheep; when I view her teams of horses and oxen, large and strong, fat and sleek; when I see her farm houses the habitations of plenty, cleanliness, and convenience; and her peasants well fed, well lodged, well clothed, tall and stout, and hale and jolly; I cannot help concluding that the people are well able to bear those impositions which the public necessities have rendered necessary. On the other hand, when I perceive such signs of poverty, misery, and dirt, among the commonalty of France, their unfenced fields dug up in despair, without the intervention of meadow or fallow ground, without cattle to furnish manure, without horses to execute the plans of agriculture; their farm houses mean, their furniture wretched, their apparel beggarly; themselves and their beasts the images of famine; I cannot help thinking they groan under oppression, either from their landlords, or their government; probably from both.

But change was on the way:

> There are, undoubtedly, many marks of relaxation in the reins of the French government, and, in all probability, the subjects of France will be the first to take advantage of it. There is at present a violent fermentation of different principles among them, which under the reign of a very weak prince, or during

a long minority, may produce a great change in the constitution. In proportion to the progress of reason and philosophy,
which have made great advances in this kingdom, superstition
loses ground; ancient prejudices give way; a spirit of freedom
takes the ascendant . . .

'You cannot imagine what pleasure I feel while I survey the white
cliffs of Dover,' he wrote from Boulogne: for all the literary and political battering he had endured, 'I am attached to my country, because
it is the land of liberty, cleanliness, and convenience; but I love it
still more tenderly, as the scene of all my interesting connections;
as the habitation of my friends, for whose conversation, correspondence and esteem, I wish alone to live.'

Back in London, the Smolletts took a house near Golden Square,
within easy walking distance of old friends like the Macaulays, David
Hume and John Home, and round the corner from William Hunter's
lecture hall and anatomical collection; they were joined, in due
course, by their heavy luggage, which had been sent by sea from
Nice. 'I am returned to England after an absence of two years, during
which I have been more than once on the brink of the grave,'
Smollett told John Moore in July 1765. 'I have been brought back
no more than the skeleton of what I was, but with proper care that
skeleton may hang for some few years together.' He planned to spend
the winter in Bath, but 'if I find that climate intolerable, I shall
once more go into exile, and never more think of returning'. In the
meantime, he busied himself completing the fifth and final volume
of his *Continuation of the Complete History of England*; it was published
in October, when the Smolletts moved to Bath, taking rooms on
South Parade. Writing to Moore the following month, Smollett said
that although he had written some pieces for his own amusement,
he had severed all connections with the *Critical Review* 'and every
other literary system' – by which he meant, presumably, the *British
Magazine*. He was, however, working on a book about his travels,
which he had 'thrown into a series of letters', to be published in the
spring in two volumes. 'I will not answer for their success with the
public,' he went on, but he hoped they might prove helpful to 'other
valetudinarians who travel for the recovery of their health'.

Composed of forty-one letters to real or imaginary friends, among them William Hunter, William Smellie, the Macaulays and John Moore, as well as the more numerous unnamed recipients, *Travels through France and Italy* combined two fashionable literary genres of which Smollett had direct experience: the travel book consisting of letters to a friend or friends, and written, ideally, by a dyspeptic, hypochondriacal narrator; and the compendium or gazetteer. Eleven years before, Smollett had edited Alexander Drummond's *Travels*, which had made use of the epistolary form, and the genre had flourished in the years between: as the imaginary bookseller put it in the preamble to *Humphry Clinker*, that most ingenious of all epistolary novels, 'there have been so many letters upon travels lately published – What between Smollett's, Sharp's, Derrick's, Thicknesse's, Baltimore's and Baretti's, together with Shandy's Sentimental Travels, the public seems to be cloyed with that kind of entertainment . . .' But *Humphry Clinker* itself – for which the *Travels* might have been, in Smollett's mind, a model or dummy run – was to combine a novelist's freedom and invention with the close observation of people, places and social trends more usually associated with a geographer, an economist or a social historian; and although some of the letters in the *Travels* may have been sent – none of them survives – it seems far more probable that Smollett used the letters as a device to combine his own experiences with detailed observations of the places he visited, and that most if not all of them were written up after his return to England.

Like many writers, Smollett was given to hyperbole, and may not have worried over-much about the less important details of time and place: Sterne may have taken authorial liberties over his alleged encounters with Smelfungus in Italy, but Smollett was happily inconsistent himself. Letters XVIII to XXII are dated from Nice between September and November 1764, yet the Smolletts had left for Italy in September; Letter XVII refers to a murder Smollett claimed to have witnessed in Florence, but is dated three months before his arrival there; the last Italian letter is dated March 1765, four months after his return to France. Genuine letters, if they ever existed, may have been polished and improved: in Letter XVIII Smollett says that he has never seen a swordfish, but then adds in a footnote, 'Since I wrote the above letter, I have eaten several times of this fish.' He combined, brilliantly, the conversational ease and vivacity inherent in good letters with the appetite for knowledge – historical, topographical, anthropological – he had picked up during his vast and seemingly interminable labours on the *Compendium of Authentic and Entertaining Voyages*, the *Universal History*, and other exhaustive if unreadable works. In between the obstreperous postilions and the filthy lavatories and the bug-ridden beds and the sullen innkeepers, the *Travels* are crammed with hard information – much of which is, especially when dealing with Roman antiquities, stunningly tedious but mercifully compacted, so that the impatient reader, spotting some antique sculpture lumbering towards him, can safely skip whole pages at a single bound and seek refuge in a verminous *auberge* or a carriage stranded, minus wheels, halfway up a Tuscan hillside. The gazetteer in Smollett, never far beneath the surface, was assiduous in his homework. He read, paraphrased and sometimes recycled a mass of material from contemporary travellers and from the ancient world; for the wearisome Roman antiquities, he drew extensively on the 1,800 pages of *Roma antiqua, e moderna* of 1750, lifting his account of the baths of Ancient Rome directly from this long-forgotten guidebook.

Smollett may not have thought much of its inhabitants, but his detailed, highly coloured account of the town's balmy climate and its perfect position between the sea and the mountains did much to popularise Nice in particular, and the Riviera in general, with English visitors, even if the full effect was not to be felt for another century at least. The Niçois may eventually have honoured him, in 1885, with a 'rue Smollet' [*sic*], but Arthur Young, visiting the town some eighteen years after Smollett's death, was warned that 'if he [Smollett] were to go again thither the Nissards would certainly knock him on the head'. Smollett's book achieved a certain notoriety as a model of its kind, as harsh about the French and the Italians as the English were about the Scots, only a good deal funnier and more entertaining. The *Critical Review*, loyal as ever to its founder, praised the *Travels* on the unliterary grounds that it did 'more service to Great Britain than fifty acts of Parliament for prohibiting French fripperies and foreign commodities, or even forbidding the exportation of fools, fops and coxcombs'; but although reactions at home were generally favourable, including that of the usually hostile *Monthly Review*, some readers were unamused. Madame Riccoboni told David Garrick (in French) that 'Smollett is a "charming author" – a low knave who's no better acquainted with the *mores* of his own country than with those of France, and all of whose works are loathsome – I said loathsome.' But the most choleric reaction of all came from the truculent and litigious Philip Thicknesse, a man who had spent part of his youth rounding up runaway slaves or 'maroons' in Jamaica, done time in the King's Bench Prison, and is probably best remembered, if at all, as the friend and biographer of Gainsborough.

In 1766, the same year in which Smollett's *Travels* were published, Thicknesse brought out his *Observations on the Customs and Manners of the French People*, described in its subtitle as 'A Series of Letters in which that Nation is Vindicated from the Misrepresentation of some Late Writers'. Unlike Smollett, Thicknesse spoke good French, and claimed to like both the people and their cuisine. Even so, he was far from complimentary at times. 'The manners of the common run of Frenchmen, who call themselves gentlemen, are so far from being agreeable, that they are to an Englishman highly disgustful,' he declared. Like Smollett, he deplored the way in which the French took snuff while eating, and, sharing the same interest in lavatorial matters, he noted how, in Flanders, 'a girl of twelve years of age will do that business in a public street here, that one of the same age in England would be ashamed to own she did in private'. Thicknesse's book was mauled in the *Critical Review* and, wrongly assuming that Smollett was still involved, he sought revenge in *Useful Hints to Those who Make the Tour of France*, published two years later. Referring to Smollett as 'Toby, the martinet in literature', and to the pro-Scots bias of the *Critical*, he nicknamed *Travels* 'Quarrels through France and Italy, for the Cure of a Pulmonic Disorder'. Its author, he declared, must have stayed in 'ale houses' and consorted with 'the lowest class of mechanic' to have written such stuff; he had either 'kept very bad company, or his own ill state of health and want of appetite, or both together, must have been the means of warping his judgement, and corrupting his imagination'. 'I forgot to tell you,' he went on, that as I passed through Boulogne, I saw the young gentleman who had so kindly received, and hospitably entertained, Mr S—— and his family. This young man, whose youth and good office ought to have saved him from the Doctor's ridicule, is now pointed out to every English traveller, as an object of contempt, because he was picked out as a subject of satire, for rendering every civility that lay in his power to the Doctor in the best manner he was able . . .

Smollett had done France 'the highest injustice in drawing so vile a portrait of its inhabitants. I do not mean to impeach his veracity, but to show his real incapacity to give an account of people with whom he never eat or conversed.'

Smollett's coarseness, rather than his Francophobia, meant that the *Travels*, like his novels, fell out of favour in the nineteenth century: Sterne's *A Sentimental Journey* had a far greater appeal to both the literary and the genteel, and its more rumbustious rival only began to be enjoyed again in the first third of the twentieth century. It was, Arnold Bennett suggested,

a fine splenetic book, thoroughly interesting. The kind of book that a few men might, and probably do, cherish as a masterpiece too special in its flavour to please the crowd. It gives the impression of a sound, sincere personality, not very cultured in the arts, but immensely well informed, and breathing a hard, comfortable common sense at every pore. A doctor's personality, and yet still more the personality of a police magistrate; slightly less *doux*, and more downright, than that of Fielding. One leaves this book in thankfulness that one is not an eighteenth-century traveller.

And for V.S. Pritchett, another devotee, it was 'the first ill-tempered, captious, disillusioned and vigorously personal travel book in modern literature . . . a tale of bad inns, illness, cheating customs officials, a thoroughly British book of grousings and manias'.

That October, the Smolletts took rooms in Bath with Dr Macaulay and his wife Catherine, a well-known historian, a republican and a bluestocking. Smollett's health must have been poor; when they made a foray to Bristol the following spring, one of the Bath papers reported that 'Dr Smollett, who is returned from the Hot Wells to Bath, is now so dangerously ill at the last mentioned place, that it is thought he cannot possibly recover.' Writing to John Moore in November 1765, Smollett gave a mixed account of his health. Though still painfully thin, he had put on some weight; despite his stated views on the matter, 'the Bath water agrees with me wonderfully well', so much so that 'some of my friends declare that they never saw me look better.' On the other hand – and here one doctor was talking to another, with learned references to the 'air vesicules' and 'the membrane that lines the trachea arteria' – the catarrh made breathing difficult, he was suffering from a 'troublesome cough', his susceptibility to the cold made it impossible for him to leave the house and get the exercise he craved – 'if I were a galley slave and kept to hard labour for two or three years, I believe I should recover my health entirely' – and the scorbutic 'eruption' on his right hand had resurfaced.

In May 1766 the Smolletts, accompanied perhaps by Ann Curry, set out for Scotland; like Matthew Bramble and party, they travelled by way of Harrogate, the waters of which were to be described, unflatteringly, in *Humphry Clinker*. They arrived in Edinburgh in early June, and after visiting his mother, who was now living with her widowed daughter, Jane Telfer, they took rooms on the second floor of a tenement off the Canongate, with a fine view over the city. Like his fictional *alter ego*, no doubt, he met many of the city's writers and intelligentsia, including Alexander Carlyle – whose 'humour and conversation', Bramble noted, 'inflamed me with a desire of being better acquainted with his person' – David Hume, John Home, William Wilkie, Adam Ferguson, Hugh Blair and William Robertson, all of whom had made of their city a 'hot-bed of genius'. Whether, like Bramble, he attended the Leith races and a hunters' ball, and watched the citizens of Edinburgh playing golf on the links at Leith, are things we may never know. A second- or even third-hand account, published in Edinburgh in the 1820s, describes him as 'dressed in black clothes, tall, and extremely handsome, but quite unlike the portraits foisted upon the public at the fronts of all his works, all of which are disclaimed by his relations . . . He was very peevish, on account of the ill health to which he had been so long a martyr, and used to complain much of a severe ulcerous disorder in his arm.'

From Edinburgh the Smolletts moved on to Glasgow, which Squire Bramble thought 'one of the prettiest towns in Europe' and 'one of the most flourishing in Great Britain'. They met up with John Moore – as did Bramble, who pronounced him a 'merry, facetious companion, sensible and shrewd, with a considerable fund of humour' and a wife who was 'well-bred, kind and obliging' (by now, Bramble was a raging Scottophile, and kindness, he notes, is 'the distinguishing characteristic of the Scotch ladies in their own country'). Moore, for his part, 'had never seen Smollett but in the bloom of health, of a vigorous make, an elegant form, and agreeable countenance', and he was 'much affected by the dismal alterations which had now taken place in his face and person'. While in Scotland, Moore went on, Smollett was

> greatly tormented by rheumatic pains, and he was seized besides with an ulcer on his arm, which had been neglected on its first appearance, and afterwards resisted every attempt to heal it. These disorders confined him much to his chamber, but did not prevent his conversation being highly entertaining when he joined society.

It is unlikely, given the state of his health, that he travelled as far out of Glasgow as Bramble and party, who sampled the farther reaches of Loch Lomond, Inverary, Jura, Islay and Mull, but, with Moore, they visited Commissary Smollett at Cameron House – the inspiration, perhaps, for his Arcadian 'Ode to Leven Water'.

Smollett left his native country for the last time in August 1766, and made his way back to Bath, where they had taken rooms in Gay Street. It was unusually cold that winter, with deep snowdrifts in the streets, and Squire Bramble reported that when Gay Street was 'covered with snow, as it was for fifteen days this very winter, I don't see how any individual could go either up or down, without the most imminent hazard of broken bones'. From there, the following spring,

Smollett wrote to Moore, giving full details of his ailments and apologising for his 'peevishness and discontent' while in Scotland. Had he been in good health, he would have enjoyed the expedition to the full, but it had been 'productive of nothing to me but misery and disgust'. He worried that his brain had been affected by his poor health, and that, where he was concerned, Mrs Moore had 'seen nothing but the wrong side of the tapestry'. No sooner had he returned to Bath than he caught a cold, which had led on to an 'orthopnea', a form of asthma in which the sufferer can only breathe in an upright position; at the same time, his ulcer had spread from three inches above the wrist to the ball of the thumb, making it impossible for him to use his right hand. By November matters had deteriorated still further: he could not sleep without an 'opiate', and his appetite had quite gone. Luckily he had been seen by two of the most eminent surgeons in the country, both of whom happened to be in Bath – one of whom, Samuel Sharp, was the author of *Letters from Italy*, and Sterne's 'Mundungus'. Between them, they had prescribed 'a double mercurial ointment without turpentine' for the ulcer, and recommended a daily swig of 'Van Sweeten's solution of corrosive sublimate' and a quart, also daily, of 'decoction of sarsaparilla'. Within no time, the ulcer had sealed over, his right hand was back in use, and 'I find myself better in health and spirits than I have at any time these seven years.' But such moments of euphoria and good health were all too ephemeral. 'I am almost stupefied with ill health, loss of memory, confinement and solitude,' he told William Hunter a mere fortnight later, and even the skinned-over ulcer, which he had been warned might be cancerous, looked 'very shabby and leprous'.

Despite his poor health, and the sporadic loss of his writing hand, Smollett was still busy with the literary life. He was almost certainly working on *Humphry Clinker*; he had been compiling, editing and writing large parts of another vast compendium-cum-gazetteer, *The Present State of All Nations*, sections of which would be incorporated – not quite verbatim, but almost so – in his last novel; and, in order to help pay doctors' fees and the cost of renting rooms in Bath, he embarked on yet another translation of Fénelon's *Les Aventures de Télémaque*.

Published in France in 1699, Fénelon's lofty tome was immensely popular and influential throughout Europe, and was translated into English at least a dozen times during the course of the eighteenth century; it was widely recommended by teachers and clerics as salutary and improving reading, and Smollett may well have read it first while at Dumbarton Grammar School. It is a sonorous, long-winded work, but, like many of his contemporaries, Smollett must have found its teachings entirely to his taste. Mentor, a moralising windbag, spends much of the book dispensing sage advice to the hapless Telemachus, warning him against luxury and corruption, praising the simple life, and exalting the enlightened ruler who governs his passions, displays moderation in all things, is scrupulously honest, and works for the good of all. Archibald Hamilton paid Smollett £70 for the copyright in his translation; he seems to have been in no hurry to publish – a rival translation had recently appeared, and was thought to be superior to Smollett's version – and *The Adventures of Telemachus, the Son of Ulysses* did not appear until 1776, five years after its translator's death.

Smollett's interest in politics, always more satirical than practical, found further release in a Swiftian squib called *The History and Adventures of an Atom*: he never owned up to being its author, partly through fear of being prosecuted for *lèse-majesté* or seditious libel, and its printer and its publisher were openly hostile to all that Smollett stood for. John Moore seems to have had no doubts about its authorship, loyally observing that 'no political allegory has been executed with equal wit and pleasantry since the days of Arbuthnot' – Arbuthnot being the Scottish physician who satirised the cost and fatuity of the War of the Spanish Succession, including in his highly recognisable cast of characters the likes of 'Lewis Baboon', or Louis XIV – and even though the *Atom* is nowadays of interest only to historians of the period, it allowed Smollett to vent his spleen on the politicians of the day, and Pitt, Newcastle, Wilkes and Bute in particular. An atom, observant and articulate, enters the brain of a solid citizen named Nathaniel Peacock, and relates its intimate memories of British politics and politicians from the start of the Seven Years War to the present day: the story is set in 'Niphon', an imaginary Japan at war with China, and the characters are provided with pseudo-Japanese names, reminiscent of those used later in *The Mikado*. The notion of a speaking, all-observing atom could, it seems, have been taken from Voltaire's 'Micromegas', which Smollett had translated back in 1752, and from Charles Johnstone's *Chrysal*, in which the spirit of gold, embodied in a guinea, tells an alchemist about its adventures with George II, Lord Chesterfield and Sir Francis Dashwood, but disappears in a huff when the alchemist tactlessly farts just as it is about to reveal the secret of making gold. The bogus oriental setting was a fashionable literary device, used in Montesquieu's *Lettres persanes*, Voltaire's *Zadig*, Goldsmith's *Citizen of the World* and Shebbeare's *History of the Sumatrans* (which, surprisingly perhaps, had been favourably reviewed in the *Critical* when it appeared in 1762). Smollett may well have refreshed his knowledge of Japan by re-reading the Japanese section of the *Universal History* in the South of France; reviewing them in the *Critical* in 1759, he had noted how the Japanese, like the English, are 'brave and warlike, quick in apprehension, solid in understanding, modest, patient, courteous, docile, industrious, studious', and that whereas 'the Chinese [like the French] are more *gay*, the Japanese [are] more *substantial* . . . The Chinese are remarkable for *dissimulation*, *complaisance*, and *effeminacy*; the Japanese are famous for their *integrity*, *plain dealing* and *manly vigour*.'

Although the Japanese (or so the atom assures his temporary host) 'value themselves upon their constitution, and are very clamorous about the words liberty and property; yet, in fact, the only liberty they enjoy is to get drunk whenever they please, to revile the government, and quarrel with one another'. Japan used to be ruled by absolute monarchs, but the emperor has become a 'cypher', and power has been assumed by the Prime Minister or 'Cuboy'. 'Fika-kaka' or Newcastle – the *Atom* is an alarmingly scatological work, and his name alone embraces both fucking and shitting – is a blithering idiot who had

> no understanding, no economy, no courage, no steadiness, no discernment, no vigour, no retention. He was reputed generous and good-humoured; but was really profuse, chicken-hearted, negligent, fickle, blundering, weak and leaky. All these

qualifications were agitated by an eagerness, haste, and impatience, that completed the most ludicrous composition which human nature ever produced.

Every day, the Prime Minister presents his 'posteriors' to be kicked by the Emperor; this proves pleasant enough, but he suffers from a chronic 'itching of the podex', and what he loves above all else, exciting an 'orgasm of pleasure', is to have his perineum – Smollett the medical man is keen to use the exact word – licked by bishops and members of his Cabinet, particularly by those with bristly beards; and much ponderous humour is extracted from the whole business of 'osculation *a posteriori*' and Rabelasian musings on the wiping of arses. (Smollett is always a very visual writer, often akin to a comic-strip artist, and Robert Adams Day has suggested that he may have been influenced by the plethora of contemporary cartoons, all hostile to Bute, many extremely scatological, with much vomiting, peeing, arse-licking and the like, one of them showing Smollett administering an enema to Britannia.)

Other politicians to come under the lash include 'Quamba-cundono' ('Butcher' Cumberland), who is sent north to crush a rebellion by the Ximians, or Scots, many of whom are condemned to death by crucifixion, evisceration or boiling oil by 'Sti-phi-rum-poo' (Hardwicke, the long-serving Lord Chancellor), and, in scenes reminiscent of Swift's *Modest Proposal*, have their livers eaten by the southerners; and 'Serluon' (Admiral Knowles, baitable once more now that the seven-year commitment to good behaviour had expired), who runs his junk aground while leading a futile attack on the coast of China. 'Yak-Strot' (Bute), is 'honest at bottom, but proud, reserved, vain and affected' and, as Cuboy, makes sure that 'every department, civil and military, was filled with Ximians', a people who 'came over in shoals to Niphon, and swarmed in the streets of Meaco, where they were easily distinguished by their lank sides, gaunt looks, lanthorn jaws, and long, sharp teeth'. Opposition to Yak-Strot is led by the demagogue 'Taycho' (Pitt), 'distinguished by a loud voice, an unabashed countenance, a fluency of abuse and an intrepidity of opposition to the measures of the Coboy, who was far from being a favourite with the plebeians'. Supported by 'that many-headed hydra, the mob', Taycho inveighs against Yak-Strot's peace negotiations with China; in this he is helped by 'Llur-Chir' (Churchill), 'a profligate Bonza [clergyman], degraded for his low life', and 'Jan-ki-dtzin' (Wilkes), who was 'the best marksman in Japan in the art and mystery of dirt-throwing. He possessed the art of making balls of filth, which were famous for sticking and stinking; and these he threw with such dexterity, that they very seldom missed their aim.'

While Smollett was working on the *Atom*, Wilkes had returned to London. Riots had broken out in 1768 after he had been elected three times as an MP, only to be refused the right to take his seat. Scots in London once again found themselves being hissed and harassed after three Scottish soldiers had been put on trial for allegedly killing a man during the disturbances, and this in turn provoked the infamous St George's Fields Massacre, during which troops fired on the Wilkesite rioters. Pelted by 'dirt-men and rhymers', the wretched Yak-Strot is 'quite overwhelmed' by a 'torrent of filth', to the extent that 'he was carried home in such an unsavoury pickle, that his family smelled his disaster long before he came in sight; and when he appeared in this woeful condition, covered with ordure, blinded with dirt, and even deprived of sense and motion, his wife was seized with *hysterica passio* . . .' For all his humiliations, Yak-Strot is the hero of the story, such as it is: 'just, upright, sincere and charitable', he was 'one of the honestest men in Japan', far outstripping the inept if ruthless Fika-kaka both as Prime Minister and as a war leader.

But enough is more than enough: the *Atom* is more readable than *Sir Launcelot Greaves*, but few modern readers will want to attempt it: professional historians, who might find it of value, seem to have passed it by. For some inexplicable reason, it was printed for John Almon, the friend and adviser of Wilkes; his nerve seems to have cracked, and, bafflingly, he passed the sheets on to George Kearsly, the printer of the *North Briton*, who in turn sold them on to the less contentious firm of Robinson & Roberts. It was finally published in April 1769, and went through a dozen editions over the next seventeen years. Smollett made no reference to it in his correspondence, but the *London Chronicle*, which had printed extracts, referred to it as 'attributed to the author of Roderick Random'. *The Political Register*, the editor of which was a Wilkesite, declared that it was 'a political, satirical and moral romance said to be written by Dr Smollett, but falls so far short of the graceful simplicity and lively entertaining humour of his other performances': the author's treatment of the old Japanese Emperor (George II) – 'he was rapacious, shallow, hot-headed, and perverse . . . His heart was meanly selfish, and his disposition altogether unprincely' – could be attributed to the fact that the 'supposed author' had been 'a prisoner in the King's Bench during the late k——'s reign', but the characters of contemporary politicians had been 'vilely mangled' to 'gratify keen resentment'.

Whereas the *Atom* is mercifully brief, *The Present State of All Nations* was the last of those mammoth compilations that had proved such a drain on Smollett's time, health and energy. Like the *Compendium*, it mirrored the contemporary passion for travel literature, and for the systematic presentation of knowledge about particular countries, starting with their physical geography, and moving on from descriptions of climate, soil and livestock to constitutions, laws and religion. Smollett may have been working on the book, on and off, for a good many years, since it was originally undertaken for James Rivington, co-publisher of the *Complete History of England*, who had made a mess of his affairs, severed relations with his more upright brother John, who continued to run the firm, and emigrated to Philadelphia in 1760: writing to an American admirer in 1763, Smollett had asked him to pass on to his former publisher 'my kindest comps'.

First published from June 1768 in weekly sixpenny numbers, and later reissued in eight volumes, *The Present State* is noteworthy – in a Smollettian context, at least – for the attention paid to Scotland: indeed, it seems likely that, whatever his hand in the rest, Smollett alone was responsible for all the Scottish material. Few such accounts of Scotland were then available: it tended to be tacked on to descriptions of England, very much as an afterthought, or ignored altogether. Spurred on, perhaps, by a combination of nostalgia, resentment at English Scottophobia, and pride in what he had seen on his return visits, Smollett was determined to rectify matters. 'A remarkable spirit of industry has of late years appeared very visibly in many parts of Scotland. We have already observed how much agriculture has been improved in the Lothians, and on all the eastern coast; nor have the Scots been more remiss in the article of manu-facturing,' he declared; and elsewhere he noted how

> this kingdom, though branded with the reproach of poverty and barrenness, might prove an inexhaustible source of wealth to the natives: they understand the nature of commerce: they see the happy effects of industry: they take example by their southern neighbours and fellow-subjects, and pursue their steps with such emulation, as hath already opened a fair prospect of opulence and importance.

Interlacing criticism with praise, he was, at times, impatient of Scottish superstitions, of lingering local beliefs in witches and second sight – and he had no hesitation about praising England where praise was called for. England, he wrote in an idyllic evocation of a vanished Arcadia,

> except in a very few places, exhibits to the view an enchanting variety of gently swelling hills, level plains, corn fields, meadow grounds, wood and water, intermingled in the most agreeable manner . . . The uncultivated part of the ground is clothed with a perpetual verdure; and the lands, in general, display the perfection of agriculture. The seats of noblemen and gentlemen rise like enchanted castles on every hand; populous villages, thriving towns, and flourishing cities, abound in every part of the kingdom, which excels all the states of Europe in beauty, opulence and cultivation.

The English were, he pronounced, the cleanest and best-looking people in Europe, though 'variable in their tempers, whimsical, capri-cious, and inconstant'. They prided themselves on speaking their minds – 'hence those shocking reflections and reproaches, national and personal, which have often been productive of quarrels and homicide' – but the Englishman was 'not naturally cruel, but rather mild and compassionate, and though extremely irascible, easily appeased by submission. He is neither tenacious of resentment, nor addicted to revenge, and soon forgets injuries, easier and sooner than the natives of some other countries could well imagine.'

'Several people, who have a particular regard and esteem for the reputed author of *The Present State of All Nations*, are sorry to find that he has too much exposed the posteriors of our brothers in the north; and made some undeserved compliments to their neighbours in the south, who have already enough share of self-conceit; and that, amongst other perfections, he allows them to be the handsomest people in Europe, which they think a very disreputable opinion,' John Armstrong wrote to Smollett in March 1769; and in *Humphry Clinker* Smollett was more critical of England and, Edinburgh sanitation excepted, more rhapsodic about Scotland, a country which seemed to provide Squire Bramble with a glimpse of paradise lost, inhabited by a people 'among whom I have met with more kindness, hospitality, and rational entertainment, in a few weeks, than ever I received in any other country during the whole course of my life'. The difference between the two countries was encapsulated in one all-explaining word: luxury. Smollett never identified the Scots, the Welsh (Bramble is, significantly, a Welsh squire) or, presumably, the Irish with luxury; and even if the Scots were making great strides towards becoming a commercial and industrial nation, they seemed somehow exempt from a vice associated, in Smollett's mind, with the vulgar *nouveaux riches* and the compromised Whig nobility of England. 'Perhaps the happiness of the golden age was never so much realised as in St Kilda,' Smollett wrote in *The Present State*, adding that its inhabitants, of whom he had no direct experience, were 'unknown to envy and ambition, ignorant of luxury and avarice'; and their fellow-Scots lived, to a lesser degree, in a similar state of prelapsarian grace. Nor was he alone in such views: back in 1754, before the days of Bute and the *North Briton*, David Hume had written to Wilkes to say that

if your time had permitted, you should have gone into the Highlands. You would there have seen human nature in the Golden Age, or rather, indeed, in the Silver: for the Highlanders have degenerated somewhat from the primitive simplicity of mankind. But perhaps you have so corrupted a taste as to prefer your Iron Age, to be met with in London and the south of England; where luxury and vice of every kind so much abound.

South of the Border, as Squire Bramble learned to his distress, even those pockets of Arcadia inhabited by old-fashioned county gentlemen had, all too often, been infected and ruined by luxury. A sad example was provided by his old friend Bayard, who had married the heiress to a fortune made in the East Indies and been reduced to misery and near-penury by her passion for modish luxury: the mellow old house that Bramble remembered from his youth had been utterly transformed into a cold and comfortless shell, the old oaks cut down, the ancient crumbling gallery replaced by a white and gleaming Grecian screen, the garden, once stocked with the best fruit trees in the land, reduced to a 'naked circus of loose sand, with a dry basin and a leaden triton in the middle'. The ancient virtues could still be found, however, in men like Bramble's old friend Dennison, who had 'really attained to that pitch of rural felicity at which I have been aspiring these twenty years in vain' and asked nothing of life other than 'wholesome air, pure water, plain diet, convenient lodging and decent apparel'.

Of course, Smollett's fondness for Scotland had been warmed by the persistent denigration of the Scots in England. As he put it in the fifth volume of his *Continuation of the Complete History of England*:

The jealousy of the English nation, towards their fellow-subjects on the other side of the Tweed, had discovered itself occasionally ever since the union of the two crowns; and ancient animosities had been kept alive by two successive rebellions which began in Scotland; but the common grudge was founded upon the success of the Scots, who had established themselves in different parts of England, and risen from very small beginnings to wealth and consideration. They had prospered in many different provinces of life, and made no contemptible figure in the cultivation of the arts and sciences. In a word, the English people looked upon them with an evil eye, as interlopers in commerce and competitors for reputation. It was not without murmuring, they had seen them aspire to the first offices in the law, the army, and the navy: but they were exasperated to find a Scot at the head of the English treasury, and the chief administration of the kingdom in his hands. These were topics on which the writers of the opposition did not fail to expatiate. They revived, and retailed with particular virulence, all the calumnies, ancient and modern, that ever had been muttered against the Scottish nation; some of them so gross and absurd, that they could not possibly obtain credit but among the very dregs of the people . . .

Although Smollett probably wrote *Humphry Clinker* as a relief from his hackwork on *The Present State* and the revising of the *Universal History*, it was not published until June 1771, only months before his death, and nearly three years after he and his wife had left England for the last time and settled in Italy. Virtually nothing is known about his last year in England. In May 1768 he wrote from Bath to Robert Cotton, an apothecary and a Chelsea friend. 'I shall never forget the cheerful hours I have spent in your company,' he told him, and his letter goes on to give a rare, nostalgic glimpse of the joshing, convivial life he must, at times, have enjoyed, when health and work permitted:

Pray, remember me to our friend Halford, who I hear is still in a single state. If I had a little health and spirits I would write a ballad upon him entitled *the old batchelor's ditty*. If he will clap on a bag wig and come down to Bath, it shall go hard but I will buckle him for life. Here is his neighbour Major Macdonald, but he does not seem to profit much by the waters. Yet he is fat and fair, and his tongue seems to go as fast as ever . . .

The portly major had been a frequenter of Don Saltero's and, like Smollett, had contributed to its collection of curiosities; no doubt Smollett revisited Chelsea from time to time, and – at the opposite end of London – he may have attended a Johnsonian club which met at the Queen's Arms in St Paul's Churchyard, from where John

Armstrong reported, in 1770, that 'our little club at the Q Arms never fails to devote a bumper to you, except when they are in the humour of drinking none but scoundrels'.

Of Smollett's farewell letters, only that to David Hume survives. Writing in late August 1768, Smollett begins by warmly recommending to Hume their fellow-Scot Robert Stobo, whose unusual character and frontiersman adventures in North America during the Seven Years War may have provided a partial model for the eccentric Lismahago in *Humphry Clinker*. 'With respect to myself,' Smollett continued,

> I am sorry I cannot have the pleasure of taking leave of you in person before I go into perpetual exile. I sincerely wish you all health and happiness. In whatever part of the earth it may be my fate to reside, I shall always remember with pleasure, and recapitulate with pride, the friendly intercourse I have maintained with one of the best men, and, undoubtedly, the best writer of the age.

Quite how well Smollett and Hume knew each other, and how often they met, is something we may never know. Held in some dread as a sceptic and an atheist – he had made his name in 1740 with *A Treatise of Human Nature*, published when he was only twenty-eight – Hume was, according to Alexander Carlyle, 'a man of great knowledge, and of a social and benevolent temper, and truly the best natured man in the world', given to writing 'the most pleasing and agreeable letters to his friends'. A year earlier, Hume had put in a word on Smollett's behalf with Lord Shelburne about the vexed matter of the Nice consulship, and Shelburne, after floating the possibility of Smollett's being stoned in the streets by outraged Niçois, had asked him how he could possibly 'take on the patronage of a person, so notorious for libelling as Dr Smollett. I should disoblige everyone whom he has abused . . .' According to Oliphant Smeaton, one of Smollett's nineteenth-century biographers, Hume once said of him that 'He is like the cocoa-nut: the outside is the worst part of him'; the tone in which he writes about his cantankerous acquaintance is amused and affectionate, and his reply to Smollett's farewell letter is, like that to which it responds, curiously touching. 'I am sensible of your great partiality, in the good opinion you express towards me,' he wrote,

> but it gives me no less pleasure than if it were founded on the greatest truth; for I accept it as a pledge of your good will and friendship. I wish an opportunity of showing my sense of it may present itself during your absence. I assure you I should embrace it with great alacrity; and you need have no scruple, on every occasion, of having recourse to me.

In the autumn of 1768, Smollett, his wife and Anne Curry made their way to Pisa, which had earlier appealed to him as a possible place in which to retire from the world. Six months later, they were still there. Armstrong wrote from London to say how much 'pleasure and entertainment' had been provided by a recent letter from his old friend. 'It is needless to say how much I rejoice in your recovery,' he went on,

> but I have all along had great confidence in the vigorous stamina with which nature has blest you. I hope you may, within a year or two, be able to weather out if not an English winter, at least an English summer. Meanwhile, if you won't come to us, I'll come to you; and shall with the help of small punch and your company laugh at the Tuscan dog days.
>
> I enjoy with pleasing sympathy the agreeable society you find among the professors at Pisa. All countries and all religions are the same to men of liberal minds . . .

In June the Smolletts went to Florence for the wedding of Anne Curry and George Renner, a German-born merchant in Livorno (better known to the English as Leghorn) with whom they became very friendly. Smollett's health may have taken a turn for the worse, for in August the *London Chronicle* announced that, according to 'some letters from Turin', the 'ingenious biographer and historian' had died the previous month at Massa Carrara; a few days later, the same paper denied the rumours, 'the last post having brought letters from him, which mention that he is in better health than for years past'. Intimations of mortality were pressing enough to convince Smollett that the time had come to make his will. Describing himself as 'late of the parish of Chelsea in Middlesex, physician', he left his 'dear wife Anne Smollett' his worldly goods, many of which – 'houses, warehouses, wharfs, offices, wherries, lands, plantations, enclosures, wells, watercourses, etc in and about the town of Kingston in Jamaica and elsewhere', plus however many slaves they still owned – he had acquired through marriage to her; the sum of £200 was left to Mrs Anne Renner 'as a small token of my esteem and gratitude for her friendship and attention to me shown in the course of my long illness'. Archibald Hamilton, a merchant named Allan Auld, Robert Graham of Gartmore and Thomas Bontein from Jamaica were appointed his executors. Every now and then the Smolletts would authorise, through their agents, the sale of plots of land or slaves, a 'negro man' or 'negro woman' realising some £80 each, but welcome as they must have been in monetary terms, the Jamaican properties proved troublesome to the end. In the month Smollett died, Robert Graham wrote to acknowledge 'a letter from Leghorn replete with various complaints', and to point out that he was unable to 'preserve old houses from decaying, or to persuade people to give a high rent for them when they are in order'; he had done all he could to advance their interests, but 'believe me, it is no easy matter to collect money in Jamaica . . .'

Writing to Horace Walpole in February 1770, Sir Horace Mann, a long-time resident of Florence, reported that he had recently encountered Smollett in Pisa, and that he was 'settled there for his health'; but later that spring the Smolletts moved to a villa called Il Giardino, situated on the slopes of Monte Nero, three miles south of Livorno. 'I am at present rusticated on the side of a mountain that overlooks the sea in the neighborhood of Leghorn, a most romantic and salutary situation,' Smollett told Caleb Whitefoord in a letter pining for literary and political gossip (was Burke the 'Junius' of the celebrated letters? What was Mrs Macaulay up to?). Nearly sixty years later, a Scottish traveller, Alexander Malcolm, waxed lyrical about the delights of the Smolletts' new home. None of the villas around, including one in which Lord Byron had lived for a while, could match Il Giardino in 'situation or elegance', he wrote. 'It commands a divine view of the Mediterranean with the islands of Gorgona and Elba on the right and left, and the snow-capped mountains of Corsica between, in the distance.' A stream ran in front of the house, and 'the road for five or six miles beyond, in the direction of Rome, forms one of the most charming rides in the country'.

John Armstrong – who, for all his indolence, was proving to be Smollett's most attentive friend – had written the previous October to say that 'notwithstanding all you tell me, I still have such confidence in your stamina that I hope to make a pleasant ramble through several parts of Italy next spring'. Armstrong travelled out to Italy by sea, a voyage of twenty-eight days, in the company of Henry Fuseli, the painter; they quarrelled over the pronunciation of an English word, and went their separate ways after their ship had been blown into Genoa harbour by a storm. Smollett and Armstrong met for dinner in Livorno in May. Armstrong was hurrying through on his way to Rome, from where he wrote to say that 'as you talked of a ramble somewhere in the south of France, I shall be extremely happy to attend you'. No such ramble took place, it seems, but Armstrong spent two weeks with the Smolletts in July. In his *Short Ramble through Some Parts of France and Italy*, published the following year under the *nom de plume* of Launcelot Temple – the writer John Gray told Smollett that he thought it 'altogether trifling, and unworthy of him' – Armstrong wrote that he had enjoyed 'above a fortnight of domestic happiness with a worthy old friend, in the agreeable company of two small families [the Smolletts and the Renners] who lived most cordially together on the side of Monte Nero, a romantic mountain which affords a great variety of situations to a number of little villas and looks over the sea about the distance of four English miles from Leghorn'. Four years later he wrote to Mrs Smollett to say that he had felt 'really ashamed of some part of the attention paid to me' on his visit. He was very upset to learn that Smollett had never received a long letter he had written him from Paris, 'as I find by your letter it hurt him so much, and must have hurt me in his honest, generous mind, under the idea of a faithless desertion from a friend whom I loved, esteemed, and admired'. He reassured his hostess that he had found 'everything perfectly agreeable, kind and obliging to the utmost degree' during his stay on Monte Nero, and that 'the fortnight I passed with you is one of the favourite morsels of my life'.

Reports of Smollett's health varied with the recipient. Contemplating a possible future behind glass in his friend's private museum, he told John Hunter – who, like his brother, had an anatomical collection – that he had 'nothing to say but that if I can prevail upon my wife to execute my last will, you shall receive my poor carcase in a box, after I am dead, to be placed among your rarities. I am already so dry and emaciated that I may pass for an Egyptian mummy without any preparation than some pitch and painted linen.' John Gray, on the other hand, wrote after a visit to say how happy he would be to 'have the agreeable news of your health daily more confirmed'. Mrs Smollett collected paintings, and Gray 'despaired of executing Mrs Smollett's commission; for there are no ultramarines to be found in the shops' in Florence. Rather more worrying was an earthquake, which, Smollett told his nephew Alexander Telfer, 'visited us in repeated shocks, some of which were violent and terrible'. The inhabitants of Livorno streamed out of the town; Smollett 'could hardly keep my own family within doors, but for my own part I thought it was better to run some small risk of being smother'd quietly in my own warm bed than expose myself to certain death from the damps of a dark winter night'.

Smollett continued to work on a revised and abridged version of the *Universal History* – Anne Smollett confessed that 'as he would never suffer anyone to come near his books, I never had any opportunity to find out what parts he wrote on' – and despite his unhappy record as a dramatist, he may have reverted to his first love, and tried his hand at a play. He also revised and corrected his *Travels*, thoughtfully adding translations to the lengthy passages in Latin and French given over to Roman remains and Dr Fizès's ineffectual diagnosis of his ills. These have only been incorporated into recent editions of the book, but his two marked-up volumes can still be consulted in the British Library; the leather-bound pages have a wonderfully musty whiff, and the margins of the amended pages, and the neatly pasted-in addenda, are covered by Smollett's tiny, meticulous handwriting, in cinnamon-coloured ink. But far and away the best use of his time was that devoted to bringing Matthew Bramble and his party home to Wales after their extended tour of England and Scotland. 'It galls me to the soul to think how much that poor dear man suffered while he wrote that novel, and that all his pains and part of his life was to be expended to serve such an unworthy and dishonest wretch, who has neither honesty nor probity in him,' Anne Smollett wrote after his death, on learning that William Johnston, its co-publisher, was in a bad way: but the hardest writing often makes for the easiest reading, and *Humphry Clinker* is pleasure undiluted.

Whether Smollett had actually read Richardson's epistolary novels is a matter of conjecture, but he was very familiar with travel books written in letter form. At a less elevated level, he may have been influenced, in technique as well as subject matter, by Christopher Anstey's *New Bath Guide* of 1766, which consists of fifteen verse letters in which various members of the Blunderhead family inveigh against unhygienic spas, quack doctors and predatory medical men; and, perhaps, by his old colleague Samuel Derrick's *Letters Written from Leverpoole, Chester, Corke, the Lake of Killarney, Tunbridge-Wells, Bath*. Derrick is, like Quin and the blithering Newcastle, one of the 'real life' characters who pop up in the novel, so reinforcing its documentary character; so too, albeit under a pseudonym, was a man Smollett had come to loathe and despise, whose appearance, also in the Bath scenes, suggests that it was almost certainly written after 1768. Among the 'clerks and factors from the East Indies, loaded with the spoil of plundered provinces' and now flaunting their wealth in Bath, is one Paunceford, who was once poverty-stricken, but has now returned from the East 'up to the very ears in affluence' and 'blazes out in all the tinsel of the times': as the embodiment of new money, he is ruthless in his neglect of old friends, and particularly those to whom he is indebted. Bramble meets his old friend Serle, who had 'rescued Paunceford from the lowest distress, when he was bankrupt, both in means and reputation' but is now being given the cold shoulder by the ungrateful wretch; and whereas

Mr Paunceford lives in a palace, feeds upon dainties, is arrayed in sumptuous apparel, appears in all the pomp of equipage, and passes his time among the nobles of the land, Serle lodges in Stall-street, up two pairs of stairs backwards, walks a-foot in a Bath-rug, eats for twelve shillings a-week, and drinks water as a preservative against the gout and gravel. Mark the vicissitude . . .

The original of Paunceford was Alexander Campbell, who had gone out to India in 1763, amassed a fortune, returned to England in 1767 with, according to the *Public Advertiser*, 'Sixty Thousand Pounds several Times told' in the bank, and settled in Bath the following year. Smollett and Archibald Hamilton had supported him in his years of penury, and offered him work on the *Critical Review*: he had written from India to say how he longed to share his new-found wealth with his benefactors, but once installed in Bath he shunned his old ally. Smollett was luckier than one of Campbell's other mentors, who was said to have become sadly 'reduced in circumstances', and ended his days as the 'collector of the toll on carts at Holborn Bars', but the slight still rankled.

> In Fortune's car behold that minion ride,
> With either India's glittering spoils oppress'd

Smollett wrote of Paunceford in his unmemorable and posthumously published 'Ode to Independence'; but in *Humphry Clinker* he took a more effective revenge on this unappealing character, along with Wilkes, Pitt and the chattering, effusive Duke of Newcastle.

Although it takes the form of a journey, *Humphry Clinker* is less picaresque in tone than its predecessors, and less populated by caricatures and humours; and although Thackeray thought it 'the most laughable story that has ever been written since the goodly art of novel-writing began', and Hazlitt 'the most pleasant gossiping novel that ever was written', it is also more serious-minded, both in its rage against luxury and the corruption of English society, and its almost sociological eagerness to inform as well as inveigh. Nowhere is this more apparent than in the letters devoted to Scotland.

Smollett not only made use of the material gleaned while working on the Scottish volume of *The Present State of All Nations*, but also drew on his own childhood memories and printed sources that were equally out of date. When writing about Highland superstitions, for example, he probably made use of Martin Martin's celebrated *Description of the Western Islands of Scotland*, published as long ago as 1703, while the kind of Highland funeral so luridly evoked in the novel may have been a thing of the past by the time it was written. Smollett's use of the epistolary method, on the other hand, was more sophisticated than most. Matthew Bramble may dominate the proceedings, but his is only one of five narrative voices; nor is his the only point of view to be allowed an airing. The same scenes and incidents are often described by different correspondents in very different ways; and even if Smollett, as puppet-master, may find Jery Melford's or Lydia's opinions naïve or idealistic, he never lets on, and is more than happy to let them have their say. The deliberate misspellings and *doubles entendres* found in the letters from Tabitha Bramble and her maid, Wynn Jenkins, have a Joycean coarseness and delight in puns: Wynn's reference to the 'holy bands of matter-money' is a fine example, while others, often sexual or scatological in nature, include 'cuntry' for 'country', 'turd' for 'third', 'beshits' for 'beseeches', 'piss' for 'piece' and 'asterisks' for 'hysterics'.

Matthew Bramble is the great exception to the notion that, for all their vigour and outward animation, Smollett's characters are, in essence, humours or caricatures, starved of internal life and seemingly incapable of introspection, ambiguity, ambivalence or change. A fine embodiment of the curmudgeon with the heart of gold, he has much in common with Goldsmith's Mr Drybones, the 'Man in Black' in *The Citizen of the World*:

> Though he is generous even to profusion, he affects to be thought a prodigy of parsimony and prudence; though his conversation be replete with the most sordid and selfish maxims, his heart is dilated with the most unbounded love. I have known him profess himself a man-hater while his cheek was glowing with compassion; and while his looks were softened into pity, I have heard him use the language of unbounded ill nature.

Some affect humanity and tenderness, others boast of having such dispositions from Nature; but he is the only man I ever knew who seemed ashamed of his natural benevolence.

Voltaire had encouraged the belief that England was a natural haven for misanthropes, and, as editor of the *Works*, Smollett may have known his play *L'Ecossaise*, which featured a benevolent misanthrope named Freeport; such characters, like Smollett himself, tended to combine scepticism about man's innate goodness and perfectibility with generosity and private good deeds.

V.S. Pritchett wrote of Bramble that 'generosity and goodness of heart go together with an impetuous temper and a touch of hypochondria', and that 'his protest and his hypochondria suggest that he felt the pleasure and the agony of a man who has a skin too few': both observations apply equally to Smollett, and complement the eighteenth-century belief that the hypochondriac was, almost by definition, a man of rare and heightened intelligence and sensibility. George Cheyne, who numbered both Samuel Richardson and the famously neurotic Dr Johnson among his patients, had popularised the notion of 'nervous distemper'. Hypochondria – sometimes referred to as 'hyppo' or 'hippo' – was thought to affect in particular those who led sedentary, thoughtful lives, like literary men; David Hume claimed to suffer from 'the disease of the learned', while Dr Johnson – 'blest with all the powers of genius and understanding to a degree far above the ordinary state of human nature,' in Boswell's opinion – was wretchedly prone to melancholia and Smollettian anxiety about his health. Bramble's letters are addressed to his doctor back in Wales, and in the very first line of his opening letter he complains that the pills Dr Lewis has prescribed are no use, and that he is rigid with constipation. Like all keen hypochondriacs, he likes to read about his ailments – Smollett had complained in the *Critical* about the 'inundation of medical books, by which the public has been lately overwhelmed' – and he has 'studied [his] own case with the most painful attention' before coming to the conclusion (which Smollett probably shared) that 'the sum of all your medical discoveries amounts to this, that the more you study the less you know'. Bramble's hypochondria is combined with hyper-sensitivity about the society in which he has to live; its excesses and vulgarities pain him in exactly the same way as the noise and dirt and bustle of London grate on his every nerve. As Bramble and his party move east through England, through Bath and Gloucester and the Wiltshire Downs, Jery Melford begins to realise that his uncle is not simply a crusty old codger and a 'complete cynic'. His 'peevishness arises from bodily pain, and partly from an excess of mental sensibility': 'splenetic with his familiars only', he is 'extravagantly delicate in all his sensations, both of soul and body'; 'his blood rises at every instance of insolence and cruelty, even where he is in no way concerned; and ingratitude makes his teeth chatter'. Bramble's background and career, and his way of life, are very different from his creator's, but in essentials the two men speak as one.

London, like Bath, embodies everything that Bramble finds most loathsome about the modern world. 'The capital is become an overgrown monster; which, like a dropsical head, will in time leave the body and extremities without nourishment and support,' he declared. Dr Johnson, while agreeing that London had become too vast, thought it 'nonsense to say that the head is too large for the body'; but Smollett's vision of London as a leech, drawing labourers off the land and leading to the decay and depopulation of the countryside, was revived some thirty years later in Cobbett's denunciation of the 'Great Wen'. Needless to say, luxury is to blame. 'About five and twenty years ago, very few, even of the most opulent citizens of London, kept any equipage, or even servants in livery,' Bramble remembers of the good old days:

> Their tables produced nothing but plain boiled and roasted, with a bottle of port and a tankard of beer. At present, every trader in any degree of credit, every broker and attorney, maintains a couple of footmen, a coachman, and a postilion. He has his own town house, and his country house, his coach, and his post-chaise. His wife and daughters appear in the richest stuffs, bespangled with diamonds. They frequent the court, the opera house, the theatre, and the masquerade. They hold assemblies in their own houses: they make sumptuous entertainments, and treat with the richest wines of Bordeaux, Burgundy, and

Champagne. The substantial tradesman, who wont to pass his
evening in the ale-house for fourpence-halfpenny, now spends
three shillings in the tavern, while his wife keeps card tables
at home; she must likewise have fine clothes, her chaise, or
pad, with country lodgings, and go three times a week to public
diversions. Every clerk, apprentice, and even waiter of tavern
or coffee-house, maintains a gelding by himself, or in partnership, and assumes the air and apparel of a petit maitre. The
gayest places of public entertainment are filled with fashionable figures; which, upon enquiry, will be found to be journeymen tailors, serving-men, and abigails, disguised like their
betters.

In short, there is no distinction or subordination left . . .

Writing to Dr Lewis in Wales, Bramble contrasts the Arcadian life
he has left behind him in Brambleton Hall with the din and stench
of London. Back home, he can breathe 'a clear, elastic, salutary air',
eat fresh bread, fruit, mutton, cheese and ham, drink the milk from
his dairy, look after his tenants, provide for the poor, and live quietly
among 'honest men, and trusty dependants, who, I flatter myself,
have a disinterested attachment to my person'; in London, he finds
himself 'pent up in frowzy lodgings', breathes foul air impregnated
with coal dust, 'a pernicious nuisance to lungs of any delicacy of
texture', is woken all night by the banging of doors and the shouting
of night-watchmen, and drinks water suffused 'with all the filth of
London and Westminster'. The wine is adulterated with 'cider, corn-
spirit, and the juice of sloes'; the greens 'taste of nothing but the
dung-hills from whence they spring'; the poultry is rotten, the fish
stink, the fruit have been polished with spit, and the milk is

the product of faded cabbage leaves and sour draff, lowered with
hot water, frothed with bruised snails, carried through the streets
in open pails, exposed to foul rinsings, discharged from doors
and windows, spittle, snot and tobacco quids from foot passengers, overflowings from mud carts, spatterings from coach
wheels, dirt and trash chucked into it for the joke's sake, the
spewings of infants . . .

Despite such tribulations, 'I never knew a hypochondriac so apt to be infected with good humour,' Jery declares of his uncle. 'He is the most risible misanthrope I ever met with.' It is this combination of crustiness and good humour, imaginative licence and journalistic observation, that makes *Humphry Clinker* so exhilarating a novel – a fictional version of sweet and sour, in which young and old, the town and the country, commerce and Arcadia, are cunningly counterpointed and intertwined. Yet for all its modernity of style and subject matter, its satirical swipes at social trends and unscrupulous or ingratiating politicians, it remains in many ways a curiously old-fashioned book. Like Dickens, Smollett made unashamed use of the conventions of coincidence: in much the same way as Roderick Random, briefly in Buenos Aires, bumps into a wistful expatriate Scot who happens to be his long-lost father, with a fortune to bestow, so Humphry Clinker, the gormless-seeming character whom Bramble takes on as his manservant, turns out to be the old gentleman's illegitimate son, a by-product of those far-off days when he was sowing his own wild oats. Wilson, the strolling actor who, to Jery's brotherly irritation, pops up the length and breadth of Britain, heavily disguised, to pay court to Lydia Melford, is revealed to be none other than the eminently eligible son of Bramble's old friend Mr Dennison. As expected, true love prevails: Bramble is delighted to bestow his niece on the bogus travelling actor, with whom Jery is now on the best of terms; Humphry – a member of the lower orders, despite Bramble's part in his procreation – finds true love with Wynn Jenkins; even the termagant Tabitha finds belated bliss with the equally cantankerous Lismahago, who, for all his fierce Scots pride, seems happy to spend the rest of his days in Wales. By now even Bramble's bowels are loosened and in perfect working order, and the time has come to bring the story to its fairy-tale conclusion.

Smollett's brutality, and his weakness for practical jokes, stayed with him to the end, often at Lismahago's expense: a brutish squire raises a false fire alarm in the middle of the night and, to Bramble's indignation, much merriment is had at the old soldier's expense as he clambers slowly down a flimsy ladder in his nightshirt, his scrawny buttocks exposed to public gaze; and one of the funniest scenes in the book is that in which Lismahago describes the terrible tortures he suffered in North America at the hands of the Badger tribe of Miami Indians (having contributed his 'History of Canada' to the *British Magazine*, Smollett thought himself something of an expert on the subject). But for all its crudities and anger, *Humphry Clinker* is a far mellower book than the others, and the good-tempered final pages are suffused with a valedictory note of acceptance and resignation. Paradise has been glimpsed if not regained as Smollett rediscovers Scotland, the lost Arcadia of his dreams, and his vanished boyhood.

Humphry Clinker was published by William Johnston of Ludgate Street and Benjamin Collins of Salisbury in June 1771: the three volumes were priced at nine shillings, and the initial print run was 1,500 copies. The Smolletts had spent the summer at Bagni di Lucca, some miles inland from Livorno, and it was there, perhaps, that Smollett received his author's copies and a letter from John Gray. 'I have read the Adventures of Humphry Clinker with great delight, and think it calculated to give a very good run, and add to the reputation of the author, who has, by the magic of his pen, turned the banks of Loch Lomond into classic ground,' Gray wrote. Shallow readers, he continued, 'are not so well satisfied with the performance as the best judges, who are lavish in its praises. Your half-animated sots say that they don't see the humour', but, admiring as ever, John Cleland 'gives it the stamp of excellence, with the enthusiastic emphasis of voice and fist . . .'

The actual reviews were many, if mixed – the *Critical* thought Smollett one of the few novelists to have 'discovered an original genius', the *Monthly* ranked it well below *Roderick Random* and *Peregrine Pickle*, but 'superior to his *Count Fathom*, and perhaps equal to *The Adventures of an Atom*', the *Universal* resented its 'flagrant partiality to Scotland, as I fear it will tend rather to widen than heal the breach that at present subsists between the South and North Britons' – but it is unlikely that Smollett read any of them. On 21 August he wrote from 'Lucca Baths' to George Renner in Livorno to say that they were about to set off home via Pisa, and that 'we propose to take pot luck with you at Leghorn so that we may proceed to the Giardino in the evening' – where, he hoped, 'you will remember to make some provision of wine'. A month later, on 14 September, he was taken ill. Dr Gentili, who visited him, diagnosed asthma, colic, chronic diarrhoea, convulsions and fever, as well as a 'scabrous condition' of the kind associated with a skin disease. Three days later Smollett died, possibly of an intestinal infection, 'asthmatic and consumptive, without trying to help himself'. His patient, Gentili noted, had been remarkable for his 'vigour' and his 'fiery temperament': he was 'a man of matured talent enduring the blows of human life, but almost misanthropic. He lived eighteen years in perfect harmony with his wife by whom he had a daughter who wrote poetry. He had a very ardent and choleric temperament but was reflective and devoted to political and historical studies.' He was only fifty when he died.

Epilogue

Two years after Smollett's death, Dr Johnson and Boswell, nearing the end of their tour of the Hebrides, called to see Commissary Smollett at Cameron House, on the shores of Loch Lomond. Their host was, Boswell later recalled, 'a man of considerable learning, with abundance of animal spirits; so that he was a very good companion for Dr Johnson, who said to me, "We have had more solid talk here than at any place where we have been."' The Commissary showed them a column he had erected 'to the memory of his ingenious kinsman, Dr Smollett', and asked Dr Johnson for advice about the wording of the inscription. Johnson angrily rejected a suggestion by Lord Kames, the eminent Edinburgh lawyer and agriculturalist, that it should be in English as a 'disgrace to Dr Smollett'; Boswell hastily agreed, adding that 'all to whom Dr Smollett's merit could be an object of respect and imitation would understand it as well in Latin; and that surely it was not meant for the Highland drovers, or other such people who pass and repass that way'. In the event, both Kames and Johnson prevailed: Kames was allowed to pay his tribute in sonorous English prose; after carefully considering the original Latin draft – itself the work of a Dr Stuart, and the John Ramsay of Ochtertyre who suggested that Smollett's old schoolmaster, Dr Love, had, after all, provoked a schoolboy rebellion – the sage 'greatly improved it by several additions and variations'. 'Stay, traveller!' it reads, put back into English,

If elegance of taste and wit,
If fertility of genius,
And an unrivalled talent
In delineating the characters of mankind,
Have ever attracted thy admiration,
Pause a while
On the memory of TOBIAS SMOLLETT, M.D.
One more than commonly indued with those virtues
Which in a man and citizen
You would praise, or imitate.
Who,
Having secured the applause
Of posterity,
By a variety of literary abilities,
And a peculiar facility of composition,
Was,
By a rapid and cruel distemper,
Snatched from this world in the 51st year of his age,
Far, alas, from his country . . .

It was just as well that Johnson was at hand to lend advice, since, far away to the south, Mrs Smollett was feeling aggrieved. Writing to her late husband's old friend and executor, Archibald Hamilton, she thought it a wretched business that 'my dear Smollett has never yet had any monument rais'd up to his memory, which in this country is looked at with astonishment'. It would be 'a triffling [sic] expense to his cousin or nephew to do it for him', yet 'I have not among so many friends any one who has wrote an epitaph to his memory.' The Commissary had indeed written to say that 'he would put up a pile near Leven, but still that does not answer, for where his body lies, there certainly ought to be the Chief Monument . . .' She wondered whether, now that her husband's library was being shipped back to Alexander Telfer in Scotland, it might be possible for her to keep back 'some of the amusing books' with which to while away the long and lonely hours in exile.

Despite the Jamaican properties, money was again in short supply:

eleven years later, in March 1784, the Theatre Royal in Edinburgh staged a benefit performance of Otway's *Venice Preserv'd* and Smollett's *The Reprisal*, and the £300 raised was dispatched to the widow in Livorno. With that the quiet and long-suffering Anne Smollett vanishes for ever from the memory of man; but she would have been gratified to learn that her husband was far from forgotten. Nearly fifty years after Smollett's death, the *Gentleman's Magazine* reported that, 'so many Britons having planted slips in honour of departed genius', Smollett's tomb was so covered with laurel as to be almost invisible; the *Literary Gazette* noted a steady stream of ships' officers and men doing 'homage to his memory in sacrifices of the finest fruit, and copious libations of the most generous *lachrymae Christi* wine', while the *London Magazine* described the 'plain and modest monument' to which 'every Englishman repairs', so much so that it had been 'scratched with over a thousand names'.

> Death's *random* darts too certainly transfix,
>   And souls unwilling Charon's sure to land 'em;
> Ah! Take some gloomier soul to gloomy Styx,
>   And give us back facetious *Roderick Random*

declared the *Royal Magazine* on learning of Smollett's death. Wherever his shade might be, his work and reputation lived on, and formed the subject of literary debate. Writing to John Moore in the summer of 1790 to thank him for sending a copy of his novel, *Zeluco*, Robert Burns told Smollett's old friend that he was planning 'a comparative view of you, Fielding, Richardson and Smollett, in your different qualities and merits as novel-writers'. He already admired Smollett 'for the sake of his incomparable humour'; by comparing him with Fielding, he was conforming to the pattern that has persisted to this day, almost invariably to Smollett's discredit. Pondering the two novelists in the *Edinburgh Review*, and *Tom Jones* and *Roderick Random* in particular, William Hazlitt conceded that

> The style of *Roderick Random*, though more scholastic and elaborate, is stronger and more pointed than that of *Tom Jones*; the incidents follow one another more rapidly, (though it must be

confessed they never come in such a throng, or are brought out with the same dramatic facility); the humour is broader, and as effectual; and there is very nearly, if not quite, an equal interest excited by the story.

'What then is it that gives the superiority to Fielding?' Hazlitt asks. His answer is very similar to that given by Coleridge in his lecture on 'Wit and Humour', in which he declared that, in *Peregrine Pickle*, 'we find an abundance of drollery, which too often degenerates into mere oddity; in short, we feel that a number of things are put together to counterfeit humour, but that there is no growth from within'. Whereas, in Hazlitt's opinion, Fielding enjoys a 'superior insight into the springs of human character, and the constant development of that character through every change of circumstance',

> Smollett's humour often arises from the situation of the persons, or the peculiarity of their external appearance, as, from Roderick Random's carroty locks, which hung down over his shoulders like a pound of candles, or Strap's ignorance of London, and the blunders which follow from it. The incidents frequently resemble detached anecdotes taken from a newspaper or magazine . . . He exhibits only the external accidents and reverses to which human life is liable – not the 'stuff' of which it is composed. He seldom probes to the quick, or penetrates beyond the surface of his characters: and therefore he leaves no stings in the minds of his readers, and in this respect is far less interesting than Fielding. His novels always enliven, and never tire us: we take them up with pleasure, and lay them down without any strong feeling of regret. We look on and laugh, as spectators of an amusing though inelegant scene, without closing in with the combatants, or being made parties in the event. We read *Roderick Random* as an entertaining story; for the particular accidents and modes of life which it describes, have ceased to exist: but we regard *Tom Jones* as a real history; because the author never stops short of those essential principles which lie at the bottom of all our actions . . . Smollett excels most as the lively caricaturist: Fielding as the exact painter and profound metaphysician.

Fielding is not the outright victor, however, for in *Roderick Random*, the 'purest of Smollett's novels', 'There is a rude conception of generosity in some of his characters, of which Fielding seems to have been incapable; his amiable persons being merely good-natured. It is owing to this, we think, that Strap is superior to Partridge; and there is a heartiness and warmth of feeling in some of the scenes between Lieutenant Bowling and his nephew, which is [sic] beyond Fielding's power of impassioned writing.' Fielding, Hazlitt concluded, was 'an observer of the characters of human life', whereas Smollett, for all his gifts, was merely a 'describer of its various eccentricities'.

'In leaving Smollett's personal for his literary character, it is impossible not to consider the latter as contrasted with that of his eminent contemporary, Fielding,' Sir Walter Scott announced in his *Lives of the Novelists*, published in 1821. Scott was well disposed towards his fellow-countrymen, but had to

> assign to Fielding, with little hesitation, the praise of a higher and purer taste than was shewn by his rival; a nearer approach to the grave irony of Swift and Cervantes; a great deal more address or felicity in the conduct of his story; and, finally, a power of describing amiable and virtuous characters, and placing before us heroes, and especially heroines, of a much higher as well as pleasing character than Smollett was able to present.

Once again comparing *Tom Jones* and *Roderick Random*, Scott notes how 'characters are introduced and dropped without scruple' by Smollett, while the 'low-minded Roderick Random' is 'not to be named in one day with the open-hearted, good-humoured, and noble-minded Tom Jones'. Fielding's women are in a different class from those of his rival, almost all of whom are 'drawn as the objects rather of appetite than of affection, and excite no higher or more noble interest than might be created by the houris of a Mahomedan paradise'. And yet

> the deep and fertile genius of Smollett afforded resources suffi-
> cient to balance these deficiencies; and when the full weight
> has been allowed to Fielding's superiority of taste and expression,

his northern contemporary will still be found fit to balance the scale with his great rival. If Fielding had superior taste, the palm of more brilliancy of genius, more inexhaustible richness of invention, must be in justice awarded to Smollett. In comparison with his sphere, that in which Fielding walked was limited; and, compared with the wealthy profusion of varied character and incident which Smollett has scattered through his works, there is a poverty of composition about his rival.

If Fielding excels in evoking pity, 'the northern novelist soars far above him in his powers of exciting terror'; but it is 'chiefly in his profusion, which amounts almost to prodigality, that we recognise the superior richness of Smollett's fancy'. Like Smollett, Scott is irritated by the way in which 'Fielding pauses to explain the principles of his art, and to congratulate himself and his readers on the felicity with which he constructs his narrative'; Smollett, to his credit, 'manages his delightful puppet-show without thrusting his head beyond the curtain, to explain what he is doing', with the result that 'our attention to the story remains unbroken'. And if Fielding is 'pre-eminent in grave irony', Smollett is the master of 'broad and ludicrous humour', so that 'perhaps no books ever written have excited such peals of inextinguishable laughter'. 'Upon the whole,' Scott concludes,

> the genius of Smollett may be said to resemble that of Rubens. His pictures are often deficient in grace; sometimes coarse, and even vulgar in conception; deficient too in keeping, and in the due subordination of parts to each other; and intimating too much carelessness on the part of the artist. But these faults are redeemed by such richness and brilliancy of colours; such a profusion of imagination – now bodying forth the grand and terrible – now the natural, the easy, and the ludicrous; there is so much of life, action, and bustle, in every group he has painted; so much force and individuality of character, that we readily grant to Smollett an equal rank with his great rival Fielding.

Surprisingly, perhaps, given their interest in the subjective and the inner man, many of the Romantics were keen admirers of

Smollett. De Quincey, who had little time for Fielding or Smollett
– 'How bestial and degrading seem many of the scenes in Smollett!'
he once wrote – remembered how Wordsworth 'read and remembered with extreme delight' the works of the two novelists; Charles
Lamb, objecting to those bossy, intrusive writers who 'continually
put a sign-post up to shew where you are to feel', looked back
with nostalgia to *Robinson Crusoe*, *Roderick Random* 'and other
beautiful bare narratives'. Leigh Hunt had mixed views on the
matter. 'There is a vein in Smollett – a Scotch vein – which is
always disgusting to people of delicacy,' he wrote to a friend in
1817, adding that 'one has no patience with his want of patience'.
Smollett's crudity and coarseness proved too much for the
Victorians, many of whom would have agreed with Charles Burney
that his novels were 'so d——d gross that they are not fit reading
for women with all their wit', yet in his *Table Talk*, published in
1851, Leigh Hunt seemed better disposed than he had been in his
youth:

> Though Smollett sometimes vexes us with the malicious boys'-
> play of his heroes, and sometimes disgusts with his coarseness,
> he is still the Smollett whom now, as in one's boyhood, it is
> impossible not to heartily laugh with. He is an accomplished
> writer, and a masterly observer, and may be called the finest of
> caricaturists . . .

The coarser kind of reader would benefit from reading the novels,
since they would realise that their heroes 'are expected to have
virtues as well as faults, and seldom get anything by being positively
disagreeable or bad'. However lurid the scenes described,

> There is no serious evil intention, however. It is all out of
> resentment of some evil, real or imaginary, or is made up of
> pure animal spirit and the love of venting a complexional sense
> of power. It is energy, humour, and movement, not particularly
> amiable, but clever, entertaining, and interesting, and without
> an atom of hypocrisy in it. No man will learn to be shabby by
> reading Smollett's writings.

Leigh Hunt's friend Dickens was more reticent on the subject, but his indebtedness to Smollett is obvious, especially in the early, picaresque novels like *The Pickwick Papers*, *Nicholas Nickleby* and *The Old Curiosity Shop*. In an 'Autobiographical Fragment' he described, in a passage he re-used almost verbatim in *David Copperfield*, how

> My father had left a small collection of books in a little room upstairs to which I had access (for it adjoined my own), and which nobody else in our house ever troubled. From that blessed little room, *Roderick Random*, *Peregrine Pickle*, *Humphry Clinker*, *Tom Jones*, *The Vicar of Wakefield*, *Don Quixote*, *Gil Blas* and *Robinson Crusoe* came out, a glorious host, to keep me company. They kept alive my fancy, and my hope of something beyond that place and time . . .

'I have sustained my own idea of Roderick Random for a month at a stretch, I verily believe,' he went on, and 'I have seen Tom Pipes go climbing up the church steeple; I have watched Strap, with the knapsack on his back, stopping to rest himself upon the wicket-gate; and I *know* that Commodore Trunnion held that club with Mr Pickle in our little village alehouse . . .' And in a letter to Frank Stone he wrote that

> *Humphry Clinker* is certainly Smollett's best. I am rather divided between *Peregrine Pickle* and *Roderick Random*, both extraordinarily good in their way, which is a way without tenderness, but you will have to read them both, and I send the first volume of *Peregrine* as the richer of the two.

Although he despised him as an historian, Thomas Carlyle, too, had fond memories of reading Smollett as a boy:

> I remember few happier days than those in which I ran off into the fields to read *Roderick Random*, and how inconsolable I was that I could not get the second volume. To this day I know of few writers equal to Smollett. *Humphry Clinker* is precious to me now as he was in those years. Nothing by Dante or anyone

else surpasses in pathos the scene where Humphry goes into the smithy made for him in the old house, and whilst he is heating the iron, the poor woman who has lost her husband, and is deranged, comes and talks to him as to her husband. 'John, they told me you were dead. How glad I am you have come!' And Humphry's tears fall down and bubble on the hot iron.

Thackeray, consumed with nostalgia for the eighteenth century, wrote fondly of Smollett in *The English Humourists*. He was, he suggested, 'manly, kindly, honest, and irascible; worn and battered, but still brave and full of heart', and (this would have particularly pleased his subject) 'You see somehow that he is a gentleman, through all his battling and struggling, his poverty, his hard-fought successes, and his defeats.' In *Vanity Fair* he wrote of how

Once, when Mr Crawley asked what the young people were reading, the governess replied, 'Smollett.' 'Oh, Smollett,' said Mr Crawley, quite satisfied. 'His history is more dull, but by no means so dangerous as that of Mr Hume. It is history you are reading?' 'Yes,' said Miss Rose; without, however, adding that it was the history of Mr Humphry Clinker.

George Eliot seems to have been more amused than censorious – in *Middlemarch* Mr Brooke advises Casaubon to 'get Dorothea to read you light things, Smollett – *Roderick Random, Humphry Clinker*: they are a little broad, but she may read anything now she's married, you know. I remember they made me laugh uncommonly – there's a droll bit about a postilion's breeches' – but it was left to Ruskin to give voice to full-blooded Victorian disapproval:

I cannot, for the life of me, understand the feelings of men of magnificent wit and intellect, like Smollett and Fielding, when I see them gloating over and licking their chops over nastiness, like hungry dogs over ordure . . . Not that I think, as many people do, that they are bad books; for I don't think these pieces of open filth are in reality injurious to the mind . . .

Trollope thought the obscenities in Smollett 'more conspicuous than in Fielding, without the great redeeming gifts'; brooding on the naval scenes in *Roderick Random*, which must have influenced *Treasure Island*, Robert Louis Stevenson decided that 'there are portions . . . over which the reader passes lightly and hurriedly, like a traveller in a malarious country'. Conan Doyle, again insisting on the comparison with Fielding, remembered 'rocking with laughter' over the 'Banquet in the Fashion of the Ancients' in *Peregrine Pickle*, but thought Smollett too gross to be borne, and, when compared with his rival, 'His view of life is far more limited, his characters less varied, his incidents less distinctive, and his thoughts less deep.' Asked whether *Pygmalion* had been in any way inspired by the scene in which Peregrine Pickle takes up a working-class girl whom he meets on the road, gives her lessons in elocution and etiquette, and lets her loose among his raffish London acquaintances, Bernard Shaw denied the charge, and said of Smollett that 'he may not have become absolutely unreadable (I have not tried him for more than forty years); but there is certainly a good deal in this book that is now simply disgusting to the class of readers that in its own day found it uproariously funny'.

In the early years of the last century Smollett began to enjoy a modest revival – his *Travels through France and Italy* and *Humphry Clinker* were reissued as World's Classics, and *Roderick Random* sold well in Everyman – but he was, and still is, largely ignored by the British academic world, and its disciples in teaching and journalism, in favour of Fielding, Sterne and Richardson. Nor has he found many champions among professional writers like himself. Katherine Mansfield told Virginia Woolf how a drawling Aldous Huxley 'lay upon the sofa, buried his head in a purple pillow and *groaned* over the "hor-rible qual-ity" of Smollett's coarseness'. But help was to hand in the more robust form of George Orwell. Writing in *Tribune* in 1944, he subtitled his piece in praise of Smollett 'Scotland's Best Novelist'. There was, he suggested, one sense in which

the stilted, artificial novelists of the eighteenth century are more 'realistic' than almost any of their successors, and that is in their attitude towards human motives. They may be weak at describing scenery, but they are extraordinarily good at describing scoundrelism. This is true even of Fielding, who in *Tom Jones* and *Amelia* already shows the moralising tendency which was to mark English novels for a hundred and fifty years. But it is much truer of Smollett, whose outstanding intellectual honesty may have been connected with the fact that he was not an Englishman.

For Orwell, 'Smollett's real masterpieces are *Roderick Random* and *Peregrine Pickle*, which are frankly pornographic in a harmless way and which contain some of the best passages of sheer farce in the English language'. He admired him for his comicality, and for his cynicism: 'by simply ruling out "good" motives and showing no respect whatever for human dignity, Smollett often attains a truthfulness that more serious novelists have missed. He is willing to mention things which do happen in real life but are invariably kept out of fiction.' 'The writers nearest to Smollett are perhaps Surtees and Marryat,' he suggested, 'but when sexual frankness ceased to be possible, picaresque literature was robbed of perhaps half of its subject matter.'

Herbert Read was another admirer – 'It has long been a commonplace of criticism that Smollett is the most neglected of our eighteenth-century authors' are the opening words of an essay in *Particular Studies* – but perhaps the most sympathetic and perceptive advocate of recent years was V.S. Pritchett. Writing in his regular *New Statesman* column under the title of 'The Shocking Surgeon', he suggests that Smollett's 'coarseness, like that of Joyce, is the coarseness of one whose senses were unprotected and whose nerves were exposed' and that, as we have seen, he felt the pleasure and the agony of the man who has a skin too few'. Turning to Rowlandson's illustrations for an edition of *Peregrine Pickle*, he sees in both the pictures and the text

the nightmare lying behind the Augustan manner. The nightmare of the pox, the scurvy, delirium tremens, of obesity and gout, the nightmare of the insanitary streets, of the stairway which was a dunghill, of the sedate Georgian window which was a place for the emptying of chamber pots; the nightmare of the suppurations which flowed into the waters of Bath, of the stenches that rose from the 'elegant' Assemblies . . .

Smollett may have remained 'the portrayer of the outside, rarely able to get away from physical externals', but for all the unpleasantnesses he described, he himself was neither brutal nor filthy: 'He enjoyed being the shocking surgeon who brings out horrors at the dinner table, but because he was shocked himself . . .'

'You will pardon the curiosity of a man distant from you by many thousand miles,' an admirer of Smollett wrote to his hero in February 1763. Richard Smith was the Recorder of Burlington, New Jersey, and later became a member of the Continental Congress. He was desperate to learn more about the working methods of a man he regarded as 'the First Genius in Britain', and 'whether *Roderick Random* or *Peregrine Pickle* contain any traces of your real adventures'. For whatever reason, American interest in Smollett has persisted to this day: in the first half of the last century, a clutch of monosyllabic American professors – Noyes, Jones, Buck, Kahrl, Martz and, above all, Knapp – pioneered the scholarly study of his life and work, and in more recent times the tradition has been sustained by Messrs Day, Beasley, Spector, Sekora, Basker, Skinner, Sena, Rousseau, Fulton, Gassman, Korte and Donoghue. Without their dedication, and that of Paul-Gabriel Boucé, Ian Campbell Ross and Frank Felsenstein, Smollett might well have vanished from scholarly sight altogether.

Biographers inevitably want their subjects to seem both exotic and familiar, denizens of a remote and vanished country who yet behave and think and feel as we do, and, if they are writers, give voice to sentiments and concerns that still affect us all. As a novelist, Smollett seems like a relic of an earlier age in his refusal, or inability, to evoke or describe the inner man, his reliance on stereotypes and humours at the expense of subjectivity, ambivalence, the unique and irreplaceable complexities of character; as a man, he is, to his biographer at least, a bundle of familiar contradictions, of vices and virtues, strengths and weaknesses, and all the more lovable for it. Nor has his world entirely vanished. Phlebotomy and spiked sulphuric acid may have gone the way of innumerable other long-discredited antidotes and remedies, but the battle still rumbles on between medics who place their trust in chemistry and the pill bottle, and those who, like the embattled followers of Galen, see the cause and cure of disease as a matter involving diet, exercise and the proper balance of humours; the world of writers, publishers, editors and hacks is much as it was two and a half centuries ago, as incestuous, gossipy, malicious, bibulous, sponging, convivial and feud-ridden as ever; the dislike and resentment once felt for the Scots is now aimed at asylum-seekers, Romanian gypsies and immigrants from the Third World. And, like the late Victorians or the Edwardians of the pluto-cratic age, we live in a time of luxury and ostentatious expenditure, when, more than ever, people are judged by what they own and wear and look like; and those of us who look on, with a mixture of envy and disdain, are torn between a Smollettian loathing for the vulgarity and crassness of a materialistic age, and a Johnsonian suspicion that this is, in part, how society renews itself, and keeps atrophy at bay. Either way, we should start reading Smollett again, for his anger, his energy, his frankness, his comicality, his coarseness and, above all, his ability to tell a good story. He deserves to be better remembered.

Bibliography

MAJOR WORKS BY SMOLLETT

The Adventures of Roderick Random (1748)
The Adventures of Peregrine Pickle (1751, revised 1758)
The Adventures of Ferdinand Count Fathom (1753)
A Complete History of England (1757–58)
The Adventures of Sir Launcelot Greaves (1761)
Travels through France and Italy (1766)
The Present State of All Nations (1768)
The History and Adventures of an Atom (1769)
The Expedition of Humphry Clinker (1771)

SECONDARY READING

Allen, Brian, *Francis Hayman* (New Haven, 1987)
Alter, Robert, *Rogues' Progress: Studies in the Picaresque Novel* (Cambridge, Massachusetts, 1964)
Anderson, *The Life of Tobias Smollett, M.D.* (London, 1797)
Barrell, John, *English Literature in History: An Equal, Wide Survey* (London, 1983)
Basker, James G., *Tobias Smollett: Critic and Journalist* (Newark, 1988)
——'Another Smollett Play?', *Notes and Queries*, 1980
——'Scotticisms and the Problem of Cultural Identity in Eighteenth-century Britain', *Eighteenth-century Life*, 1991

Battestin, Martin, *Henry Fielding: A Life* (London, 1989)

Beasley, Jerry C., *Tobias Smollett, Novelist* (Athens, Georgia, 1998)

——Introduction and notes to *The Adventures of Ferdinand Count Fathom* (Athens, Georgia, 1988)

Black, Jeremy, *The British and the Grand Tour* (London, 1985)

——*The British Press in the Eighteenth Century* (London, 1987)

——*The British Navy and the Use of Naval Power in the Eighteenth Century* (Leicester, 1988)

——*Robert Walpole and the Nature of Politics in Early Eighteenth-century England* (London, 1990)

——and Porter, Roy (eds) *A Dictionary of Eighteenth-century History* (Oxford, 1996)

Boege, F.W., *Smollett's Reputation as a Novelist* (Princeton, 1947)

Bold, Alan (ed.) *Smollett: Author of the First Distinction* (London, 1982)

Boswell, James, *Life of Johnson*, ed. Pat Rogers (Oxford, 1980)

Boucé, Paul-Gabriel, *The Novels of Tobias Smollett* (London, 1976)

——Introduction and notes to *Roderick Random* (Oxford, 1978)

——Introduction and notes to *The Adventures of Ferdinand Count Fathom* (Harmondsworth, 1990)

——(ed.) *Sexuality in Eighteenth-century Britain* (Manchester, 1982)

Brewer, John, *The Pleasures of the Imagination* (London, 1997)

Bruce, Donald, *Radical Doctor Smollett* (London, 1964)

Buck, Howard Swazey, *A Study in Smollett: Chiefly Peregrine Pickle* (New Haven, 1925)

——*Smollett as Poet* (New Haven, 1927)

Bynum, W.F. and Porter, Roy (eds) *William Hunter and the Eighteenth-century Medical World* (Cambridge, 1985)

Carlyle, Alexander, *Anecdotes and Characters* (Oxford, 1973)

Chilton, Leslie A., Introduction and notes to *The Adventures of Telemachus, the Son of Ulysses* (Athens, Georgia, 1997)

Clifford, James L., Introduction and notes to *The Adventures of Peregrine Pickle* (Oxford, 1964)

Cochrane, J.A., *Dr Johnson's Printer: The Life of William Strahan* (London, 1964)

Colley, Linda, *Britons: Forging the Nation* (London, 1992)

Cranfield, G.A., *The Press and Society: From Caxton to Northcliffe* (London, 1978)

Crawford, Robert, *Devolving English Literature* (Oxford, 1992)

Cunninghame Graham, R.B., *Doughty Deeds: An Account of the Life of Robert Graham of Gartmore* (London, 1925)

Daiches, David, *The Paradox of Scottish Culture: The Eighteenth-century Experience* (Oxford, 1994)

Day, Robert Adams, Introduction and notes to *The History and Adventures of an Atom* (Athens, Georgia, 1989)

——'Ut Pictura Poesis: Smollett, Satire and the Graphic Arts', *Studies in Eighteenth-century Culture*, 1981

Deutsch, O.E., 'Poetry Preserved in Music', *Modern Language Notes*, 1948

Devine, T.M., *The Scottish Nation* (London, 1999)

Dobson, Austin, *Eighteenth-century Vignettes* (London, 1923)

Donoghue, Frank, *The Fame Machine: Book Reviewing and Eighteenth-century Literary Careers* (Stanford, 1996)

Douglas, Aileen, *Uneasy Sensations: Smollett and the Body* (Chicago, 1997)

Dow, Derek A. (ed.) *The Influence of Scottish Medicine: An Historical Assessment of the International Impact* (Glasgow, 1988)

Dudden, F. Homes, *Henry Fielding: His Life, Works and Times* (Oxford, 1952)

Duncan Eaves, T.C. and Kimbel, Ben D., *Samuel Richardson: A Biography* (Oxford, 1971)

Epstein, William H., *John Cleland: Images of a Life* (New York, 1974)

Evans, David L., '*Humphry Clinker*: Smollett's Tempered Augustanism', *Criticism*, 1967

Fadel, Robin, 'Tobias Smollett and English Politics, 1756–1771', *Eighteenth-century Studies*, 1, 1974

Feather, John, *A History of British Publishing* (London, 1988)

Felsenstein, Frank, Introduction and notes to *Travels through France and Italy* (Oxford, 1979)

Foster, James R., 'Smollett's Pamphleteering Foe Shebbeare', *Proceedings of the Modern Language Association*, 1942

Fuentes, Carlos, Introduction to *Don Quixote*, translated by Tobias Smollett (New York, 1986)

Fulton, Henry L., 'Smollett's Apprenticeship in Glasgow', *Studies in Scottish Literature*, 15

Gassman, Byron, Introduction and notes to *Poems, Plays and the Briton* by Tobias Smollett (Athens, Georgia, 1993)

——'*Humphry Clinker* and the Two Kingdoms of George III', *Criticism*, 1974

George, Dorothy, *London Life in the Eighteenth Century* (London, 1930)

——*England in Transition* (London, 1931)

Gibson, William, 'All Together Exquisite: Tobias Smollett and Fine Art' (PhD thesis, Leeds University, 2001)

Giddings, Robert, *The Tradition of Smollett* (London, 1967)

Ginger, John, *The Notable Man: The Life and Times of Oliver Goldsmith* (London, 1977)

Gosse, Philip, *Dr Viper: The Querulous Life of Philip Thicknesse* (London, 1952)

Grant, Damian, Introduction and notes to *The Adventures of Ferdinand Count Fathom* (Oxford, 1971)

——*Tobias Smollett: A Study in Style* (Manchester, 1977)

Hamilton, David, *The Healers: A History of Medicine in Scotland* (Edinburgh, 1981)

Harvie, David I., *Limeys: The True Story of One Man's War against Ignorance, the Establishment and the Deadly Scurvy* (Stroud, 2002)

Herman, Arthur, *The Scottish Enlightenment: The Scots' Invention of the Modern World* (London, 2002)

Hook, Andrew and Sher, Richard B., *The Glasgow Enlightenment* (Glasgow, 1995)

Humphries, A.R., 'Fielding and Smollett', in *From Dryden to Johnson: Volume 4 of the Pelican Guide to English Literature*, ed. Boris Ford (Harmondsworth, 1957)

Joliat, Eugene, 'Smollett, Editor of Voltaire', *Modern Language Notes*, 1939

Jones, Claude E., *Smollett Studies* (California, 1942)

——Introduction to *An Essay on the External Use of Water* by Tobias Smollett (Baltimore, 1935)

Kahrl, George M., *Tobias Smollett: Traveller and Novelist* (Chicago, 1945)

Kelly, Lionel, *Tobias Smollett: The Critical Heritage* (London, 1987)

Kernan, Alvin, *Printing Technology, Letters and Samuel Johnson* (Princeton, 1987)

Knapp, Lewis M., *Tobias Smollett: Doctor of Men and Manners* (Princeton, 1949)

——(ed.) *The Letters of Tobias Smollett* (Oxford, 1970)

——'Anne Smollett, Wife of Tobias Smollett', *Proceedings of the Modern Language Association*, 1930

——'Elizabeth Smollett, Daughter of Tobias Smollett', *Review of English Studies*, 1932

——'Rex versus Smollett: More Data on the Smollett–Knowles Libel Case', *Modern Philology*, 1943

——'Smollett and the Elder Pitt', *Modern Language Notes*, 1944

——'John Armstrong, Littérateur and Associate of Smollett, Wilkes and Other Celebrities', *Publications of the Modern Language Association of America*, 1944

——'Smollett's Self-Portrait in *The Expedition of Humphry Clinker*', in F. W. Hilles (ed.) *The Age of Johnson: Essays Presented to Chauncey Brewster Tinker* (New Haven, 1949)

——'The "Prophecy" Attributed to Smollett', *Review of English Studies*, 1965

——'Smollett's Translation of Fénelon's *Télémaque*', *Philological Quarterly*, 1965

——'Comments on Smollett by the Rev Dr Thomas Birch', *Notes and Queries*, 1965

——Introduction and notes to *The Expedition of Humphry Clinker* (Oxford, 1966)

——'Scottish Attitudes towards Smollett', *Philological Quarterly*, 45, 1966

——'Smollett and Johnson: Never Cater-cousins?', *Modern Philology*, 66, 1968–70

Korte, Donald M., 'Smollett's "Advice" and "Reproof": Apprenticeship in Satire', *Studies in Scottish Literature*, 1971

Langford, Paul, *A Polite and Commercial People: England 1727–1783* (Oxford, 1989)

Le Fevre, Peter and Harding, Richard, *Precursors of Nelson* (London, 2000)

Lenman, Bruce, *The Jacobite Risings in Britain, 1689–1746* (London, 1980)

Linsalata, Carmine Rocco, *Smollett's Hoax: Don Quixote in English* (Stanford, 1956)

Lloyd, Christopher and Coulter, Jack, *Medicine and the Navy, 1200–1900*. Vol. III, 1714–1815 (Edinburgh, 1961)

Macdonald, Fiona A. 'The Infirmary of the Glasgow Town's Hospital, 1733–1800: A Case for Voluntarism?', *Bulletin of the History of Medicine*, 1999

——'The Infirmary of the Glasgow Town's Hospital: Patient Care, 1733–1800', in Paul Wood (ed.) *The Scottish Enlightenment: Essays in Reinterpretation* (Rochester, New York, 2000)

McKendrick, Neil, Brewer, John and Plumb, J.H., *The Birth of a Consumer Society* (London, 1982)

Mackie, J.B., *History of Scotland* (Harmondsworth, 1964)

Mackillop, A.D., *The Early Masters of English Fiction* (London, 1962)

Martz, Louis, *The Later Career of Tobias Smollett* (New Haven, 1942)

——'Smollett and the Expedition to Cartagena', *Publications of the Modern Languages Association of America*, 1941

Mathias, Peter, *The Transformation of England* (London, 1979)

Maxwell, Constantia, *The English Traveller in France* (London, 1932)

Mayo, Robert D., *The English Novel in the Magazines, 1740–1815* (Oxford, 1962)

Melville, Lewis, *The Life and Letters of Tobias Smollett* (London, 1926)

Middleton, Richard, *The Bells of Victory: The Pitt–Newcastle Administration and the Conduct of the Seven Years' War, 1757–62* (Cambridge, 1985)

Moore, John, 'The Life of T. Smollett, MD', in *The Works of Tobias Smollett, MD*, Vol. I (London, 1797)

Moore, Lucy, *Amphibious Thing: The Life of Lord Hervey* (London, 2000)

Mullen, John, *Sentiment and Sociability: The Language of Feeling in the Eighteenth Century* (Oxford, 1988)

Mumby, F.A. and Norrie, Ian, *Publishing and Bookselling* (London, 1974)

Neale, R.S., *Bath 1680–1850: A Social History* (London, 1981)

Noyres, Edward S. (ed.) *The Letters of Tobias Smollett* (Cambridge, Massachusetts, 1926)

Ollard, Richard (ed.) *The Diaries of A.L. Rowse* (London, 2003)

Oman, Carola, *David Garrick* (London, 1958)

Orwell, George, 'Tobias Smollett: Scotland's Best Novelist', *Tribune*, 22 September 1944

Pares, Richard, *War and Trade in the West Indies, 1739–1763* (Oxford, 1936)

Parker, Alice, 'Tobias Smollett and the Law', *Studies in Philology*, 1942

Paulson, Ronald, *Hogarth*, Vol. III, *Art and Politics* (Cambridge, 1993)

——*Satire and the Novel in Eighteenth-century England* (New Haven, 1967)

Picard, Liza, *Dr Johnson's London* (London, 2000)

Plant, Marjorie, *The English Book Trade: An Economic History of the Making and Sale of Books* (London, 1974)

Plumb, J.H., *England in the Eighteenth Century* (Harmondsworth, 1950)

——*The First Four Georges* (London, 1956)

——*Georgian Delights* (London, 1980)

Porter, Dorothy and Porter, Roy, *Doctors and Doctoring in Eighteenth-century England* (Cambridge, 1989)

——*Doctors, Medicine and Society in England, 1550–1860* (London, 1987)

Porter, Roy, *English Society in the Eighteenth Century* (Harmondsworth, 1982)

——*The Greatest Benefit to Mankind: A Medical History of Humanity from Antiquity to the Present* (London, 1997)

——*Enlightenment: Britain and the Creation of the Modern World* (Harmondsworth, 2000)

Postgate, Raymond, *That Devil Wilkes* (London, 1930)

Pottle, Frederick (ed.) *James Boswell: London Journal* (London, 1950)

——(ed.) *Journal of a Tour of the Hebrides with Samuel Johnson, LID* (London, 1963)

Powell, L.F., 'William Huggins and Tobias Smollett', *Modern Philology*, 34, 1936–37

Preston, Thomas R., 'Smollett and the Benevolent Misanthrope Type', *Proceedings of the Modern Language Association*, 1964

——Introduction and notes to *The Expedition of Humphry Clinker* (Athens, Georgia, 1990)

Pritchett, V.S., 'The Shocking Surgeon', *The Living Novel* (London, 1946)

Putney, Rufus D.S., 'Smollett and Lady Vane's Memoirs', *Philological Quarterly*, 1946

Read, Herbert, *Collected Essays in Literary Criticism* (London, 1951)

Richmond, H.W., *The Navy in the War of 1739–48* (Cambridge, 1920)

Roberts, Marie and Porter, Roy (eds) *Literature and Medicine during the Eighteenth Century* (London, 1993)

Rodger, N.A.M., *The Wooden World: An Anatomy of the Georgian Navy* (London, 1986)

Roper, Derek, *Reviewing before the 'Edinburgh'* (London, 1978)

——'Smollett's "Four Gentlemen": the First Contributors to the Critical Review', *Review of English Studies*, 1959

Rogers, Pat, *Grub Street: Studies in a Sub-culture* (London, 1972)

——*Henry Fielding: A Biography* (London, 1979)

——*The Augustan Vision* (London, 1978)

Ross, Ian Campbell, *Laurence Sterne: A Life* (Oxford, 2001)

——'Tobias Smollett: Gentleman by Birth, Education and Profession', *British Journal for Eighteenth-century Studies*, 1982

Rothstein, Eric, 'Scottophilia and *Humphry Clinker*: The Politics of Beggary, Bugs and Buttocks', *University of Toronto Quarterly*, 1982

Rousseau, G.S., *Tobias Smollett: Essays of Two Decades* (Edinburgh, 1982)

——and Boucé, Paul-Gabriel *Bicentennial Essays Presented to Lewis M. Knapp* (New York, 1971)

Rudé, George, *Wilkes and Liberty* (Oxford, 1962)

——*Hanoverian London, 1714–1808* (London, 1971)

Scott, William, 'Smollett, Dr John Hill, and the Failings of *Peregrine Pickle*', *Notes and Queries*, 1955

Sekora, John, *Luxury: The Concept in Western Thought, Eden to Smollett* (Baltimore and London, 1977)

Sena, John F., 'Smollett's Persona and the Melancholic Traveller', *Eighteenth-century Studies*, 1967–68

Simpson, Kenneth, *The Protean Scot: The Crisis of Identity in Eighteenth-century Scottish Literature* (Aberdeen, 1988)

Skinner, John, *Constructions of Smollett: A Study of Genre and Gender* (Delaware, 1966)

Smeaton, Oliphant, *Tobias Smollett* (Edinburgh, 1897)

Smout, T.C., *A History of the Scottish People* (London, 1969)

Speck, W.A., *Stability and Strife: England 1714–60* (London, 1977)

——*Society and Literature in England, 1700–60* (London, 1983)

Spector, R.D., *English Literary Periodicals and the Climate of Opinion during the Seven Years' War* (The Hague, 1966)

——*Tobias Smollett* (New York, 1968)

——'Eighteenth-century Political Controversy and Linguistics', *Notes and Queries*, 1955

Taylor, Richard C., *Goldsmith as Journalist* (Rutherford, New Jersey, 1993)

Thomas, P.D.G., *John Wilkes: A Friend to Liberty* (Oxford, 1991)

Tierney, James T., *The Correspondence of Robert Dodsley, 1733–64* (Cambridge, 1988)

Turbeville, A.S. (ed.) *Johnson's England: An Account of the Life and Manners of his Age* (Oxford, 1933)

Turner, E.S., *Taking the Cure* (London, 1967)

Uglow, Jenny, *Hogarth: A Life and a World* (London, 1997)

Vernon, W.L., *Memorial of Admiral Vernon from Contemporary Authorities* (London, 1861)

Vincent, H.P., 'Tobias Smollett's Assault on Gordon and Groom', *Review of English Studies*, 1940

Watt, Ian, *The Rise of the Novel* (London, 1967)

Wilkes, R.M., *Serial Publication in England before 1750* (Cambridge, 1957)

Williams, Basil, *The Whig Supremacy* (Oxford, 1939)

Worden, Blair, *Roundhead Reputations: The English Civil Wars and the Passions of Posterity* (London, 2001)

Index